THE NATURE OF HU

MW00623141

The study of human intelligence features many points of consensus, but there are also many different perspectives. In this unique book Robert J. Sternberg invites the 19 most highly cited psychological scientists in the leading textbooks on human intelligence to share their research programs and findings. Each chapter answers a standardized set of questions on the measurement, investigation, and development of intelligence – and the outcome represents a wide range of substantive and methodological emphases including psychometric, cognitive, expertise-based, developmental, neuropsychological, genetic, cultural, systems, and group-difference approaches. This is an exciting and valuable course book for upper-level students to learn from the originators of the key contemporary ideas in intelligence research about how they think about their work and about the field.

ROBERT J. STERNBERG is Professor of Human Development at Cornell University and Honorary Professor of Psychology at the University of Heidelberg. Formerly he was IBM Professor of Psychology and Education at Yale University. He holds a PhD from Stanford University, along with 13 honorary doctorates. He has won both the James and Cattell Awards from the Association for Psychological Science and is a member of the National Academy of Education and the American Academy of Arts and Sciences. He is a former president of the American Psychological Association and the Federation of Associations in Behavioral and Brain Sciences. He is among the most cited psychologists in the world, with roughly 138,000 citations and an h–citation index of 182.

THE NATURE OF HUMAN INTELLIGENCE

EDITED BY

ROBERT J. STERNBERG

Cornell University

CAMBRIDGE
UNIVERSITY PRESS

CAMBRIDGE
UNIVERSITY PRESS

One Liberty Plaza, 20th Floor, New York, NY 10006, USA

Cambridge University Press is part of the University of Cambridge.

It furthers the University's mission by disseminating knowledge in the pursuit of education, learning, and research at the highest international levels of excellence.

www.cambridge.org
Information on this title: www.cambridge.org/9781316629642
DOI: 10.1017/9781316817049

First published 2018

A catalogue record for this publication is available from the British Library.

Library of Congress Cataloging-in-Publication Data
Names: Sternberg, Robert J., editor.
Title: The nature of human intelligence / edited by Robert J. Sternberg.
Description: New York: Cambridge University Press, 2018. |
Includes bibliographical references and index.
Identifiers: LCCN 2017044205| ISBN 9781107176577 (hardback) |
ISBN 9781316629642 (paperback)
Subjects: LCSH: Intellect.
Classification: LCC BF431.N384 2018 | DDC 153.9–dc23
LC record available at https://lccn.loc.gov/2017044205

ISBN 978-1-107-17657-7 Hardback
ISBN 978-1-316-62964-2 Paperback

This book is dedicated to the memory of Earl Hunt, a pioneer in the field of intelligence and a scholar whose influence only will become stronger in the years to come.

Contents

Contributors

ACKERMAN, PHILLIP L. Georgia Institute of Technology

BOUCHARD, THOMAS J., JR. University of Minnesota

BUTLER, HEATHER A. California State University, Dominguez Hills

CECI, STEPHEN J. Cornell University

CHEN, JIE-QI. Erikson Institute

CONWAY, ANDREW R. A. Claremont Graduate University

DEARY, IAN J. University of Edinburgh

ENGLE, RANDALL W. Georgia Institute of Technology

ERICSSON, K. ANDERS. Florida State University

FLYNN, JAMES R. University of Otago

GARDNER, HOWARD. Harvard University

GINTHER, DONNA K. University of Kansas

GOTTFREDSON, LINDA S. University of Delaware

GRIGORENKO, ELENA L. Baylor College of Medicine, St. Petersburg University, Russia, University of Houston, Yale University

HAIER, RICHARD J. University of California, Irvine

HALPERN, DIANE F. Claremont-McKenna College and Minerva Schools at KGI

KAHN, SHULAMIT Boston University

KAUFMAN, ALAN S. Yale University

KAUFMAN, SCOTT BARRY. University of Pennsylvania

KORNHABER, MINDY. Pennsylvania State University

KOVACS, KRISTOF. Eszterhazy Karoly University

LUBINSKI, DAVID. Vanderbilt University

LYNN, RICHARD. University of Ulster

MAYER, JOHN D. University of New Hampshire

RITCHIE, STUART J. University of Edinburgh

SHIPSTEAD, ZACH. Alma College

STERNBERG, ROBERT J. Cornell University

WILLIAMS, WENDY M. Cornell University

Preface

"The field of intelligence is dead." So said one of my graduate-school mentors, Lee Cronbach, himself an expert on intelligence, in 1972. I had just started as a graduate student at Stanford and had gone to see him about possibly doing some work with him in the field of intelligence; but he displayed no optimism about the field. Perhaps I should not have been surprised. About a decade earlier, one of his colleagues at Stanford, Quinn McNemar, had written a paper published under the title "Lost: Our Intelligence? Why?" (McNemar, 1964).

The collaboration with Cronbach never happened, and it was not until my second year as a graduate student that I started working in the field of intelligence under the mentorship of my primary adviser, Gordon Bower. But the year that I started working on intelligence, unbeknownst to me, the field that McNemar suggested was lost was found again – or, to put it in terms of Cronbach's metaphor, it became undead and resurrected. Earl Hunt, to whom this volume is dedicated, and two of his colleagues had just published a book chapter that, in some respects, would bring intelligence to life (Hunt, Lunneborg, & Lewis, 1975). Hunt and his colleagues showed that a productive path to understanding intelligence would be through the cognitive analysis of intellectual functioning. Hunt and colleagues followed up two years later with a cognitive analysis specifically of verbal ability (Hunt, Lunneborg, & Lewis, 1975). Two years after that, I proposed a related although in some respects competing approach to studying intelligence (Sternberg, 1977). The rest, as they say, is history. Today, the field of intelligence research is about as active as any field could be. Indeed, its form seems to change every few years, or, arguably, every few months!

Once upon a time, recognizing that the field of intelligence was thriving, I edited a series that updated advances in the field on a regular basis. The series started in 1982 and was called *Advances in the Psychology of Human Intelligence* (Sternberg, 1982a). But that series lasted only through five volumes. A few years after my first edited volume, Douglas Detterman (1985) started a related series, *Current Topics in Human Intelligence*. But that series too is long gone. The field continued to be updated through a series of handbooks edited by myself (e.g., Sternberg, 1982b, 2000; Sternberg & Kaufman, 2011) and others (e.g., Goldstein, Princiotta, & Naglieri, 2015; Wolman, 1985), but these handbooks were intended to be comprehensive reviews rather than updates regarding current research on particular topics. Yet, the field continued to advance rapidly.

So I recently decided to edit a volume of updates on intelligence research. In the past, I had just chosen colleagues to write whose work I admired because of its impact on the field. But at the same time, I realized that my selections were always colored by my own biases about what kinds of research were worthwhile to the field. Those biases led to some kinds of work being included, but not others. This time I wanted to do things a bit differently.

When I started this volume, I recently had coedited a volume of essays by eminent psychologists who were chosen in an objective (statistically based) way (Sternberg, Fiske, & Foss, 2016), and I decided to try an analog to this approach for the current volume. I started with what I considered to be the three principal contemporary textbooks on intelligence – ones by Hunt (2011), Mackintosh (2011), and Sternberg and Kaufman (2011) – and tabulated citations in these volumes to the various authors whose work was mentioned. I then chose as my potential authors the scholars whose work was most frequently cited. Almost everyone I wrote to then agreed to write. Earl Hunt was an exception, and I later realized that the reason was that he was in the last months of his life. It therefore is fitting that this volume is dedicated to him. (I have written elsewhere about his landmark contributions to the field – Sternberg, 2017). This volume thus represents the contributions of the most-cited authors in the field of intelligence, at least as represented in three textbooks published in 2011. Because one of the textbooks, the *Cambridge Handbook of Intelligence*, is edited, I believe it fair to say that the authors have been chosen to represent those scholars who the field believes to have made the highest-impact contributions to the study of intelligence.

Regrettably, some of the most highly cited scholars in the field of human intelligence have died in recent years, not just Hunt but also John B. Carroll (e.g., Carroll, 1993), John Horn (e.g., Horn, Donaldson, & Engstrom, 1981), and Arthur Jensen (e.g., Jensen, 1998), among others. This book would have been enriched greatly had these scholars lived and been willing to contribute.

The scholars who have written for this volume represent diverse perspectives, or "metaphors of mind" (Sternberg, 1990). These perspectives include primarily biological (including behavior-genetic), cognitive, cultural, developmental, psychometric, and group-difference approaches. This book does not include all possible approaches, and there are many excellent scholars, especially ones early in their careers, who have not written for it. But this certainly will not be the last edited book of advances in the field of human intelligence, and later volumes (edited by others) doubtless will include approaches that may be underrepresented here.

Although intelligence always has been important to society, one might argue that, in some respects, it is more important now than ever before. On the one hand, intelligence as measured by IQ tests increased greatly in the 20th century (Flynn, 2009). On the other hand, we are seeing in the 21st century more stupid behavior than one might have believed possible, given these rising IQs (Sternberg, 2002). Earl Hunt (1995) asked, before the dawn of the 21st century, "Will we be smart enough?" It was a good question to ask. I hope the essays in this book provide some enlightenment as to the answer!

References

Carroll, J. B. (1993). *Human cognitive abilities: A survey of factor-analytic studies.* New York: Cambridge University Press.

Detterman, D. K. (Ed.) (1985). *Current topics in human intelligence* (Vol. 1). Norwood, NJ: Ablex.

Flynn, J. R. (2009). *What is intelligence? Beyond the Flynn effect.* Cambridge: Cambridge University Press.

Goldstein, S., Princiotta, D., & Naglieri, J. (Eds.) (2015). *Handbook of intelligence: Evolutionary theory, historical perspective, and current concepts.* New York: Springer.

Horn, J. L., Donaldson, G., & Engstrom, R. (1981). Apprehension, memory, and fluid intelligence decline in adulthood. *Research on Aging*, 3(1), 33–84.

Hunt, E. B. (1995). *Will we be smart enough? Cognitive capabilities of the coming workforce.* New York: The Russell Sage Foundation.

    (2011). *Human intelligence.* New York: Cambridge University Press.

Hunt, E. B., Lunneborg, C., & Lewis, J. (1975). What does it mean to be high verbal? *Cognitive Psychology*, 1, 194–227.

Jensen, A. R. (1998). *The g factor: The science of mental ability.* Westport, CT: Praeger.

Mackintosh, N. J. (2011). *IQ and human intelligence.* New York: Oxford University Press.

McNemar, Q. (1964). Lost: Our intelligence? Why? *American Psychologist*, 19, 871–882.

Sternberg, R. J. (1977). *Intelligence, information processing, and analogical reasoning: The componential analysis of human abilities*. Hillsdale, NJ: Lawrence Erlbaum Associates.

(Ed.) (1982a). *Advances in the psychology of human intelligence* (Vol. 1). Hillsdale, NJ: Erlbaum.

(Ed.). (1982b). *Handbook of human intelligence*. New York: Cambridge University Press.

(1990). *Metaphors of mind: Conceptions of the nature of intelligence*. New York: Cambridge University Press.

(Ed.). (2000). *Handbook of intelligence*. New York: Cambridge University Press.

(Ed.). (2002). *Why smart people can be so stupid*. New Haven, CT: Yale University Press.

(2017). Acute angles: Parallels and near-parallels in two careers studying human intelligence. *Intelligence*. https://doi.org/10.1016/j.intell.2017.09.003. http://www.sciencedirect.com/science/article/pii/S016028961730274X.

Sternberg, R. J., Fiske, S. T., & Foss, D. J. (Eds.) (2016). *Scientists making a difference: One hundred eminent behavioral and brain scientists talk about their most important contributions* New York: Cambridge University Press.

Sternberg, R. J., & Kaufman, S. B. (Eds.) (2011). *Cambridge handbook of intelligence*. New York: Cambridge University Press.

Wolman, B. (Ed.) (1985). *Handbook of intelligence*. New York: Wiley.

CHAPTER I

Intelligence as Potentiality and Actuality

Phillip L. Ackerman

In two seminal articles, David Wechsler emphasized the importance of non-ability determinants of adult intelligence, and called for a more inclusive consideration of traits beyond that which is assessed by traditional intelligence quotient (IQ)–type measures. Wechsler's main point was that in order to predict an individual's ability to "understand the world about him and his resourcefulness to cope with its challenges" (Wechsler, 1950, 1975, p. 139), one needs to have a much broader understanding of the individual beyond a single IQ score. A second issue with modern intelligence assessment is that at various times, an IQ score has been seen to reflect an individual's 'capacity' for intellectual competence, rather than a snapshot of the individual's performance from which inferences can be made, such as the likelihood that a child will succeed academically (Anastasi, 1983). In the current chapter, an effort will be made to explicitly distinguish between the concept of intelligence as a 'potentiality' from intelligence as an 'actuality,' and inclusion of non-ability constructs, especially with respect to the abilities of older adolescents and adults.

Fundamental Issues about Intelligence

Ever since Binet and Simon published the first modern scales to measure child intelligence, the fundamental purpose of intelligence assessment has been for *prediction* – whether it be performance in the classroom, laboratory, workplace, or in success at other life tasks. Although there have been many basic research efforts that purport to focus on finding basic properties of intelligence, the majority of research and application efforts during the past century has focused on the utilitarian value of predicting the rank-ordering of individuals on some criterion performance measure. Once one understands this fundamental issue in the study of intelligence, several key concepts must be considered, as follows:

First, intelligence is, more or less, contextually (and culturally) bounded. That is, because performance criteria (such as success in school or work) differ to some degree from one cultural environment to another, the underlying components of intelligence that are relevant to predicting success may differ from one environment to another. For example, 'intelligence' for writing a novel is not *exactly* the same as 'intelligence' for solving calculus problems. That is not to say that these two intelligences are unrelated to one another. Indeed, there are many intelligences that are highly related to each other, which ultimately gives rise to the notion of 'general intelligence' (or *g*).

Second, intelligence is a 'relative' or normative construct. One of Binet's seminal contributions to the assessment of intelligence was to introduce the idea that we can best index intelligence, especially during childhood when rapid cognitive development occurs, as the individual's performance *in comparison to* a reference group (e.g., all six-year-old children). It is almost universally accepted that one can only quantify an individual's intelligence by referring to the reference or norming group. The principal advantage to this approach is that an individual's intelligence is indexed in a way that it has the same meaning, even though norming groups may change from one decade to the next (e.g., in terms of the core knowledge and skills that are within the capabilities of the larger reference group). The principal disadvantage to this approach is that it renders comparisons *across* norming groups somewhat problematic. For example, it is arguably nonsensical to say that a large sample of today's 18-year-olds is more or less 'intelligent' than a large sample of 18-year-olds in 1930. The average 18-year-old today has very different knowledge and skills from the 18-year-old in 1930, in areas of math, science, arts and literature, and so on (see, e.g., Learned & Wood, 1938). An intelligence test designed for 18-year-olds in 1930 would be expected to yield very different performance norms if administered today, yet an IQ score for 18-year-olds in 1930 on a then-current test has the same normative meaning as an IQ score for an 18-year-old today on a current test. The IQ score only tells us the individual's standing with respect to other members of the norming sample.

Third, intelligence is dynamic. That is, although one's IQ score may be relatively constant (e.g., see Thorndike, 1940), the underlying capabilities of the individual (and the reference group) change with age. Over the course of the life span, intellectual development is quite rapid in early childhood, slows in adolescence and early adulthood, and then, for many components of intellectual ability, shows declines in middle-to-late adulthood (e.g., see Schaie, 1996).

Fourth, because prediction is the key determinant of the utility of intelligence assessments, one can make a critical distinction between intelligence *potentiality* and intelligence *actuality*. These terms are derived from Aristotle's *Metaphysics* (see Gill, 2005), but they are especially appropriate for understanding the construct of intelligence, the practicalities of intelligence assessment, and the insights that can be derived from individual intelligence scores. Moreover, as will be introduced later, this particular consideration illustrates the importance of non-ability constructs in the development and expression of intelligence.

Potentiality, in Aristotle's view, can be imagined in terms of a block of bronze (metal). It has the 'potential' to become a statue of a person or many other objects. Yet, in order to realize the goal of a statue, 'work' must be done to transform the block of bronze, by carving or hammering and so on. A completed bronze statue represents an actuality – which is the result of the work done to it by the artist. In terms of intelligence, performance scores on an IQ test are an actuality, but they are not generally of interest, in and of themselves, for many of the reasons provided previously. Consistent with Wechsler's (1975) suggestions, the goal for an intelligence assessment is an index of the individual's *potential* for intellectually demanding learning and task performance. Yet, there are three problems that prevent one from reasonably equating an IQ score with an individual's potential: (a) the test score only represents the individual's actual performance, and as such, potential can only be indirectly inferred (see Anastasi, 1983); (b) although one may be able to make effective predictions of later academic and occupational achievement from a current IQ score, it is impossible to know what future scientific and/or medical developments might be made that would fundamentally change the capability of individuals of different IQ levels to acquire new intellectual skills and knowledge (e.g., so-called brain drugs or new educational instructional techniques); and (c) like Aristotle's example, the translation from the block of bronze to a statue requires the substantial investment of work time and effort on the part of the artist. For an individual to acquire new intellectually demanding knowledge and skills, he/she must invest time and effort, which in turn, implicates non-ability constructs, such as personality and motivation. In the next sections, I will discuss how these key concepts relate to the scientific study of intellectual development and expression.

Adolescent and Adult Intellectual Development

Prior to adolescence in the developed world, nearly all children are subjected to a set of relatively common educational topics (e.g., the traditional reading, writing, and arithmetic). Once they reach early adolescence, however, educational experiences become differentiated across individuals. In addition to core courses in language, math, and sciences, most secondary schools allow students to select a subset of 'elective' or optional courses across the arts, humanities, sciences, and technology domains. These opportunities present both an opportunity and a challenge to researchers who hope to use intelligence assessments for predicting individual differences in subsequent educational and occupational success. The opportunity is represented by the fact that students can choose among courses that have greater or lesser intellectual demands, and they can choose to specialize in a particular domain or to broaden their intellectual horizons across multiple domains. Selective enrollment in these courses provides the researcher with natural experiments, where the researcher can examine differences in the acquisition of knowledge and skills of students who have varied educational experiences. Researchers can examine how such enrollments lead to changes in the depth and breadth of an individual's intellectual repertoire.

The challenge for intellectual assessment, though, is perhaps more daunting than is the opportunity for understanding of intellectual growth and diversification. That is, when students no longer have educational experiences in common, it becomes problematic to compare them using a standard intelligence test. If one student chooses to complete elective courses in Spanish throughout high school, and another student chooses instead to take courses in computer programming, then it becomes difficult to figure out how to rank-order the individuals on their respective levels of intelligence. An intelligence test that included Spanish vocabulary knowledge would put the computer science student at a disadvantage, because he/she would receive no credit for knowledge of computer science, and vice versa. On one hand, an intelligence test that excluded both Spanish and computer science would inadequately sample the knowledge of these individuals, but, on the other hand, an intelligence test that sampled all of the different domains of both in-school elective courses and out-of-school courses of study would be unreasonably long and impractical to administer. This challenge only gets more difficult as students transition from secondary school to higher education or occupations, because the content of their respective intellectual repertoires gets increasingly differentiated and specialized.

The traditional solution to such challenges has been to focus only on what knowledge and skills are common to most students (i.e., not directly sampling knowledge and skills from elective courses), and is further compromised when testing adults, who are many years beyond their high school educational experience. For example, the SAT and ACT tests, used for college/university selection, only assess mathematics knowledge and skills through algebra and geometry, because only a portion of the college-applying population advances to elective courses beyond these topics (e.g., calculus). Four years after the student completes the SAT or ACT, he/she might be considering postgraduate study. Yet, because of the lack of common core courses at the college/university level, the most widely used entrance examination for graduate study, the Graduate Records Examination (GRE) is still only testing algebra and geometry – topics that some students may have only encountered in high school, while other students may have continued with a rigorous study of advanced mathematics at university. Cattell (1957) called this testing of 'historical' crystallized intelligence (Gc), as opposed to 'current' Gc.

As individuals reach adulthood, what they can accomplish on intellectually demanding tasks becomes much more importantly determined by their prior specialized experience. Nearly every profession or expert performance depends on knowledge that has been acquired over a long period of learning and practice. Indeed, I have previously argued (e.g., Ackerman, 1996) that most of the tasks that adults perform on a day-to-day basis are much more highly associated with an adult's specialized knowledge and skills, rather than the kinds of intelligence associated with abstract reasoning and working memory. Jobs that vary broadly share this fundamental property, whether in health care (doctors, nurses), other knowledge work (e.g., accounting, law, science), and in various 'trades' (e.g., carpentry, plumbing). Ultimately, this turns out to be fortuitous for adults, because with increasing age into the middle-adult years, there is typically a decline in the 'fluid' intellectual abilities (Gf), relative to adolescents and younger adults (Cattell, 1943; Hebb, 1942). The implication of these changes is that middle-aged and older adults are less effective in performing abstract reasoning kinds of tasks, that in turn, appear to be important for the acquisition of novel task knowledge and skills. But adults who have acquired expertise in their own professions or other areas often have an advantage in acquiring new knowledge and skills within their own areas of expertise, because transfer-of-training/transfer-of-knowledge is a very powerful positive influence for acquisition of new knowledge, when it can be incorporated into existing knowledge structures (e.g., see Ferguson, 1956).

Intelligence of Young and Middle-Aged Adults

For much of the modern period of intelligence theory and assessment, it has been claimed that intelligence declines in middle-aged years, compared to adolescents and young adults (for a review, see Ackerman, 2000). The evidence for this is somewhat complex, because as noted earlier, IQ scores for different age cohorts – those born in different decades – are fundamentally incommensurable, because intelligence tests are normed for particular cohort groups. Thus cross-sectional studies, where groups of individuals of different age cohorts are given the same intelligence test, yield results where age effects are confounded with cohort differences (Schaie & Strother, 1968). Longitudinal studies, where the same individuals are given the same intelligence test repeatedly, are more informative about the effects of aging compared to cross-sectional studies, but they have other confounds that must be taken into account (such as practice effects). Nonetheless, the accumulated evidence across these studies strongly supports the notion that in adulthood, there is a normative decline in Gf abilities, but much less decline or stability in 'historical' Gc, at least into later adulthood, when there are normative declines, with stronger decline gradients for Gf, compared to Gc (Schaie, 1996). Great efforts have been expended in recent decades to determine factors that may slow or stop the decline of intellectual abilities with increasing age in adulthood, ranging from so-called brain-training games to physical exercise. A discussion of the efficacy of such programs is beyond the scope of this chapter, but see Hertzog and colleagues (2009).

Directly Assessing the Knowledge Components of Intelligence

In studies examining *current* Gc in young and middle-aged adults, we developed tests of content knowledge across a wide spectrum of domains of intellectual expertise. While one cannot reasonably hope to sample all different types of knowledge possessed by adults, we obtained a representative sampling of areas of knowledge that are found in both traditional classrooms and advanced study areas in postsecondary education (e.g., physical and social sciences, literature, art, business, and law), and also domains outside the traditional educational context (knowledge of current events, health and safety, technology, financial planning). Performance was indicated by raw scores rather than norm-based, so that direct comparisons are made between age groups, while keeping in mind that different cohort groups may have different levels of experience and

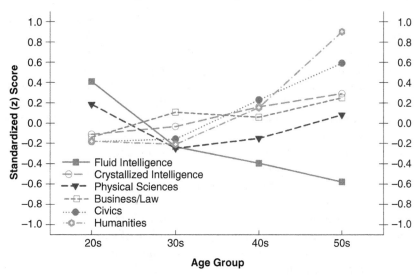

Figure 1.1 Patterns of traditional intellectual ability scores (fluid intelligence and crystallized intelligence) and domain knowledge composite scores as a function of age group in a cross-sectional study (Ackerman, 2000, *N* = 228).
Copyright 2014. Association for Psychological Science.

exposure to the knowledge being sampled. As such, these studies cannot separate aging effects from cohort differences, but they do provide a snapshot of the relative levels of knowledge of different age groups. At the same time, we collected data on traditional measures of Gf and (historical) Gc.

First of all, these studies showed that, consistent with earlier cross-sectional studies, with increasing age, measures of Gf tend to show a decline, while tests of historical Gc are stable or even show small increases. If one were to equally weight Gf and Gc components to yield a general intelligence (*g*) composite, a reasonable conclusion is that older adults are less intelligent, on average, when compared with late adolescents and young adults. In contrast, knowledge assessments show higher levels of average performance among middle-aged adults, with the greatest differences in the areas of the arts and humanities and the smallest differences in the domains of physical sciences (see Figure 1.1 for example results from a study of adults between 21 and 60; Ackerman, 2000). Similar results are found, favoring middle-aged adults in knowledge domains of current events, health, and financial planning (e.g., see Ackerman & Beier, 2006; Beier & Ackerman, 2001, 2003).

As we have argued elsewhere, there is no *inherent* reason why global estimates of adult intelligence should be based on an equal weighting of Gf and historical Gc measures. Indeed, *if* the goal is to predict the 'actuality' of adult intelligence, meaning a representation of what intellectual tasks an adult can actually accomplish, there are many reasons to prefer a measure that gives greater weight to historical Gc (because of the importance of transfer-of-training in acquisition of new knowledge – see Ackerman & Beier, 2006), and includes a substantial weighting for *current* Gc. Estimates of global intelligence that are designed in this way can be expected to show that middle-aged adults have, on average, higher levels of actual intelligence, compared with adolescent and young adults.

Such a result would be entirely consistent with the notion that if one desired a completed task along a great number of dimensions, such as accounting, law, art, literature, and so on, the greatest expertise would be found among middle-aged adults. However, this is *not* to say that any middle-aged adult would be capable to perform tasks in each of these domains. Rather, as common sense indicates, those adults who have developed expertise in a particular area would be expected to be able to accomplish the respective task successfully. It would be silly to approach a typical skilled carpenter for a radiological consultation, much as it would be nonsensical to ask a typical skilled radiologist to make a wood cabinet. As obvious as these hypothetical examples are, they should give one great pause when researchers or practitioners claim the importance of Gf over historical Gc and current Gc in representing the *actuality* of adult intelligence. Few 18-year-olds, who have the highest raw Gf scores, would be capable, for example, of successfully completing heart bypass surgery or constructing a competent legal argument before a jury.

One interesting finding from these studies is that in contrast to general intelligence assessments, there are many examples of significant, and sometimes profound, sex differences in domain knowledge. There is an important historical reason why there are negligible gender differences in omnibus IQ assessments. That reason is that one individual psychologist, Lewis Terman, decided that boys and girls should have equal scores on his Stanford-Binet intelligence test (Terman, 1916). That is, both Terman and other researchers realized that girls and boys often showed consistent average differences in scores on various intelligence subtests (e.g., verbal, math, and spatial domains). Other researchers suggested that intelligence assessments reflect these differences in whatever manner they appeared, and that separate norms be created for boys and girls, so that an intelligence score would be referenced to the sex of the examinee (Yerkes, Bridges, & Hardwick, 1915). Terman, however, decided that there was adequate justification for equality of IQ scores across the sexes, and so he constructed his IQ test to be specifically balanced by including subtests where the sex differences in the overall scale were eliminated. Subsequent IQ tests generally adopted this same approach to eliminating sex differences.

But, when it comes to individual domain knowledge tests that are content-referenced rather than norm-referenced, sex differences are clearly observed. The majority of the academic domain knowledge tests (e.g., Ackerman & Rolfhus, 1999) show advantages to males, though such differences are not typically found in current-events knowledge tests, and women have a distinct advantage in domains of health knowledge (Beier & Ackerman, 2001, 2003). When one examines sex differences in knowledge tests where the individuals self-select into particular areas of study, these differences are also seen in young adults (College Board, 2011). Ultimately, these results suggest that both individual and sex differences relate to the *direction* and *intensity* of effort devoted to the acquisition of domain-specific knowledge and skills.

Ability and Non-ability Traits and Intellectual Investment

Elementary education is largely a system for transmitting core educational content, and as such, there is great commonality among students in terms of the instruction they receive. Homework, for example, starts off relatively modest in demands for time and effort on the part of students. Once students reach secondary school, they have options toward or away from the investment of their time and effort for acquiring knowledge in intellectually demanding domains. Homework often increases in terms of time and effort, and demands consequently increase for self-regulated cognitive investments. It is during this critical period that an individual's personality and motivational traits appear to increase in influence on the direction and intensity of intellectual investments. For a conceptual discussion of investment and intellectual development, see Cattell (1971; also see Schmidt, 2014; von Stumm & Ackerman, 2013). Intellectual investments continue through decisions about postsecondary education, including whether to attend university study, selection of a major, and choice of early career paths. Together with Gf and both historical and current Gc abilities, non-ability traits also appear to be influential in determining how individuals invest their cognitive resources well into middle adulthood, in terms of seeking out or avoiding intellectual challenges, such as acquiring new knowledge and skills in and out of the workplace, and in terms of refining and improving one's performance on relatively routine tasks.

Several personality and motivational traits are, or become, associated with individual differences in intellectual abilities and domain knowledge during adolescent and adult development. Affective (personality) traits such as openness to experience and conscientiousness are positively related to individual differences in domain knowledge in many areas, while personality traits like neuroticism and extroversion tend to be negatively related to domain knowledge. Similarly, conative (will, motivation) traits such as a mastery orientation or a desire to learn are positively related to individual differences in domain knowledge, while worry and anxiety in achievement contexts are negatively related to individual differences in domain knowledge. In addition, there is a moderate association of vocational interests to differences in domain knowledge, such as investigative interests and artistic interests being positively associated with domain knowledge in the sciences and humanities, and a negative association between social and enterprising interests and a variety of academic knowledge domains. These non-ability traits are related to one another, even though they represent different aspects of individuals. This commonality has been a major factor in the development of the concept of "trait complexes" (Ackerman & Heggestad, 1997) – that is, constellations of personality, motivation, and other traits that: (a) appear more frequently in the population, and (b) are associated with orientations toward or away from intellectual development. Trait complexes of intellectual/cultural traits and science/math traits are associated with higher levels of domain knowledge in the arts, humanities, and social sciences, and in STEM (science, technology, engineering, and math) domains, respectively. Complexes of social and conventional traits are associated with lower levels of knowledge in a variety of academic and other intellectually demanding domains (Ackerman, 2000). Based on these considerations, a general framework for understanding adult intellectual development can be illustrated as shown in Figure 1.2.

In the figure, early adolescent intellectual potentiality is represented in terms of what is measured with an IQ test, that is, Gf and historical Gc. As individuals develop into adulthood, non-ability trait complexes interact with levels of intellectual potentiality to determine the investment (time and effort) the individual makes into one or more of a variety of different directions, both intellectual and non-intellectual. The result is found in an adult's breadth and depth of domain knowledge and skills, which represent the vocational and avocational (e.g., hobbies) intellectual repertoire of the individual. I propose this is the *main* source of individual differences in

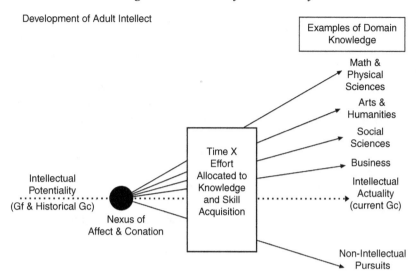

Figure 1.2   An abstracted illustration of the influences on intellectual growth from adolescent intellectual potentiality to adult intellect actuality, based on Ackerman (1996).

adult intelligence. This is *not* to say that Gf-type abilities are unimportant in adulthood (Deary et al., 2004), but it is to say that for the majority of day-to-day activities, Gf abilities are much less influential in determining an individual's performance, in comparison to the individual's current domain-specific and domain-general Gc abilities. In a nutshell, the proposition is that it is easier and more effective to *know and recall* the answer to an intellectually demanding problem than it is to figure it out from scratch using abstract reasoning (Ackerman, 1996) – which in essence, is the difference between an 'expert system' and a 'general-problem-solving' engine. One would hardly be advised to get onto an airplane piloted by an individual with high Gf but no pilot experience, over an individual with perhaps an average level of Gf but 20 years of experience piloting commercial aircraft.

Current Issues

From the theoretical foundation outlined earlier, and the body of research reviewed, two issues are important for educational and public policy perspectives. First and foremost is the finding of sex differences in domain knowledge among adolescents and adults. Large sex differences in knowledge about STEM areas among adolescents are likely a nontrivial determinant of disparities between men and women who select and persist in STEM majors in postsecondary study, and in later career choices (Ackerman, Kanfer, & Calderwood, 2013). That these differences are manifest during the high school years suggests that it may generally be too late to remedy these differences by the time an adolescent starts college. Efforts are needed to understand whether there are systematic influences external to the individual that are responsible for these differences (e.g., school policies, parental or peer influences), or whether the influences are largely internally driven, in terms of the student's interests, preferences, and personality characteristics.

The second issue is related to the first. That is, what is needed is a better understanding of the malleability of the connections between non-ability traits and an individual's investment of effort toward acquisition of knowledge and skills in particular domains, and overall. While a scientific consensus exists that Gf and historical Gc are limited in malleability, at least within the variety of environments students encounter in the developed world, substantially less research has been conducted that explores the limits of guidance or instruction on either developing affective and conative traits to better focus student efforts toward acquisition of domain knowledge, or to modifying the connections between these non-ability traits and acquisition of domain knowledge. Efforts in this area might have benefits both in reducing sex differences in STEM achievements and in generally improving the educational and occupational outlooks for many students.

Future Directions

In many ways, theory and research on traditional IQ assessment for children and early adolescents has become moribund, perhaps partly because of the clear success of the Binet-inspired tests for predicting overall academic success in the elementary school system. Yet, if one considers that adult intelligence differs fundamentally from Gf and historical Gc, in that it includes the breadth and depth of current Gc knowledge and skills, understanding of adult intelligence is woefully incomplete. Assessments that give credit to adults for the wide variety of knowledge and skills that they possess have yet to be developed. A high proportion of an adult's day-to-day intellectual life is simply unaccounted for by modern IQ assessments. As a result, there is little knowledge about how current Gc develops, is maintained, or declines, especially in older-age populations. Current Gc is essentially equivalent to the 'dark matter' hypothesized by physicists.

That is, current Gc is clearly necessary to gain a complete understanding of how adults function in an intellectually demanding society, even as Gf abilities decline with each additional decade of adult life, yet it has not been adequately measured and described. Perhaps the second century of modern intelligence theory and assessments will usher in a reorientation to both the intellectual and nonintellectual determinants of the adult repertoire for intelligent task performance.

References

Ackerman, P. L. (1996). A theory of adult intellectual development: Process, personality, interests, and knowledge. *Intelligence*, 22, 229–259.

(2000). Domain-specific knowledge as the "dark matter" of adult intelligence: gf/gc, personality and interest correlates. *Journal of Gerontology: Psychological Sciences*, 55B (2), P69–P84.

Ackerman, P. L., & Beier, M. E. (2006). Determinants of domain knowledge and independent study learning in an adult sample. *Journal of Educational Psychology*, 98, 366–381.

Ackerman, P. L., & Heggestad, E. D. (1997). Intelligence, personality, and interests: Evidence for overlapping traits. *Psychological Bulletin*, 121, 219–245.

Ackerman, P. L., Kanfer, R., & Calderwood, C. (2013). High school Advanced Placement and student performance in college: STEM majors, non-STEM majors, and gender differences. *Teachers College Record*, 115 (10), 1–43.

Ackerman, P. L., & Rolfhus, E. L. (1999). The locus of adult intelligence: Knowledge, abilities, and non-ability traits. *Psychology and Aging*, 14, 314–330.

Anastasi, A. (1983). Evolving trait concepts. *American Psychologist*, 38, 175–184.

Beier, M. E., & Ackerman, P. L. (2001). Current events knowledge in adults: An investigation of age, intelligence and non-ability determinants. *Psychology and Aging*, 16, 615–628.

(2003). Determinants of health knowledge: An investigation of age, gender, abilities, personality, and interests. *Journal of Personality and Social Psychology*, 84 (2), 439–448.

Cattell, R. B. (1943). The measurement of adult intelligence. *Psychological Bulletin*, 40, 153–193.

(1957). *Personality and motivation structure and measurement*. Yonkers-on-Hudson, NY: World Book Company.

(1971/1987). *Abilities: Their structure, growth and action*. Amsterdam: North-Holland.

College Board (2011). AP Data 2011. http://professionals.collegeboard.com/data-reports-research/ap/data

Deary, I. J., Whiteman, M. C., Starr, J. M., Whalley, L. J., & Fox, H. C. (2004). The impact of childhood intelligence on later life: Following up the Scottish Mental Surveys of 1932 and 1947. *Journal of Personality and Social Psychology*, 86, 130–147.

Ferguson, G. A. (1956). On transfer and the abilities of man. *Canadian Journal of Psychology*, 10, 121–131.

Gill, M. L. (2005). Aristotle's *Metaphysics* reconsidered. *Journal of the History of Philosophy*, 43, 223–241.

Hebb, D. O. (1942). The effect of early and late brain injury upon test scores, and the nature of normal adult intelligence. *Proceedings of the American Philosophical Society*, 85, 275–292.

Hertzog, C., Kramer, A. F., Wilson, R. S., & Lindenberger, U. (2009). Enrichment effects on adult cognitive development: Can the functional capacity of older adults be preserved and enhanced? *Psychological Science in the Public Interest*, 9, 1–65.

Learned, W. S., & Wood, B. D. (1938). *The student and his knowledge*. New York: The Carnegie Foundation for the Advancement of Teaching.

Schaie, K. W. (1996). *Intellectual development in adulthood: The Seattle longitudinal study*. New York: Cambridge University Press.

Schaie, K. W., & Strother, C. R. (1968). A cross-sequential study of age changes in cognitive behavior. *Psychological Bulletin*, 70, 671–680.

Schmidt, F. L. (2014). A general theoretical integrative model of individual differences in interests, abilities, personality traits, and academic and occupational achievement: A commentary on four recent articles. *Perspectives on Psychological Science*, 9, 211–218.

Terman, L. M. (1916). *The measurement of intelligence*. Boston: Houghton Mifflin Co.

Thorndike, R. L. (1940). "Constancy" of the IQ. *Psychological Bulletin*, 37, 167–186.

von Stumm, S., & Ackerman, P. L. (2013). Investment and intelligence: A review and meta-analysis. *Psychological Bulletin*, 139, 841–869.

Wechsler, D. (1950). Cognitive, conative, and non-intellective intelligence. *American Psychologist*, 5, 78–83.

(1975). Intelligence defined and undefined. *American Psychologist*, 30, 135–139.

Yerkes, R. M., Bridges, J. W., & Hardwick, R. S. (1915). *A point scale for measuring mental ability*. Baltimore, MD: Warwick & York.

CHAPTER 2

Hereditary Ability: g Is Driven by Experience-Producing Drives

Thomas J. Bouchard, Jr.

Intelligence boasts numerous definitions, but the one I like very much and that I find useful as a starting point is:

> Intelligence is a very general mental capability that, among other things, involves the ability to reason, plan, solve problems, think abstractly, comprehend complex ideas, learn quickly and learn from experience. It is not merely book learning, a narrow academic skill, or test-taking smarts. Rather, it reflects a broader and deeper capability for comprehending our surroundings – "catching on," "making sense" of things, or "figuring out" what to do. (Gottfredson, 1994, 1997)

This definition captures the now quite prevalent lay view that individuals differ considerably from each other on a dimension of mental capacity that has important implications for everyday functioning (Gottfredson, 2011), as well as outstanding achievement (Makel et al., 2016). Interestingly, this is a quite modern idea that has taken root largely because of the work of British polymath Francis Galton and his followers (Bouchard, 1996; Tuddenham, 1962).

Galton, in his book *Hereditary Genius*[1] (1869/1914), formulated the idea that individuals differ from one another in mental ability and noted that the range of differences was quite wide, had consequences for everyday life, and, like all the features of the organic world, was influenced by inheritance or what today we call genetics.

That this idea was new and enlightening is confirmed by Darwin's comments on the book:

> I do not think I ever in all my life read anything more interesting and original. And how well and clearly you put every point! … You have made a convert of an opponent in one sense, for I have always maintained that, excepting fools, men did not differ much in intellect, only in zeal and hard work; and I still think there is an eminently important difference, I congratulate you on producing what I am convinced will prove a memorable work. (Pearson, 1914–1930, Vol. I, p. 6)

It is worth emphasizing Darwin's astute comment that there is a difference between intelligence and motivation (zeal) and effort (hard work), and that the difference is important. Galton himself was well aware of the difference and argued that all three were influenced by heredity. "The triple event, of ability combined with zeal and with capacity for hard labour[,] is inherited" (Galton, 1892/1962, p. 78). Galton's speculative proposal has been nicely confirmed. We now know that virtually all traits (human and nonhuman, psychological and otherwise) are influenced by heredity (Bouchard, 2004; Lynch & Walsh, 1998, p. 175; Polderman et al., 2015).

What Is *g*?

The definition of intelligence given previously in this chapter, like almost all others, implies that many mental processes (abilities) underlie intelligence and that they are related at a deeper level. The idea that there are many independent mental abilities (faculties) is a very old one and used to be called faculty psychology. It continues to be manifest today in the brilliant work of Tooby and Cosmides (2015). These authors argue strongly that many abilities evolved to solve very specific problems – they are modular and adaptive. I largely agree with this view. What intelligence researchers like myself are concerned with is the fact that virtually all measures of mental abilities correlate positively and in many instances quite strongly. Guttman and Levey (1991) call this the first law of intelligence testing. This empirical fact can be characterized as a general factor, or, more specifically, as Spearman's *g*, in honor of the investigator who first described it mathematically (Spearman, 1904). For investigators who approach the question "What is intelligence?" from a factor point of view, the more technical question is, "What is *g*?"

A useful way to address this question is by looking at it from the point of view of its most severe critics. Steven J. Gould[2] (1981, 1996), the distinguished paleontologist, evolutionary biologist, and historian of science, argued strongly against the idea of a general factor of intelligence. He argued that belief in *g* constituted an error of reification:

> The notion that such a nebulous socially defined concept as intelligence might be identified as a "thing" with a locus in the brain and a definite degree of heritability – and that it might be measured as a single number, thus permitting a unilinear ranking of people according to the amount they possess. (Gould, 1981, p. 239)

In addition he argued that *g* was chimerical.

> Spearman's g is not an ineluctable entity; it represents one mathematical solution among many equivalent alternatives. The chimerical nature of g is the rotten core of Jensen's edifice, and the entire hereditarian school. (Gould, 1981, p. 320)

Spearman's *g* is a theoretical construct, not a "thing." Whether it has a "locus in the brain" is an empirical question (Korb, 1994). Is there a physical substructure to intelligence? Modern brain mapping suggests that there may well be (Haier, 2017). Indeed, I believe that advances in this domain, in conjunction with molecular genetics, are among the most promising future avenues of research in the domain of intelligence (Colom, 2014; Ponsoda et al., 2016).

Is *g* chimerical or ineluctable? Gould's understanding of factor analysis was, in Bartholomew's words, "half a century out of date" (Bartholomew, 2004, p. 70). Experts in the field strongly reject Gould's views (Reeve & Charles, 2008, p. 685). There is simply no doubt that a *g* factor is unavoidable (ineluctable) when correlation matrices of mental abilities are examined empirically (Reeve & Blacksmith, 2009). It is sometimes asserted that the *g* in one battery of tests is different from the *g* derived from a different battery. This is simply not true if each battery contains a reasonable number of tests and samples a broad set of abilities (Major, Johnson, & Bouchard, 2011). When such an assessment is carried out appropriately, there is just one *g* (Johnson & Bouchard, 2011; Salthouse, 2013).

Do we need a definition of intelligence? My answer is yes. The literature is rife with poor measures of *g* and claims that "this or that *g*" fails to predict key outcomes (i.e., academic achievement, etc.) better than some alternative (e.g., so-called complex problem solving) (Lotz, Sparfeldt, & Greiff, 2016). As pointed out earlier, my preferred definition requires numerous mental abilities (reasoning, planning, solving problems, thinking abstractly, comprehending complex ideas). Without such a guide, the choice of tests to include in a battery designed to measure *g* will be much too narrow. The classic case is the use of the Raven as a substitute for *g*; it is far from sufficient, as no single measure is adequate (Gignac, 2015). This is the problem of factor indeterminacy. Lee and Kuncel (2015) provide a thoughtful discussion applicable to any general factor. There is no substitute for careful measurement of the construct of interest and that requires both a meaningful definition implemented in the form of a theory and adequate quantification of the theoretical construct. To paraphrase my former colleague Paul Meehl, "theories built around poorly conceived constructs are scientifically unimpressive and technologically worthless" (Meehl, 1978, p. 806). I and others (Borsboom, 2013) believe that his arguments continue to be valid.

For those who prefer *Grit* and *Practice* over *g*, and zeal and hard work as alternative explanations of achievement, I refer them to Simonton(2016), who found the arguments of the major proponents of these constructs less than adequate. Others agree with this argument (Crede, Tynan, & Harms, 2016; Hambrick et al., 2016). I continue to prefer the terms "zeal" and "hard work." As McNemar pointed out long ago, the first cardinal principle of psychological progress is: "Give new names to old things" (1964, p. 872).

Those who believe in the threshold hypothesis – "there is little evidence that those scoring at the very top of the range in standardized tests are likely to have more successful careers in the sciences" (Muller et al., 2005) – are simply wrong (Arneson, Sackett, & Beatty, 2011). Monotonicity even applies when one looks at the top 1% of the ability distribution (Makel et al., 2016). Indeed the opposite of a threshold effect (increasing predictive power at higher levels) may be true (Coyle, 2015).

The Heritability of Intelligence

I have always had an interest in biology, and my fondest memory of high school was laboratory work in a biology course. Early exposure to biological and genetic thinking (Bouchard, 2016b) prepared me for my most influential work, a study of twins reared apart (Bouchard et al., 1990a; Segal, 2012). I would like to emphasize two important facts about this work. It is an experimental study, a fact that is widely underappreciated and often barely recognized. First, twins are an experiment of nature. In simple terms, monozygotic twins (MZ) share all their genes and dizygotic twins (DZ) share half their genes. When they are reared apart, they allow us to estimate the magnitude of genetic influence on any trait. In particular, the correlation for IQ of monozygotic twins reared apart (MZA) directly estimates the heritability (Bouchard et al., 1990b). There are additional complexities (Segal, 2017) but, as I show in what follows, it is a very good model when used in conjunction with other designs. Second, adoption is an experiment of society. Again there are complexities, but it is still a very good model. Thus, we have a combination of an experiment of nature and an experiment of nurture. Unlike laboratory experiments, the adoption experiment is a very powerful one in terms of magnitude of influence, as it involves a treatment that is applied day in and day out for many years.[3] Before turning to work on the genetics of intelligence, I will again discuss the point of view of an intense critic.

Gould Again

The idea that intelligence has a heritable component has been vigorously attacked for a very long time, sometimes viciously, as noted by Gould's use of the term "rotten core" cited earlier. Gould's attacks focused on the works of Cyril Burt with monozygotic twins reared apart and Burt's work on social mobility (1981, chap. 6). Gould drew largely on the writings of Leon Kamin (1974) and Donald Dorfman (1979). I hesitate to argue that this long-running controversy is over, but I will assert that the so-called evidence brought to bear against Burt in support of the accusation of fraud is far from conclusive. Dorfman claimed that "The eminent Briton is shown, beyond reasonable doubt, to have fabricated data on IQ and social class"[4] (p. 117). According to a panel that reexamined the "Burt Affair" (Mackintosh, 1995), the data on IQ and social class were key in deciding that Burt was guilty of fraud, as there was reasonable doubt about other charges. Tredoux (2015) has shown that critics of Burt's social mobility work did not understand his procedures and demonstrated that methods available to Burt at the time of his analysis easily explain his purportedly falsified results. Gould's larger focus, captured in his title "The Mismeasure of Man," argued that work in this domain was largely characterized by bias. There is now striking evidence to suggest that it was Gould who was biased in his analysis and interpretation of the data gathered by others (Fancher, 1987; Glenn & Ellis, 1988; Lewis et al., 2011; Zenderland, 1988). Even more interestingly, data Gould took at face value – work by Franz Boas (1912) – rather than examining for bias, and that he used as a basis of criticism of the hereditarian paradigm (Gould, 1981, p. 108), have turned out to support the hereditarian paradigm (Sparks & Jantz, 2002). For a more thorough analysis of Gould's many errors, omissions, and distortions, see Bouchard (2014) and Rushton (1997). Pinker discusses the similar role Gould played in the larger "sociobiology wars" (Pinker, 2002, chap. 6).

The Wilson Effect

A major reason why there was so much controversy regarding the magnitude of genetic influence on intelligence is the fact that there is a massive age (developmental) effect. For many years, psychologists believed that genetic influence was manifest at birth and experience altered behavioral and other traits. For example, J. P. Scott, one of the founders of behavior genetics as a systematic discipline, asserted:

> We thought that the best time to study the effects of genetics would be soon after birth, when behavior still had little opportunity to be altered by experience. On the contrary, we found that the different dog breeds were most alike as newborns; that is, genetic variation in behavior develops postnatally, in part as a result of the timing of gene action and in part from the interaction of gene action and experience, social, and otherwise. (Scott, 1990, p. vii)

This effect appears to be rather general (Bergen, Gardner, & Kendler, 2007). In the domain of intelligence, the effect is now called the Wilson Effect (Bouchard, 2013), and the results of the various relevant studies are shown in Figure 2.1.

Figure 2.1 illustrates that the results are consistent a) across multiple research designs (twins, adoptees, various combinations of kinships), b) measure of intelligence, c) Westernized industrialized countries, and d) kinds of samples, some very comprehensive and others much more restricted.

I have always thought it was amazing that while psychologists and others heavily emphasize the role of family environment, thus the emphasis on socioeconomic status (SES), in the shaping of intelligence in children, they conducted almost no studies of unrelated individuals reared together (URT). The URT design is the most powerful one to assess this source of influence. As Figure 2.1 shows, this design suggests a value near zero in adulthood for shared environment (see the asterisks in Figure 2.1), a value below that suggested by twin designs, namely, about 10%. My view is that psychologists have been plagued by confirmation bias and highly resistant to strong inference and refutation of their theories (Bouchard, 2009). The influence of genes on IQ and SES was laid out for us a great many years ago by a brilliant and highly underappreciated psychologist, namely Barbara Burks (Burks, 1938; King, Montanez-Raminez, & Wertheimer, 1996).

The Structure of Mental Abilities

It is important to realize that g is not the only mental ability. There are important special abilities. One of the goals of the Minnesota Study of Twins Reared Apart (MISTRA) was to formally test competing models regarding the structure of mental abilities. Advances in confirmatory factor analysis had made clear that it would be possible to pit models against each

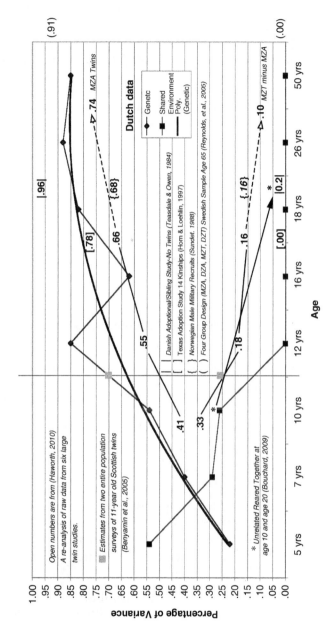

Figure 2.1 Estimates of genetic and shared environmental influence on *g* by age. The age scale is not linear.

other in meaningful ways if the appropriate test batteries were assembled (Jöreskog, 1969). The MISTRA battery was assembled with this goal in mind and that body of data, gathered over 20 years, has been made publicly available (Johnson & Bouchard, 2011).[5] The process of pitting theories against each other is called "Strong Inference" (Platt, 1964), a practice in short supply in the social sciences (Bouchard, 2009). The first good example of the application of this methodology in the domain of intelligence was published by Gustafsson (1984). He explicated the rationale lucidly, but his test battery was somewhat limited. Surprisingly, this procedure was not fully implemented again until we developed the Verbal, Perceptual, Rotation (VPR) model of mental abilities (Johnson & Bouchard, 2005b) and provided multiple replications (Johnson & Bouchard, 2005a; Johnson, te Nijenhuis, & Bouchard, 2007; Major, Johnson, & Deary, 2012). Even the classic work of John Carroll (1993) did not involve pitting the various theories against each other, a drawback he readily admitted (Carroll, 2003, p. 12). I only briefly mention the VPR here to make clear that the MISTRA research program attempted to deal with our understanding of mental abilities in a comprehensive manner.

What Influences the Development of g? Experience-Producing Drives!

My research team and I have always been clear about how we believe genes influence IQ and other traits (Bouchard et al., 1990a, p. 227).

> Specific mechanisms by which genetic differences in human behavior are expressed in phenotypic differences are largely unknown. It is a plausible conjecture that a key mechanism by which the genes affect the mind is indirect, and that genetic differences have an important role in determining the effective psychological environment of the developing child. (Hayes, 1962; Scarr & McCartney, 1983)

Note the citation of the Hayes paper (Genes, Drives and Intellect). Scarr's theory (How people make their own environments: A theory of genotype -> environment effects) was influenced by Hayes, although she does not cite him. Hayes called his model "Experience-Producing Drives" (EPD). Put simply EPD theory asserts:

> Intelligence is acquired by learning, and inherited motivational makeup influences the kind and amount of learning which occurs. The hereditary basis of intelligence consists of drives, rather than abilities as such. (Hayes, 1962, p. 302)

I have revised the theory somewhat and applied it to intelligence (Bouchard, 2014), genius (Johnson & Bouchard, 2014), and personality (Bouchard, 2016a). The "theory" is admittedly weak in the sense it is difficult to refute as currently formulated and it should perhaps be called a "meta-theory" or a "heuristic" pointing investigators in a potentially fruitful direction. What it does do, however, is give a specific name to what I believe is a widely held point of view, namely, that the mind has been shaped by the environment, via evolution, and that the content of individual minds is shaped to an important extent by the content of the environment.

Behavior geneticists have long held this view. A nice example applied to genetic influence on social attitudes is given next.

> In no way does our model minimize the role of learning and social interaction in behavioral development. Rather, it sees humans as exploring organisms whose innate abilities and predispositions help them select what is relevant and adaptive from the range of opportunities and stimuli presented by the environment. The effects of mobility and learning, therefore, augment rather than eradicate the effects of the genotype on behavior. (Martin et al., 1986, p. 4368)

EPD theory needs to be more rigorously formulated, but, if correct, it has the virtue of answering the "how" question (Anastasi, 1958). The answer is "nature via nurture"; that is, "the genome impresses itself on the psyche largely by influencing the character, selection, and impact of experience during development" (Bouchard et al., 1990a. p. 228).

Notes

1 The book was originally published in 1869. In the 1892 edition Galton admitted that the title was misleading, that it had little to do with genius, and that it should have been titled *Hereditary Ability* (Galton, 1892/1962, p. 26). As Darwin noted in the quote that follows, the idea of "intellect," a fixed characteristic or a trait in which individuals did not differ, has a very long history.

2 Gould was one of the most widely read scientists of the 20th century and was highly influential among both academics and the literate public (Shermer, 2002).

3 It is not widely recognized that any given experimental manipulation is simply one of many possible implementations of a causal mechanism and is not an infallible procedure (Johnson & Bouchard, 2014, footnote 1). The "fadeout effect" is a dramatic example in the domain of intelligence research. Interventions appear to influence g, but the effect fades with time (Protzko, 2016).

4 The reason the IQ and social class issue enters the discussion is because it relates to the hereditarian argument that higher-IQ individuals migrate to higher social classes via the influence of IQ on education and occupational success.

Ipso facto higher-social-status individuals are genetically superior, at least with respect to IQ. This has been a taboo topic (Bouchard, 1995). The classic adoption studies on IQ and social class are, in my view, dispositive (Scarr & Weinberg, 1978), and molecular genetic techniques have begun to confirm that conclusion (Kong et al., 2017; Selzam et al., 2016), although the actual effect sizes remain quite small.

5 I had a special interest in spatial and mental rotation abilities (Bouchard & McGee, 1977; Lubinski, 2010), and, as a result, the MISTRA test batteries more adequately represent this domain relative to most other batteries. Work on the VPR model was spearheaded by my colleague Wendy Johnson.

References

Anastasi, A. (1958). Heredity, environment, and the question "how?" *Psychological Review*, 65, 197–208. doi:10.1037/h0044895.

Arneson, J. J., Sackett, P. R., & Beatty, A. S. (2011). Ability–performance relationships in education and employment settings: Critical tests of the more-is-better and the good-enough hypotheses. *Psychological Science*, 22(10), 1336–1342. doi:10.1177/0956797611417004.

Bartholomew, D. J. (2004). *Measuring intelligence: Facts and fallacies*. Cambridge: Cambridge University Press.

Bergen, S. E., Gardner, C. O., & Kendler, K. S. (2007). Age-related changes in heritability of behavioral phenotypes over adolescence and young adulthood: A meta-analysis. *Twin Research and Human Genetics*, 10(3), 423–433. doi:10.1375/twin.10.3.423.

Boas, F. (1912). Changes in the bodily form of descendants of immigrants. *American Anthropologist*, 14, 530–562.

Borsboom, D. (2013). Theoretical amnesia. *Centre for Open Science*. Retrieved from: http://centerforopenscience.github.io/osc/2013/11/20/theoretical-amnesia/.

Bouchard, T. J., Jr. (1995). Breaking the last taboo. Review of "The Bell Curve." *Contemporary Psychology*, 40, 415–421.

(1996). Behavior genetic studies of intelligence, yesterday and today: The long journey from plausibility to proof – the Galton lecture. *Journal of Biosocial Science*, 28, 527–555. doi:10.1017/S0021932000022574.

(2004). Genetic influence on human psychological traits: A survey. *Current Directions in Psychological Science*, 13, 149–151.

(2009). Strong inference: A strategy for advancing psychological science. In K. McCartney & R. Weinberg (Eds.), *Experience and development: A festschrift in honor of Sandra Wood Scarr* (pp. 39–59). London: Taylor and Francis.

(2013). The Wilson effect: The increase in heritability of IQ with age. *Twin Research and Human Genetics*, 16, 923–930. doi:10.1017/thg.2013.54.

(2014). Genes, evolution and intelligence. *Behavior Genetics*, 44, 549–577. doi:10.1007/s10519-014-9646-x.

(2016a). Experience producing drive theory: Personality "writ large." *Personality and Individual Differences*, 90, 302–314. doi:10.1016/j.paid.2015.11.007.

(2016b). Genes and behavior: Nature via nurture. In R. J. Sternberg, S. T. Fiske, & D. Foss (Eds.), *Scientists making a difference: One hundred eminent behavioral and brain scientists talk about their most important contributions.* Cambridge: Cambridge University Press.

Bouchard, T. J., Jr., Lykken, D. T., McGue, M., Segal, N. L., & Tellegen, A. (1990a). Sources of human psychological differences: The Minnesota Study of Twins Reared Apart. *Science*, 250(4978), 223–228. doi:10.1126/science.2218526.

(1990b). When kin correlations are not squared. *Science*, 250, 1498.

Bouchard, T. J., Jr., & McGee, M. (1977). Sex differences in human spatial ability: Not an X-linked recessive gene effect. *Social Biology*, 24, 225–232.

Burks, B. S. (1938). On the relative contributions of nature and nurture to average group differences in intelligence. *Proceedings of the National Academy of Sciences*, 24, 276–282.

Carroll, J. B. (1993). *Human cognitive abilities: A survey of factor-analytic studies.* New York: Cambridge University Press.

(2003). The higher-stratum structure of cognitive abilities: Current evidence supports *g* and about ten broad factors. In H. Nyborg (Ed.), *The science of general intelligence: Tribute to Arthur R. Jensen* (pp. 5–22). Oxford: Elsevier.

Colom, R. (2014). From the earth to the brain. *Personality and Individual Differences*, 61–62, 3–6. doi:10.1016/j.paid.2013.12.025.

Coyle, T. R. (2015). Relations among general intelligence (g), aptitude tests, and GPA: Linear effects dominate. *Intelligence*, 53, 16–22. doi:10.1016/j.intell.2015.08.005.

Crede, M., Tynan, M. C., & Harms, P. D. (2016). Much ado about grit: A meta-analytic synthesis of the grit literature. *Journal of Personal Social Psychology*, doi:10.1037/pspp0000102.

Dorfman, D. D. (1979). The Cyril Burt question: New findings. *Science*, 201, 1177–1186.

Fancher, R. E. (1987). Henry Goddard and the Kallikak family photographs: "Conscious skullduggery" or "Whig history"? *American Psychologist*, 42, 585–590.

Galton, F. (1869/1914). *Hereditary genius: An inquiry into its laws and consequences.* London: Macmillan.

(1892/1962). *Hereditary genius: An inquiry into its laws and consequences (with an introduction by C. D. Darlington).* Cleveland, OH, and New York: World Publishing Company.

Gignac, G. E. (2015). Raven's is not a pure measure of general intelligence: Implications for *g* factor theory and the brief measurement of *g*. *Intelligence*, 50, 71–79. doi:10.1016/j.intell.2015.07.006.

Glenn, S. S., & Ellis, J. (1988). Do the Kallikaks look "menacing" or "retarded"? *American Psychologist*, 43, 742–743.

Gottfredson, L. S. (1994, Tuesday, December 3). Mainstream science on intelligence. *Wall Street Journal*.

(1997). Editorial: Mainstream science on intelligence: An editorial with 52 signatories, history, and bibliography. *Intelligence*, 24, 13–24.

(2011). Intelligence and social inequality: Why the biological link? In T. Chamorro-Premuzic, S. von Stumm, & A. Furnham (Eds.), *The Wiley-Blackwell handbook of individual differences*. Malden, MA: Wiley-Blackwell.

Gould, S. J. (1981). *The mismeasure of man*. New York: W. W. Norton.

(1996). *The mismeasure of man* (2nd edn.). New York: Norton.

Gustafsson, J. (1984). A unifying model for the structure of intellectual abilities. *Intelligence*, 8, 179–203.

Guttman, L., & Levey, S. (1991). Two structural laws for intelligence tests. *Intelligence*, 15, 79–103.

Haier, R. J. (2017). *The neuroscience of intelligence*. New York: Cambridge University Press.

Hambrick, D. Z., Macnamara, B. N., Campitelli, G., Ullén, F., & Mosing, M. A. (2016). Beyond born versus made: A new look at expertise. In B. H. Ross (Ed.), *The psychology of learning and motivation* (Vol. 64, pp. 1–55). Elsevier Academic Press.

Hayes, K. J. (1962). Genes, drives, and intellect. *Psychological Reports*, 10, 299–342. doi:10.2466/pr0.1962.10.2.299.

Johnson, W., & Bouchard, T. J., Jr. (2005a). Constructive replication of the visual-perceptual-image rotation model in Thurstone's (1941) battery of 60 tests of mental ability. *Intelligence*, 33, 417–430.

(2005b). The structure of human intelligence: It's Verbal, Perceptual, and Image Rotation (VPR), not Fluid Crystallized. *Intelligence*, 33, 393–416. doi:10.1016/j.intell.2004.12.002.

(2011). The MISTRA data: Forty-two mental ability tests in three batteries. *Intelligence*, 39(2–3), 82–88. doi:10.1016/j.intell.2011.02.010.

(2014). Genetics of intellectual and personality traits associated with creative genius: Could geniuses be Cosmobian Dragon Kings?. In D. K. Simonton (Ed.), *The Wiley handbook of genius* (pp. 269–296). Oxford: Wiley.

Johnson, W., te Nijenhuis, J., & Bouchard, T. J., Jr. (2007). Replication of the hierarchical visual-perceptual-image rotation model in de Wolff and Buiten's (1963) battery of 46 tests of mental ability. *Intelligence*, 35, 69–81. doi:10.1016/j.intell.2006.05.002.

Jöreskog, K. G. (1969). A general approach to confirmatory maximum likelihood factor analysis. *Psychometrika*, 34(2), 183–202. doi:10.1007/bf02289343.

Kamin, L. J. (1974). *The science and politics of IQ*. Potomac, MD: Erlbaum.

King, D. B., Montanez-Raminez, L. M., & Wertheimer, M. (1996). Barbara Stoddard Burks: Pioneer behavioral geneticist and humanitarian. In G. A. Kimble, C. A. Boneay, & M. Wertheimer (Eds.), *Portraits of pioneers in psychology; Volume II* (pp. 213–225). Washington, DC: American Psychological Association.

Kong, A., Frigge, M. L., Thorleifsson, G., Stefansson, H., Young, A. I., Zink, F., ... Stefansson, K. (2017). Selection against variants in the genome associated with educational attainment. *Proceedings of the National Academy of Science USA*, 114(5), E727–E732. doi:10.1073/pnas.1612113114.

Korb, K. B. (1994). Stephen Jay Gould on intelligence. *Cognition*, 52(2), 111–123.

Lee, J. J., & Kuncel, N. R. (2015). The determinacy and predictive power of common factors. *Industrial and Organizational Psychology*, 8(03), 467–472. doi:10.1017/iop.2015.64.

Lewis, J. E., Degusta, D., Meyer, M. R., Monge, J. M., Mann, A. E., & Holloway, R. L. (2011). The mismeasure of science: Stephen Jay Gould versus Samuel George Morton on skulls and bias. *PLoS Biology*, 9(6), e1001071. doi:10.1371/journal.pbio.1001071.

Lotz, C., Sparfeldt, J. R., & Greiff, S. (2016). Complex problem solving in educational contexts – Still something beyond a "good g"? *Intelligence*. doi:10.1016/j.intell.2016.09.001.

Lubinski, D. (2010). Spatial ability and STEM: A sleeping giant for talent identification and development. *Personality and Individual Differences*, 49, 344–351. doi:10.1016/j.paid.2010.03.022.

Lynch, M., & Walsh, B. (1998). *Genetics and analysis of quantitative traits.* Sunderland, MA: Sinauer.

Mackintosh, N. J. (Ed.) (1995). *Cyril Burt: Fraud or framed.* Oxford: Oxford University Press.

Major, J. T., Johnson, W., & Bouchard, T. J., Jr. (2011). The dependability of the general factor of intelligence: Why small, single-factor models do not adequately represent *g*. *Intelligence*, 39, 418–433. doi:10.1016/j.intell.2011.07.002.

Major, J. T., Johnson, W., & Deary, I., J. (2012). Comparing models of intelligence in Project TALENT: The VPR model fits better than the CHC and extended Gf–Gc models. *Intelligence*, 40, 543–559. doi:10.1016/j.intell.2012.07.006.

Makel, M. C., Kell, H. J., Lubinski, D., Putallaz, M., & Benbow, C. P. (2016). When lightning strikes twice: Profoundly gifted, profoundly accomplished. *Psychological Science*, 27(7), 1004–1018. doi:10.1177/0956797616644735

Martin, N. G., Eaves, L. J., Heath, A. C., Jardine, R., Feingold, L. M., & Eysenck, H. J. (1986). Transmission of social attitudes. *Proceedings of the National Academy of Science USA*, 83(12), 4364–4368.

McNemar, Q. (1964). Lost: Our intelligence? Why? *American Psychologist*, 19, 871–882.

Meehl, P. E. (1978). Theoretical risks and tabular asterisks: Sir Karl, Sir Ronald, and the slow progress of soft psychology. *Journal of Consulting and Clinical Psychology*, 46, 806–834.

Muller, C. B., Ride, S. M., Fouke, J., Whitney, T., Denton, D. D., Cantor, N., ... Robinson, S. (2005). Gender differences and performance in science. *Science*, 307(5712), 1043. doi:10.1126/science.307.5712.1043b.

Pearson. (1914–1930). *The life, letters and labours of Francis Galton, Volume 1.* Cambridge: Cambridge University Press.

Pinker, S. (2002). *The blank slate: The modern denial of human nature.* New York: Viking.

Platt, J. R. (1964). Strong inference. *Science*, 146, 347–353.

Polderman, T. J. C., Benyamin, B., De Leeuw, C. A., Sullivan, P. F., Van Bochoven, A., Visscher, P. M., & Posthuma, D. (2015). Meta-analysis of the heritability of human traits based on fifty years of twin studies. *Nature Genetics*, 47, 702–709. doi:10.1038/ng.3285.

Ponsoda, V., Martinez, K., Pineda-Pardo, J. A., Abad, F. J., Olea, J., Roman, F. J., ... Colom, R. (2016). Structural brain connectivity and cognitive ability differences: A multivariate distance matrix regression analysis. *Human Brain Mapping*. doi:10.1002/hbm.23419.

Protzko, J. (2016). Does the raising IQ–raising g distinction explain the fadeout effect? *Intelligence, 56*, 65–71. doi:10.1016/j.intell.2016.02.008.

Reeve, C. L., & Blacksmith, N. (2009). Identifying g: A review of current factor analytic practices in the science of mental ability. *Intelligence, 37*, 487–494. doi:10.1016/j.intell.2009.06.002.

Reeve, C. L., & Charles, J. E. (2008). Survey of opinions on the primacy of g and social consequences of ability testing: A comparison of expert and non-expert views. *Intelligence, 36*(6), 681–688. doi:10.1016/j.intell.2008.03.007.

Rushton, J. P. (1997). Race, intelligence, and the brain: The errors and omissions of the "revised" edition of S. J. Gould's *The mismeasure of man* (1996). *Personality and Individual Differences, 23*, 169–180.

Salthouse, T. A. (2013). Evaluating the correspondence of different cognitive batteries. *Assessment*. doi:10.1177/1073191113486690.

Scarr, S., & McCartney, K. (1983). How people make their own environments: A theory of genotype -> environment effects. *Child Development, 54*, 424–435. doi:10.2307/1129703.

Scarr, S., & Weinberg, R. A. (1978). The influence of "family background" on intellectual attainment. *American Sociological Review, 43*, 674–692.

Scott, J. P. (1990). Foreword. In M. E. Hahn, J. K. Hewitt, N. D. Henderson, & R. H. Benno (Eds.), *Developmental behavior genetics: Neural, biometrical, and evolutionary approaches*. New York: Oxford.

Segal, N. L. (2012). *Born together–reared apart: The landmark Minnesota twin study*. Cambridge, MA: Harvard University Press.

(2017). *Twin mythconceptions: False beliefs, fables, and facts about twins*. New York: Academic Press.

Selzam, S., Krapohl, E., Von Stumm, S., O'Reilly, P. F., Rimfeld, K., Kovas, Y., ... Plomin, R. (2016). Predicting educational achievement from DNA. *Molecular Psychiatry, 22*(2), 267–272. doi:10.1038/mp.2016.107.

Shermer, M. B. (2002). Stephen Jay Gould as historian of science and scientific historian, popular scientist and scientific popularizer. *Social Studies of Science, 32*, 489–525.

Simonton, D. K. (2016). Intelligence, inheritance, motivation, and expertise. Review of *Grit: The power of passion and perseverance*, A. Duckworth, and *Peak: Secrets from the new science of expertise*, A. Ericsson & R. Pool. *Intelligence, 58*, 80–81. doi:10.1016/j.intell.2016.05.005.

Sparks, C. S., & Jantz, R. L. (2002). A reassessment of human cranial plasticity: Boas revisited. *Proceedings of the National Academy of Sciences, 99*(23), 14636–14639. doi:10.1073/pnas.222389599.

Spearman, C. (1904). General intelligence: Objectively determined and measured. *American Journal of Psychology, 15*, 201–293.

Tooby, J., & Cosmides, L. (2015). The theoretical foundations of evolutionary psychology. In D. M. Buss (Ed.), *The handbook of evolutionary psychology, second edition* (Vol. Volume 1: Foundations, pp. 3–87). Hoboken, NJ: Wiley.

Tredoux, G. (2015). Defrauding Cyril Burt: A reanalysis of the social mobility data. *Intelligence, 49*, 32–43. doi:10.1016/j.intell.2014.12.002.

Tuddenham, R. D. (1962). The nature and measurement of intelligence. In L. Postman (Ed.), *Psychology in the making: Histories of selected research problems* (pp. 469–525). New York: Knopf.

Zenderland, L. (1988). On interpreting photographs, faces and the past. *American Psychologist, 42*, 743–744.

CHAPTER 3

Culture, Sex, and Intelligence

Stephen J. Ceci, Donna K. Ginther, Shulamit Kahn, &
Wendy M. Williams

In this chapter we focus on findings from our research on sex differences in academic achievement and what they say about the role of culture in shaping mathematical and spatial cognition. Our research focuses on the policy and educational implications of spatial and mathematical ability that are correlated with psychometric data (e.g., SAT, GRE, NAEP) and raises questions about the nature and development of these differences and what role policy has in ameliorating them.

Sex Differences in Quantitative Fields

Women are underrepresented in all math-intensive fields in the academy. According to the NSF's 2010 Survey of Doctorate Recipients (SDR), women in Geoscience, Engineering, Economics, Math/Computer science, and the Physical sciences (**GEEMP**) in 2010 comprised only 25%–44% of tenure-track assistant professors and only 7%–16% of full professors. There is debate over why women are so conspicuously absent in these fields compared with the Life sciences, Psychology, and Social sciences (**LPS**), where the comparable figures show women at 66% of tenure-track assistant professorships in psychology, 45% in social sciences (excluding economics), and 38% in life sciences; for full professors, the figures are 35%, 23%, and 24%, respectively. So, compared with their presence in LPS fields, women's presence in mathematically intensive (GEEMP) fields is much lower. Why is this? What does it say about spatial and quantitative aptitude? And what, if anything, ought to be done to narrow this gap between the sexes? To answer these questions, we have taken a developmental perspective, starting early in life and tracking cohorts through adulthood. Before examining early sex differences, however, we review sex differences at the college, graduate school, and professional levels.

Females comprise 57% of college graduates and 57% of STEM (Science, Technology, Engineering, and Mathematics) majors. Figure 3.1 shows the

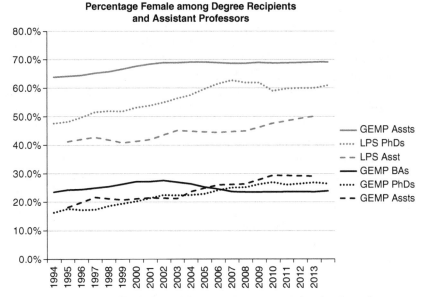

Figure 3.1   Percent of bachelor and doctorate degrees awarded to females and percent female of assistant professors, by STEM category. Data drawn from the NSF's WebCASPAR database. (ncsesdata.nsf.gov/webcaspar/) and the NSF's 1973–2010 Survey of Doctorate Recipients.

percentages of females among college graduates, PhD recipients, and assistant professors. Since 2000, 69% of majors in the life sciences, psychology, and social sciences (LPS) are women. In contrast, women comprise only a quarter of undergraduates in GEEMP fields. Because of these disparities across fields, combining across all STEM majors misses important field-specific sex differences.

As seen in this figure, women have made significant gains in both categories of STEM at each of these levels over the past 40 years. By 2011, there was little difference in women's and men's advancement from baccalaureate to PhD and then to tenure-track assistant professorships – *in GEEMP fields only*. Thus, although far fewer women begin in GEEMP fields, of those who do, their progress resembles male GEEMP majors and in fact slightly exceeds males in transitioning from baccalaureate to PhD (Ceci et al., 2014, fig. 11). Recently, research showed that women with undergraduate engineering degrees persisted in the workforce 7–8 years post-baccalaureate degree nearly identically to males (Kahn & Ginther, 2015).

In contrast, in 2011, the probability of advancing from an LPS baccalaureate to a PhD was not as high for women as for men, nor as high as in GEEMP fields. Further, the gap in the probability of advancing from PhD to assistant professorship was particularly large for women in LPS, with fewer women than men advancing at each stage. Using a different methodology, Miller and Wai (2015) reported no consistent sex difference in persisting through the STEM pipeline.

There has been much speculation about the causes of the dearth of women in GEEMP fields (Ceci & Williams, 2007, 2010a, 2010b, 2011; Ceci, Williams, & Barnett, 2009; Williams & Ceci, 2015), some invoking girls' lower math and spatial ability, others favoring early socialization/ stereotypes that tilt girls away from GEEMP fields, and still others focusing on gendered preferences for people-vs.-thing occupations. The four of us reported the results of several hundred analyses, and concluded that the reason for women's shortage in GEEMP fields probably has less to do with their relative mathematical and spatial disadvantage (Ceci et al., 2014). Before delving into the arguments for this conclusion, we summarize the descriptive data on math ability.

Sex Differences in Mathematical Ability

Discussions of early sex differences in mathematical ability primarily focus on mean performance rather than on performance at the extreme right tail of the ability distribution, where we assume most mathematicians, computer scientists, physicists, and engineers score (top 5%, top 1%, perhaps even top 0.01%).

Figure 3.2 illustrates the strong negative relation between the mathematical intensity of the PhD – reflected by the average GRE-Q scores of applicants (170 is the highest score possible) – and the fraction of women receiving advanced degrees in the field. The most math-intensive fields have mean GRE-Q scores around 159–160 (~85th percentile), while the LPS fields hover around 150 (~53rd percentile), leading us to opine: "Simply put, the more math, the fewer women" (Ceci et al., 2014, p. 87). Moreover, the further you go out on the right tail of the quantitative distribution, the more men relative to women are found.

According to one view, sex differences in mathematical ability result from biological differences that interact with the environment, with early differences growing into larger gender gaps, hence fewer females at the right tail. According to this view, women's lower quantitative scores reduce their chances of admittance into GEEMP PhD programs. A number of researchers have challenged this as the main cause of the dearth of women in these fields (e.g., Andreescu et al., 2008; Ceci & Williams, 2010a, 2010b; Halpern & Miller, 2014; Hyde & Mertz, 2009).

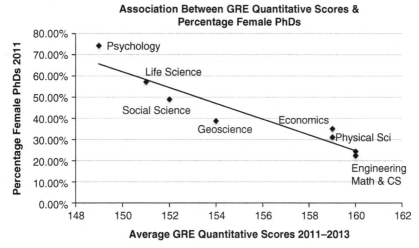

Figure 3.2 Association between average GRE-Quantitative scores and % PhDs awarded to females (CS refers to computer science).
Source: Ceci et al., 2014, data from ETS and Webcaspar.

For example, sex differences favoring men in spatial 3-D tasks do not translate directly to superiority in geometry, but depend on whether the dependent variable is grades in geometry or scores on standardized tests that cover materials not directly taught (Else-Quest, Hyde, & Linn, 2010; Lindberg et al., 2010). For that matter, sex differences in mathematics scores do not translate into grades in math classes, including complex math classes in college (Ceci et al., 2009): women obtain slightly higher grades in college classes and 40–48% of baccalaureates in mathematics for two decades (see Ceci et al., 2014, table A1A). None of this means that biological sex differences play no role in the shortage of women in GEEMP fields. But it does mean that care must be taken in touting them as *the* primary causal factor.

At the midpoint of the quantitative distribution, there are no systematic sex differences through middle school (see Ceci et al., 2014). Hyde and her colleagues have analyzed the sex gap in average mathematics ability, using large-scale national probability samples (Hyde, Fennema & Lamon, 1990; Hyde et al., 2008). They showed that mean scores highly overlap (ds between 0.05–0.26 favoring males): Hyde and colleagues' 1990 meta-analysis of 100 studies found no significant sex differences for children at any age and for any type of mathematical problem – the only exception was a small male advantage, d = 0.29, for complex math problems for high school–aged students. Hyde and colleagues (2008) even found small female advantages for most years through ninth grade. However, they also found significant male advantages in grades 10 and 11.

By the early 2000s, average U.S. sex differences were small even on the most complex items, leading Hyde and Mertz (2009) to conclude: "effect sizes were found to average d = 0.07, a trivial difference. These findings provide further evidence that the average U.S. girl has now reached parity with the average boy, even in high school, and even for measures requiring complex problem solving" (p. 8802).

Some have found small differences on math tests earlier than middle school, but not at entrance to kindergarten. For instance, Fryer and Leavitt (2010) and Penner and Paret (2008), studying the same 1998–1999 kindergarten cohort, found no differences entering kindergarten but differences starting at tiny levels by the end of kindergarten that rose to 0.15–0.20 SDs by fifth grade. Cross-national studies found countries differ. For instance, Mullis and colleagues (2000b) reported no U.S. average sex difference on the fourth-grade TIMSS, but a male advantage for Korea and Japan.

In sum, there is agreement that in the United States, there are either nonexistent male advantages in average math scores, or very small ones relative to the overlap of the distributions, on the order of less than 0.001, or less than 0.1% SD.

Sex differences at the right tail. Perhaps the shortage of women in GEEMP fields is the result of sex differences in high math ability. As seen in Figure 3.3, most graduate students in GEEMP fields at one of our universities have GRE-Q scores in the top 18% (750), which is equivalent to the updated scale used earlier.

What is known about sex differences at the right tail? A male advantage in math ability is unreliable until early adolescence (Ceci et al., 2009). Lohman and Lakin (2009) analyzed more than 300,000 American 9- to 17-year-olds and found a higher proportion of boys in in the top 4% of the math distribution, which was stable across national samples from 1984 to 2000 (Figure 3.4). Strand and colleagues (2006) reported a similar male overrepresentation at the right tail of this test for more than 300,000 11-year-olds from the UK, with boys significantly more likely to score in the top group (+1.75 SDs above the mean); boys are also more likely to score in the bottom 4% in quantitative ability. Hedges and Nowell's (1995) analyses of six national data sets also showed consistency in the sex ratios at the top tail over a 32-year period.

Wai and colleagues (2010); Wai and Putallaz (2011), and Hyde and colleagues (2008) also reported substantial sex differences at the right tail

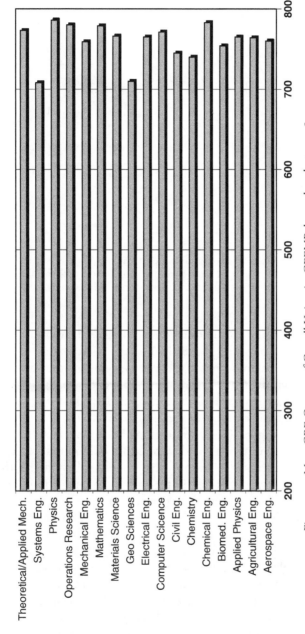

Figure 3.3   Mean GRE-Q scores of Cornell University GEEMP doctoral students, 2008–2009.

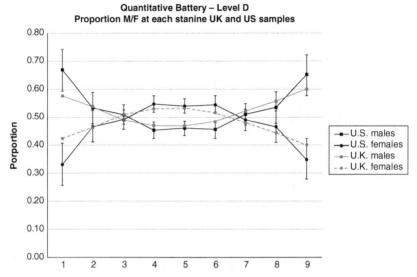

Figure 3.4   Male-to-female proportions at each stanine ($M = 5$, $SD = 2$) based on data from 318,599 students in the United States and 320,000 10- to 11-year-olds in the UK. (Data are from Lohman & Lakin, 2009. Reproduced with permission of the authors.)

of the mathematics distribution. And Ellison and Swanson (2010) and Andreescu and colleagues (2008) found large sex differences in students achieving top rankings on the most challenging mathematics competitions. However, the magnitude of these differences changes as a function of epoch, nation, and schools within countries, indicating sociocultural factors are the basis for some of them.

Wai and colleagues' (2010) findings are based on a stability analysis of right tail ratios over 30 years and involved 1.6 million non-randomly chosen seventh graders (all of whom were intellectually gifted). They show that the large sex gap reported in the early 1980s (13.5:1 ratio of males to females among those seventh graders scoring at the top 0.01% on the SAT-Mathematics) had shrunk by the early 1990s to 3.8:1 and has remained near that ratio. However, on the ACT-math test among a similar intellectually gifted group, the ratio of those scoring in the top .01% was 2.6:1 males-to-females, and *had* been falling since the early 1990s. Hyde and colleagues (2008) also found a 2.09:1 sex ratio among the top 1% of 11th grade math scorers on the National Assessment of Educational Progress (NAEP) for whites, but a 0.91:1 ratio (small female advantage) for Asians. Mullis and colleagues (2000a) reported small and inconsistent sex differences on

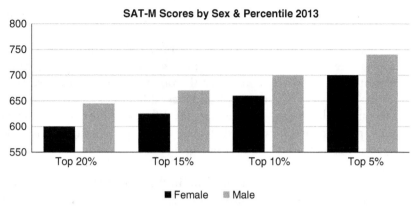

Figure 3.5   SAT-Math scores by sex and percentile, 2013.
Source: Ceci et al., 2014, data from College Board.

TIMSS at grade 8, but consistent male superiority by grade 12, particularly among the highest quartile of mathematics scorers. Relatedly, Stoet and Geary (2013) analyzed PISA data for the 33 countries that participated in all waves from 2000–2009. They, too, found slowly narrowing sex differences of 15-year-olds at the right tail, ending at 1.7:1 favoring males at the top 5% and 2.3:1 at the top 1%. Thus, large-scale analyses converge on the conclusion that there is a sizable male advantage at the right tail of the math distribution.

Sex differences favoring males on the SAT-Mathematics are similar: the same score that gets a girl into the top 5% of the female mathematics distribution gets a boy into only the top 10% of the male distribution; the same score that gets a girl into the top 10% gets a boy into only the top 20% (Figure 3.5).

There is inconsistency in sex differences at the right tail, even when comparing large national samples or meta-analyses (for review, see Ceci et al., 2009). For instance, among certain age children in Iceland, Singapore, and Indonesia, more girls scored in the top 1% than boys (Hyde & Mertz, 2009). Further, the male advantage at the right tail has been decreasing, more in some countries than in others, and the greater male variance in math scores is not always the case. In Lohman and Lakin's (2009) data, females narrowed the right tail gap on the Cognitive Abilities Test Nonverbal Battery: ninth stanine female-to-male ratios changed from 0.72 in 1984, to 0.83 in 1992, to 0.87 in 2000. Relatedly, the male-to-female ratio at the top 4% is larger in the United States (two to one) than it is in the UK (roughly three to two), further illustrating the influence of cultural factors.

Researchers have reported variations across ethnic groups in the United States. Hyde and Mertz (2009) found large differences favoring white males at the extreme right tail, but the opposite for Asian Americans, with more females at the right tail, and these differences varied by cohort. Miller and Halpern (2014), note that "sex differences in high mathematics test performance are reversed (female advantage) among Latino kindergarteners, indicating the early emerging effects of family and culture" (p. 39).

Finally, there are cross-state variations in the United States in the male/female ratio at the 95th percentile, with sex differences in some states less than half the size in others (Pope & Sydnor, 2010): the males-to-females ratio among the top 5% scorers in math/science is approximately 1.8 in the Eastern South Central states, but only 1.4 in the New England states. However, the ratio of *females-to-males* NAEP 95th percentile scores in reading is approximately 2.1 in the New England states and 2.6 in the East South Central states. States with more gender-equal math and science scores also have more gender-equal reading scores at the right tail (which otherwise has more girls), suggesting gender norms strongly influence mathematic and verbal achievement at the top tail. Along these lines, Ellison and Swanson (2010) found that local school culture was highly influential in determining how many girls competed at the highest level of mathematics in national competitions.

Boys are overrepresented in both tails of the distribution. Transnational mathematics analyses (TIMMS, PISA) show boys' higher variance ratios (VRs) – the male variance divided by the female variance (e.g., Else-Quest et al., 2010; Penner, 2008). Else-Quest and colleagues report VRs ~1:1.19 in the United States, 1:1.06 in the UK, 1:0.99 in Denmark, and 1:0.95 in Indonesia. In representative studies, VRs average 1.15, and on average there is at least a 2-to-1 ratio favoring males among the top 1% of math scorers. These sex differences are real. However, transnational and trans-state differences suggest that something more than mathematical potential is driving the higher male variability. Yet VRs may underestimate population variance because more males are developmentally delayed and not included in assessments (see Halpern, 2012). Thus, state-by-state, transnational, cohort, and ethnic data all indicate that sex differences at the right tail are fluid; these ratios can and do change.

Moreover, data sources used in these analyses are vulnerable to variations in context, (e.g., changes over time in test content that favor one sex,

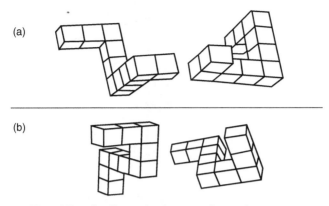

(a)

(b)

Mental Rotation Test—Are these two figures the same except for their orientation?

Figure 3.6   Shepard-Meltzer (1971) display.

changes in participation rates in testing, changes in coursework, etc.; see Ceci et al., 2009).

Finally, the asymmetry at the right tail cannot explain women's under-representation in GEEMP because even if potential PhD candidates favored males by two to one, that cannot explain gaps of up to six to one among senior professors. Further, as seen in Figure 3.3, the average quantitative scores of PhD candidates in GEEMP fields hover around 750, which is the 82nd percentile, a region where the sex gap is considerably lower than two to one.

Sex Differences in Spatial Ability

Tasks with a heavy spatial component are correlated with measures of fluid intelligence, sometimes almost perfectly (Chuderski, 2013). On mental rotation tasks, 2-D or 3-D figures must be rotated to make a correct match (Figure 3.6).

Numerous studies have examined sex differences on these tasks. They uniformly report large effect sizes favoring males in 3-D processing, with effect sizes often >0.80 (e.g., see Linn & Petersen, 1985; Voyer, Voyer, & Bryden et al., 1995). (No systematic sex differences are found for 2-D processing or on tasks involving spatial memory.)

Interestingly, some spatial tasks show a male advantage when they are framed as geometry problems but a female advantage when the same task

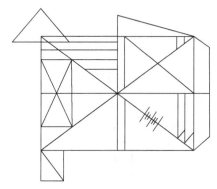

Figure 3.7a Spatial task used by Huguet and Regner (2009); can be framed as geometry or art.

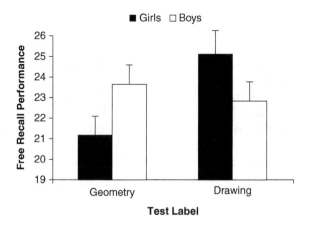

Figure 3.7b Shows the interaction between framing and sex differences.

is framed as an art task. Huguet and Regner (2009) presented Figure 3.7a to middle school students for 90 seconds and gave them five minutes to reproduce it from memory.

Boys outperformed girls when the task was presented as a geometry problem, but the reverse was true when it was presented as an artistic task (Figure 3.7b).

Various interventions to teach spatial processing demonstrate that the sex gap can be narrowed, though not fully closed within the confines of the training durations, which have been one semester or less (Ceci et al., 2009).

If boys' spatial superiority is due to playing dynamic video games, Lincoln logs, erector sets, Legos, etc., then exposing girls to these activities could narrow the gap. Some research shows that spatial activities between the ages of two and four years (e.g., shaping clay, drawing, and cutting 2-D figures) predicts mathematical skills at age four and a half (Grissmer et al., 2013). They showed that an intervention based on transforming spatial materials to 2-D and 3-D elevated disadvantaged children on the Woodcock-Johnson Applied Problems and KEYMATH3-Numeration tests from ~ 32nd to the 48th percentile; visual-spatial ability was also elevated due to play activity, from 33% to 47%.

There is some evidence, however, of sex differences in spatial processing prior to the onset of activities. Four studies have shown that male infants outperform females on rotation tasks. However, this depends on whether they are speeded and/or entail rigid surface transformations (see Miller & Halpern, 2014). And there is some evidence that crawling experience fosters spatial ability. Moore and Johnson (2011) employed a habituation paradigm using the spatial task in Figure 3.6. Following habituation to an object, when infants are shown it in a new perspective, three-month-old boys prefer the novel display over the rotated version of the familiar display, whereas girls look at the familiar and novel objects equally, indicating that only the boys mentally rotated objects. This suggests that boys' spatial intelligence is evident somewhat earlier than girls'. (Quinn and Liben, 2008, found a similar result for three–four-month-olds with 2-D rotation though, as noted, sex differences are primarily found for 3-D rotations.) Although these studies strongly suggest an early biological basis of early sex differences, some argue they cannot rule out environmental causes (see Miller & Halpern, 2014, p. 39).

As noted, 3-D mental rotation is linked to seemingly small differences favoring infants who engage in early crawling and manual manipulation. Researchers presented nine-month-olds with a 3-D rotation task; half had been crawling for nine weeks, and some were likely to manipulate five objects presented to them. The infants were habituated to a video of an object rotating back and forth through a 240° angle around its longitudinal axis. When tested with the same object rotating through the unseen 120° angle, the crawlers focused longer at the novel (mirror) object, regardless of their manual manipulation scores. In contrast, the non-crawlers' rotation was influenced by their manual manipulation (Schwarzer, Freitag, & Schum, 2013). These findings indicate that subtle environmental differences, such as early crawling and object manipulation, influence spatial cognition. Of course this does not preclude a biological role in male spatial superiority (perhaps early crawling is biologically determined and occurs earlier for male babies), but it suggests an intervention to induce infant girls to manipulate and crawl.

A Seeming Paradox

There is a seeming paradox: females outperform males on classroom mathematics achievement. Yet males are more numerous at the right tail of mathematics performance on standardized tests such as the SAT-Math, the NAEP, PISA, and GRE-Q. Males are also more likely to major in GEEMP disciplines, obtain GEEMP masters and PhDs, and work in GEEMP fields.

Explanations for this paradox may lie in gender stereotypes that associate math with boys and reading with girls. Cvencek, Meltzoff, and Greenwald (2011) report that by second grade, boys and girls demonstrated implicit and explicit stereotypes associating math with maleness and reading with femaleness.

Paradoxically, these stereotypes are incongruent with what children observe in classrooms, including math and science. Part of the paradox may be related to girls associating in early grades brilliance with being male. This stereotype has a sudden onset, sometime between kindergarten and second grade. Bian, Leslie, and Cimpian (2017) demonstrated that children's sense of what it means to be brilliant changes between five and seven. In their study, children had to guess which of two boys and two girls was "really, really smart" and most likely to solve a hard problem. Five-year-old boys *and* girls associated brilliance with their own gender. Yet between five and seven, girls become less likely than boys to associate brilliance with their gender. This also extended to children rating adults, they begin to exhibit a bias in favor of males between six and seven. However, there is no bias in favor of males in predicting who had better academic achievement; there was an expectation that girls will get better grades, consistent with the actual data showing girls do get better grades. Finally, additional experiments in Bian and colleagues (2017) found that girls were less interested than boys in a game they associated with smart children: "Many children assimilate the idea that brilliance is a male quality at a young age. This stereotype begins to shape children's interest as soon as it is acquired and is thus likely to narrow the range of careers they will one day contemplate" (Bian et al., 2017, pp. 390–391).

There is some evidence that a belief that math ability can be developed is self-fulfilling, and that girls are less likely to have this so-called growth mindset. For middle schoolers or high schoolers, Blackwell, Trzesniewski, and Dweck (2007), Nix, Perez-Felkner, and Thomas (2014), and Good, Aronson, and Harder (2008) found evidence of a correlation between a math growth mindset and math performance, math interest, and math course-taking in middle school and high school. Moreover, the lack of a growth mindset is particularly evident in math, which is perceived as difficult. And at least by high school, boys are much more likely to have a math growth mindset than girls: controlling for scores on standardized math tests, by 10th grade, boys are 0.2 standard deviations more likely (p < 0.001) than girls to believe that math can be learned (Nix et al., 2014).

Teachers may have a role in developing gender stereotypes. For instance, elementary/middle school teachers' biases play an important role in high school students' likelihood of taking advanced math and science courses, more so for girls from lower SES backgrounds and those from families in which the father is more educated than the mother (Lavy & Sand, 2015). Sometimes, the impact of teachers on stereotypes is more complex. Beilock and colleagues (2009) found that first- and second-grade girls who had female teachers with math anxiety were likely to believe that "boys are good at math and girls good at reading" and to have lower math achievement than both boys and girls with female teachers without math anxiety. Antecol, Eren, and Ozbeklik (2015), using a natural experiment, found that primary school girls taught by women teachers with weak math backgrounds did worse on their math scores, but not if taught by women with stronger math backgrounds. However, instructor gender itself did not seem to be creating stereotype bias.

Unanswered Questions

Can the early gender stereotyping findings explain why even at a young age, children have gender-differentiated career aspirations that not only persist but get enlarged to the extent that they deter females from pursuing GEEMP fields? Can such stereotypes affect sex differences in spatial cognition? When asked whether they are interested in becoming engineers or computer scientists, few adolescent girls respond positively, whereas about a quarter of boys aspire to such careers. In contrast, girls are more likely to aspire to careers as physicians, veterinarians, teachers, biologists, and nurses. For example, 24% of 8- to 17-year-olds boys indicated interest in engineering versus only 5% of girls; in another survey of 13- to 17-year-olds, 74% of boys expressed interest in computer science versus only 32% of girls (Hill, Corbett, & Rose, 2010). While these early preferences are not stable until later in high school and they do not predict the later specific gender segregation observed in college majors (Legewie & DiPrete, 2012), they nevertheless reveal early career leanings.

However, several enigmas remain. Even if sex differences in math and science orientation/identification begin as early as ages six and seven and solidify by the end of middle school, it is unclear why they should result in the particular gendered pattern of career aspirations observed. Among high school students, sex differences in STEM courses and plans to major in STEM fields are well-established and demonstrated by the lower participation rates (23% to 42% female) in AP exams such as Calculus BC, computer science, and Physics C, and between 20% and 60% more males receive top scores of 5 (Ceci et al., 2014). Yet, even among those women who escape stereotypical influences, who take and excel in math-intensive advanced coursework in high school and college (where almost half of baccalaureates in mathematics are awarded to women), we still see far fewer women entering GEEMP careers; instead, they choose careers in microbiology, medicine, or statistics, fields in which women have achieved significant presence.

Thus, research converges on the following three conclusions. a) Stereotypes are important: girls/boys learn them early, although it does not translate into lower average math ability in testing until puberty. b) There is higher variance and more representation at the right tail for males. This appears to be mutable to some degree, although we do not know fully whether this can be eliminated. Yet this alone is not enough to explain the difference in GEEMP representation. And c) in addition to stereotypes and math ability differences (that may or may not be due to biology), there are gender differences in interests, with females more interested in people-related careers and males more interested in nonsocial things (e.g. Auyeung, Lombardo, & Baron-Cohen, 2013; Thorndike, 1911). Lippa has repeatedly documented very large sex differences in occupational interests, including in transnational surveys, with men more interested in "thing"-oriented activities and occupations, such as engineering and mechanics, and women more interested in people-oriented occupations, such as nursing, counseling, and elementary school teaching (e.g., Lippa, 1998, 2001, 2010). In an extensive meta-analysis of more than half a million people, Su, Rounds, and Armstrong (2009) reported a sex difference on this dimension of a full standard deviation (see also Su & Rounds, 2015). However, the extent to which these gendered interests and outcomes are influenced by early biases and stereotypes remains to be demonstrated.

References

Andreescu, T., Gallian, J. A., Kane, J., & Mertz, J. E. (2008). Cross-cultural analysis of students with exceptional talent in mathematical problem solving. *Notices of the American Mathematical Society, 55,* 1248–1260.

Antecol, H., Eren, O., & Ozbeklik, S. (2015). The effect of teacher gender on student achievement in primary school. *Journal of Labor Economics, 33*(1), 63–89.

Auyeung, B., Lombardo, M. V., & Baron-Cohen, S. (2013). Prenatal and postnatal hormone effects on the human brain and cognition. *Pflügers Archiv-European Journal of Physiology, 465,* 557–571. doi:10.1007/s00424-013-1268-2.

Beilock, L. S., Gunderson, E. A., Ramirez, G., & Levine, S. C. (2009). Female teachers' math anxiety affects girls' math achievement. *Proceedings of the National Academy of Sciences, 107*(5), 1860–1863.

Bian, L., Leslie, S.-J., & Cimpian, A. (2017). Gender stereotypes about intellectual ability emerge early and influence children's interests. *Science, 355,* 389–391.

Blackwell, L. S., Trzesniewski, K. H., & Dweck, C. S. (2007). Implicit theories of intelligence predict achievement across an adolescent. *Child Development, 78*(1), 246–263.

Ceci, S. J., Ginther, D. K., Kahn, S., & Williams, W. M. (2014). Women in academic science: A changing landscape. *Psychological Science in the Public Interest,* http://psi.sagepub.com/content/15/3/75.abstract?patientinform-links=yes&legid=sppsi;15/3/75. doi:10.1177/1529100614541236.

Ceci, S. J. & Williams, W. M. (2007). Sex differences in cognition: Moving closer and closer apart. In S. J. Ceci & W. M. Williams (Eds.). *Do women belong in science?: Eminent thinkers weigh the evidence.* (pp. 213–236). Washington, DC: American Psychological Association Books.

(2010a). *The mathematics of sex: How biology and society conspire to limit talented women and girls.* New York: Oxford University Press.

(2010b). Sex differences in math-intensive fields. *Current Directions in Psychological Science, 19*(5), 275–279.

(2011). Understanding current causes of women's underrepresentation in science. *Proceedings of the National Academy of Sciences, 108,* 3157–3162.

Ceci, S. J., Williams, W. M., & Barnett, S. M. (2009). Women's underrepresentation in science: Sociocultural and biological considerations. *Psychological Bulletin, 135,* 218–261.

Chuderski, A. (2013). When are fluid intelligence and working memory isomorphic and when are they not? *Intelligence, 41,* 244–262. doi:10.1016/j.intell.2013.04.003 Google Scholar CrossRef.

Cvencek, D., Meltzoff, A. N., & Greenwald, A. (2011). Math-gender stereotypes in elementary schoolchildren. *Child Development, 82*(3) May/June, 766–779.

Ellison, G. & Swanson, A. (2010). The gender gap in secondary school mathematics at high achievement levels: Evidence from the American Mathematics Competitions. *Journal of Economic Perspectives, 24,* 109–128.

Else-Quest, N., Hyde, J., & Linn, M. (2010). Cross-national patterns of gender differences in mathematics: A meta-analysis. *Psychological Bulletin*, 136, 103–127.

Fryer, R. G., Jr. & S. D. Levitt. (2010). An empirical analysis of the gender gap in mathematics. *American Economic Journal: Applied Economics*, 2(2), April, 210–240. www.jstor.org/stable/25760212.

Good, C., Aronson, J., & Harder J. A. (2008). Problems in the pipeline: Stereotype threat and women's achievement in high-level math courses. *Journal of Applied Developmental Psychology*, 29, 17–28.

Grissmer, D. W., Mashburn, A., Cottone, E., Chen, W.-B., Brock, L. L., Murrah, W. M., ... Cameron, C. E. (2013). Effects of a play-based after-school curriculum for high risk K–1 children. In N. Newcombe (Ed.), *Educating spatial skills at varied ages with varied approaches: Are STEM outcomes affected?* Seattle, WA: Society for Research in Child Development.

Halpern, D. F. (2012). *Sex differences in cognitive abilities* (4th edn.). New York: Psychology Press.

Hedges, L. V. & Nowell, A. (1995). Sex differences in mental test scores, variability, and numbers of high-scoring individuals. *Science*, 269, 41–45.

Hill, C., Corbett, C., & St. Rose, A. (2010). *Why so few? Women in science, technology, engineering, and mathematics.* Washington, DC: American Association of University Women.

Huguet, P. & Regner, I. (2009). Counter-stereotypic beliefs in math do not protect school girls from stereotype threat. *Journal of Experimental Social Psychology*, 45, 1024–1027.

Hyde, J. S., Fennema, E., & Lamon, S. (1990). Gender differences in mathematics performance: A meta-analysis. *Psychological Bulletin*, 107, 139–155.

Hyde, J. S., Lindberg, S., Linn, M. C., Ellis, A. B., & Williams, C. C. (2008). Gender similarities characterize math performance. *Science*, 321, 494–495.

Hyde, J. S. & Mertz, J. (2009). Gender, culture, and mathematics performance. *Proceedings of the National Academy of Sciences, USA*, 106, 8801–8809.

Kahn, S. & Ginther, D. K. (2015). Are recent cohorts of women with engineering bachelors less likely to stay in engineering? *Frontiers in Psychology*, https://doi.org/10.3389/fpsyg.2015.01144.

Lavy, V. & Sand, E. (2015). On the origins of gender human capital gaps: Short and long term consequences of teachers' stereotypical biases. NBER Working Paper 20909. www.nber.org/papers/w20909.pdf.

Legewie, J. & DiPrete, T. A. (2012). High school environments, STEM orientations, and the gender gap in science and engineering degrees. http://ssrn.com/abstract=2008733.

Lindberg, S. M. et al. (2010). New trends in gender and mathematics performance: a meta-analysis. *Psychological Bulletin*, 136, 1123–1135.

Linn, M. C. & Petersen, A. C. (1985). Emergence and characterization of sex differences in spatial ability: A meta-analysis. *Child Development*, 56, 1479–1498.

Lippa, R. (1998). Gender-related individual differences and the structure of vocational interests: The importance of the people-things dimension. *Journal of Personality and Social Psychology,* 74, 996–1009.

Lippa, R. A. (2001). On deconstructing and reconstructing masculinity-femininity. *Journal of Research in Personality,* 35, 168–207.

——— (2010). Sex differences in personality traits and gender-related occupational preferences across 53 nations: Testing evolutionary and social-environmental theories. *Archives of Sexual Behavior,* 39, 619–636.

Lohman, D. F. & Lakin, J. M. (2009). Consistencies in sex differences on the cognitive abilities test across countries, grades, test forms, and cohorts. *British Journal of Educational Psychology,* 79, 89–407.

Miller, D. I. & Halpern, D. F. (2014). The new science of cognitive sex differences. *Trends in Cognitive Sciences,* 18, 37–45.

Miller, D. I. & Wai, J. (2015). The bachelor's to Ph.D. STEM pipeline no longer leaks more women than men: A 30-year analysis. *Frontiers in Psychology,* https://doi.org/10.3389/fpsyg.2015.00037.

Moore, D. S. & Johnson, S. P. (2011). Mental rotation of dynamic, three-dimensional stimuli by 3-month-old infants. *Infancy,* 16, 435–445.

Mullis, I., M., Fierros, M., Goldberg, E., & Stemler, A. S. (2000a). Gender differences in achievement. http://timssandpirls.bc.edu/timss1995i/gender.html

Mullis, I., Martin, M. O., Fierros, E. G., & Goldberg, A. L. (2000b). *Gender differences in achievement: IEA's Third International Mathematics and Science Study.* Chestnut Hill, MA: Boston College. International Study Center. Retrieved May 1, 2008, from timss.bc.edu/timss1995i/TIMSSPDF/T95_GChapter%201.pdf.

Nix, S., Perez-Felkner, L., & Thomas, K. (2014). Perceived mathematical ability under challenge: A longitudinal perspective on sex segregation among STEM degree fields. *Frontiers in Psychology.*

Penner, A. M. (2008). Gender differences in extreme mathematical achievement: An international perspective on biological and social factors. *American Journal of Sociology,* 114, 138–170.

Penner, A. M. & Paret, M. (2008). Gender differences in mathematics achievement: Exploring the early grades and the extremes. *Social Science Research,* 37, 239–253.

Pope, D. G. & Sydnor, J. R. (2010). Geographic variation in the gender differences in test scores. *Journal of Economic Perspectives,* 24, 95–108.

Quinn, P. C. & Liben, L. S. (2008). A sex difference in mental rotation in young infants. *Psychological Science,* 19, 1067–1070.

Schwarzer, G., Freitag, C., & Schum, N. (2013). How crawling and manual object exploration are related to the mental rotation abilities of 9-month-old infants. *Frontiers in Psychology,* 4, 97–110. doi:10.3389/fpsyg.2013.00097.

Shepard, R. N. & Metzler, J. (1971). Mental rotation of three-dimensional objects. *Science,* 171, 701–703.

Stoet, G. & Geary, D. C. (2013). Sex differences in mathematics and reading achievement are inversely related: Within-nation assessment of ten years of PISA data. *PLoS One*, 8(3): e57988. doi:10.1371/journal.pone.0057988.

Strand, S., Deary, I. J., & Smith, P. (2006). Sex differences in cognitive abilities test scores: A UK national picture. *British Journal of Educational Psychology*, 76, 463–480.

Su, R. & Rounds, J. (2015). All STEM fields are not created equal: People and things interests explain gender disparities across STEM fields. *Frontiers in Psychology*, doi: 10.3389/fpsyg.2015.00189.

Su, R., Rounds, J., & Armstrong, P. (2009). Men and things, women and people: A meta-analysis of sex differences in interests. *Psychological Bulletin*, 135, 859–884.

Thorndike, E. L. (1911). *Individuality*. New York: Houghton & Mifflin.

Voyer, D., Voyer, S., & Bryden, M. P., 1995. Magnitude of sex differences in spatial abilities: A metaanalysis and consideration of critical variables. *Psychological Bulletin*, 117, 250–270.

Wai, J., Cacchio, M., Putallaz, M., & Makel, M. (2010). Sex differences in the right tail of cognitive abilities: A 30 year examination. *Intelligence*, 38, 412–423. doi:10.1016/j .intell.2010.04.006.

Wai, J., & Putallaz, M. (2011). The Flynn effect puzzle: A 30-year examination from the right tail of the ability distribution provides some missing pieces. *Intelligence*, 39, 443–455.

Williams, W. M. & Ceci, S. J. (2015). National hiring experiments reveals 2-to-1 preference for women faculty on STEM tenure-track. *Proceedings of the National Academy of Sciences*, 112(17), 5360–5365. www.pnas.org/content/early/2015/04/08/1418878112.abstract. doi:10.1073/pnas.1418878112.

CHAPTER 4

The Nature of the General Factor of Intelligence

Andrew R. A. Conway & Kristof Kovacs

In the current chapter, we present an overview of our program of research on the relationship between working memory, executive attention, and intelligence. This line of work has culminated in a new theory of the positive manifold of intelligence and a corresponding new model of the general factor, g. We refer to this new framework as process overlap theory (POT) (Kovacs & Conway, 2016b). We present here an overview of POT and review initial empirical support of the theory. We conclude this chapter by addressing a series of questions posed by the editor.

When describing our research on intelligence, we find it useful to start with a description of the positive manifold, which refers to the pattern of all-positive correlations that is observed when a battery of mental tests is administered to a large, heterogeneous sample of people. Even when the battery of tests includes rather diverse tasks, such as a vocabulary test and a mental rotation test, the correlations observed among all tests tend to be positive. It is also true that, among this pattern of all-positive correlations, there are clusters of correlations that are stronger than others, and these clusters of strong correlations are thought to reflect what are known as group factors, representing broadly interpreted abilities. For example, a vocabulary test, a reading comprehension test, and a listening comprehension test might reveal relatively strong positive correlations within the positive manifold, and this cluster is thought to reflect a group factor that we might refer to as verbal ability. This pattern of all-positive correlations and clusters of particularly strong positive correlations is best explained by confirmatory factor analysis that includes a hierarchical general factor. That is, multiple group factors, such as verbal ability and spatial ability, account for the clusters of strong positive correlations, and a higher-order general factor, or g, accounts for the positive manifold.

The Cattell-Horn-Caroll (CHC) (McGrew, 2009) model nicely captures this factorial structure of intelligence (see Figure 4.1). The CHC

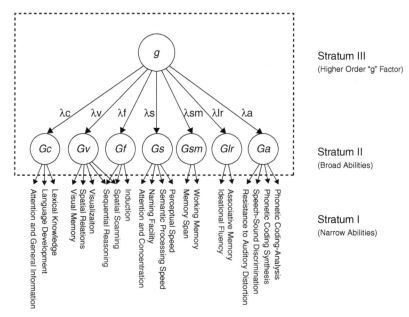

Figure 4.1 The Cattell-Horn-Carroll psychometric model of intelligence. Ovals
represent latent variables. Directional arrows depict causality. *g*: general intelligence;
Gc: crystallized knowledge; Gv: visual-spatial ability; Gf: fluid reasoning; Gs: processing
speed; Gsm: short-term/working memory; Glr: memory retrieval; Ga: auditory
processing; λ: Factor loading of each broad ability on *g*.

model consists of seven group factors, including fluid and crystallized
intelligence, as well as a higher-order *g* factor, which represents general
intelligence. We find the CHC model to be a useful description of the
structure of intelligence but we take issue with the interpretation of the
general factor as reflective of a general cognitive ability. According to POT,
which we describe in more detail in the next section, the general factor is
"not a thing," and therefore cannot have a causal influence on mental test
scores.

Process Overlap Theory

POT is motivated by the theory of fluid and crystallized intelligence (Blair,
2006; Cattell, 1971; Horn, 1994; McGrew, 2009). This model makes a distinction between fluid reasoning and crystallized knowledge. Fluid reasoning is the ability to solve novel problems, the solution of which does not

depend on previously acquired skills and knowledge. It is usually measured with tests that require inductive reasoning, such as Raven's Progressive Matrices. Crystallized knowledge, in contrast, depends on experience and existing skills, and is usually measured by tests of general knowledge or vocabulary.

POT also builds upon research on the relationship between working memory and fluid intelligence. Working memory refers to the "the ensemble of components of the mind that hold a limited amount of information temporarily in a heightened state of availability for use in ongoing information processing" (Cowan, 2016). For example, to comprehend this chapter, you must maintain information in an accessible state and at the same time continue to process new words, phrases, sentences, and paragraphs. Measures of working memory capacity, such as complex span tests, require this type of parallel storage and processing. For example, in the operation span test, participants have to remember a list of words while also solving a series of mathematical operations. Complex span tests are therefore different from so-called simple span tests, such as digit span, letter span, or word span, in which participants simply have to recall a list of items. And in contrast to simple span tests, variance in complex span tests is primarily domain-general (Kane et al., 2004). Therefore, similar to intelligence tests, a general factor of working memory capacity can be extracted, and this factor correlates strongly with fluid intelligence (Kane, Hambrick, & Conway, 2005; Oberauer et al., 2005).

POT is also inspired by empirical results on the relationship between working memory and fluid reasoning. Specifically, our prior work suggests that whatever working memory tasks measure beyond simple storage correlates most strongly with fluid reasoning (Conway & Kovacs, 2013; Kovacs, 2010). Furthermore, the processes that working memory tasks measure, beyond storage, most likely reflect individual differences in the executive attention component of working memory (Engle & Kane, 2004; Engle et al., 1999; Kane et al., 2001; Kane & Engle, 2002).

The main premise of POT is that a battery of intelligence tests requires a number of domain-general processes, such as those involved in working memory and attention, as well as a number of domain-specific processes. Importantly, domain-general processes are required by the majority (but not all) of test items, whereas domain-specific processes are required less frequently, depending on the nature of the test (e.g., verbal vs. spatial). Such a pattern of overlapping processes explains the positive manifold and thus the general factor. POT is, in this respect, similar to Thomson's sampling model (Thomson, 1916), but is also different in crucial ways (Kovacs & Conway, 2016a).

The most important and novel aspect of POT, and its main divergence from Thomson's ideas, is that it proposes that the processes involved in test performance are non-additive. Since executive attention processes are involved in the majority of test items, individual differences in executive attention pose general limits on total performance, acting as a bottleneck and masking individual differences in more domain-specific processes.

Besides providing an account of the positive manifold, POT also explains a number of important phenomena observed in the study of human intelligence. The first such phenomenon is ability differentiation, which refers to the finding that cross-domain correlations are higher in samples with lower average ability and so g explains more variance in such samples. The second is the worst performance rule, the finding that worst performance on a test (e.g., slowest reaction times on a speeded test) is a better predictor of g than average or best performance. The third is that the more complex a task, the higher its correlation with g. Finally, through proposing that the positive manifold is caused by the overlapping activation of the executive attention processes that are involved in both working memory and fluid reasoning, the theory accounts for the central role of fluid reasoning in the structure of human abilities, and for the finding that the fluid reasoning factor (Gf) seems to be statistically identical or near-identical to g (Gustafsson, 1984).

POT is therefore able to explain why g is both population- and task-dependent, i.e., it explains the most variance in 1) populations with lower ability, 2) worst performance, and 3) cognitively demanding tasks. POT focuses on the limitations of executive attention processes in explaining g, and proposes an interaction between the executive demands of the task and the executive functioning of the individual. This is expressed in a formal mathematical model (a multidimensional item response model) that specifies the probability of arriving at a correct answer on a given mental test item as the function of the level of domain-specific as well as domain-general cognitive processes (see Kovacs & Conway, 2016b).

The most important consequence of the theory is that g is "not a thing" but instead is the consequence of a set of overlapping cognitive processes sampled by a battery of tests. Therefore the general factor is a *formative* latent variable (Bagozzi, 2007), and as such it can be thought of as an index of mental functioning. Scores on the general factor represent a summary statistic that can be used to predict various phenomena, ranging from everyday cognitive performance (e.g., academic achievement and job performance) to non-cognitive life outcomes (e.g., socioeconomic status or longevity). Thus POT does not deny the existence of *g*, but, contrary to the standard view, interprets it as an emergent rather than a latent property.

Internal Consistency of POT

Kan, Van der Maas, and Kievit (2016) conducted a series of simulations to test whether a mathematical model of test performance, consistent with POT, would in fact generate a latent variable model consistent with the theory. They first created a specific version of the general mathematical model, which they then used in their simulation. Consistent with POT, fluid, verbal, and visuospatial reasoning were determined by a number of processes that each have a capacity, and the probability that a domain-general process is sampled was high (p = 0.50–0.60), while the probability that a domain-specific process is sampled was relatively low (p = 0.35).

Based on these equations and parameter settings, Kan and colleagues simulated test scores on three fluid intelligence tests, three verbal tests, and three visuospatial tests. The simulation resulted in a three-factor model in which all three factors were correlated and the correlations with the fluid reasoning factor were stronger than the correlation between the verbal and visuospatial factor. This is exactly what POT predicts. The results of the simulation are presented in Figure 4.2.

Besides providing evidence for POT, this simulation also demonstrates that it is possible for the positive manifold to emerge, and for a general factor model to be statistically appropriate even if there is no single process involved in all kinds of cognitive activities that a causal (non-formative) general factor could meaningfully represent.

Empirical Support of POT

One of the central claims of POT is that domain-general processes associated with working memory and executive attention will constrain performance on most items on most intelligence tests. To be clear, these processes are not essential for all items on all tests; for example, if one knows the definition of words on a vocabulary test, then working memory capacity will not constrain performance. But on most tests, and especially those that require fluid reasoning, working memory capacity and executive attention are vital. It therefore follows that scores on tests of

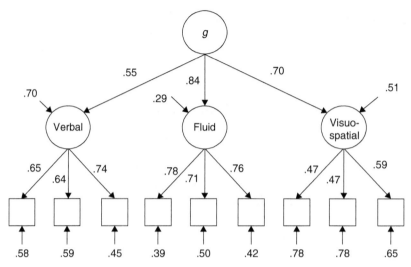

Figure 4.2   A latent variable model illustrating the results of a simulation by Kan et al. (2016). Ovals represent latent variables and squares represent manifest variables (representing nine simulated tasks, three for each construct). Directional arrows depict causality. *g*: general intelligence; Verbal: verbal ability; Fluid: fluid reasoning; Visuospatial: visuospatial ability.

working memory and executive attention should be strongly correlated (but not perfectly correlated) with fluid intelligence and the general factor of intelligence.

It is now well established that working memory capacity is strongly correlated with fluid intelligence. While some researchers have gone as far as to say that working memory capacity and reasoning are perfectly correlated (Kyllonen & Christal, 1990), two meta-analyses of latent variable studies investigating the relationship between working memory and fluid intelligence estimate that the correlation is somewhere between $r = 0.72$ to $r = 0.81$ (Kane et al., 2005; Oberauer et al., 2005). This estimate is consistent with a recent large sample study that found a correlation of $r = 0.77$ between the two constructs (Gignac, 2007).

According to the executive attention theory of individual differences in working memory capacity (Engle & Kane, 2004; Kane et al., 2001), the reason working memory and fluid intelligence are so strongly related is that both constructs rely to a great extent on executive functions, such as updating, inhibition, and task-switching. Therefore, measures of executive function should also be strongly related to fluid intelligence. Indeed, several recent latent variable studies have demonstrated strong correlations between executive attention and fluid intelligence (Engelhardt et al., 2016; Shipstead et al., 2014; Unsworth et al., 2014).

Editor's Questions

What Is Intelligence?

Intelligence researchers rarely agree on a definition of intelligence (Sternberg & Detterman, 1986). However, most definitions refer to a "general mental capability," or "general intelligence," or something similar. As discussed, POT rejects the notion of a general ability that permeates all of cognition; hence we reject this family of definitions.

In fact, our definition of intelligence is twofold. Our primary focus is on abilities that, unlike *g*, can be substantively interpreted. This, together with the functional overlap of processes in cognitive performance that POT proposes, translates to the following definition:

> Intelligence is a system of separate abilities, some of which are domain-general, such as fluid reasoning, working memory, and executive attention, while others are domain-specific, such as verbal, spatial, or numerical skills. Each ability is in fact the result of a set of processes that are activated in an overlapping fashion by cognitive activity, such that many of the processes involved in working memory are also tapped to some extent by tests that purportedly measure domain-specific cognition.

Second, however, our model also includes *g*, albeit as a kind of index rather than a casual factor. This aspect of POT invokes the infamous definition by Edwin Boring (Boring, 1923), which recently gained new support (Van der Maas, Kan, & Borsboom, 2014), and which claims that *intelligence is what tests of intelligence measure*. If intelligence tests do not *measure* *g* per se, but rather *g* is the result of measurement, there is substantial flexibility in what kind of abilities one can include in intelligence. This is the reason we did not specify a list of specific abilities (like Thurstone's Primary Mental Abilities) in our definition.

Intelligence can be composed of different abilities for different "purposes," making the construct largely dependent on the cultural context in which one is trying to achieve success (Sternberg & Grigorenko, 2004). Having said that, we find it important to emphasize that fluid intelligence, as well as the overlapping constructs of working memory and executive attention, appear to be tremendously important cognitive skills in modern Western societies (e.g., Raven, 2000; St Clair-Thompson & Gathercole, 2006).

How Is Intelligence Best Measured?

It is important to consider the goal of measurement when choosing an appropriate assessment tool. Intelligence is best measured using a diverse battery of tests that can provide a profile-type assessment, highlighting individual strengths and weaknesses. A diverse set of tests is optimal if the goal is the diagnosis of learning disabilities because it allows for the detection of anomalous scores.

If, however, the goal of assessment is to predict a more specific outcome, then a narrow range of tests may be more appropriate. If the circumstances only allow a rough and ready evaluation of one's cognitive abilities, or if for some reason a single overall estimate is sufficient, a test of fluid intelligence is probably the best solution, as the fluid intelligence factor (Gf) is statistically near-identical to g (Gustafsson, 1984; Matzke, Dolan, & Molenaar, 2010); therefore tests of fluid reasoning tap central aspects of the variation in cognitive abilities. Finally, from a technical perspective, the best method for the measurement of cognitive abilities is *computerized adaptive testing* (Kovacs & Temesvari, 2016; Van der Linden & Glas, 2002; Weiner & Dorans, 2000).

The rise in popularity of websites like Lumosity and Cogmed raises another important related question: **can intelligence be measured through video games?** Angeles Quiroga and colleagues (2015) found that scores on the general factor derived from video games were very strongly correlated with scores on the general factor derived from the intelligence tests ($r = 0.93$). This is an exciting finding because it suggests that g scores can be reliably obtained from games. This obviously makes assessment more fun for the participants, but it presents other benefits as well; the use of games for assessment allows for repeated measurements and the tracking of performance relative to one's own baseline.

How Is Intelligence Best Developed?

In the past decade, online training programs, or "brain games," such as Lumosity, CogniFit, and Cogmed, have become incredibly popular. These websites claim to provide broad and general cognitive enhancement. Despite these claims, a recent independent review of "brain training" websites is rather pessimistic. Their conclusion: "we find extensive evidence that brain-training interventions improve performance on the trained tasks, less evidence that such interventions improve performance on closely related tasks, and little evidence that training enhances performance on distantly related tasks or that training improves everyday cognitive performance" (Simons et al., 2016). This is consistent with a recent meta-analysis of working memory training experiments, which provides evidence for near transfer but "no convincing evidence" for far transfer (Melby-Lervåg, Redick, & Hulme, 2016). Overall, our current state of knowledge does not seem to substantiate the strong claims of the marketers of such products, and careful future research is needed for such methods to be validated.

At the same time, most studies on training have focused on adults, in particular the elderly. The verdict on such studies does not necessarily transfer to children, whose brains are much more plastic and for whom such training might therefore be more beneficial. Indeed, it seems possible to improve executive attention in children with targeted interventions (Diamond et al., 2007; Thorell et al., 2009). Besides, regardless of the efficiency of recent cognitive training programs, there is a well-established brain-training method aimed particularly at children that clearly has the capability of raising intelligence: it is called education (Cahan & Cohen, 1989; Nisbett, 2009).

What Are Some of the Most Interesting Empirical Results from Your Own Research and Why Are They Important to the Field?

The most important result of our own research is process overlap theory, a new explanation of the more-than-a-century-old problem of the positive manifold (Kovacs & Conway, 2016b). In terms of empirical results, the most relevant findings from our own research concern the relationship between working memory and fluid intelligence and between working memory and executive attention. We have contributed to the now large literature demonstrating a strong relationship between working memory capacity and fluid intelligence (e.g., Conway et al., 2002; Conway & Kovacs, 2013; Engle et al., 1999; Kane et al., 2001, 2005), and we have provided empirical support for the executive attention theory of individual differences in working memory capacity, demonstrating that working memory capacity is related to the performance of attention tasks that have minimal memory demands (e.g., Colflesh & Conway, 2007; Conway, Cowan, & Bunting, 2001; Conway et al., 1999). All of these empirical results are important in the current context because POT is influenced, to a great extent, by the executive attention theory of working memory.

We have also demonstrated that the processes that working memory tasks measure beyond pure storage and retrieval are most strongly related to fluid reasoning and least strongly to crystallized intelligence and processing speed (Conway & Kovacs, 2013; Kovacs, 2010).

Finally, as a work in progress, our preliminary results suggest that ability differentiation also takes place in working memory capacity, meaning that the correlations between domain-specific working memory tasks are stronger when overall capacity is lower and thus the general working memory capacity factor explains more variance in populations with lower working memory capacity (Kovacs, Molenaar, & Conway, in progress). This result can greatly inform debates about the domain-generality of working memory capacity.

What Do You See as the Most Important Educational or Social Policy Issue Facing the Field of Intelligence Today?

In our view, the most important educational issue facing the field of intelligence is the need to educate society with regard to the science of intelligence. That is, we intelligence researchers need to do a better job communicating our work to a broader audience. Mackintosh (2014) provides several compelling arguments as to why we all should be teaching a course on intelligence. We argue that such courses should be taught not only in psychology departments, but also in schools of education.

Besides, the field of education should move toward more evidence-based policies and interventions, and a dialog with researchers of cognitive ability should be an important milestone. All too often, ideas become fashionable among educators without thorough research having demonstrated their validity with prior evidence. For instance, the concept of learning styles seems to be immensely popular, even though there seems to be no solid evidence to back up the utility of matching teaching styles accordingly (Pashler et al., 2009; Rogowsky, Calhoun, & Tallal, 2015). Similarly, the so-called 10,000 hour rule has received enormous hype, even though the empirical evidence is far from univocal (Macnamara, Hambrick, & Oswald, 2014).

What Are the Most Important Questions about Intelligence that Future Research on Intelligence Should Address?

According to the United Nations 2015 report on aging, older persons are expected to account for more than 25% of the populations in Europe and in North America by 2030 (United Nations Department of Economic and Social Affairs Population Division, 2015). Therefore, one of the most important questions that future research on intelligence should address is **how do components of intelligence decline with age?** It is clear that some components of intelligence, such as fluid reasoning and processing speed, demonstrate sharp declines with age, while other components, such as crystallized intelligence, remain relatively stable and might even peak quite late (Hartshorne & Germine, 2015). An important area for future research is gaining a better understanding of the cognitive aging process and exploring ways in which declines in ability can be prevented or slowed.

As discussed before, one of the most important questions to be addressed by future research is whether intelligence can be enhanced through cognitive training. Finally, an ever-important question, which our own recent work addresses, is one of the most fundamental questions about intelligence: **what is the nature of g?** According to POT, g is "not a thing," but instead is a summary statistic. It remains to be seen whether such a view of g is correct, but if it is, that has implications for how the science of intelligence should proceed. For example, if g is nothing but a summary statistic, then the search for the neural basis of g is meaningless. Likewise, if g is just a summary statistic, then the search for general intelligence genes is also meaningless. In their commentary on process overlap theory, Kan and colleagues (2016) put it this way: "if a constructivist conceptualization of the higher order factor is most appropriate, this informs and constrains our search for neural and genetic antecedents: The most fruitful path in such cases would be to focus on those lower order variables that do allow for a realist, causal interpretation." We couldn't agree more.

Acknowledgment: The second author's research was supported by the grant EFOP-3.6.1-16-2016-00001 ("Complex improvement of research capacities and services at Eszterhazy Karoly University").

References

Angeles Quiroga, M., Escorial, S., Roman, F. J., Morillo, D., Jarabo, A., Privado, J., ... Colom, R. (2015). Can we reliably measure the general factor of intelligence (g) through commercial video games? Yes, we can! *Intelligence*, 53, 1–7. http://doi.org/10.1016/j.intell.2015.08.004.

Bagozzi, R. P. (2007). On the meaning of formative measurement and how it differs from reflective measurement: Comment on Howell, Breivik, and Wilcox (2007). *Psychological Methods*, 12(2), 229-237-245. http://doi.org/10.1037/1082-989X.12.2.229.

Blair, C. (2006). How similar are fluid cognition and general intelligence? A developmental neuroscience perspective on fluid cognition as an aspect of human cognitive ability. *The Behavioral and Brain Sciences*, 29(2), 109-25-60. http://doi.org/10.1017/S0140525X06009034.

Boring, E. G. (1923). Intelligence as the tests test it. *New Republic*, 36, 35–37.

Cahan, S., & Cohen, N. (1989). Age versus schooling effects on intelligence development. *Child Development*, 60(5), 1239–1249. http://doi.org/10.2307/1130797.

Cattell, R. B. (1971). *Abilities: Their structure, growth, and action*. Boston, MA: Houghton Mifflin. http://books.google.com/books?id=10EgAQAAIAAJ&pgis=1.

Colflesh, G. J. H., & Conway, A. R. A. (2007). Individual differences in working memory capacity and divided attention in dichotic listening, 14(4), 699–703.

Conway, A. R. A., Cowan, N., & Bunting, M. F. (2001). The cocktail party phenomenon revisited: The importance of working memory capacity. *Psychonomic Bulletin & Review*, 8(2), 331–335. http://doi.org/10.3758/BF03196169.

Conway, A. R. A., Cowan, N., Bunting, M. F., Therriault, D. J., & Minkoff, S. R. (2002). A latent variable analysis of working memory capacity, short-term memory capacity, processing speed, and general fluid intelligence. *Intelligence*, 30(2), 163–183. http://doi.org/10.1016/S0160-2896(01)00096-4.

Conway, A. R. A., & Kovacs, K. (2013). Individual differences in intelligence and working memory. In B Ross (Ed.), *Psychology of Learning and Motivation* (Vol. 58, pp. 233–270). Cambridge, MA: Academic Press. http://doi.org/10.1016/B978-0-12-407237-4.00007-4.

Conway, A. R. A., Tuholski, S. W., Shisler, R. J., & Engle, R. W. (1999). The effect of memory load on negative priming: An individual differences investigation. *Memory & Cognition*, 27(6), 1042–1050. http://doi.org/10.3758/BF03201233.

Cowan, N. (2016). The many faces of working memory and short-term storage. *Psychonomic Bulletin & Review*, 24(4), 1–13. https://doi.org/10.3758/s13423-016-1191-6.

Diamond, A., Barnett, W. S., Thomas, J., & Munro, S. (2007). Preschool program improves cognitive control. *Science*, 318(5855), 1387–1388. http://doi.org/10.1126/science.1151148.

Engelhardt, L. E., Mann, F. D., Briley, D. A., Church, J. A., Harden, K. P., & Tucker-Drob, E. M. (2016). Strong genetic overlap between executive functions and intelligence. *Journal of Experimental Psychology. General*, 145(9), 1141–59. http://doi.org/10.1037/xge0000195.

Engle, R. W., & Kane, M. J. (2004). Executive attention, working memory capacity, and a two-factor theory of cognitive control. *The Psychology of Learning and Motivation*, 44, 145–199.

Engle, R. W., Tuholski, S. W., Laughlin, J. E., & Conway, A. R. A. (1999). Working memory, short-term memory, and general fluid intelligence: A latent-variable approach. *Journal of Experimental Psychology. General*, 128(3), 309–31. www.ncbi.nlm.nih.gov/pubmed/10513398.

Gignac, G. E. (2007). Working memory and fluid intelligence are both identical to g?! Reanalyses and critical evaluation. *Psychology Science*, 49(3), 187.

Gustafsson, J.-E. (1984). A unifying model for the structure of intellectual abilities. *Intelligence*, 8(3), 179–203. http://doi.org/10.1016/0160-2896(84)90008-4.

Hartshorne, J. K., & Germine, L. T. (2015). When does cognitive functioning peak? The asynchronous rise and fall of different cognitive abilities across the life span. *Psychological Science*, 26(4), 433–443. http://doi.org/10.1177/0956797614567339.

Horn, J. L. (1994). Theory of fluid and crystallized intelligence. In R. Sternberg (Ed.), *Encyclopedia of human intelligence* (pp. 443–451). New York: MacMillan Reference Library.

Kan, K.-J., Van der Maas, H. L. J., & Kievit, R. A. (2016). Process overlap theory: Strengths, limitations, and challenges. *Psychological Inquiry*, 27(3), 220–228. http://doi.org/10.1080/1047840X.2016.1182000.

Kane, M. J., Bleckley, M. K., Conway, A. R. A., & Engle, R. W. (2001). A controlled-attention view of working-memory capacity. *Journal of Experimental Psychology: General*, 130(2), 169–183. http://doi.org/10.1037/0096-3445.130.2.169.

Kane, M. J., & Engle, R. W. (2002). The role of prefrontal cortex in working-memory capacity, executive attention, and general fluid intelligence: An individual-differences perspective. *Psychonomic Bulletin & Review*, 9(4), 637–671. http://doi.org/10.3758/BF03196323

Kane, M. J., Hambrick, D. Z., & Conway, A. R. A. (2005). Working memory capacity and fluid intelligence are strongly related constructs: Comment on Ackerman, Beier, and Boyle (2005). *Psychological Bulletin*, 131, 66-71-75. http://doi.org/10.1037/0033-2909.131.1.66.

Kane, M. J., Hambrick, D. Z., Tuholski, S. W., Wilhelm, O., Payne, T. W., & Engle, R. W. (2004). The generality of working memory capacity: A latent-variable approach to verbal and visuospatial memory span and reasoning. *Journal of Experimental Psychology. General*, 133(2), 189–217. http://doi.org/10.1037/0096-3445.133.2.189.

Kovacs, K. (2010). A component process account of the general factor of intelligence. Unpublished PhD thesis. University of Cambridge.

Kovacs, K., & Conway, A. R. A. (2016a). Has *g* gone to POT? *Psychological Inquiry*, 27(3), 241–253. http://doi.org/10.1080/1047840X.2016.1202744.

(2016b). Process overlap theory: A unified account of the general factor of intelligence. *Psychological Inquiry*, 27(3), 151–177. http://doi.org/10.1080/1047840X.2016.1153946.

Kovacs, K., Molenaar, D., & Conway, A. R. A. (in progress). The domain-specificity of working memory: A matter of ability.

Kovacs, K., & Temesvari, E. (2016). Számítógépes, adaptív IQ-mérés: Egy gyakorlati példa. *Magyar Pszichológiai Szemle*, 71, 143–163.

Kyllonen, P. C., & Christal, R. E. (1990). Reasoning ability is (little more than) working-memory capacity?! *Intelligence*. http://doi.org/10.1016/S0160-2896(05)80012-1.

Mackintosh, N. J. (2014). Why teach intelligence? *Intelligence*, 42, 166–170. http://doi.org/10.1016/j.intell.2013.08.001.

Macnamara, B. N., Hambrick, D. Z., & Oswald, F. L. (2014). Deliberate practice and performance in music, games, sports, education, and professions: A meta-analysis. *Psychological Science*, 25(8), 1608–1618. http://doi.org/10.1177/0956797614535810.

Matzke, D., Dolan, C. V., & Molenaar, D. (2010). The issue of power in the identification of "g" with lower-order factors. *Intelligence*, 38(3), 336–344. http://doi.org/10.1016/j.intell.2010.02.001.

McGrew, K. S. (2009). CHC theory and the human cognitive abilities project: Standing on the shoulders of the giants of psychometric intelligence research. *Intelligence*, 37(1), 1–10. http://doi.org/10.1016/j.intell.2008.08.004.

Melby-Lervåg, M., Redick, T. S., & Hulme, C. (2016). Working memory training does not improve performance on measures of intelligence or other measures of "far transfer" evidence from a meta-analytic review. *Perspectives on Psychological Science*, 11(4), 512–534.

Nisbett, R. E. (2009). *Intelligence and how to get it: Why schools and cultures count.* New York: WW Norton & Company.

Oberauer, K., Schulze, R., Wilhelm, O., & Süss, H.-M. (2005). Working memory and intelligence – their correlation and their relation: Comment on Ackerman, Beier, and Boyle (2005). *Psychological Bulletin*, 131, 61-65-75. http://doi.org/10.1037/0033-2909.131.1.61.

Pashler, H., Mcdaniel, M., Rohrer, D., & Bjork, R. (2009). Concepts and evidence. *Psychological Science*, 9(3), 105–119. http://doi.org/10.1111/j.1539-6053.2009.01038.x.

Raven, J. C. (2000). Psychometrics, cognitive ability, and occupational performance. *Review of Psychology*, 7(1–2), 51–74.

Rogowsky, B. A., Calhoun, B. M., & Tallal, P. (2015). Matching learning style to instructional method: Effects on comprehension. *Journal of Educational Psychology*, 107(1), 64–78. http://doi.org/10.1037/a0037478.

Shipstead, Z., Lindsey, D. R. B., Marshall, R. L., & Engle, R. W. (2014). The mechanisms of working memory capacity: Primary memory, secondary memory, and attention control. *Journal of Memory and Language*, 72, 116–141.

Simons, D. J., Boot, W. R., Charness, N., Gathercole, S. E., Chabris, C. F., Hambrick, D. Z., & Stine-morrow, E. A. L. (2016). Do "brain-training" programs work ? http://doi.org/10.1177/1529100616661983.

St Clair-Thompson, H. L., & Gathercole, S. E. (2006). Executive functions and achievements in school: Shifting, updating, inhibition, and working memory. *Quarterly Journal of Experimental Psychology*, 59(4), 745–759. http://doi.org/10.1080/17470210500162854.

Sternberg, R. J., & Detterman, D. K. (Eds.). (1986). *What is intelligence?: Contemporary viewpoints on its Nature and definition.* New York: Ablex Publishing Corporation.

Sternberg, R. J., & Grigorenko, E. L. (2004). Intelligence and culture: How culture shapes what intelligence means, and the implications for a science of well-being. *Philosophical Transactions of the Royal Society of London.*

Series B, Biological Sciences, 359(1449), 1427–1434. http://doi.org/10.1098/rstb.2004.1514.

Thomson, G. H. (1916). A hierarchy without a general factor. *British Journal of Psychology, 1904–1920*, 8(3), 271–281. http://doi.org/10.1111/j.2044-8295.1916.tb00133.x.

Thorell, L. B., Lindqvist, S., Bergman Nutley, S., Bohlin, G., & Klingberg, T. (2009). Training and transfer effects of executive functions in preschool children. *Developmental Science*, 12(1), 106–113. http://doi.org/10.1111/j.1467-7687.2008.00745.x.

United Nations Department of Economic and Social Affairs Population Division. (2015). *World population ageing 2015*. New York: United Nations.

Unsworth, N., Fukuda, K., Awh, E., & Vogel, E. K. (2014). Working memory and fluid intelligence: Capacity, attention control, and secondary memory retrieval. *Cognitive Psychology*, 71, 1–26.

Van der Linden, W. J., & Glas, G. A. W. (2002). *Computerized adaptive testing: Theory and practice*. New York: Kluwer Academic Publishers.

Van der Maas, H. L. J., Kan, K.-J., & Borsboom, D. (2014). Intelligence is what the intelligence test measures. Seriously. *Journal of Intelligence*, 2(1), 12–15. http://doi.org/10.3390/jintelligence2010012.

Weiner, H., & Dorans, N. J. (2000). *Computerized adaptive testing: A primer* (2nd edn.). Mahwah, NJ: Lawrence Erlbaum Associates.

CHAPTER 5

Intelligence in Edinburgh, Scotland: Bringing Intelligence to Life

Ian J. Deary & Stuart J. Ritchie

What Is Intelligence?

Being asked for a definition of intelligence is a routine conversation-opener whenever we tell people what we do for a living. We have both written a popular book on intelligence that, near the beginning, shies away from offering a definition, and passes the buck to Linda Gottfredson's (Deary, 2001, p. 17; Ritchie, 2015, p. 3). Here is a joint attempt. Intelligence is the massive accruing pyramid, the strongly knitted nomological network of facts relating to cognitive ability test scores: how they correlate, what they predict, and why they come about. It's the quality that we recognise as showing differences between people when we (correctly) understand that people who tend to be good at one mental ability tend to be good at others also; these include remembering things, manipulating information, working out general principles from a set of examples and then applying them more broadly, thinking quickly, organising mental work, working things out in two or three dimensions, knowing word meanings, and knowing facts about the world.

How Is Intelligence Best Measured?

Intelligence is not best measured by high-tech methods, be they brain imaging, physiological, or fancy information-processing apparatuses. We think academics are too inclined to look a gift horse in the mouth: the truth is that, to a rough approximation, intelligence is ludicrously easy to measure. It needs hardly more than a sheet of paper, and it hardly matters how one does it.

A sheet of paper. Look at the images of the original Binet tests online; they are just a few pages, and the tests for any one age group are a fraction of a page. Look at the National Adult Reading Test (NART), or the very similar Test of Premorbid Function; the stimuli are irregularly pronounced words that can be printed on a single page, and the testing takes a couple of minutes as the subject reads the words aloud. Yet, the Binet test at age 11 years correlates 0.72 with the NART at age 77 (Deary & Brett, 2015). At age 11, not many of the NART's words will be known. Of course, we are aware that there are good reasons for using much larger, thorough, and diverse cognitive test batteries, as we do in our older cohorts (Deary et al., 2012a), and especially to obtain a latent trait of general fluid cognitive ability; however, especially for crystallised intelligence in adults, it is hard to better such straightforward, single-sheet-of-paper measures.

It hardly matters how one measures intelligence. Spearman (1927) told us that, and he remains correct:

> Theorem of indifference of the indicator … This means that, for the purpose of indicating the amount of *g* possessed by a person, any test will do just as well as any other, provided only that its correlation with *g* is equally high. With this proviso, the most ridiculous 'stunts' will measure the selfsame *g* as the highest exploits of logic or flight of imagination. (p. 197).

Our Edinburgh colleague Wendy Johnson and her colleagues showed that one obtains the same *g* from different batteries of cognitive tests (Johnson, Bouchard, & Krueger, 2004). Of course, there are caveats here too: that the tests chosen for the batteries are psychometrically sound and cover a range of mental abilities.

So, let's reflect on the fact that the score people obtain after less than an hour's interaction with a paper-and-pencil test in childhood will: tap into cognitive differences that are pretty stable into older age; predict educational achievements and occupational status in midlife; and predict health, illness, and survival (Deary, Whalley, & Starr, 2009). There can be few objections to seeking ever-sharper psychometric tools, but our and our team's main worry is not about how best to measure intelligence differences. Our more pressing head-scratchers are finding the biological and social foundations of such persistent and pervasively important cognitive differences, and their mechanisms of association with real-life outcomes.

Some Intelligent Results from Edinburgh and Scotland

Our contributions focus on the foundations and practical implications of intelligence differences, and occasionally on intelligence's psychometric structure. We largely eschew theory (Deary, 2000, p. 108). Well, not quite, because we have become Godfrey Thomson's bairns (Scots for 'children'). Many of our recent empirical findings rely on data from his intelligence tests given across Scotland in the first half of the 20th century, and we have found that his non-*g* theory of intelligence holds about as much water as Spearman's *g* theory (Bartholomew, Allerhand, & Deary, 2013; Bartholomew, Deary, & Lawn, 2009; Deary, Cox, & Ritchie, 2016). Our follow-up studies of the Scottish Mental Surveys of 1932 and 1947 are important in what follows (Deary et al., 2009b). We looked for the narrative thread in our contributions and out popped 'life': from our Edinburgensian viewpoint, we think we've brought intelligence to life, and made progress towards understanding how intelligence plays a part in the human life course.

Bringing the Scottish Mental Surveys' Intelligence Data to Life

One of us (IJD) started research on intelligence in the 1980s, mostly studying the association between intelligence and speed of processing (Brand & Deary, 1982). This work was based on visual and auditory tests of the 'inspection time' concept, and showed that more efficient low-level processing was associated with higher intelligence (e.g., Deary & Stough, 1996). This work continues to this day, with longitudinal and cross-sectional reports in our Lothian Birth Cohort studies showing the importance of mental speed's slowing for predicting (and potentially explaining?) more general cognitive ageing (Deary & Ritchie, 2016; Ritchie, Tucker-Drob, & Deary, 2014). This work on processing speed also included reaction time, where again one finds that more intelligent people tend to have faster responses, especially in choice reaction-time procedures (Deary, Der, & Ford, 2001). However, although processing speed correlates of intelligence are well replicated, they have not led to a reductionistic understanding of intelligence differences; this failure was the theme of Deary's (2000) *kommos* to the field, *Looking Down on Human Intelligence*.

A career-changing event occurred for IJD in 1997 when, with his friend Professor Lawrence Whalley, he discovered that the Scottish Mental Surveys of 1932 (SMS1932) and 1947 (SMS1947) had been performed, and that the data had been retained (Deary et al., 2009b, pp. x–xi). Much of our narrative will deal with follow-up studies and re-analyses of these Surveys' data.

The test used in both Scottish Mental Surveys was a version of the Moray House Test No. 12 (MHT; see Deary et al., 2004). It was devised by Godfrey Thomson and his research team in the Education Department at the University of Edinburgh. It was a paper-and-pencil test with five pages and a maximum total score of 76. It had mostly verbal-reasoning items, with some arithmetic, spatial, and other items. It had a concurrent validity coefficient of about 0.8 with the Stanford revision of the Binet Test (Scottish Council for Research in Education, 1933). Thomson made the test available for free to the Scottish Council for Research in Education (SCRE), the body that organised the Scottish Mental Surveys, and of which Thomson was a member. On 1 June 1932, SCRE tested almost every Scottish school pupil born in 1921 on the MHT: N = 87,498 (SCRE, 1933). On 4 June 1947, SCRE tested almost every Scottish school pupil born in 1936 on the MHT: N = 70,805 (SCRE, 1949). (See Deary and colleagues, 2009b, pp. 5–40, for a summary of the rationales and results of these Surveys.)

In their days, the SMS1932 and SMS1947 were internationally famous. After the SMS1947 was performed, Godfrey Thomson wrote a leading article about the two Surveys in *The Times* of London. But by the time Whalley and Deary came across the data ledgers in 1997, the Surveys had been mostly forgotten and had been unused for many years. Two uses of these intelligence test score data occurred pretty quickly to Whalley and Deary: first, they would make a good baseline from which to study lifetime cognitive ageing, if the participants could be traced several decades on; and, second, they could be used to predict survival and health, if the data could be linked to national death and health records. The participants were traced and the data were linked (a process that was burdensome; e.g., Brett & Deary, 2014), resulting in the hundreds of research reports we have produced, based on the SMS1932 and SMS1947 (see Deary et al., 2009b, and Deary et al., 2012a, for not-now-up-to-date summaries of the results).

Intelligence and the Length of Life

In our first study of what we later called 'cognitive epidemiology' (Deary & Der, 2005, p. 64), we sought the vital status – using death and marriage records in Scotland – of the 2,792 children who sat the SMS1932 in Aberdeen (Whalley & Deary, 2001). We found the vital status of 79.9% of those children as of 1 January 1997, about 65 years after they sat the MHT in the SMS1932. The main result was that a standard deviation disadvantage in MHT score at age 11 was associated with a 21% reduced likelihood of being alive at age 76.

The association between intelligence in childhood and youth and mortality has been replicated in other samples of the SMS1932 and SMS1947, and in samples from several other countries. Meta-analysis of these studies confirms the direction and size of the association (Calvin et al., 2011). Childhood intelligence is also associated with death from several specific causes, such as cardiovascular disease, dementia, respiratory disease, and external causes (accidents, suicide, homicide), though generally not with cancer, with the exception of lung cancer (Deary, Weiss, & Batty, 2010). Our most comprehensive study of childhood intelligence and causes of death up to older age linked about 94% of the Scottish Mental Survey 1947 intelligence test score data from age 11 years to death records up to age 79. There were strong associations between childhood intelligence and all-cause mortality (Cukic et al., 2017), and deaths from cardiovascular disease, coronary heart disease, stroke, cancer overall, non-smoking-related cancers specifically, respiratory disease, digestive disease, dementia, and injury (Calvin et al., 2017).

In addition to replicating the original childhood intelligence–mortality association, and extending it to different countries, to various causes of death, and to illnesses and health behaviours, we have sought to explain the association. In the first report in 2001 we put forward a number of non-exclusive possibilities, including that childhood intelligence might be: a marker of accumulated pathology; an indicator of system integrity (Deary, 2012); a predictor of healthy behaviours; and a predictor of safer and more affluent environments in adulthood. All of these remain tenable. Our studies with the large UK Biobank sample have shown that some of the intelligence-health association can be traced to shared genetic factors (Hagenaars et al., 2016). It is interesting that reaction time accounts for a substantial portion of the association between intelligence and survival (Deary & Der, 2005). The SMS1947 has extra data collected on the children born on the first days of the even-numbered months of 1936 (the 6-Day Sample); they were followed up for 16 years with almost-annual interviews and questionnaires, from age 11 to age 27. We have found from them that, in addition to intelligence, a personality trait akin to conscientiousness (rated by teachers) and belonging to a club in youth are independent pre-dictors of survival to old age (Calvin et al., 2015; Deary et al., 2008).

The Lifetime Stability of Intelligence Differences

In the Aberdeen and Edinburgh (Lothian) areas of Scotland, we obtained permission to trace and recall participants of the SMS1932 and SMS1947. They were enrolled into, first, the Aberdeen Birth Cohort studies of 1921 and 1936 (ABC1921, ABC1936; Deary et al., 2009b; Whalley et al., 2011), and then the Lothian Birth Cohort studies of 1921 and 1936 (LBC1921, LBC1936; Deary et al., 2012a). As we write (December 2016), IJD has just sent the last batch of 80th-birthday cards to the LBC1936 members, and has signed Christmas cards to several hundred of the LBC1921/LBC1936 participants. The LBC1936 have been seen by IJD's team at ages 70, 73, 76, and 79, and the LBC1921 have been seen at ages 79, 83, 87, 90, and 92. At each visit they undertake many cognitive tests, extensive medical and physical testing, blood testing (for biomarkers, genetics, epigenetics, etc.), brain imaging (Wardlaw et al., 2011), and testing on many psychological and social questionnaires.

One of the tests taken by the Cohort studies' participants in older age was the MHT, which they had taken at age 11. That afforded our studying the very long-term stability and change in intelligence differences. Before we report that, we did establish that the MHT – devised for school selection in children – had concurrent validity in older age, by showing its high correlations with, for example, the Wechsler Adult Intelligence Scale and Raven's Progressive Matrices (Deary, 2014). In the LBC1921 we found an uncorrected correlation of 0.66 between MHT at age 11 and MHT at age 79 (Deary et al., 2004), and, later, a correlation of 0.54 between MHT at age 11 and MHT at age 90 (Deary, Pattie, & Starr, 2013). ABC1921 and LBC1936 studies had similar results (Deary et al., 2000; Gow et al., 2011). A raw coefficient of 0.72 was found between the Binet test score of the 6-Day Sample of the SMS1947 at age 11 and a verbal intelligence test taken at age 77 (Deary & Brett, 2015).

These longest-ever studies of the stability of intelligence differences show that about half of the variance in intelligence test scores is stable from childhood to older age. Our research programme has focussed on the other half, that is, the instability, to which we now turn.

What Affects Lifetime Changes in Intelligence Differences?

We seek those factors – social, psychological, health, genetic, etc. – that contribute to variance in older-age intelligence that is not accounted for by childhood intelligence. We exclude dementia; that is, we study the variation in normal cognitive ageing. We want to find the protecting and damaging determinants of lifetime cognitive change. Few studies of cognitive ageing have the valuable baseline of a valid childhood intelligence test score. Our starting point was to include as wide a range of determinants as our participants could cope with. We reckoned that the reasons for relatively good, average, or poor cognitive ageing would include fate (genetics, and we emphasise that genetic associations do not mean unmodifiable influences), providence (lifestyle), and chance (stochasticity).

Let's take genetics first. Among the 20,000 or so individual human genes, only the gene for apolipoprotein E (*APOE*) appears, as yet, reliably to show variation associated with changes in intelligence across the life course. Those individuals with the e4 allele tend to score relatively less well in intelligence tests in older age – after adjusting for MHT at age 11 – than those who lack this allele (Deary et al., 2002), and also tend to decline faster in old age (Ritchie et al., 2016). These effects are small, accounting for only around 1% of the variance in older-age intelligence. This variation in *APOE* is well known to be associated with risk of dementia.

We then moved from single gene variants to looking at the combined effect of all genetic variation on lifetime cognitive change. The Aberdeen and Lothian 1921 and 1936 cohorts were all tested for more than half a million genetic variants, called single nucleotide polymorphisms (SNPs). A then-new method called bivariate GCTA-GREML allowed us to reckon how similar these unrelated individuals were across their genomes and whether this correlated with how much their intelligence changed from childhood to older age (Deary et al., 2012b). Recall from the previous section that about 50% of the variance in intelligence in older age was not due to variance in childhood intelligence. We found that about a quarter of the change in intelligence from childhood to older age was associated with all genetic factors (all tested SNPs, at least) combined. If replicated, this means that up to as much as three quarters of lifetime cognitive ageing might be due to lifestyle factors and health, at least some of which could be modifiable.

In testing for contributors to lifetime cognitive change in the Lothian cohorts, our model is as follows: we examine whether the candidate exposure variable, which might be protective or damaging, is associated with intelligence in older age after adjusting for the MHT at age 11. We found that the following lifestyle and health factors are associated with having a better intelligence test score in older age than expected from the score in childhood, that is, associated with healthy cognitive ageing: not smoking (Corley et al., 2012), being physically active (Gow et al., 2012), being physically fit (Deary et al., 2006), having had a complex occupation (Smart, Gow, & Deary, 2014), having had more education (Ritchie, Bates, & Deary, 2015), being able to speak additional languages (Bak et al., 2014), having a well-connected brain (healthy white matter; Penke et al., 2012), having a symmetrical body (Penke et al., 2009), having few minor physical anomalies such as abnormal finger curvature (Hope et al., 2012), and having a low allostatic load (e.g., no hypertension, no diabetes, not being obese, having low inflammatory biomarkers in the bloodstream, etc.; Booth et al., 2015). We emphasise that most of these effects are small, typically accounting for around 1% of the variance in intelligence in older age, and that they require replication. Also, when many of them are entered together in multivariate analyses, the main significant independent predictors of cognitive change are variation in the *APOE* e4 allele and physical fitness (Ritchie et al., 2016). Clearly, a great deal more work needs to be done on finding new biosocial predictors of cognitive ageing differences, and interactions among the ones we already know. We should not rule out the so-called gloomy prospect; that is, that substantial portions of the variance are explained by unique, individual-specific, chance factors (e.g., Davey Smith, 2011).

The data from the age-11 MHT tests enabled us to find something else about intelligence in the life course, that is, the detection of those apparent contributors to cognitive ageing that were confounded with childhood intelligence (that is, variation in childhood intelligence is associated with variation in the putative contributor and later-life intelligence and that any correlation between the latter two is spurious), and maybe subject to reverse causation (i.e., higher or lower intelligence may cause variation in the putative contributor, rather than that factor causing higher or lower intelligence in later life). Here is an example. We found that drinking more caffeine was associated with better intelligence scores in older age in the LBC1936 (Corley et al., 2010b). So, does that make coffee drinking a protective factor for cognitive ageing? Well, no, because the association did not survive adjustment of the MHT score at age 11, taken 60 years earlier. What those results might mean is that smarter children are both more likely to have higher intelligence scores in older age and drink more coffee (perhaps as part of a cluster of lifestyle choices associated with higher education and a more professional social class, to which childhood intelligence is related), but that those latter two variables are not causally related. We found the same pattern of confounding for alcohol drinking (Corley et al., 2011), body mass index (Corley et al., 2010a), several dietary intakes (antioxidants, B vitamins, flavonoids, Mediterranean diet, etc.; e.g., Butchart et al., 2011; McNeill et al., 2011), blood cholesterol (Corley, Starr, & Deary, 2015), the blood inflammatory marker called C-reactive protein (Luciano et al., 2009), and social and intellectual engagement (Gow et al., 2012). All of these factors, then, are unlikely to be causal of cognitive change from childhood to old age, but variation in them in older age appears to be associated with childhood intelligence. A few variables, such as higher vitamin B12 blood levels (Starr et al., 2005) and negative cytomegalovirus infection status (Gow et al., 2013), appeared to show both confounding and a small contribution to healthy cognitive ageing.

The Heritability of Intelligence

For many years of our studies into intelligence, we were observers of the results appearing on heritability. We have written some overviews on the topic and pieces that included a summary of genetic findings (Deary, Penke, & Johnson, 2010; Deary, Spinath, & Bates, 2006; Plomin & Deary, 2015), and we reported genetic contributions to cognitive ageing, as recounted previously. The SMS1932 and SMS1947 contained twins, but no zygosity information. We devised a way to estimate the heritability of childhood intelligence using same- and opposite-sex twins, and obtained results similar to more modern twin studies, with heritability estimates around 0.7. That had the benefit of having been done in two near-entire populations of twins, so selection bias was not an issue (Benyamin et al., 2005).

Our most significant contribution to the study of the heritability of intelligence was using the molecular-genetic data we described earlier. We combined the Aberdeen and Lothian Birth Cohorts' molecular genetic data on about half a million SNPs with those of a cohort from England. Using our total N of more than 3,000, we estimated the heritability of fluid and crystallised intelligence using data based on DNA testing of unrelated individuals, that is, not from twins, adoptees, or families (Davies et al., 2011). What we did was a genome-wide association study (GWAS), with analyses using a method known as GCTA-GREML to estimate heritability. The method can test the extent to which unrelated people with similar DNA have similar intelligence test scores. It was the first report of the heritability of intelligence that was based on DNA testing of unrelated individuals, and not based on the assumptions that twin or family studies entail. Our estimate was about 0.4 or above. It is typical of DNA SNP-based heritability estimates to be about half of that obtained from twin studies, in part, it is thought, because SNPs do not tap into all of the genetic variation. Subsequent, larger studies, including some led by us, have put the estimate of the SNP-based heritability of intelligence nearer to 0.3 (Davies et al., 2015).

Following our first GWAS of intelligence report, the mode of working has been to combine greater numbers of GWAS studies in meta-analyses. We led the largest study to date, with an N of more than 53,000 (Davies et al., 2015). In addition to heritability, these studies have enabled us to do three things. First, we are beginning to find the individual genetic variants that contribute to intelligence differences; we now know that they are very many – thus intelligence is called a polygenic trait – and that contributions from individual genetic variants are minuscule. Second, using only the summary genetic association data from these large studies, one can take the information about which genetic variants are associated with intelligence and significantly predict intelligence test scores in new, independent samples (this is known as 'polygenic profiling'; see later in this chapter for more). Third, the results from GWAS studies of intelligence have been used to reveal substantial genetic correlations between intelligence and other cognitive functions, education, anthropometric traits, and a number of physical and mental health variables and illnesses (Hagenaars et al., 2016). That is, for reasons we are still investigating, intelligence shares genetic influences with many of the traits with which intelligence is phenotypically correlated: some of the same genes are involved across these many different traits, including intelligence.

Structural Brain Imaging Correlates of Intelligence

The LBC1936 was unusual, in addition to what we said previously, in having 700 of its members undertake a detailed structural magnetic resonance (MR) brain scan at about age 73 (Wardlaw et al., 2011). This N is unusually large for brain-imaging studies, and even more useful because all were done on the same brain scanner. One part of the scan was diffusion-tensor MR imaging, which can examine the health of the white matter, that is, the connections in the brain. Our first novel finding was that people who had healthy connections in one part of the brain tended to have healthy connections in other regions; that is, there was a general factor of the health of the brain's white matter connections, akin to the general factor of intelligence (Penke et al., 2010). Second, we found that this white matter general factor accounted for about 10% of the variation in general cognitive function at about age 73, and that this is mostly mediated by processing speed (Penke et al., 2012).

Beyond just looking at white matter connections, we showed in the LBC1936 that one can account for up to about 20% of variation in later-life general intelligence with a combination of total brain volume, brain cortical thickness, and white matter damage (Ritchie et al., 2015). It will be of interest to see how much of the remaining 80% can be explained by newer, more detailed brain structural and functional measures. We have also found some confounding by childhood intelligence in brain structural-intelligence associations: in the LBC1936 we found widespread associations across the brain between the thickness of the cerebral cortex and intelligence at age 73 (Karama et al., 2014). However, almost all of the associations disappeared after adjusting for MHT intelligence score at age 11, taken 60 years earlier. Thus we were prevented from incorrectly concluding that brain cortical thickness was a cause of better intelligence in older age. More likely, cortical thickness and intelligence ran in parallel, that is, they were correlated from childhood onwards.

Sex Differences, Getting on in Life, and Estimating Premorbid Intelligence

Showing sex differences in intelligence variance but not its mean. We used the data from the SMS1932 and SMS1947 to show that, at age 11, in Scotland at least, the mean intelligence test (MHT) scores for both sexes were about the same (Deary et al., 2003; Johnson, Carothers, & Deary, 2008). However, boys had greater variance: there were more male lower scorers and higher scorers, and the girls were more bunched around the mean. The importance of this finding was that it was based on a near-entire population and so was not prey to the possible differential sex bias in sample selection that affects other studies. Subsequent studies by us and others on other very large samples (Strand, Deary, & Smith, 2006), and in sibling designs (Deary et al., 2007a) confirmed the 'same-mean, different-variance' result with respect to sex differences in intelligence. There is still no clear theory as to why this variance difference exists; some biologists argue it may have an evolutionary basis (e.g. Lehre et al., 2009), and we have speculated that the variance differences might be traced in part to the X-chromosome (Johnson, Carothers, & Deary, 2009). However, data that allow a decisive test of these ideas have not yet been gathered.

Getting on in life. Two types of study with the Scottish Mental Survey data have been revealing about social mobility and social position. First, data linkage between the SMS1932 and the Scottish Midspan Health study showed that parental social class, childhood intelligence, education, and the social class of the person's own first job all contributed to social position in mid-life (Deary et al., 2005). Moreover, intelligence made a stronger contribution to mid-life social position than to the first job. This provided some evidence for the 'gravitational' hypothesis, which posits that people with higher intelligence will tend eventually to rise to high-status jobs even if they are initially from more disadvantaged backgrounds (consistent with the existence of some degree of 'meritocracy', at least in our UK context). Studies using the LBC1921 and LBC1936 have looked across three generations – because the participants reported on the educations and occupations of their parents and children – and found that even grandparental social class and education are associated with education and social class two generations later (Johnson, Brett, & Deary, 2010a, 2010b). We have also contributed by showing, using DNA testing in the very large UK Biobank sample, that intelligence, education, and social class correlate in part because of shared genetic variation (Hill et al., 2016).

Validating estimates of premorbid/prior intelligence. In research on dementia and cognitive decline, it is useful to have an estimate of someone's prior intelligence level, which may be compared with current cognitive testing. One then can estimate how far they have fallen. Word-pronunciation tests, such as the National Adult Reading Test (NART) and the Test of Premorbid Function, are widely used for this purpose. However, how well do the scores on these brief irregular-word pronunciation tests correlate with actually tested prior ability? In a series of studies, we reported correlations of well over 0.6 between NART scores in older age and MHT at age 11 (Crawford et al., 2001; Deary & Brett, 2015; Dykiert & Deary, 2013). Moreover, we found that the correlation was about the same in healthy older people and in early dementia (McGurn et al., 2004). These findings provided some validation of these tests as estimators of premorbid intelligence. And we further showed that the Mini-Mental State Examination – widely used to test for cognitive decline in older age – is sensitive to prior intelligence and so should be adjusted for it (Crawford et al., 2001; Dykiert et al., 2016).

More Intelligence Research with Good Epidemiological Samples

We think we have filled in some of the story of how intelligence affects life and vice versa. We also try to do unusually well-powered studies using samples others than the SMSs. In this vein, our finding correlations of above 0.4 between four-choice reaction time and intelligence in the West of Scotland Twenty-07 Study was a lesson in how population-representative samples make a difference to effect sizes: 0.4 estimates replaced estimates around 0.2 from student samples (Deary et al., 2001; Der & Deary, 2003). Our much-cited correlation of about 0.8 between a latent trait of intelligence at age 11 and national education examination results in England at age 16 showed that the combination of a good intelligence test battery, a huge population-representative sample, and linkage to standardised national exams can give a definitive effect size (Deary et al., 2007b). And an even larger study in two countries showed that some of this correlation was due to shared genetic factors (Calvin et al., 2012).

Educational and Social Policy Matters in Intelligence

Many of our intelligence research findings are relevant to those making educational or social policy, though we recognise that results do not mandate policy, and that policy follows people's values. We find three areas of particular interest. First, we think intelligence is relevant for healthcare: the results from cognitive epidemiology suggest that scores from intelligence tests are predictive and informative about people's health outcomes, regardless of the ultimate explanation for the correlation (Deary & Johnson, 2010). Second, there has been a long-running debate in the United Kingdom over selective schooling, something we would be remiss not to mention given the Moray House Test's origins as an 'Eleven-Plus'-style selective test. We won't delve into the details of this debate here, except to note that the evidence for the benefits of a selective system seems equivocal, at least in the history of education in the UK; the disadvantages to the 'unselected' students seem to balance out any benefits for those who pass the test (e.g., Boliver & Swift, 2011).

Third, the major advances being made in the genetics of intelligence – see earlier in this chapter – raise the question: what will people do with the summary information from genome-wide association studies? The polygenic profile that we can create for each individual, indexing his or her propensity to have high or low intelligence, is proving an interesting variable to include in scientific studies. It is becoming more accurate: a GWAS-derived polygenic profile for educational attainment – strongly genetically correlated with intelligence – has explained around 9% of the variance in exam success at age 16 in an independent sample (Selzam et al., 2016). The predictive accuracy will increase in the future as the GWAS become larger. As the polygenic profile scores become more and more accurate, what will happen outside of scientific research?

Will prospective parents begin to demand DNA testing of embryos, selecting for IVF-style implantation only those that have high-end polygenic profiles for intelligence (and/or other traits that the parents deem desirable)? Will governments and health services regulate this technology? Will they take steps to restrict their use among the well-off and encourage their use in the poor (as suggested by Young, 2015), so as to avoid the exacerbation of current inequalities and, in fact, reduce them? We do not have answers to these questions; nor do we have the expertise to make policy recommendations. A frank, informed (bio)ethical debate is required on the potential uses of our growing knowledge of the genetics of intelligence and its genetic correlations with education, social status, and health.

Questions for Future Research

The validating evidence for the concept of intelligence, its measurement, its foundations, and its practical importance is colossal, and still accumulating. So why are there still so many anti-IQ critics (e.g. Dorling & Tomlinson, 2016; Gillborn, 2016; Murdoch, 2007)? The idea of intelligence differences just pushes too many moral hot buttons, we think, and there are a great many confusions, strawman arguments, and get-out clauses in our scientific conversation about it. But just as a thought experiment, we will now briefly consider what future intelligence researchers might do to try and convince the unconvinced that this kind of research is worthwhile.

As the sample sizes in genome-wide association studies continue to increase, we are finding more and more genetic variants linked to performance on cognitive tests. There is little reason to expect this to stop in the future, especially as whole-genome sequencing becomes cheaper and thus rarer genetic variants can be examined alongside common SNPs. The so-called missing heritability (that is, the gap between the full heritability we get from twin studies and the heritability we get directly from DNA; Manolio et al., 2009) will – if current theoretical models and empirical findings are anything to go by – shrink. Finding correlations between genes and cognitive ability is one thing, but understanding the biological mechanisms that explain these correlations is far harder. A great deal of careful work needs to be done in understanding the functions of the many genetic variants (each with minuscule contributions to intelligence differences), how they are expressed in the brain, and the pathways linking them to the complex phenotype of intelligence. Initial steps are being taken on this deeper biology (e.g., Johnson et al, 2016), and we anticipate that the advances in genomics – and related 'omics' such as epigenetics, gene expression, etc. – will make the task of understanding the genetics of intelligence more feasible.

Currently, neuroimaging research into intelligence generally uses broad, gross measures like total brain volume, with which there appears to be a solid correlation (Pietschnig et al., 2015). However, to get a handle on the neuroscience of intelligence differences, we need to drill deeper into the relevant aspects of brain structure and functioning. Whenever a new brain-imaging measure is developed, it is usually tested for a correlation with intelligence; see the preceding discussion on diffusion-tensor imaging, and recent papers on the connectome (Santarnecchi, Rossi, & Rossi, 2015) and regional gyrification (Gregory et al., 2016). As with genetics, as sample sizes accumulate, we can sort out which of these brain measures is doing the real work in explaining intelligence differences.

Intelligence is a prominent, important, and valued trait (see Deary et al., 2009a discussing Thomson, 1936). Its lineaments, reach, and origins deserve more attention from careful, sceptical – but not dismissive – researchers.

References

Bak, T. H., Nissan, J. J., Allerhand, M., & Deary, I. J. (2014). Does bilingualism influence cognitive aging? *Annals of Neurology*, 75, 959–963.

Bartholomew, D. J., Allerhand, M., & Deary, I. J. (2013). Measuring mental capacity: Thomson's bonds model and Spearman's g-model compared. *Intelligence*, 41, 222–233.

Bartholomew, D. J., Deary, I. J., & Lawn, M. (2009). A new lease of life for Thomson's bonds model of intelligence. *Psychological Review*, 116, 567–579.

Benyamin, B., Wilson, V., Whalley, L. J., Visscher, P. M., & Deary, I. J. (2005). Large, consistent estimates of heritability of cognitive ability in two entire populations of 11-year-old twins from Scottish Mental Surveys of 1932 and 1947. *Behavior Genetics*, 35, 525–534.

Boliver, V., & Swift, A. (2011). Do comprehensive schools reduce social mobility? *The British Journal of Sociology*, 62, 89–110.

Booth, T., Royle, N. A., Corley, J., Gow, A. J., Valdes Hernandez, M. A., Maniega, S. M., Ritchie, S. J., Bastin, M. E., Starr, J. M., Wardlaw, J. M., & Deary, I. J. (2015). Association of allostatic load with brain structure and cognitive ability in later life. *Neurobiology of Aging*, 36, 1390–1399.

Brand, C. R., & Deary, I. J. (1982). Intelligence and inspection time. In H. J. Eysenck (Ed.), *A model for intelligence* (pp. 133–148). New York: Springer.

Brett, C. E., & Deary, I. J. (2014). Realising health data linkage from a researcher's perspective: Following up the 6-Day Sample of the Scottish Mental Survey 1947. *Longitudinal and Life Course Studies*, 5, 283–298.

Butchart, C., Kyle, J., McNeill, G., Corley, J., Gow, A., Starr, J., & Deary, I. J. (2011). Flavonoid intake in relation to cognitive function in later life in the Lothian Birth Cohort 1936. *British Journal of Nutrition*, 106, 141–148.

Calvin, C. M., Batty, G. D., Brett, C. E., & Deary, I. J. (2015). Childhood club participation and all-cause mortality in adulthood: A 65-year follow-up study of a population-representative sample of Scotland. *Psychosomatic Medicine*, 77, 712–720.

Calvin, C., Batty, G. D., Der, G., Brett, C. E., Pattie, A., Cukic, I., & Deary, I. J. (2017). Childhood intelligence in relation to major causes of death in 68 year follow-up: prospective population study. *British Medical Journal*, 357, j2708.

Calvin, C. M., Deary, I. J., Fenton, C., Roberts, B., Der, G., Leckenby, N., & Batty, G. D. (2011). Intelligence in youth and all-cause mortality: Systematic review with meta-analysis. *International Journal of Epidemiology*, 40, 626–644.

Calvin, C. M., Deary, I. J., Webbink, D., Smith, P., Fernandes, C., Lee, S. H., Luciano, M., & Visscher, P. M. (2012). Multivariate genetic analyses of cognition and education from two population samples of 174,000 and 166,000 school children. *Behavior Genetics*, 42, 699–710.

Corley, J., Gow, A. J., Starr, J. M., & Deary, I. J. (2010a). Is body mass index in old age related to cognitive abilities? The Lothian Birth Cohort 1936 study. *Psychology and Aging*, 25, 867–875.

(2012). Smoking, childhood IQ, and cognitive function in old age. *Journal of Psychosomatic Research*, 73, 132–138.

Corley, J., Jia, X., Brett, C. E., Gow, A. J., Starr, J. M., Kyle, J. A. M., McNeill, G., & Deary, I. J. (2011). Alcohol intake and cognitive abilities in old age: The Lothian Birth Cohort 1936 study. *Neuropsychology*, 25, 166–175.

Corley, J., Jia, X., Kyle, J. A. M., Gow, A. J., Brett, C., Starr, J. M., McNeill, G., & Deary, I. J. (2010b). Caffeine consumption and cognitive function at age 70: The Lothian Birth Cohort 1936 study. *Psychosomatic Medicine*, 72, 206–214.

Corley, J., Starr, J. M., & Deary, I. J. (2015). Serum cholesterol and cognitive functions: The Lothian Birth Cohort 1936. *International Psychogeriatrics*, 27, 439–453.

Crawford, J. R., Deary, I. J., Starr, J., & Whalley, L. J. (2001). The NART as an index of prior intellectual functioning: A retrospective validity study covering a 66 year interval. *Psychological Medicine*, 31, 451–458.

Cukic, I., Brett, C. E., Calvin, C. M., Batty, G. D., & Deary, I. J. (2017). Childhood IQ and survival to 79: Follow-up of 94% of the Scottish Mental Survey 1947. *Intelligence*, 63, 45–50.

Davey Smith, G. (2011). Epidemiology, epigenetics, and the 'gloomy prospect': Embracing randomness in population health research and practice. *International Journal of Epidemiology*, 40, 537–562.

Davies, G., Armstrong, N., Bis, J. C., Bressler, Chouraki, V. et al. (2015). Genetic contributions to variation in general cognitive function: A meta-analysis of genome-wide association studies in the CHARGE consortium (N = 53,949). *Molecular Psychiatry*, 20, 183–192.

Davies, G., Tenesa, A., Payton, A., Yang, J., Harris, S. E., Liewald, D., et al. (2011). Genome-wide association studies establish that human intelligence is highly heritable and polygenic. *Molecular Psychiatry*, 16, 996–1005.

Deary, I. J. (2000). *Looking down on human intelligence: From psychometrics to the brain*. Oxford: Oxford University Press.

(2001). *Intelligence: A very short introduction*. Oxford: Oxford University Press.

(2012). Looking for 'system integrity' in cognitive epidemiology. *Gerontology*, 58, 545–553.

(2014). The stability of intelligence from childhood to old age. *Current Directions in Psychological Science*, 23, 239–245.

Deary, I. J., Batty, G. D., Pattie, A., & Gale, C. G. (2008). More intelligent, more dependable children live longer: A 55-year longitudinal study of a representative sample of the Scottish Nation. *Psychological Science*, 19, 874–880.

Deary, I. J., & Brett, C. E. (2015). Predicting and retrodicting intelligence between childhood and old age in the 6-Day Sample of the Scottish Mental Survey 1947. *Intelligence*, 50, 1–9.

Deary, I. J., Cox, S. R., & Ritchie, S. J. (2016). Getting Spearman off the sky-hook: One more in a century (since Thomson, 1916) of attempts to vanquish g. *Psychological Inquiry*, 27, 192–199.

Deary, I. J., & Der, G. (2005). Reaction time explains IQ's association with death. *Psychological Science*, 16, 64–69.

Deary, I. J., Der, G., & Ford, G. (2001). Reaction times and intelligence differences: A population-based cohort study. *Intelligence*, 29, 389–399.

Deary, I. J., Gow, A. J., Pattie, A., & Starr, J. M. (2012a). Cohort profile: The Lothian Birth Cohorts of 1921 and 1936. *International Journal of Epidemiology*, 41, 1576–1584.

Deary, I. J., Irwing, P., Der, G., & Bates, T. C. (2007a). Brother-sister differences in the g factor in intelligence: Analysis of full, opposite-sex siblings from the NLSY1979. *Intelligence*, 35, 451–456.

Deary, I. J., & Johnson, W. (2010). Intelligence and education: causal perceptions drive analytic processes and therefore conclusions. *International Journal of Epidemiology*, 39(5), 1362–1369.

Deary, I. J., Lawn, M., Brett, C., & Bartholomew, D. J. (2009a). 'Intelligence and civilisation': A Ludwig Mond lecture delivered at the University of Manchester on 23rd October 1936 by Godfrey H. Thomson. A reprinting with background and commentary. *Intelligence*, 37, 48–61.

Deary, I. J., Pattie, A., & Starr, J. M. (2013). The stability of intelligence from age 11 to age 90 years: The Lothian Birth Cohort 1921. *Psychological Science*, 24, 2361–2368.

Deary, I. J., Penke, L., & Johnson, W. (2010). The neuroscience of human intelligence differences. *Nature Reviews Neuroscience*, 11, 201–211.

Deary, I. J., & Ritchie, S. J. (2016). Processing speed differences between 70- and 83-year-olds matched on childhood IQ. *Intelligence*, 55, 28–33.

Deary, I. J., & Stough, C. (1996). Intelligence and inspection time: Achievements, prospects and problems. *American Psychologist*, 51, 599–608.

Deary, I. J., Strand, S., Smith, P., & Fernandes, C. (2007b). Intelligence and educational achievement. *Intelligence*, 35, 13–21.

Deary, I. J., Taylor, M. D., Hart, C. L., Wilson, V., Davey Smith, G., Blane, D., & Starr, J. M. (2005). Intergenerational social mobility and mid-life status attainment: Influences of childhood intelligence, childhood social factors, and education. *Intelligence*, 33, 455–472.

Deary, I. J., Thorpe, G., Wilson, V., Starr, J. M., & Whalley, L. J. (2003). Population sex differences in IQ at age 11: The Scottish Mental Survey 1932. *Intelligence*, 31, 533–542.

Deary, I. J., Weiss, A., & Batty, G. D. (2010). Intelligence and personality as predictors of illness and death: How researchers in differential psychology and chronic disease epidemiology are collaborating to understand and address health inequalities. *Psychological Science in the Public Interest*, 11, 53–79.

Deary, I. J., Whalley, L. J., Batty, G. D., & Starr, J. M. (2006). Physical fitness and lifetime cognitive change. *Neurology*, 67, 1195–1200.

Deary, I. J., Whalley, L. J., Lemmon, H., Crawford, J. R., & Starr, J. M. (2000). The stability of individual differences in mental ability from childhood to old age: Follow-up of the 1932 Scottish Mental Survey. *Intelligence*, 28, 49–55.

Deary, I. J., Whalley, L. J., & Starr, J. M. (2009b). *A lifetime of intelligence: Follow-up studies of the Scottish Mental Surveys of 1932 and 1947*. Washington, DC: American Psychological Association.

Deary, I. J., Whiteman, M. C., Pattie, A., Starr, J. M., Hayward, C., Wright, A. F., Carothers, A., & Whalley, L. J. (2002). Cognitive change and the APOE e4 allele. *Nature*, 418, 932.

Deary, I. J., Whiteman, M. C., Starr, J. M., Whalley, L. J., & Fox, H. C. (2004). The impact of childhood intelligence on later life: Following up the Scottish Mental Surveys of 1932 and 1947. *Journal of Personality and Social Psychology*, 86, 130–147.

Deary, I. J., Yang, J., Davies, G., Harris, S. E., Tenesa, A., Liewald, D., Luciano, M., Lopez, L. M., Gow, A. J., Corley, J., Redmond, P., Fox, H. C., Rowe, S. J., Haggarty, P., McNeill, G., Goddard, M. E., Porteous, D. J., Whalley, L. J., Starr, J. M., & Visscher, P. M. (2012b). Genetic contributions to stability and change in intelligence from childhood to old age. *Nature*, 482, 212–215.

Der, G., & Deary, I. J. (2003). IQ, reaction time and the differentiation hypothesis. *Intelligence*, 31, 491–503.

Dorling, D., & Tomlinson, S. (2016). The creation of inequality: Myths of potential and ability. *Journal for Critical Education Policy Studies*, 14, retrieved from: www.jceps.com/archives/3204.

Dykiert, D., & Deary, I. J. (2013). Retrospective validation of WTAR and NART scores as estimators of prior cognitive ability using the Lothian Birth Cohort 1936. *Psychological Assessment*, 25, 1361–1366.

Dykiert, D., Der, G., Starr, J. M., & Deary, I. J. (2016). Why is Mini-Mental State Examination performance correlated with estimated premorbid ability? *Psychological Medicine*, 46, 2647–2654.

Gillborn, D. (2016). Softly, softly: Genetics, intelligence and the hidden racism of the new geneism. *Journal of Education Policy*, 1–24.

Gow, A. J., Corley, J., Starr, J. M., & Deary, I. J. (2012). Reverse causation in activity-cognitive ability associations: The Lothian Birth Cohort 1936. *Psychology and Aging*, 27, 250–255.

Gow, A. J., Firth, C., Harrison, R., Starr, J.M., Moss, P., & Deary, I. J. (2013). Cytomegalovirus infection and cognitive abilities in old age. *Neurobiology of Ageing*, 34, 1846–1852.

Gow, A. J., Johnson, W., Pattie, A., Brett, C. E., Roberts, B., Starr, J. M., & Deary, I. J. (2011). Stability and change in intelligence from age 11 to ages 70, 79 and 87: The Lothian Birth Cohorts of 1921 and 1936. *Psychology and Aging*, 26, 232–240.

Gregory, M. D., Kippenhan, J. S., Dickinson, D., Carrasco, J., Mattay, V. S., Weinberger, D. R., & Berman, K. F. (2016). Regional variations in brain gyrification are associated with general cognitive ability in humans. *Current Biology*, 26, 1301–1305.

Hagenaars, S. P., Harris, S. E., Davies, G. et al. (2016). Shared genetic aetiology between cognitive functions and physical and mental health in UK Biobank (N = 112 151) and 24 GWAS consortia. *Molecular Psychiatry*, 21, 1624–1632.

Hill, W. D., Hagenaars, S. P., Marioni, R. E., Harris, S. E., Liewald, D. C. M., Davies, G., Okbay, A., McIntosh, A. M., Gale, C. R., & Deary, I. J. (2016). Molecular genetic contributions to social deprivation and household income in UK Biobank. *Current Biology*, 26, 3083–3089.

Hope, D., Bates, T., Gow, A. J., Starr, J. M., & Deary, I. J. (2012). Minor physical anomalies, intelligence, and cognitive decline. *Experimental Aging Research*, 38, 265–278.

Johnson, M. R., Shkura, K., Langley, S. R., Delahaye-Duriez, A., Srivastava, P., Hill, W. D., ... & Rotival, M. (2016). Systems genetics identifies a convergent gene network for cognition and neurodevelopmental disease. *Nature Neuroscience*, 19, 223–232.

Johnson, W., Bouchard, T. J., & Krueger, R. F. (2004). Just one *g*: consistent results from three test batteries. *Intelligence*, 32, 95–107.

Johnson, W., Brett, C. E., & Deary, I. J. (2010a). Intergenerational class mobility in Britain: A comparative look across three generations in the Lothian Birth Cohort 1936. *Intelligence*, 38, 268–281.

(2010b). The pivotal role of education in the association between ability and social class attainment: A look across three generations. *Intelligence*, 38, 55–65.

Johnson, W., Carothers, A., & Deary, I. J. (2008). Sex differences in variability in general intelligence: A new look at the old question. *Perspectives on Psychological Science*, 3, 518–531.

(2009). A role for the X chromosome in sex differences in variability in general intelligence?. *Perspectives on Psychological Science*, 4, 598–611.

Karama, S., Bastin, M. E., Murray, C., Royle, N. A., Penke, L., Maniega, et al. (2014). Childhood cognitive ability accounts for associations between cognitive ability and brain cortical thickness in old age. *Molecular Psychiatry*, 19, 555–559.

Lehre, A. C., Lehre, K. P., Laake, P., & Danbolt, N. C. (2009). Greater intrasex phenotype variability in males than in females is a fundamental aspect of the gender differences in humans. *Developmental Psychobiology*, 51, 198–206.

Luciano, M., Marioni, R. E., Gow, A. J., Starr, J. M., & Deary, I. J. (2009). Reverse causation in the association between C reactive protein and fibrinogen levels and cognitive abilities in an aging sample. *Psychosomatic Medicine*, 71, 404–409.

Manolio, T. A., Collins, F. S., Cox, N. J., Goldstein, D. B., Hindorff, L. A., Hunter, D. J., ... & Cho, J. H. (2009). Finding the missing heritability of complex diseases. *Nature*, 461, 747–753.

McGurn, B., Starr, J. M., Topfer, J. A., Pattie, A., Whiteman, M. C., Lemmon, H. A., Whalley, L. J., & Deary, I. J. (2004). Pronunciation of irregular words is preserved in dementia, validating premorbid IQ estimation. *Neurology*, 62, 1184–1186.

McNeill, G., Jia, X., Whalley, L. J., Fox, H. C., Corley, J., Gow, A. J., Brett, C., Starr, J. M., & Deary, I. J. (2011). Antioxidant and B vitamin intake in relation to cognitive function in later life in the Lothian Birth Cohort 1936. *European Journal of Clinical Nutrition*, 65, 619–626.

Murdoch, S. (2007). *IQ: A smart history of a failed idea*. Hoboken, NJ: John Wiley & Sons.

Penke, L., Bates, T. C., Gow, A. J., Pattie, A., Starr, J. M., Jones, B. C., Perrett, D. I., & Deary, I. J. (2009). Symmetric faces are a sign of successful cognitive aging. *Evolution and Human Behavior*, 30, 429–437.

Penke, L., Maniega, S. M., Bastin, M. E., Hernandez, M. C. V., Murray, C., Royle, N. A., Starr, J. M., Wardlaw, J. M., & Deary, I. J. (2012). Brain white matter integrity as a neural foundation for general intelligence. *Molecular Psychiatry*, 17, 1026–1030.

Penke, L., Munoz Maniega, S., Murray, C., Gow, A. J., Valdes Hernandez, M. C., Clayden, J. D., Starr, J. M., Wardlaw, J. M., Bastin, M. E., & Deary, I. J. (2010). A general factor of brain white matter integrity predicts information processing speed in healthy older people. *Journal of Neuroscience*, 30, 7559, 7674.

Pietschnig, J., Penke, L., Wicherts, J. M., Zeiler, M., & Voracek, M. (2015). Meta-analysis of associations between human brain volume and intelligence differences: how strong are they and what do they mean? *Neuroscience and Biobehavioral Reviews*, 57, 411–432.

Plomin, R., & Deary, I. J. (2015). Genetics and intelligence differences: Five special findings. *Molecular Psychiatry*, 20, 98–108.

Ritchie, S. J. (2015). *Intelligence: All that matters*. London: John Murray Learning.

Ritchie, S. J., Booth, T., Valdes Hernandez, M. C., Corley, J., Munoz Maniega, S., Gow, A. J., Royle, N. A., Pattie, A., Karama, S., Starr, J. M., Bastin, M. E., Wardlaw, J. M., & Deary, I. J. (2015). Beyond a bigger brain: Multivariable brain imaging and intelligence. *Intelligence*, 51, 47–56.

Ritchie, S. J., Tucker-Drob, E. M., Cox, S. R., Corley, J., Dykiert, D., Redmond, P., Pattie, A., Taylor, A. M., Sibbett, R., Starr, J. M., & Deary, I. J. (2016).

Predictors of age-related decline across multiple cognitive functions. *Intelligence*, 59, 115–126.

Ritchie, S. J., Tucker Drob, E. M., & Deary, I. J., (2014). A strong link between speed of visual discrimination and cognitive ageing. *Current Biology*, 24, R681–R683.

Santarnecchi, E., Rossi, S., & Rossi, A. (2015). The smarter, the stronger: Intelligence level correlates with brain resilience to systematic insults. *Cortex*, 64, 293–309.

Scottish Council for Research in Education (1933). *The intelligence of Scottish children*. London: University of London Press.

(1949). *The trend of Scottish intelligence*. London: University of London Press.

Selzam, S., Krapohl, E., von Stumm, S., O'Reilly, P. F., Rimfeld, K., Kovas, Y., ... & Plomin, R. (2016). Predicting educational achievement from DNA. *Molecular Psychiatry*. Advance online publication, doi: 10.1038/mp.2016.107.

Smart, E. L., Gow, A. J., & Deary, I. J. (2014). Occupational complexity and lifetime cognitive abilities. *Neurology*, 83, 2285–2291.

Spearman, C. (1927). *The abilities of man*. New York: MacMillan.

Starr, J. M., Pattie, A., Whiteman, M. C., Whalley, L. J., & Deary, I. J. (2005). Vitamin B12, serum folate, and cognitive change from age 11 to age 79. *Journal of Neurology, Neurosurgery and Psychiatry*, 76, 291–292.

Strand, S., Deary, I. J., & Smith, P. (2006). Sex differences in cognitive ability test score: A UK national picture. *British Journal of Educational Psychology*, 76, 463–480.

Thomson, G. H. (1936). Intelligence and civilisation: A Ludwig Mond lecture delivered at the University of Manchester on 23rd October 1936. Edinburgh, UK: T. & A. Constable.

Wardlaw, J. M., Bastin, M. E., Valdes Hernandez, M. C., Munoz Maniega, S., Royle, N. A., Morris, Z., Clayden, J. D., Sandeman, E. M., Eadie, E., Murray, C., Starr, J. M., & Deary, I. J. (2011). Brain ageing, cognition in youth and old age, and vascular disease in the Lothian Birth Cohort 1936: Rationale, design and methodology of the imaging protocol. *International Journal of Stroke*, 6, 547–559.

Whalley, L. J., & Deary, I. J. (2001). Longitudinal cohort study of childhood IQ and survival up to age 76. *British Medical Journal*, 322, 819–822.

Whalley, L. J., Murray, A. D., Staff, R. T., Starr, J. M., Deary, I. J., Fox, H. C., Lemmon, H., Duthie, S. J., Collins, A. R., & Crawford, J. R. (2011). How the 1932 and 1947 mental surveys of Aberdeen schoolchildren provide a framework to explore the childhood origins of late onset disease and disability. *Maturitas*, 69, 365–372.

Young, T. (2015). The fall of the meritocracy. *Quadrant Online*. Retrieved from: https://quadrant.org.au/magazine/2015/09/fall-meritocracy/.

CHAPTER 6

Intelligence as Domain-Specific Superior Reproducible Performance
The Role of Acquired Domain-Specific Mechanisms in Expert Performance

K. Anders Ericsson

The concept of intelligence has many descriptions and many attempts have been made to measure corresponding individual differences. To find the definition of intelligence, I went to the Oxford Dictionary. It states that intelligence is "[T]the ability to acquire and apply knowledge and skills" (Oxford Dictionary, 2016a). The same dictionary defines the ability as "[P] possession of the means or skill to do something" (Oxford Dictionary, 2016b), which I interpret to be measureable by observing individuals successfully performing some task in a given domain of activity.

Individual differences in intelligence according to the definition should be measureable by the performance among individuals who have had an opportunity to acquire knowledge and skills in a domain of activity. Accordingly, the individuals with the highest level of attained performance should be viewed as the most "intelligent."

For the past several decades I have studied individuals and groups of individuals who have attained a level of performance in a domain that varies from an amateur level to that of world-class experts (Ericsson, 2006; Ericsson & Pool, 2016). The vast majority of individuals who attain the highest levels of performance in their respective domains have reported that they have followed a relatively similar developmental path. They started in the domain of activity when they were quite young with the help of their parents and other significant adults. Their parents often provided them with access to regular focused training at a young age (often under the guidance of a teacher or coach), and frequently, they reached their highest level of achievement in the domain at ages ranging from 20 to 40. There is evidence of the need to specialize in a particular domain to reach the highest levels in that domain, because it is very rare that the same individual wins at international competitions in two or more clearly different domains (Ericsson & Lehmann, 1996). This limitation implies that individuals have only a single opportunity to find a domain where they can attain their highest level of performance. This empirical measurement of the highest level of performance as "intelligence" does not prejudge the nature of the individual differences that are necessary to attain their highest level of performance ("intelligence"). These individual differences could correspond to unique genes or types of engagement in practice activities. It is also possible that the differences could be due to some interaction between these two types of factors. It is generally accepted that the necessary training is typically extended for years and decades and is thus very costly. Consequently, parents and teachers have tried to find predictive signs in children and adolescents of future adult success in a domain.

The Original Approaches to the Measurement of Intelligence

In the original approach to the measurement of intelligence, Binet and Simon (1905) did not try to identify individuals with the most potential for success as adults, but rather tried to identify weaker students in the French school system who would not be likely to succeed in the normal classrooms and would need an alternative and more supportive educational environment. Their test consisted of a wide range of comprehension and knowledge questions along with tests that had been developed by earlier investigators, such as the digit-span and substitution tests (Boake, 2002). The digit-span test was developed to measure the ability to reproduce immediately a presented series of random digits (assumed to be a meaningless list of symbols). The precursor of the digit-span test (Jacobs, 1887) initially involved reading a series of nonsense syllables for immediate recall of the types used by Ebbinghaus, but schoolchildren had difficulty recalling the symbols, so the nonsense syllables were exchanged for random digits (Boake, 2002). Binet and Simon (1908) found that older children were able to recall longer digit sequences and developed a procedure where the test administrator would present increasingly longer sequences of digits until the children would consistently fail (Boake, 2002). The Binet-Simon test of intelligence was validated by other investigators and demonstrated that it could differentiate normal and cognitively impaired children and also that test scores increased with the age of the children (Peterson, 1925).

Although the initial focus had been on identifying children with below-average cognitive abilities, Terman (1916) adapted Binet-Simon's intelligence assessment to American conditions and initiated research on gifted children. Contrary to earlier beliefs that gifted children are emotionally abnormal, Terman (1925) reported on a study of gifted children and found their health to be comparable to that of regular children. In a review, Boake (2002) showed that modern IQ tests are remarkably similar to the original tests developed by Binet and Simon (1908), the Army Alpha (Yerkes, 1921), and the Wechsler Scale (Wechsler, 1939).

The original definition of intelligence focused on individual differences in the development of general abilities during childhood and adolescence and their relatively strong relations to success in general education in grades K-12 and college. There is an implied assumption that children are born with a genetic endowment that may support the development of a superior intellectual capacity. This development attains a stable level in adulthood around 18–20 years of age and corresponds to a general "ability to acquire and apply knowledge and skills" (Oxford Dictionary, 2016a), and "is an important predictor of performance in training and on the job, especially in higher level work" (Gottfredson, 1997, p. 79). As I will argue in this chapter, there is much less evidence that tests of intelligence can successfully predict who will attain expert and elite performance as adults in a domain.

Brief Outline of Chapter

My research has been focused on the effects of training and the identification of the acquired cognitive processes associated with changes in performance. This research has not examined performance on tasks that measure intelligence with one single exception. In collaboration with Bill Chase (Chase & Ericsson, 1981, 1982), I examined the effect of extended practice on the performance on a subtest of many of the intelligence tests, namely the digit-span test. This work showed how training can qualitatively change performance as well as provide insights into how expert performance can be attained by the acquisition of new and refined cognitive mechanisms over an extended period of time. I will also briefly discuss some of the current knowledge about how virtually any characteristic of a human adult can be improved by particular types of training.

I will then describe the work on the expert-performance approach and new insights into the structure of acquired expert performance and, in particular, I will review how the correlation between basic cognitive abilities, such as IQ, and performance differs for beginners' and skilled individuals' performance in different domains.

Can Short-Term Memory Capacity in Adults
Be Changed with Practice?

My research career started with studies attempting to study thinking processes during solving problems by having participants give verbal expression to their thoughts ("think aloud," Ericsson & Simon, 1993). In my doctoral dissertation, participants solved a popular puzzle while thinking aloud (Ericsson, 1976) in order to understand the detailed processes mediating individual differences in problem-solving performance. As a postdoc at Carnegie-Mellon University (CMU), I looked for collaborators who would be interested in using this methodology to study other types of performance. One of the professors at CMU, Bill Chase, was studying individual differences in short-term memory (STM) capacity. One of the primary tests used to measure STM capacity was the digit-span test, which was included in the original tests of intelligence (Boake, 2002). After reviewing some earlier studies showing some improvements with practice on the digit-span task, Bill and I decided to try to replicate these practice effects and collect verbal reports after each memory trial to hopefully learn how the thought processes might have changed to permit these increases in digit-span performance.

The two of us started a long-term practice study with a CMU student, Steve Faloon (SF), whose initial span was around seven digits. After several hundred hours of practice with the digit-span task, SF attained a digit-span of 82 digits, which is an improvement of more than 1,000%. This research has been described in considerable detail elsewhere (Chase & Ericsson, 1981, 1982; Ericsson, 2013; Ericsson, Chase, & Faloon, 1980), so I will focus on the implications for immutable mental capacities as well as for how very high levels of performance in domains of expertise can be acquired.

The most obvious finding is that performance on the digit-span task can be improved dramatically with practice and with immediate feedback. More importantly, Bill Chase and I (Chase & Ericsson, 1981, 1982) found that the cognitive processes during the presentation of the list of digits changed qualitatively over the testing sessions during the two years of extended practice. At the initial start of training, SF would simply listen to the digits and rehearse them during presentation and then rehearse them out loud at recall. SF then discovered that he could attend to the first three digits and encode them as if they were a running time, such as 413 as a time of 4 minutes and 13 seconds for the mile, and then rapidly redirect his attention to the remaining digits that he kept rehearsing. With more practice, SF was then able to store away in long-term memory (LTM) several consecutive groups of three digits. Eventually he encoded groups of three-digit groups into "super groups" in LTM in order to memorize and later recall as many as 82 digits. Given that Bill Chase was initially skeptical of the validity of the retrospective verbal reports given by SF after each memory trial, we identified testable hypotheses about SF's encoding processes and then designed tailored experiments to test them. This combination of immediate retrospective reports and designed experiments validated each theoretical hypothesis, and made our research compelling (Ericsson, 2013).

The most important implication of this research is a rejection of the assumptions that the ability to keep information accessible in the short term is a fixed and severely limited capacity and that it is general across domains of activity. This research shows that, with extended practice with a certain type of material, such as lists of digits, it is possible for an individual to store presented information rapidly in LTM with virtually unlimited capacity, and yet be able to retrieve the information with access characteristics of STM. Most importantly, this expanded storage of information in LTM is specific to the material used in practice. In fact, when SF was presented rapidly with lists of consonants (digit span for consonants), his span was unchanged (around six consonants) even after SF's digit span had been increased by well over 300%. Some of my colleagues argued that these demonstrations of improved memory for rapidly presented digits, but only for digits, were relatively uninteresting because nobody cares about acquiring such a useless memory skill with no obvious real-world benefits. A fundamentally different interpretation of our findings is that they demonstrate evidence that anybody interested in acquiring increased ability to rapidly store and retrieve information in a particular domain of activity should be able to do so by acquiring domain-specific memory skills. In an early publication, Chase and Ericsson (1982) described this type of acquired memory skill and named it skilled memory. They showed how this skill supported memory for dinner orders by an expert waiter and for intermediate products during mental calculation of the square of five-digit numbers. Subsequently, Ericsson and Kintsch (1995) proposed a wider range of encoding methods and associated memory skills that are used in expert performance, referred to as long-term working memory (LTWM). The characteristics of LTWM were found to be consistent with the evidence for superior storage of presented information in LTM in many types of skilled activities, such as text comprehension, and performance in domains of expertise, such as chess, medicine, and music.

The second implication is that these memory skills and their associated increases in memory ability for storing and retrieving a certain type of information require considerable amounts of practice with immediate feedback. The first participant in the digit-span study, SF, needed several hundred hours to reach a span of 80 digits (Chase & Ericsson, 1981). The second participant (DD) was instructed by SF about his method of encoding digits before the start of DD's training, and DD showed a steeper initial improvement; but he eventually required a similar number of practice hours to reach a span of 80 digits (Richman, Staszewski, & Simon, 1995). In many domains, it takes many hundreds or even several thousands of hours of practice to acquire certain skills, such as professional performance in music or ballet, or grandmaster status in chess, which makes it virtually impossible to study the detailed development of these memory skills by the same data-intensive methods used to study the acquisition of expert performance in digit span.

A third important implication is that the acquisition of expert digit-span performance differs in many respects from traditional models of everyday skill and expertise (Dreyfus & Dreyfus, 1986; Fitts & Posner, 1967). These models encompass three different phases of development, where performance is mediated by different types of cognitive mechanisms (see Figure 6.1). According to these models, beginners in a domain receive instruction about rules and other knowledge necessary to generate acceptable behavior. The beginner, such as a medical student or a beginning chess player, is assumed to start in the domain by reasoning from basic principles and then generating the behavior by applying step-by-step cognitive procedures (the cognitive phase in Figure 6.1). During this first phase, failure to understand leads to gross errors and is noticed by the teacher, or even the student, and then corrected, thus decreasing error frequency. With increasing opportunities for performing similar tasks during the second associative phase, the student becomes more able to generate the appropriate actions faster, more smoothly, and with less hesitation and effort (Dreyfus & Dreyfus, 1986; Fitts & Posner, 1967). During the third and final phase individuals are able to generate their behavior with minimal concentration in an almost effortless fashion – the automatic phase. Some researchers of expertise (Dreyfus & Dreyfus, 1986) argue that individuals after extensive experience in the domain become experts who are able to respond rapidly and intuitively without ability to report mediating thoughts.

Our research on the digit-span experts (Chase & Ericsson, 1981, 1982; Ericsson, 2013; Ericsson et al., 1980) showed a completely different pattern of development of cognitively mediated processes. The amount of thinking and encoding was not reduced as the digit-span performance increased from fewer than 10 digits to more than 80 digits. In fact, the types of

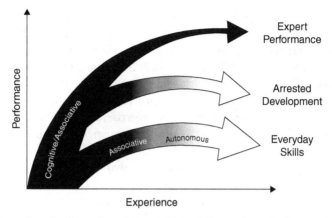

Figure 6.1 An illustration of the qualitative difference between the course of
improvement of expert performance and of everyday activities.
(adapted from "The scientific study of expert levels of performance: General implications
for optimal learning and creativity" by K. A. Ericsson in *High Ability Studies, 9*, p. 90.
Copyright 1998 by European Council for High Ability)

generated thoughts for encoding digit groups with their serial position
within a list were continually improved and elaborated to reduce interference during the subsequent retrieval at the time of recall. According to our
model of acquisition of expert performance, the individuals never leave the
cognitive phase and are engaged in refining their thinking to improve performance by identifying new goals to improve performance (see top curve
in Figure 6.1). Some individuals decide to stop their efforts to improve at
some point and thus start automating their performance at an intermediate level (see middle curve for arrested development in Figure 6.1).

Based on the different developmental paths outlined in the previous
paragraph, there are at least two different relations between attained objective performance and the amount of experience in a given domain. The
traditional models of skill acquisition and expertise describe the typical
relation, namely that when individuals have attained an acceptable level of
performance, they tend to automate their performance during additional
experience, but their level of performance remains stable without improvements. It is well known that the vast majority of amateur golfers and tennis players do not reach a higher level of performance after reaching an
acceptable level after a few months or years in spite of engaging in weekly
activities for decades. Reviews show a surprisingly weak relation between
the length of experience and objective performance in a wide range of

domains (Ericsson, 2006; Ericsson & Lehmann, 1996). For example, the accuracy of heart sound diagnosis and many types of measurable activities of nurses and general physicians do not improve as a function of professional experience (Choudhry, Fletcher, & Soumerai, 2005; Ericsson, 2004; Ericsson, Whyte, & Ward, 2007). In direct contrast to these findings, there are many other demonstrations of improvement of performance for years and decades in traditional domains of expertise, such as music, sports, and chess. Consistent with our findings of improvement of digit-span performance as a function of practice, the individuals who keep improving are not just carrying out their professional activities or engaging in playing with friends, but engaging in designed practice activities with immediate feedback frequently supervised by a teacher or coach (Ericsson, 2006; Ericsson, Krampe, & Tesch-Römer, 1993).

Expert-Performance Approach

The fact that the development of expert levels of performance takes years and decades and is attained only by a small number of the individuals who started out as beginners presents difficulties for anyone wanting to study its decade-long development, starting with the first exposure to related domains. In response to these problems Ericsson and Smith (1991), proposed a fundamentally different approach to the study of expertise, namely, the expert-performance approach.

The expert-performance approach involves three major steps. During the first step, individuals with reproducibly superior performance are identified, such as runners completing a 100m race in national competitions, chess players winning chess tournaments, and winners in regional and national competitions in music and ballet. In some domains of expertise, the events are standardized and controlled and these test situations can be easily reproduced in the laboratory. In other cases, especially domains involving competition between two or more individuals, it is essential to identify standardized representative tasks where the individuals' performance is highly correlated with their performance in actual competitions. For example, it is possible to present one or more positions extracted from a chess game between chess masters and ask a range of players with different levels of skill to select the best move for that position (see Figure 6.2, top and middle panels). Similarly, one can have athletes or other individuals respond with the best action in situations presented by a simulator or by a video sequence from an actual game (see Figure 6.2, bottom panel).

The Stream of Expert's Actions in Context

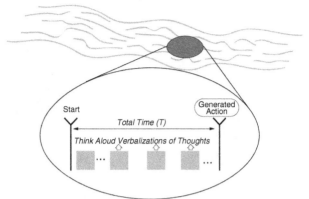

Task: Select best move for presented chess position

Context:

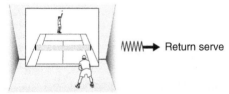

Make move

Task: Anticipate and return opponent's tennis serve

Context:

Return serve

Figure 6.2   A procedure for capturing expert performance in the laboratory. The top of the figure shows the stream of naturally occurring situations. As shown in the bottom part of the figure, one can present a particular challenging chess position from an actual game and ask for the best next move in a laboratory setting. Alternatively, one can project a film of a player serving a tennis ball and ask the participants to attempt to return the "imaged ball" with the best shot using their racket.
(Re-publication of figure 1 in Ericsson, K. A., & Ward, P. (2007). *Current Directions in Psychological Science*, 16, 347).

During the second step, the scientists collect data on the processes that mediate their superior performance, using reaction times, eye-fixation patterns, and think-aloud protocols to generate hypotheses about the associated mental mechanisms. Many of these hypotheses have been tested by designing experimental manipulations of the standardized tasks. From the analyses in the second step of expert-performance approach, there are

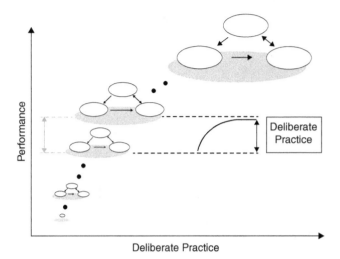

Figure 6.3   A schematic illustration of the acquisition of expert performance as a series
of states with mechanisms of increasing complexity for monitoring and guiding future
improvements of specific aspects of performance.
(Adapted from "The scientific study of expert levels of performance can guide training
for producing superior achievement in creative domains" by K. A. Ericsson in *Proceedings
from International Conference on the Cultivation and Education of Creativity and Innovation*
(p. 14). Beijing, China: Chinese Academy of Sciences. Copyright 2009 International
Research Association for Talent Development and Excellence)

extensive data showing that experts engage in generating plans and examine alternative options when they perform challenging tasks, such as selecting the best next move for a presented chess position, or preparing a music
piece for public performance (Ericsson, in press a). There is evidence that
expert performers acquire mental representations for imaging the desired
outcome, for executing behavior to produce that outcome, and for monitoring the produced behavior, as is illustrated in Figure 6.3. These collections
of representations provide an internalized feedback loop permitting experts
to monitor their practice and make incremental improvements. Over time
these representations become more refined and capable of supporting the
generation of increasingly accurate and reliable performance (see progression in Figure 6.3). Some of the primary evidence for the development
of these representations as a function of attained superior performance
comes from the expert performers' superior memory for relevant aspects
of the current situation, which are kept accessible by information stored
in LTM consistent with characteristics of LTWM (Ericsson, in press b;
Ericsson & Kintsch, 1995).

The uncovered complex and domain-specific structure of the cognitive mechanisms mediating the experts' superior performance in many different domains suggests that these mechanisms are acquired. Furthermore, their acquisition and continued refinement would not likely result from additional experience of doing the same or similar activities, but would require engagement in particular types of goal-directed training supervised and designed by a teacher for an extended period of time. Research from the third step confirms that attaining adult levels of expert performance requires a long period of preparation and practice. In most cases there is compelling evidence that individuals who eventually reached an international level of performance started engaging in activities related to the domain at a young age and spent extended periods working closely with a teacher or coach (Ericsson, 2006; Ericsson, in press c).

The Role of Intelligence and Basic Cognitive Abilities in the Acquisition of Expert Performance

In a recent paper (Ericsson, 2014), I reviewed evidence of the relation between tests of basic cognitive abilities, such as intelligence, and participation and success in domains of expertise. This review found that skilled participants in many domains, such as science, chess, and music, have higher scores on IQ and cognitive ability tests than the normal population. In contrast, in other domains, such as American football and GO, no reliable superiority was observed. The higher IQ for skilled performers in science and music is consistent with the selection of students to higher levels of education who attend colleges and universities based on above-normal performance on academic achievement tests, which are correlated with performance on IQ tests (Frey & Detterman, 2004). In some other domains, such as American football and GO, access to training is not dependent on above-average scores on academic tests. In these domains, skilled performers do not show a reliably superior performance on tests of cognitive ability and intelligence compared with the normal population.

The more critical relation between expert performance and basic cognitive abilities concerns the existence of correlations between individual differences in domain-specific performance and basic abilities. The expert-performance framework predicts an interaction with attained level of performance, showing different results for beginners, on the one hand, and skilled performers on the other. For beginners, a positive correlation is predicted between performance on domain-specific tasks and cognitive ability. Beginners in a domain must by definition rely on their preexisting abilities, such as general cognitive abilities. Initial performance in the domain should benefit from the beginners' superior ability to comprehend instructions and to learn from books and other general abilities. All of these general abilities are known to be correlated with scores on tests of general basic cognitive abilities, as well as with academic success in schools. Consistent with this hypothesis, beginners' performance on domain-related tasks is correlated with higher scores on IQ and some other tests of basic cognitive abilities in several domains (see Ericsson, 2014, for a review). For example, Ruthsatz, Detterman, Griscom, and Cirullo (2008) found a significant correlation between music performance by players in a high school band and an intelligence test. In a recent review Ruthsatz, Ruthsatz, and Stephens (2014) reviewed evidence for a correlation in the 0.3 to 0.4 range between performance on tests of general intelligence and performance on memory and perceptual tasks involving music stimuli for children without musical training. These findings were presented to support the existence of measureable innate music talent that could be used to guide young "talented" children toward engaging in early music instruction.

The expert-performance framework predicts a different pattern of correlation for skilled performers in a domain (Ericsson, 2014). The skilled performers will have acquired a wide range of mental representations and memory skills to support their performance and are therefore mediating their skilled performance rather than using the preexisting mechanisms measured by general ability tests. Consistent with these predictions, researchers have not found a correlation between intelligence measures and domain-specific performance among skilled performers (with the acquired domain-specific mechanisms illustrated in Figure 6.3) in domains such sports, chess, GO, science, and music. For example, Ruthsatz and colleagues (2008) did not find any significant correlations between intelligence and music performance for a group of university majors with intermediate levels of practice nor for a group of conservatory musicians with extensive practice. Ericsson (2014) analyzed the relation between intelligence and success as football players in the NFL and found a nonsignificant correlation for more than 1,000 participants. Similarly, several studies of 200 to 400 scientists did not find significant correlations between their intelligence scores and their success as scientists as measured by their numbers of publications and citations (Ericsson, 2014).

Concluding Remarks

The Oxford Dictionary (2016a) defined intelligence as "the ability to acquire and apply knowledge and skills." This chapter supports the argument that there are at least two types of phenomena related to intelligence that are not closely correlated. The first type of intelligence refers to the traditional definition of intelligence as the ability to attain superior performance as a beginner, due to better ability to comprehend instructions and use them to generate a superior performance. Individual differences in this type of intelligence are predictive of performance in the traditional educational system, which is currently focused on relatively superficial mastery of a number of different domains of knowledge. The second type of intelligence refers to the ability to attain an expert and exceptional level of performance in a particular domain after an extended period of practice with feedback and guidance by teachers and coaches. The research on expert performance has shown that reproducibly superior performance at the highest levels reflects the acquisition of a large number of complex and integrated mechanisms, which are attained by successive refinement during practice over many years or even decades. The traditional view has been that the two types of intelligent phenomena are mediated by the same processes, but my review (Ericsson, 2014) showed that traditional tests of intelligence and IQ are not predictive of individual differences in attained performance among skilled performers.

Our society is committed to helping individuals develop expert levels of performance in their chosen professions and domains of expertise. The discovery of at least two types of intelligence has important societal implications. First, the standard practice of selecting children and adolescents for future advanced-level education based on the traditional tests of intelligence needs to be reconsidered, given their lack of relation to performance among skilled performers. Second, our educational system should not simply train students to rapidly acquire introductory and relatively superficial knowledge in many domains. Students should be taught and trained to attain an advanced level of performance in at least one domain, so they will know how they can improve performance in their future profession and how expert performance can be attained with appropriate practice with feedback under the guidance of teachers. Serious consideration of these issues should help to improve the effectiveness of our school system and in turn help students acquire improved levels of adult performance that will benefit everyone.

References

Binet, A., & Simon, T. (1905). Méthodes nouvelles pour le diagnostic du niveau intellectuel des anormaux [New methods for the diagnosis of intellectual level of subnormals]. *L'Année Psychologique*, 11, 191–244.

(1908). Le developpement de l'intelligence chez les enfants [The development of intelligence in children]. *L'Année Psychologique*, 14, 1–90.

Boake, C. (2002). From the Binet-Simon to the Wechsler-Bellevue: Tracing the history of intelligence testing. *Journal of Clinical and Experimental Neuropsychology*, 24, 383–405.

Chase, W. G., & Ericsson, K. A. (1981). Skilled memory. In J. R. Anderson (Ed.), *Cognitive skills and their acquisition* (pp. 141–189). Hillsdale, NJ: Lawrence Erlbaum Associates.

Chase, W. G., & Ericsson, K. A. (1982). Skill and working memory. In G. H. Bower (Ed.), *The psychology of learning and motivation* (Vol. 16, pp. 1–58). New York: Academic Press.

Choudhry, N. K., Fletcher, R. H., & Soumerai, S. B. (2005). Systematic review: The relationship between clinical experience and health care. *Annals of Internal Medicine*, 142, 260–273.

Dreyfus, H. L., & Dreyfus, S. E. (1986). *Mind over machine: The power of human intuition and expertise in the era of the computer*. New York: Free Press.

Ericsson, K. A. (1976). *Approaches to descriptions and analyses of problem-solving processes: The 8-puzzle*. Stockholm, Sweden: Department of Psychology, University of Stockholm.

(2004). Deliberate practice and the acquisition and maintenance of expert performance in medicine and related domains. *Academic Medicine*, 79, S70–S81.

(2006). The influence of experience and deliberate practice on the development of superior expert performance. In K. A. Ericsson, N. Charness, P. Feltovich, & R. R. Hoffman (Eds.). *Cambridge handbook of expertise and expert performance* (pp. 685–706). Cambridge, UK: Cambridge University Press.

(2009). The scientific study of expert levels of performance can guide training for producing superior achievement in creative domains. In: *International Conference on the Cultivation and Education of Creativity and Innovation*. Beijing, China: Chinese Academy of Sciences.

(2013). Exceptional memory and expert performance: From Simon and Chase's theory of expertise to skilled memory and beyond. In J. Staszewski (Ed.), *Expertise and skill acquisition* (pp. 201–228). Abington, Oxon, UK: Taylor & Francis.

(2014). Why expert performance is special and cannot be extrapolated from studies of performance in the general population: A response to criticisms. *Intelligence*, 45, 81–103.

(in press a). Capturing expert thought with protocol analysis: Concurrent verbalizations of thinking during experts' performance on representative tasks.

In K. A. Ericsson, R. R. Hoffman, A, Kozbelt, & A. M. Williams (Eds.). *2nd revised edition of Cambridge handbook of expertise and expert performance.* Cambridge, UK: Cambridge University Press.

(in press b). Superior working memory in experts. In K. A. Ericsson, R. R. Hoffman, A, Kozbelt, & A. M. Williams (Eds.). *2nd revised edition of Cambridge handbook of expertise and expert performance.* Cambridge, UK: Cambridge University Press.

(in press c). The differential influence of experience, practice, and deliberate practice on the development of superior individual performance of experts. In K. A. Ericsson, R. R. Hoffman, A, Kozbelt, & A. M. Williams (Eds.). *2nd revised edition of Cambridge handbook of expertise and expert performance.* Cambridge, UK: Cambridge University Press.

Ericsson, K. A., Chase, W. G., & Faloon, S. (1980). Acquisition of a memory skill. *Science,* 208, 1181–1182.

Ericsson, K. A., & Kintsch, W. (1995). Long-term working memory. *Psychological Review,* 102, 211–245.

Ericsson, K. A., Krampe, R. T., & Tesch-Römer, C. (1993). The role of deliberate practice in the acquisition of expert performance. *Psychological Review,* 100, 363–406.

Ericsson, K. A., & Lehmann, A. C. (1996). Expert and exceptional performance: Evidence of maximal adaptations to task constraints. *Annual Review of Psychology,* 47, 273–305.

Ericsson, K. A., & Pool, R. (2016). *Peak: Secrets from the new science of expertise.* New York: Eamon Dolan Books/ Houghton Mifflin & Harcourt.

Ericsson, K. A., & Simon, H. A. (1993). *Protocol analysis: Verbal reports as data* (revised edition). Cambridge, MA: Bradford Books/MIT Press.

Ericsson, K. A., & Smith, J. (1991). Prospects and limits in the empirical study of expertise: An introduction. In K. A. Ericsson & J. Smith (Eds.), *Toward a general theory of expertise: Prospects and limits* (pp. 1–38). Cambridge: Cambridge University Press.

Ericsson, K. A., & Ward, P. (2007). Capturing the naturally occurring superior performance of experts in the laboratory: Toward a science of expert and exceptional performance. *Current Directions in Psychological Science,* 16, 346–350.

Ericsson, K. A., Whyte, J., & Ward, P. (2007). Expert performance in nursing: Reviewing research on expertise in nursing within the framework of the expert performance approach. *Advances in Nursing Science,* 30, E58–E71.

Fitts, P., & Posner, M. I. (1967). *Human performance.* Belmont, CA: Brooks/ Cole.

Frey, M. C., & Detterman, D. K. (2004). Scholastic assessment or g? The relationship between the scholastic assessment test and general cognitive ability. *Psychological Science,* 15(6), 373–378.

Gottfredson, L. S. (1997). Why g matters: The complexity of everyday life. *Intelligence,* 24, 79–132.

Jacobs, J. (1887). Experiments on "prehension." *Mind,* 45, 75–79.

Oxford Dictionary (2016a). Retrieved on November 1, 2016 from https:// en.oxforddictionaries.com/definition/intelligence.

(2016b). Retrieved on November 1, 2016 from https://en.oxforddictionaries .com/definition/ability.

Peterson, J. (1925). *Early conceptions and tests of intelligence.* Yonkers-on-Hudson, NY: World Book.

Richman, H. B., Staszewski, J. J., & Simon, H. A. (1995). Simulation of expert memory using EPAM IV. *Psychological Review,* 102, 305–330.

Ruthsatz, J., Detterman, D. K., Griscom, W. S., & Cirullo, B. A. (2008). Becoming an expert in the musical domain: It takes more than just practice. *Intelligence,* 36, 330–338.

Ruthsatz, J., Ruthsatz, K., & Stephens, K. R. (2014). Putting practice into per-spective: Child prodigies as evidence of innate talent. *Intelligence,* 45, 60–65.

Terman, L. M. (1916). *The measurement of intelligence: An explanation of and a com-plete guide for the use of the Stanford revision and extension of the Binet-Simon intelligence scale.* New York: Houghton Mifflin.

(1925). *Mental and physical traits of a thousand gifted children. Genetic studies of genius, Vol. 1,* Stanford, CA: Stanford University Press.

Wechsler, D. (1939). *The measurement of adult intelligence.* Baltimore, MD: Williams & Wilkins.

Yerkes, R. M. (Ed.) (1921). Psychological examining in the United States Army. *Memoirs of the National Academy of Sciences,* 15 (Parts 1–3), Washington, DC: Government Printing Office.

CHAPTER 7

Intelligence, Society, and Human Autonomy

James R. Flynn

As recently as 10 years ago, a steel chain of ideas dominated the minds of those who studied and measured intelligence. Much of my own contribution has been to break its links and therefore I must describe them in some detail. Arthur Jensen was its best advocate. The enemies of truth tried to silence Jensen. Science progresses not by labeling some ideas as too wicked to be true, but by debating their truth.

The Steel Chain of Ideas

Jensen believed that intelligence is something that transcends culture, social history, and even species; a name for certain traits of a properly developed brain that allow us to solve the wide variety of cognitive problems presented in everyday life. He based his beliefs on four pillars: factor analysis, kinship studies, the dominance of g (the general intelligence factor), and the method of correlated vectors.

Factor Analysis

There can be an inter-correlation between several factors. For example, Wechsler IQ tests have at least 10 subtests. These measure vocabulary, general information, comprehension, arithmetic, memory, solving novel problems, how quickly you process information, and logical analysis. There is a positive manifold: people who do better than average on one subtest (say, vocabulary) tend to do better on the other subtests as well. Factor analysis calculates the size of this tendency and this is called g (Jensen, 1998, pp. 18–21).

You can calculate how much performance on each subtest predicts performance on the 10 collectively. This is called the g loading of a subtest (Jensen, 1998, pp. 24–30). Something interesting: the higher the g loading, the more complex the cognitive problems the subtest poses. For example, digit span forward just tests for short-term memory: when someone reads out numbers at random, how many of them can you repeat in order? But digit span backward asks you to repeat them in reverse of the order in which they were read out. Clearly the latter has greater cognitive complexity than the former, and this is reflected in a much larger g loading. This encouraged some to identify g with intelligence. They argued that intelligent people ought to exceed the average person more the more complex the cognitive task.

The Tale of the Twins

Twin studies were interpreted as suggesting that the primary explanation of g lays in certain facets of the human brain, whose potential was largely determined by one's genes. Take identical twins raised apart from birth. If despite randomly separated environments (say one raised in a farm family and the other in a professional home), they grew up with identical IQs, we would know that their identical genes were all-powerful. Raising identical twins in the same home offers additional information. If there were a gap between their adult IQs, we would know that neither genes nor common environment exhausted the influences on IQ. There would be a third factor present, uncommon environment, which I will call "luck" environment. Even though the twins had the same genes and the same family environment, one girl might be dropped on her head, or in later years, the death of a child might cause deep depression.

Although family environment is a huge influence on IQ among preschoolers, genes absorb environmental influence by the late teens or early 20s. IQ differences evolve from 70 percent due to shared family environment and 10 percent due to genes toward 0 percent due to family environment and 80 percent due to genetic differences (Jensen, 1998, pp. 177–182). The 20 percent due to luck holds at every age: bad or good luck can happen at any time (Haworth et al., 2010).

Jensen believed that the weakness of environment within a race or a culture applied across all races and cultures, which left genetic differences between races and cultures dominant. He poked fun at those who think environment rather than genes must explain group differences. What would they say about the Watusi and Pygmies, the tallest and shortest subpopulations within Africa, whose average heights differ by one foot? (Jensen, 1973, pp. 135–145, 149).

Raven's and the Martians

Raven's Progressive Matrices has the highest *g* loading of any test (Jensen, 1998, pp. 37–38). Therefore, Jensen believed that it measures the kind of intelligence that allows a bright person to better the average person the more complex the task. It differs from tests of *crystallized* intelligence. They measure the mental abilities that bright people are likely to develop as they live their lives in a given society. Bright people are likely to acquire a large vocabulary, learn more of whatever they are taught in school, and better comprehend their culture's peculiar social arrangements (what mailing a letter is all about). Thanks to their content, they are culturally sensitive.

Raven's Progressive Matrices, on the other hand, is a test of *fluid* intelligence and appears culturally reduced (Jensen, 1980, pp. 645–647). It presents you with simple shapes and poses problems that assume a minimum of learned content. Jensen (1973, p. 320) believed that the members of every culture would find the symbols familiar and the tasks congenial, even Polar Eskimos. The symbols are presented in a matrices format and make logical sense in every direction (across, down, diagonally). One piece is missing. You must select the symbol that logically completes the design.

Jensen also argued that when Raven's measures *g*, it measures logical abilities that rank species. Raven's assumes a working memory that "sizes up" a problem. A chicken cannot solve the barrier problem. If it sees food through a wire fence, and the fence is long enough so that it loses sight of the food, it will not go around the fence. A dog can solve the barrier problem, but it cannot select the odd object out of three (say, hitting a triangle as different from two circles) to unlock a door. On the other hand, a monkey can solve a simple oddity problem, so its intelligence is equivalent to a human infant. Jensen said that we cannot imagine calling an extraterrestrial intelligent if it had "no *g*, or whose *g* is qualitatively rather than quantitatively different from *g* as we know it" (Jensen, 1980, pp. 178–182, 248, 251).

The Method of Correlated Vectors

Jensen used the method of correlated vectors to test whether an IQ difference between groups was a true intelligence difference. He thought *g* a better measure of intelligence than IQ; indeed at one point he suggested that thanks to *g*, we could junk the word "intelligence" entirely (Jensen, 1998, 45–49). The obvious method was to compare two hierarchies. Rank the 10 Wechsler subtests in order of their g loadings; rank two groups in term of the size of the score advantage one group opens up on the other subtest by subtest; see if the two tally. If one group outscores the other more on digit span backward (high g) than on digit span forward (low g), you have the beginnings of a "g pattern" and the score differences are g differences. When you rank black versus white score differences, blacks fall behind more on those subtests that have the highest g loading (the greatest cognitive complexity); and these are the ones that are the most genetically influenced (Jensen, 1998, p. 322).

What if the correlation is nil? What if there is no tendency for the score differences between two groups to predict g loadings (say all subtest score differences are much the same)? As we will see, there have been massive IQ gains over time and these separate the generations. But however large they may be, IQ gains over time flunk the test set by the method of correlated vectors (te Nijenhuis & van der Flier, 2013). The magnitudes of the subtest gains one generation enjoys over the preceding generation have nil correlation with the g loadings of the subtests; and therefore, they are non-g gains. On these grounds Jensen (1998, p. 332) calls them "hollow." He suggests that helter-skelter gains on the subtests are simply a matter of mastering specific cognitive tasks and thus less important than g gains. Only the latter signal that general intelligence is progressing.

A Better Theory

I pass from describing ideas that constricted thinking about intelligence to make a case for a better theory. It is based on an analysis of massive IQ gains over time, a reassessment of the method of correlated vectors, the Dickens-Flynn model, and a refutation of genetic determination.

The Flynn Effect

Massive IQ gains over time are sometimes called the "Flynn effect." Others had shown that IQ gains occurred at a particular time and place, but I showed that it was an international phenomenon. Americans gained 14 IQ points between 1932 and 1978 (Flynn, 1984). Fourteen nations (those for whom data were available at the time) made massive gains on a wide variety of tests over as little as one generation (Flynn, 1987). Dutch males gained 20 points on Raven's between 1952 and 1982, which meant that the average Dutchman in 1982 was at the 90th percentile of his father's generation. There are now data for continental Europe, virtually all

English-speaking nations, three nations of predominately European culture (Israel, Brazil, and Argentina), three Asian nations that have adopted European technology (Japan, China, and Korea), and three developing nations just beginning to enjoy gains – rural Kenya, Dominica, and the Sudan (Flynn, 2012a).

In developed nations, gains have averaged about nine points per generation, culminating in a huge gain of 30 points over 100 years. On the face of it, this would imply that the average person in 1900 had a mean IQ of 70 and was on the border of intellectual disability. No one can seriously contend that this is so, or contend that these gains are intelligence gains in the sense of genetically improved brains. Those who were baffled by them were scholars who could not break out of a measurement paradigm to embrace a historical paradigm. Let me tell a fable.

An archeologist from the distant future excavates the ruins of America and finds a record of performances over time on measures of marksmanship. These tests show how many bullets soldiers could put in a target 100 meters away in one minute. Records from 1865 (the U.S. Civil War) show best scores of 5, records from 1898 (Spanish–American War) show 10, and records from 1918 (World War I) show 50. The gains seem far too huge to measure gains in marksmanship "genes" over 53 years. Then the archeologist discovers battlefields specific to each time. The 1865 battlefields show the presence of non-repeating rifles, the 1898 ones yield repeating rifles, and the 1918 ones yield machine guns. This explains why it was easier to get more bullets into the target over time and confirms that the score gains were not a measure of enhanced genes for marksmanship (Flynn, 2009, pp. 179–180).

We must distinguish between measuring individual differences in shooting performance at a given time and place (when everyone has the same weapons) and measuring differences between generations. If I shoot better than my contemporaries, I may be favored by genes that give me a steadier hand and better vision. If I shoot better than my father, I may be favored by the fact that social change has given me better equipment. I may have no better genes than he did (there is no real difference in genetic quality between generations), but society may have altered the whole context.

Here I wish to introduce some all-important concepts: that the brain is like a *muscle* that profits from exercise; over time, society changes in terms of *what* cognitive exercise it asks us to do; and the very stuff of our brain *alters* to allow us to meet the challenges of our time and place. These concepts apply to our physique. If we all went from swimming to weight-lifting in a generation, our physical muscles would alter dramatically. If no one drives a car in 1900 and everyone drives a car in 1950 and all cars have an automatic guidance system in 2000, the size of the hippocampus (the map-reading area of the brain) would increase and then decrease in a few generations (Maguire et al., 2000). What IQ gains over time deliver is a historical message about new demands on our cognitive abilities.

What has really changed over the past century? In the 1920s, Luria (1976) interviewed rural Russians largely untouched by modernity. He asked them to classify and to do logical inference:

> **Fish and crows.** Question: What do a fish and a crow have in common? Answer: Nothing. A fish – it lives in water. A crow flies. If the fish just lies on top of the water, the crow could peck at it. A crow can eat a fish, but a fish can't eat a crow.
>
> **Camels and Germany.** Question: There are no camels in Germany; the city of B is in Germany; are there camels there or not? Answer: I don't know; I have never seen German cities. If B is a large city, there should be camels there. If B is a small village, there is probably no room for camels.

These examples show people three generations ago struggling with both classification (as on the Wechsler similarities subtest) and using logic in a hypothetical context, one removed from real-world problems (as on Raven's). Their minds were "handicapped" because they had on "utilitarian spectacles." The important thing for them was to manipulate the world to their advantage. This meant focusing on the differences between objects and demanding that descriptions of concrete reality be based on evidence. Why did society ask them to do these things? Ninety percent of people worked as subsistence farmers or did undemanding factory or service jobs. Few bothered with more than six years of formal schooling – they simply did not need additional cognitive skills. There were other social factors. Families tended to be large and children dominated the vocabulary level. Leisure (what there was of it) offered no intellectual challenge like video games (Flynn, 2009, pp. 23–35).

Today, people in developed nations still want to manipulate the concrete world. But they are also open to ignoring the specificity of objects in favor of classifying them using abstract categories. Take the similarities-type item: what do dogs and rabbits have in common? A schoolchild in 1900 might say, "You use dogs to hunt rabbits." She might know that "they are both mammals" – but not offer so trivial a response. The important thing is what they are used for. In 2000, schoolchildren find the correct response perfectly natural. Today they have a new habit of mind – that it is important to classify the world in terms of abstract categories as a prerequisite to understanding it. Take Raven's-type items all of which involve using logic to perceive sequences in a series of abstract shapes. In 1900, schoolchildren found such an application of logic alien. Today, children are habituated to it.

Schooling through the 12th grade has become almost universal; and schooling eventually requires classification (the theory of evolution) and logical analysis. The very nature of schooling changed (Genovese, 2002). Exams given 14-year-olds early in the 20th century ask for socially valued knowledge: what are the capitals of the 46 states? Exams late in the century ask for general explanations: Why is the largest city of a state rarely the capital? Because rural-dominated state legislatures hated the big city and located the capital in a rural center. Today society challenges us to do cognitively demanding jobs. People whose ancestors were unskilled workers or farmers are now journalists, teachers, junior executives, and computer programmers. Are they more intelligent in the Jensen sense? Now we can be more sophisticated.

Four things happened or did not happen over the past century: (1) No genetic progress enhanced our brains at conception. Our ancestors were just as able as we are in terms of coping with the cognitive tasks their society asked them to do. (2) If our ancestors were alive today, our society would give them the mental exercise needed to cope with more schooling and modern jobs. The only reason they would get a mean IQ of 70 compared to us is that we have had the advantage of modern exercise, just as the jogging craze has produced a lot more fit people. (3) The new exercise we do would make our brains look different at death. The prefrontal lobes with which we do logical analysis would be larger; whether the hippocampus would be larger would depend on whether they had to depend on mapping and memory more than we do. (4) We probably do face a wider range of cognitively complex problems than they did and you can call us more intelligent because of that. But others would say we are better adapted to our time (Flynn, 2012a, pp. 27–28).

Note the cash value of this. Once we understand the four things that actually happened to our brains and minds over time, whether we label some or one of them "intelligence" has no independent meaning. Those who insist on using it in this context are slave to a word. They are like a person who rejects the historical paradigm for the measurement paradigm. Since IQ test compare individuals for traits much influenced by genes at a given time (eyesight, steadiness of hand), some think they must function much the same over time. Well, they do measure trait differences, of course. Thanks to the spread of education, the average person today has a larger vocabulary than the average person in 1900. But you are not measuring a difference in the genetic potential of brains; you are measuring the effect of different cognitive exercise at two historical times.

Why doesn't this apply to groups within the same historical period same year

Correlated Vectors Revisited

Recall that IQ gains over time flunk the test of correlated vectors. The sizes of the subtest gains one generation enjoys over the preceding generation have nil correlation with the g loadings of the subtests and are therefore non-g gains. The fact that they do not correlate with g may imply that IQ gains are not a symptom of genetically enhanced brains. That seems to me a self-evident truism. When the Dutch gained 20 points on Raven's over 30 years, who could have thought that the genetic potential of the Dutch brain in 1982 was at the 90th percentile of the potential of the Dutch brain in 1952? Dutch society was simply making people exercise the prefrontal lobes much more than in the past.

There is now a body of evidence that shows that IQ gains are historically important despite the fact that they are not g gains. The historical trend of IQ gains parallels and predicts the growth in GDP per capita experienced by Western nations over the past 10 decades: the correlation = 0.930 (Woodley, 2012b). Education in particular cultivates specialized patterns of cognitive abilities and these improve independently of whether they correlate with g (Woodley, 2012a). Ireland enhanced education, its test scores rose, and its per capita gross domestic product rose above that of England *in that order*. Finland enhanced the education of its poorest students and duplicated Ireland's trend (Nisbett, 2015). The cognitive skills measured by the SAT predict university grades even after g has been removed (Coyle & Pillow, 2008).

A final nail in the coffin: those who suffer from iodine deficiency, prenatal cocaine exposure, fetal alcohol syndrome, and traumatic brain injury were compared with typical subjects on the Wechsler. The typical subjects were higher on every subtest. However, the magnitude of their advantages by subtest had zero correlation with the size of the subtest g loadings. It is difficult to deny that the typical subjects had a significant cognitive advantage over the four comparison groups. In sum, helter-skelter or piecemeal advantages on IQ subtests are causally potent, whether between generations or between individuals (Flynn, te Nijenhuis, & Metzen, 2014).

There is an irony here: Jensen was at pains to show that IQ gains were not g gains. How fortunate he succeeded. If they were, we might be confused about why they are so potent. They have been potent enough to take us from the society of 1900 to the society of 2000, and that is good enough for me.

There is also evidence that the fact that a group flunks the test of correlated vectors does not mean its members are genetically deficient. Recall that when American blacks are compared to American whites on the 10 Wechsler subtests, their performance falls further behind whites the greater the *g* loading (complexity) of the subtest. After World War II, the occupation army of American blacks and whites in Germany left behind children, all of whom were reared by their white German mothers. When they became old enough, samples of both the half-black and all-white children were compared on Wechsler subtests. The tendency for blacks to fall behind as the *g* loading increased had completely disappeared, suggesting that blacks show this tendency only when raised in the environment of the black American subculture, which was of course absent in Germany (Flynn, 2008, pp. 88–91).

Elsie Moore (1986) showed that you could not measure the effects of black subculture as Jensen did. Jensen compared black and white Americans as we would compare whites to one another: match them for SES (socioeconomic status: the years of education and profession of the children's parents). She studied 46 black adoptees, half raised by white parents of high SES and half raised by black parents of equal SES. The blacks reared by the whites had an advantage of 13.5 IQ points by age 8.5. Maternal attitudes toward the children's problem-solving attempts were overwhelmingly positive among white mothers and negative among black mothers (e.g., "let's try this" vs. "you're not that dumb"). It is significant that black Americans gained 5.5 IQ points on whites between 1972 and 2002, about one-third of the IQ gap that used to separate them (Dickens & Flynn, 2006).

The Dickens-Flynn Model

The Dickens-Flynn model attests to Bill Dickens's inspiration and skill at modeling (Dickens & Flynn 2001a, 2001b). Let us go back to the twin studies. These supposedly showed that at maturity, genes largely determined individual difference in IQ, and that environment was weak. I have already suggested that the twin studies cannot bridge cultures. The difference between U.S. white culture and U.S. black subculture could dictate different IQs for two children with identical genetic quality (much less for two children raised in America and Syria, respectively). But let us cons̅ ' the significance of twin studies even where they do work. Within the normal range of environments of white America, do they really show, even within that context, that environment disappears with age? The model lays bare the sociology behind these "facts" by using basketball as an example.

Two identical twins are separated at birth in the basketball-mad state of Indiana. Thanks to their identical genes, they will both be taller than average and have a faster reflex arc. Therefore, both will progressively access environments whose quality matches their genetic quality. Despite seemingly random environments, both will get picked more often to play basketball informally. Both will be likely to be chosen by their school to play on the school team, both will be more likely to play high school basketball and get really professional coaching.

In effect, the genetic identity between the twins tends to be a more and more powerful predictor of their basketball performance and the role of environment as a predictor fades. But even so, environment has not disappeared. It is as if two horses were pulling a chariot. During childhood, they tend to pull in different directions. But by adulthood, quality of genes and quality of environment tend to match. The two horses now pull in the same direction because the environment horse has been taught to follow the lead of the gene horse. The environment has as much *causal* potency as ever: it is simply hiding behind a mask. It is concealed by the fact that it adds little independent *predictive* potency to genes.

Let us shift from basketball to cognitive ability. Here again the context is the range of genes and environments available within the dominant culture of white America. As separated identical twins go through school, assuming higher-quality genes than average, they are both more likely to respond better to their math teachers, be given extra work, join the math club, take more advanced math courses, and so forth. But does it make any sense to say that environment is diminishing when it is simply a matter that both horses are beginning to pull the chariot together?

This phenomenon holds even at the top of the curve. My son is now a professor of pure mathematics at Oxford. At seven, he came to me with questions about infinity. He said: there are an infinite number of numbers; but there are an infinite number of even numbers; so one kind of infinity has twice as many members as another. I pointed out that this means you can do arithmetic with kinds of infinity. Subtract the infinity of even numbers from the infinity of all numbers, and you get the infinity of odd numbers. In other words, I (plus his teachers) recognized his genetic promise and tried to make sure that his quality of genes began to match an environment of similar quality. But we were essential causal factors. Imagine his teachers and I eliminated his environment by jumping out of a window. True, as we began to make sure his genes and environment pulled in the same direction, we made his genes a better and better predictor of his cognitive skill. This reduced the potency of environment as an independent predictor, but it did not eliminate the causal potency of environment. The causal potency of environment *never* disappears.

How do we know that environment is always potent? At least when environmental changes are favorable, it can cause the Flynn effect. Between generations, there are no significant genetic differences available to correlate with (and thereby mask) the impact of cognitive evolution, smaller families, more schooling, more demanding jobs, and better health in old age. These environmental factors upgrade the *average* IQ, although in each generation different people profit from them to different degrees as always. The enormous size of IQ gains over time shows how much environmental potency was still there, hiding behind the mask of the gene–environment correlation that exists at a given time and place.

Genes and Human Autonomy

Many who read this would be from middle-class America, Britain, the Netherlands, etc. Perhaps you will now have a less condescending attitude to preindustrial societies and alienated groups that have a lower mean IQ than your own. Even if the IQ difference is large (30 or more points), nothing about factor analysis or twins shows that environment is intrinsically weak. That environment has the potential to explain a group difference of this size does not, of course, show that genes lack that potential. Whether black–white ability differences are more like height differences or cognitive exercise differences (my own view) has to be debated on its merits – stripped of any presupposition that environment *must* lose (Flynn, 1980; 2008, chs. 2–4; 2012a, pp. 132–141; Rushton & Jensen, 2010).

I doubt many of you will take a time machine to a different generation or want to move to a less privileged culture. Therefore, you may feel intimidated by genetic determination: your genes (with help) determine your current environment and thus determine your cognitive abilities. Therefore, I want to emphasize that even within a generation, when you are competing with your own age cohort, the correlation between quality of genes and quality of environment never becomes perfect. Within America and other advanced nations, there is that 20 percent of IQ variance that is ascribed to luck, chance events like being drafted or losing your job, events that plunge you into a current environment that does not match your genetic potential (it must be even larger in less stable and more risk-prone societies).

Now reflect: At least half of the time, you make your own luck by an exercise of human autonomy. In a fit of patriotism, you may leave your job as a computer programmer to join the army; you may be disgusted with a humdrum job and decide to go back to university to immerse yourself into a more challenging environment (we hope). There is no way of interpreting the existence of that 20 percent except to assume that a lot of people are "unlucky" enough to be in an environment below their genetic capacity and could move up, and that a lot of people are in an environment above their genetic capacity that they created by welcoming cognitive challenge more than most of us. Your exercise of autonomy can leapfrog you over four-fifths of those presently above you on a cognitive ladder (Flynn, 2016, pp. 22–29).

Sociological Spectacles

The Flynn effect and the Dickens-Flynn model brought a change in mood. It became more respectable to pose environmental hypotheses and appeal to cultural differences.

That university women have a mean IQ two or three points below men was taken as evidence of female inferiority. This ignores the difference between the female and male school subculture. A girl with an IQ of 100 tends to get A's and B's and goes on to university, while a boy with an IQ of 100 tends to get B's and C's. Therefore, the upper 50 percent of women may be at your university and only the upper 40 percent of men (those with an IQ of 104 and above). That university women have a lower average IQ says nothing about the genders in general (Flynn, 2012a, pp. 141–157).

Some mental health questionnaires assume that women with a negative attitude toward marriage are more likely to be psychotic. Black women in America are more likely to have a negative attitude, but why is that? Black males suffer from premature death, imprisonment, drug addiction, AIDS, unemployment, and simply going missing. Thus, for every 100 black women of marriageable age, there are only 57 black men who are viable partners. The fact that any black woman is optimistic is symptomatic of romanticism (Flynn, 2008, ch. 2).

There is the ice ages thesis. The fact that the ancestors of the Chinese were trapped north of the Himalayas during the last ice age is supposed to show that they were rigorously selected for intelligence to cope with that harsh environment. A genetic analysis of Chinese society reveals that only those settled in the north were ever north of the Himalayas, and that the south Chinese reached China by a coastal route through India and Southeast Asia. Yet the mean IQ of the south is equivalent to the mean IQ of the north. If the Chinese have superior genes for intelligence, the ice ages have nothing to do with it (Flynn, 2012a, pp. 33–36).

Philosophy and Science

Social scientists should learn some philosophy. Jensen (1972, p. 76) once defined "intelligence" as what IQ tests measure. Philosophy calls this "instrumentalism": thinking you can define something by reference to the instrument that measures it. If the early developers of thermometers had defined "heat" as what their thermometers measured, they by definition could never have invented a better thermometer.

Psychologists waste time trying to add precision to their definitions of "intelligence." Actually a rough definition will do: a person is more intelligent if he or she can better solve the cognitive problems his society poses as most important – assuming of course that all have an equal opportunity to access that society and are not segregated by either culture (Kalahari Bushmen) or subculture (many black Americans). Precision is needed when you begin to measure a working cognitive skill (like vocabulary). The concept of *g* was appealing because Raven's could measure it so precisely. But as the history of the 20th century showed, it was just another learned cognitive skill. (Remember Luria's subjects who could not do logical analysis of general concepts and would not take the hypothetical seriously.)

Awareness of moral philosophy reveals a dividend of IQ gains over time – cognitive progress has encouraged moral progress (Flynn, 2013, pp. 72–74). All moral debate begins with taking the hypothetical seriously: "What if your skin turned black?" A literal response ends the argument: "That is crazy – who do you know whose skin has ever turned black?" Better political debate means rejection of the anecdotal in favor of generalized evidence: congressmen in 1918 were quite capable of saying, "my wife says she does not want to vote and that is good enough for me." None of this means that young people today are more likely to be honest, brave, or altruistic. But the way in which their thinking differs from their ancestors means that fewer of them are prey to primitive racism and sexism.

The Future

Better mapping of the brain may predict which child will do better than another on Wechsler tests – by producing images of neurons, connections between neurons, and the "spray" from dopaminergic neurons that thickens neural connections with use. If so, we will have the physiology that underlies intelligent problem solving. However, other levels of knowledge would still be relevant. Brain physiology cannot duplicate history's insights into the habits of mind acquired in the 20th century. It cannot replace the sociology of how these transformed school, work, leisure, and moral debate. I hope that research into brain physiology will be accompanied by greater sociological and philosophical sophistication.

As for IQ gains over time, after 1995, Scandinavian 18-year-olds began to perform worse on mental tests. In the Netherlands, families seem to be offering a static cognitive environment for preschoolers, high schools may be in mild decline, jobs are still cognitively demanding, and the aged profit from better health and more exercise (Flynn, in press). The worrying things are social trends contrary to those of the 20th century. Solo parenthood may be reducing the ratio of adults to children in the home, students may be more alienated from school culture, and industrial progress is beginning to create more undemanding service work rather than professional jobs.

These trends do not destroy individual autonomy. Just as a runner may follow a training schedule no matter what others do, nothing forbids you from creating a gymnasium of the mind that gives your brain cognitive exercise throughout life. You can develop the habit of reading widely, thinking critically, and seeking the truth in all things. I have tried to give you a guide in my book, *How to improve your mind* (Flynn, 2012b).

References

Coyle, T. R., & Pillow, D. R. (2008). SAT and ACT predict college GPA after removing "g". *Intelligence* 36: 719–729.

Dickens, W. T., & Flynn, J. R. (2001a). Great leap forward: A new theory of intelligence. *New Scientist* 21 April, 2001: 44–47.

(2001b). Heritability estimates versus large environmental effects: The IQ paradox resolved. *Psychological Review* 108: 346–369.

(2006). Black Americans reduce the racial IQ gap: Evidence from standardization samples. *Psychological Science* 17: 913–920.

Flynn, J. R. (1980). *Race, IQ, and Jensen*. London: Routledge.

(1984). The mean IQ of Americans: Massive gains 1932 to 1978. *Psychological Bulletin* 95: 29–51.

(1987). Massive IQ gains in 14 nations: What IQ tests really measure. *Psychological Bulletin* 101: 171–191.

(2008). *Where have all the liberals gone? Race, class, and ideals in America*. Cambridge: Cambridge University Press.

(2009). *What is intelligence? Beyond the Flynn Effect.* Cambridge: Cambridge University Press.

(2012a). *Are we getting smarter: Rising IQ in the twenty-first century.* Cambridge: Cambridge University Press.

(2012b). *How to improve your mind: Twenty keys to unlock the modern world.* London: Wiley-Blackwell.

(2013). *Intelligence and human progress: The story of what was hidden in our genes.* London: Elsevier.

(2016). *Does your family make you smarter? Nature, nurture, and human autonomy.* Cambridge: Cambridge University Press.

(in press). Male and female balance sheet. *Mankind Quarterly.*

Flynn, J. R., te Nijenhuis, J., & Metzen, D. (2014). The *g* beyond Spearman's *g*: Flynn's paradoxes resolved using four exploratory meta-analyses. *Intelligence* 44: 1–10.

Genovese, J. E. (2002). Cognitive skills valued by educators: Historic content analysis of testing in Ohio. *Journal of Educational Research* 96: 101–114.

Haworth, C. M. A. et al. (23 others) (2010). The heritability of general cognitive ability increases linearly from childhood to young adulthood. *Molecular Psychiatry* 15: 1112–1120.

Jensen, A. R. (1972). *Genetics and education.* New York: Harper & Row.

(1973). *Educability and group differences.* London: Methuen.

(1980). *Bias in mental testing.* London: Methuen.

(1998). *The g factor.* Westport, CT: Praeger.

Luria, A. R. (1976). *Cognitive development: Its cultural and social foundations.* Cambridge, MA: Harvard University Press.

Maguire, E A., Gadian, D. G., Johnsrude, I. S., Good, C. D., Ashburner, J., Frackowiak, R. S. J., & Firth C. D. (2000). Navigation-related structural change in the hippocampi of taxi drivers. *Proceedings of the National Academy of Sciences* 79: 4398–4403.

Moore, E. G. J. (1986). Family socialization and the IQ test performance of traditionally and transracially adopted black children. *Developmental Psychology* 22: 317–326.

Nisbett, R. E. (2015). *Mindware: Tools for smart thinking.* New York: Farrar, Straus and Giroux.

Rushton, J. P., & Jensen, A. R. (2010). Editorial: The rise and fall of the Flynn effect as a reason to expect a narrowing of the black/white IQ gap. *Intelligence* 38: 213–219.

te Nijenhuis, J., & van der Flier, H. (2013). Is the Flynn effect on *g*?: A meta-analysis. *Intelligence* 41: 803–807.

Woodley, M. A. (2012a). A life history model of the Lynn-Flynn effect. *Personality and Individual Differences* 53: 152–156.

(2012b). The social and scientific temporal correlates of genotypic intelligence and the Flynn effect. *Intelligence* 40: 189–204.

CHAPTER 8

The Theory of Multiple Intelligences
Psychological and Educational Perspectives

Howard Gardner, Mindy Kornhaber, & Jie-Qi Chen[1]

Introduction

In their textbook of psychology, Roger Brown and Richard Herrnstein commented on the two areas of psychology that had the greatest practical influence in the 20th century (Brown & Herrnstein, 1975). One was marketing and public relations; the other was the measurement of intelligence. We suspect that both authors had mixed feelings about the control of human behavior through manipulations; but at least for Richard Herrnstein, the senior author of *The Bell Curve*, the measurement of intelligence was an unalloyed success (Herrnstein & Murray, 1994).

Psychological testing began at the start of the 20th century, chiefly in Western Europe; it moved to the United States soon thereafter. In the United States, technologies of measurement and machine scoring combined to make the IQ test – and its variations, including the initial SAT – a ubiquitous and highly influential part of the educational landscape. And indeed, so long as one was attempting to predict whether individuals would succeed in a 20th-century secular school, the IQ test fulfilled its chosen niche.

Over the decades there have been numerous efforts to identify which abilities are being tested, what are the constituents of intellect, to what extent intellectual measures can predict aspects of human personality, behaviors, even life chances and fates. Yet fundamentally, the insight voiced many decades ago by E. G. Boring (1923) has been regnant: intelligence is what the tests test. From a pragmatic point of view, nothing more needs to be said.

It's not possible – and perhaps inadvisable – to ignore the history of intelligence testing and the manifold uses (and misuses) to which intelligence testing has been subjected in the past century (Gould, 1981). That being said, the theory of multiple intelligences (hereafter MI theory), and the uses to which it has been put, are best understood if one strives to switch mind-set – to think afresh about the ideas introduced in the following pages.

A Thought Experiment

Suppose that you were the proverbial visitor from a remote galaxy whose mission was to identify the cognitive powers that human beings have developed over the millennia. You could review the achievements and the challenges that confronted various hominid species over the course of tens of thousands of years; the skills and capacities valued across a diverse set of cultures; the unusual configurations of abilities and disabilities that can be observed at home, in schools, offline and online; performances by human beings on a range of tests and experiments, both in formal and in informal settings (athletic fields, the workplace, the marketplace); the configuration of capacities that can be related to specific parts of the cortex, as well as key subcortical structures; and knowledge about the genetic bases of various human capacities.

With the collaboration of a talented research team, Gardner conducted such a survey in the late 1970s and the early 1980s. His stated mission, formulated by the funder, was to describe what had been established to that point about human potential. From his earlier research on the cognitive development of children (Gardner, 1978) and on the breakdown of human cognitive capacities under various conditions of brain damage (Gardner, 1975), Gardner had concluded that the notion of a single intellect, measurable by a single instrument, was inadequate. Gardner offered a new definition of intelligence; delineated criteria that allowed evaluation of candidate abilities or skills; and specified a limited set of capacities. Gardner then took a crucial step: he decided to pluralize the word "intelligence." Others had delineated various human skills; but the coining of the word "intelligences" and the delineation of a set of defining criteria were original contributions to psychology.

Definition

As initially formulated, an intelligence is a set of skills that allow individuals to solve problems or create products in various cultures (Gardner, 1983, pp. 60–61). In subsequent writings, Gardner offered a more formal definition: "An intelligence is the biopsychological capacity to process information in order to solve problems or to create products that are valued in at least one cultural setting" (Gardner 1999, p. 33).

This formulation has distinctive features:

- There is no assumption that intelligence is a singular capacity;
- An intelligence is rooted both in human biology (brain, genes) and in human psychology (mental processes);
- Reflecting its postulation in a digital/computational era, the concept of "information processing" is introduced;
- While conceptions of intelligence typically valorize problem-solving, this definition incorporates the creation of products, ranging from works of art to technological inventions;
- An intelligence may only be expressed or valorized in certain loci at certain times.

Criteria

The most novel feature of Gardner's investigation was the delineation and application of a set of criteria to ascertain whether or not a candidate capacity qualifies as a separate human intelligence. A candidate capacity qualifies as *an intelligence* only if it fits the following criteria reasonably well:

- Potential isolation by brain damage (e.g., a capacity is either undermined or spared subsequent to focal brain damage) or other neuropsychological evidence;
- The existence of exceptional individuals (e.g., prodigies, savants) who display an intelligence prominently or conspicuously lack it;
- A distinctive developmental history and a definable set of "end-state" performances. Counter to traditional developmental theory (Piaget, 1970), stages of development in one intelligence (e.g., linguistic) are not yoked to stages that characterize another intelligence (e.g., interpersonal);
- An evolutionary history and evolutionary plausibility: one should be able to identify analogues or homologues of human intelligence in other species (e.g., spatial intelligence in rats, logical intelligence in higher primates);
- Support from psychometric findings: Gardner acknowledges the "positive manifold" across standardized tests, but correlations will be much reduced if the intelligence can be assessed in context;
- Support from experimental psychological tests: exercise of one intelligence should transfer to tasks that draw on that intelligence and far less to tasks that marshal other intelligences;
- Core operations can be defined: each intelligence consists of a small number of defining information-processing capacities. For example,

sensitivity to rhythm is important in musical intelligence, while sensitivity to syntax is important in linguistic intelligence;

• Susceptibility to encoding in a symbol system: key components or operations can be captured (or coded) in a distinctive symbol system (e.g., maps for spatial intelligence, scores for musical intelligence);

• Intelligences are not tied to sensory organs. For example, linguistic intelligence will be activated whether language is presented in written, oral, or tactile (braille) form.

Invoking these criteria, Gardner and colleagues surveyed a large number of human information-processing capacities with the aim of determining which qualified as distinct intelligences. Admittedly the ultimate judgment is a subjective one; there is no clear cut-off point for when a candidate capacity qualifies or fails to qualify. In *Frames of Mind*, Gardner presented the evidence on the basis of which intelligences were identified. Notably, while the theory has been extensively critiqued (cf. Schaler, 2006), few commentators have engaged critically with the criteria or their application.

Original Set of Intelligences

Herewith a brief definition and some examples of adult roles that typically exhibit high amounts of that intelligence:

• *Linguistic intelligence:* processing the syntax, semantics, and pragmatics of language – poets, journalists, lawyers;

• *Logical-mathematical intelligence:* calculating, computing, mathematical, and scientific knowledge – scientists, logicians, computer programmers.

Standard intelligence tests are heavily skewed toward these two forms of intelligence. Piaget's (1970) studies of cognitive development focus on logical-mathematical intelligence.

• *Spatial intelligence:* computing location, orientation, navigation in two- and three-dimensional space – sculptors, navigators, billiard players;

• *Musical intelligence:* processing melodic, harmonic, rhythmic, signals – composers, performers, musical connoisseurs;

• *Bodily-kinesthetic intelligence:* using one's body to solve problems or make things – athletes, dancers, craftspersons, technicians;

• *Interpersonal intelligence:* understanding and responding appropriately to others – salespersons, clinicians, politicians;

• *Intrapersonal intelligence:* understanding oneself and making appropriate use of that self-understanding – individuals with demonstrable self-knowledge, as discerned by clinicians and informed observers.

Other Possible Intelligences

Gardner has entertained many proposals for additional intelligences. Best known is "emotional intelligence" – as proposed by Salovey and Mayer (1990) and publicized by Goleman (1995). Goleman's concepts of emotional and social intelligence are akin to the interpersonal and intrapersonal intelligences. Note that Gardner's intelligences are non-evaluative (one can use any intelligence benignly or malignantly), while Goleman's intelligences include a value component (it's good to be emotionally intelligent).

A decade after his initial publications, Gardner added an eighth intelligence. "*Naturalist intelligence*" denotes the ability to make consequential distinctions among types of plants, animals, clouds, rocks, etc. Clearly this capacity was vital in preindustrial times. But even in our "shopping mall era" we use our naturalist intelligence to distinguish among pairs of shoes, car makes, and other commercial products.

Gardner has considered two additional intelligences: an *existential intelligence*, the capacity to pose and ponder large philosophical questions, and a *pedagogical intelligence*, the capacity to impart knowledge effectively to others. As of this writing, he has not carried out research sufficient to determine whether these candidates adequately meet the aforementioned criteria and can be distinguished from the eight validated intelligences.

Scientific Implications

As an attempt to organize a copious data according to a set of criteria, MI theory lays claim to the status of a scientific theory. It is clearly an *empirical theory* – one based on findings from numerous scientific inquiries. But it is not an *experimental theory*; it cannot be proved or disproved experimentally. Its longevity will ultimately be determined by its potential for generating scholarly work as well as useful applications. There are three scientific implications:

1. As a species, human beings are characterized by the possession and potential for developing these capacities.
2. Unless grossly impaired, all humans possess this set of intelligences, but because of different experiences (and, in nearly all cases, different genomes), no two human beings exhibit the same profiles of intellectual strengths and weaknesses.

3. Each intelligence has subcomponents; while of scientific interest, such a delineation of scores of subcomponents can undermine the utility of the theory (cf. Guilford, 1956).

At present, little scientific work is being carried out directly on MI theory. Relevant findings and implications are reviewed on multipleintelligencesoasis.com. Shearer and Karanian (2016) have surveyed neuroscientific evidence for the existence and relative neural independences of the several intelligences.

The Theory in Education

Social psychologist Kurt Lewin once said, "there's nothing so practical as a good theory" (1951). In contrast to the tepid reception of MI by mainstream psychology, educational researchers and practitioners have shown considerable interest in MI theory (Chen, Moran, & Gardner, 2009; Kornhaber, Fierros, & Veenema, 2004; Martin, 2005; Schneider, 2014). Part of the interest presumably reflects the hope harbored in the theory: while IQ was long seen as unmodifiable and thus a signal of one's life prospects, MI theory foregrounds different kinds of expertise and makes no assumptions about heritability. Part of the interest also comports with the intuition – certainly held by most teachers – that individuals display different strengths (Kornhaber & Krechevsky, 1995).

In the wake of the immediate interest among educators in the theory, Gardner and colleagues developed an assessment instrument for young children (cf. Chen, 2004; Krechevsky, 1998). Other rough-and-ready instruments have been developed, including MIDAS by Shearer (2007, www.MIResearch.org) and DISCOVER by Maker (2005, www.discover.arizona.edu).

Gardner has pointed out that "MI theory" is not in itself an educational recipe. *All* educational recommendations presuppose a set of values; only if these values are explicit can one ascertain whether MI can help realize those values. That said, Gardner emphasizes two ways in which MI ideas may help educators to convey content and skills that they value (Gardner, 2006). They are individuation and pluralization.

- *Individuation* entails discovering as much as possible about each learner, then adjusting mode of instruction and assessment as appropriate for each learner.
- *Pluralization* entails presenting important content in a variety of ways, thereby activating several intelligences and exhibiting what it means to understand a topic fully.

Both individuation and pluralization may be enabled by online resources. In what follows, we chronicle two lines of educational work that MI theory has catalyzed. The first illustrates the ways in which MI ideas have informed early childhood education. The second summarizes a study of MI-informed education at elementary and secondary levels.

Education of Young Children

MI theory has served as a conceptual framework for implementing developmentally appropriate practice in early education. Three knowledge sets are essential in this discussion: children and their development; subject matter and curriculum goals; and teaching and assessment.

Knowledge of children and their development. Development of the whole child – physically, cognitively, and social/emotionally – is a well-established concept in early education. Knowledge of children in the MI framework goes beyond describing general growth to identify a wider range of more specific developmental potentials (Chen & Gardner, 2012). Because each intelligence exhibits particular problem-solving features, information-processing capacities, and developmental trajectories, knowing about one area of a child's development does not necessarily generalize to others. In-depth understanding requires a careful review of each child's intellectual profile – his or her proclivities, strengths, vulnerabilities, and interests. Although all normally developing children possess all of the intelligences in the MI framework, from early on they characteristically exhibit different strengths and have distinctive profiles. Individual differences are the norm rather than the exception in describing children and their development.

Development from MI's perspective is domain-specific. The development of young children's intellectual abilities is tied to specific bodies of knowledge and skill. Strengths and weaknesses exhibited in a child's intellectual profile may change over time. Development is also contextualized in that intelligences develop among individuals when they interact with each other, use specific cultural tools, or engage in specific activities. Accordingly, to foster young children's intellectual abilities, early childhood educators should attend to cultural values and tools, community goals, and motivations of the child.

Knowledge of subject matter and curriculum goals. Early childhood curriculum is inclusive; activities in the areas of language, math, music, visual arts, and movement are seen regularly in most preschool classrooms.

However, their significance for the development of young children's minds is not typically deemed equal. Oral language, reading, and math are the top priorities for learning, and other activities tend to be marginalized. Developing the capacity to create and/or to acquire varied symbol systems is the foremost task during the early years. Limited exposure decreases possibilities for young children to express themselves with diverse tools and to develop their potentials to the greatest extent. It also reduces the likelihood of discovering interests and abilities that parents and teachers can then nurture.

Trained as generalists, early childhood educators typically integrate a range of content areas using themes and project-based approaches to teaching. An MI-based approach to curriculum development invites teachers to use multiple entry points to promote children's in-depth exploration and understanding of topics and concepts essential to early learning and development. MI theory can assist teachers in organizing curriculum around pivotal topics; supporting children's learning of key concepts and skills in relation to these topics; and promoting the development of varied intellectual potentials supported by multiple symbol systems. Our research indicates that this approach to curriculum and instruction engages children in active learning, deepens their understanding, and advances their academic performance (Chen, 2004; Chen & McCray, 2012).

Knowledge of teaching and assessment. Early childhood teaching is known for its play-based, emergent, and constructivist techniques. MI theory differentiates the pedagogy of early teaching by emphasizing building on children's particular strengths and using them to build bridges to other areas of learning. In contrast to approaches that focus on children's deficits, teachers in MI classrooms attend to areas in which a child excels. Teachers invite children to participate in learning activities that further develop their strengths in ways they are motivated to pursue. Teachers also give children opportunities to use their strengths as tools to express what they have learned. Teacher support for children's strengths contributes to a positive self-image and an increased likelihood for success in other learning areas. The strategy of building on children's strengths has also proven effective in helping children identified as at risk for school failure (Chen, 2004).

Effective teaching requires appropriate uses of assessment. Assessment based on MI theory is consistent with the principles of developmentally appropriate assessment advocated by many early childhood educators. The primary purpose of assessment is to aid development and learning, rather than to sort, track, or label. Features of appropriate assessment include ongoing observation in the classroom, documentation of children's behavior when engaged in meaningful activities, and linking assessment results to teaching and learning processes. Of additional importance to MI-based assessment is the use of intelligence-fair instruments to assess children's strengths in the unique qualities of each intelligence. This approach is accomplished by using media appropriate to each domain assessed and sampling a wide range of abilities in the assessment process. The Spectrum assessment, the tool based on MI theory, exemplifies the ways one can meaningfully capture diverse intellectual strengths in young children and assist educators in selecting appropriate instructional materials and approaches based on a full and in-depth understanding of each child (Chen & Gardner, 2012; Krechevsky, 1998).

Why and How Educators Use MI

In addition to their application with respect to young children, MI ideas have been used with other age groups (Coreil, 2003; Kornhaber et al., 2004). The application of MI across the age span motivated Kornhaber and her colleagues to understand *why* educators have adopted the theory (Kornhaber, 1994; Kornhaber & Krechevsky, 1995) and what practices are in place in schools that associate MI with improvements for students (Kornhaber et al., 2004).

Understanding why MI has moved into practice has import for and beyond the theory itself. Prior to the mandated approaches employed under standards-based reforms, researchers and policymakers found that ideas intended to alter classroom practice gained substantive traction slowly, if at all. (Tyack & Cuban, 1995). Understanding *why* educators found MI compelling – even in the absence of official policy or attendant threat of sanction – could shed light on qualities of the theory, on policy development, and on education reform.

To understand why a diverse array of educators had adopted the theory, Kornhaber and Krechevsky (1995) held in-person interviews lasting typically 45 minutes with more than 100 teachers in 12 diverse elementary schools across the United States. All but one was a public school. The analysis of the interview data revealed that educators adopted the theory for five reasons.

First, MI comported with teachers' beliefs and everyday experience: students are more variable than their standardized test scores reveal: some get along well with peers while others struggle to do so. Some readily succeed in gym class whereas others find success in building models or telling stories.

Second and relatedly, MI helped validate an array of classroom practices that provide varied opportunities for students to engage, learn, and demonstrate understanding, including project-based curriculum, hands-on learning, arts-enriched curriculum, and collaborative work.

Third, MI provided a vocabulary for considering variation within and across students. Teachers used MI to communicate with colleagues, parents, and sometimes students themselves about students' strengths and needs.

Fourth, MI served as a mental "closet organizer" for teachers' practices and materials. That is, the theory offered teachers a framework for reflecting on their repertoire and scanning it for resources that might be useful for particular students or curriculum units.

Fifth, examining their repertoire through an MI lens helped teachers see gaps in their practice and spurred their own professional development to meet different students' needs.

In short, MI not only comported with teachers' existing beliefs and practices – it was also useful. It furthered their understanding of different learners and helped them develop practices to meet students' varied needs. To understand how MI was realized in educational practice, Kornhaber and colleagues further undertook a three-year study, *Schools Using MI Theory* (SUMIT) (Kornhaber et al., 2004).

In its first phase, SUMIT researchers conducted interviews with leaders of 41 public schools. The schools had been using the theory for at least three years and had reputations as thoughtful implementers of MI. The schools were located in 20 U.S. states and one Canadian province. The schools served rural, suburban, and urban communities and also represented diverse student populations, with about a quarter serving high percentages of low SES students and about a third having racially and ethnically heterogeneous populations. The interviews averaged about one hour. Interviewers asked about practices the schools used to learn about the theory, the applications of theory in practice, and benefits for students associated with the application of MI. In the second phase, researchers conducted three or four day site visits to 10 schools to observe classes, interview teachers, and gather written and visual documentation of school practice. These materials were used to develop case studies of five elementary schools and six classrooms.

Where MI was associated with benefits for students – including improved achievement, greater parental involvement, and reduced disciplinary problems – six organizational features were common to classrooms and schools. These features or "compass points" may serve as guideposts for sound implementation of the theory (Kornhaber et al., 2004):

- *School culture* is marked by pervasive beliefs that all children have strengths and can learn. There are also beliefs that learning should be exciting and joyful, even as both students and teachers work hard. In addition, there is an emphasis on care and respect for everyone, by everyone, in the school culture.
- *Time is allowed for new ideas.* MI was introduced through readings and discussion among educators and developed in practice with small scale applications, conversational feedback with colleagues, and refinement. The time from introduction of MI to more wide-scale school use averaged 18 months.
- *MI is a means, not a goal.* The aim of the theory's adoption was not to be "an MI school," but rather to support students' engagement in disciplinary content and to enable students to produce high-quality work. For the most part, the theory was a tool for teachers' curricular and instructional work rather than a piece of curriculum explicitly taught to children.
- *Collaboration is widespread among educators.* The theory allowed teachers to appreciate one another's strengths and complement weaknesses and areas of expertise. There was widespread formal collaboration – for example, team teaching of project-based curriculum or arts-enriched curriculum, as well as ongoing, informal collaboration.
- *Controlled choice was afforded to students*, with respect to both curriculum and assessments. These options were intended to engage students' varied strengths, address their weaknesses, and foster substantive disciplinary learning. For example, in some project-based curriculums, teachers instituted learning centers that drew more heavily on particular intelligences. Students could pick which centers they might like to start with, but over time they rotated through each center so that they could acquire a more rounded set of skills and understandings.
- *The arts are widespread and play a significant role in the school.* Both art for art's sake and arts-integrated curricula were pervasive, even in schools that lacked regular art teachers. For example, science and social studies units featured sketching to help students develop visual documentation of their observations in the natural and man-made world. A school serving inner city children collaborated with a major opera company to engage students in music, drama, and set design. While SUMIT's

findings are based on studies of U.S. schools, analogous efforts have been undertaken elsewhere. One collection of papers chronicles how 42 educators in 15 countries on five continents have adopted or adapted the theory (see Chen, Moran, & Gardner, 2009). Gardner has described the theory as something of an educational Rorschach test. As an example, MI's widespread popularity in China is partly attributable to long-held views that an educated person manifests skills in social relations, language, and the arts and indeed should be strong across the spectrum of intelligences (Chen, 2009; Cheung, 2009; Shen, 2009). In contrast, in the United Kingdom, MI offers an antidote to long-held narrow conceptions of intelligence, teaching, and learning that underserve a diverse population of young people living in the 21st century (Craft, 2009; Fleetham, 2009).

While there are varied reasons for the theory's adoption, and varied approaches to putting the theory into practice, it is fair to say that across the globe, educators see the theory as a way of engaging a wide range of students and enriching their learning opportunities. Across the globe, it is also true that whether public school educators can draw on the theory is influenced by educational policies. Where policies emphasize achievement in limited subjects and limited test performances, teachers' ability to draw on MI will be undermined. Where policymakers seek to broaden opportunities for all students to learn a rich curriculum, the theory will continue to be educationally catalytic.

Concluding Note

Among contemporary theories of intelligence, MI theory is unusual. It was among the first to challenge the notion of intelligence as a single mental capacity, adequately assessed by a single instrument. It took seriously a wide range of disciplinary inputs (from neuropsychology to anthropology), kinds of populations (from prodigies to savants), and forms of assessment (contextual, informal). And it helped to spawn a popular explosion of various candidate intelligences – ranging from the reasonable (emotional, social) to the exotic (sexual, financial, culinary). And yet it has had remarkably little effect within the mainstream of scholarship in psychology and psychometric.

MI theory – and its offshoots – has had its main impact in two far more practical realms. In schools all over the world, "MI thinking" and "MI practices" have affected leaders, classroom teachers, specialists, and the students with whom they work. And discussion of different intelligences has also infused the workplace, cultural institutions, and talk in the playground and around the dinner table.

We are left with the question of what the visitor from another galaxy might conclude about human cognitive capacities. It would depend on where she looked; whom she consulted; which paradigms of theorizing and assessment she prioritized; and, no doubt, on how she and her fellow space travelers use their own minds. Perhaps, indeed, she might reveal some intelligences that we earthlings cannot even imagine.

Note

1 Correspondence concerning this chapter should be addressed to Howard Gardner, Harvard Graduate School of Education, 13 Appian Way, Longfellow 235, Cambridge, MA 02138.

References

Boring, E. G. (1923) Intelligence as the tests test it. *New Republic, 26,* 35–37.

Brown, R. & Herrnstein, R. (1975) *Psychology.* Boston: Little Brown.

Chen, J. Q. (2004). The Project Spectrum approach to early education. In J. Johnson & J. Roopnarine (Eds.), *Approaches to early childhood education (4th ed.),* pp. 251–279. Upper Saddle River, NJ: Pearson.

Chen, J. Q. (2009). China's assimilation of MI theory in education: Accent on the family and harmony. In J. Chen, S. Moran, & H. Gardner (Eds.). *Multiple intelligences around the world,* pp. 29–42. San Francisco: Jossey-Bass.

Chen, J. Q. & Gardner, H. (2012). Assessment of intellectual profile: A perspective from multiple intelligences theory. In D. P. Flanagan & P. L. Harrison (Eds.), *Contemporary intellectual assessment: Theories, tests, and issues (3rd ed.),* pp. 145–155. New York: Guilford.

Chen, J. Q. & McCray, J. (2012). A conceptual framework for teacher professional development: The whole teacher approach. *NHSA Dialog: A Research-to-Practice Journal for the Early Intervention Field,* 15(1), 8–23.

Chen, J., Moran, S., & Gardner, H. (2009). *Multiple intelligences around the world.* San Francisco: Jossey-Bass.

Cheung, H. H-P. (2009) Multiple intelligences in China: Challenges and hopes. In J. Chen, S. Moran, & H. Gardner (Eds.). *Multiple intelligences around the world,* pp. 43–54. San Francisco: Jossey-Bass.

Coreil, C. (Ed.), (2003). *Multiple intelligences, Howard Gardner, and new methods in college teaching.* Jersey City: New Jersey City University.

Craft, A. (2009). An English translation? Multiple intelligences in England. In J. Chen, S. Moran, & H. Gardner (Eds.). *Multiple intelligences around the world,* pp. 184–196. San Francisco: Jossey-Bass.

Fleetham, M. (2009). Does every child matter in England? In J. Chen, S. Moran, & H. Gardner (Eds.). *Multiple intelligences around the world*, pp. 197–205. San Francisco: Jossey-Bass.

Gardner, H. (1975). *The shattered mind*. New York: Knopf.

(1978). *Developmental psychology*. Boston: Little Brown.

(1983). *Frames of mind*. New York: Basic Books.

(1999). *Intelligence reframed*. New York: Basic Books.

(2006) *Multiple intelligences: New horizons*. New York: Basic Books.

Goleman, D. (1995). *Emotional intelligence*. New York; Bantam.

Gould, S. J. (1981). *The mismeasure of man*. New York: Norton & Company.

Guilford, J. P. (1956). The structure of intellect. *Psychological Bulletin*, 53(4), 267–293.

Herrnstein, R. & Murray, C. (1994. *The bell curve*. New York: Free Press.

Kornhaber, M. L. (1994). *The theory of multiple intelligences: Why and how schools use it*. Cambridge, MA: Harvard Graduate School of Education.

Kornhaber, M. L., Fierros, E., & Veenema, S. (2004). *Multiple intelligences: Best ideas from research and practice*. New York: Pearson.

Kornhaber, M. L. & Krechevsky, M. (1995). Expanding definitions of teaching and learning: Notes from the MI underground. In P. Cookson & B. Schneider (Eds.), *Transforming schools*. New York: Garland Press.

Krechevsky, M. (1998). *Project Spectrum preschool assessment handbook*. New York: Teachers College Press.

Lewin, K. (1951). *Field theory in social science*. New York: Harper and Row.

Martin, J. (2005). *Profiting from multiple intelligences in the work place*. Carmathan, UK: Crown House Publishing.

Piaget, J. (1970). Piaget's theory. In P. Mussen (Ed.), *Manual of child psychology*, Volume 1. New York: Wiley.

Salovey, P. & Mayer, J. (1990) Emotional intelligence. *Imagination, Cognition, and Personality*, 9, 185–211.

Schaler, J. (2006). *Howard Gardner under fire*. Chicago: Open Court.

Schneider, J. (2014). *From the ivory tower to the schoolhouse*. Cambridge, MA: Harvard Education Press.

Shearer, B. & Karanian, J. (2016). *The neuroscience of intelligence: Empirical support for the theory of multiple intelligences?* International Mind, Brain, and Education Society.

Shen, Z. (2009). *Multiple intelligences theory on the mainland of China*. In J. Chen, S. Moran, & H. Gardner (Eds.). *Multiple intelligences around the world*, pp. 55–65. San Francisco: Jossey-Bass.

Tyack, D. & Cuban, L. (1995). *Tinkering toward utopia: A century of public school reform*. Cambridge, MA: Harvard University Press.

g *Theory*

How Recurring Variation in Human Intelligence and the Complexity of Everyday Tasks Create Social Structure and the Democratic Dilemma

Linda S. Gottfredson

Prologue to a Theory of *g*

As a new PhD in 1977, I had no particular interest in intelligence. I was, however, skeptical of my fellow sociologists' conception of it. Their status-attainment path models assumed that offspring IQ ("cognitive ability") is a product of parents' socioeconomic advantage. These models reflected the discipline's general consensus that intelligence, real or perceived, predicts school and work success only because it transmits the parent generation's social privileges to its offspring.

Where psychologists saw individual differences, sociologists saw social inequality. Where psychologists suspected genetic influences on cognitive competence, influential figures in sociology alleged an elite perpetuating itself under the guise of intellectual merit. Career-development psychologists asked how young people choose among different occupations; status-attainment researchers asked what bars the less privileged from entering the most desirable ones. Both theories of occupational attainment pointed to factors the other ignored. One classified occupations horizontally, by field of work; the other ordered them vertically, by prestige. One looked at the nature of work performed and interests rewarded in different occupations; the other only at the socioeconomic benefits flowing to workers in them. Both approaches had venerable histories and vast bodies of evidence, yet contradicted the other's most fundamental assumptions and conclusions.

I set out to reconcile the two disciplines' positions by testing the validity of their guiding assumptions. I began with the most basic premise in sociological explanations of social inequality: higher intelligence matters only for getting a good job, not for performing it well. Testing it required marshaling evidence on job duties, requirements, working conditions, and rewards for a large number of occupations from diverse sources, including vocational guidance research, employee selection psychology, and socio-logical studies of status attainment, plus civilian and military databases on jobs and employment testing, plus proprietary job analyses. My question: does the inherent nature of some work tasks and jobs require workers to do more difficult mental processing to carry out the tasks? Evidence that cognitive ability predicts job performance (then, mostly supervisor ratings) could not answer that question.

This initial research did double duty because my immediate concern was to fill a gap in vocational guidance: what types and levels of ability do different occupations inherently require of workers to do the job well? Ability profiles influence career choice, but I wanted to provide counselors and counselees a two-dimensional map of occupations, by the type and level of abilities they require, so they could assess and improve a counselee's odds of entering their preferred occupation and performing it well (Gottfredson, 1986, 2005b).

I mention this history because it would shape my intelligence research in distinctive ways. First, I studied populations of jobs, not persons. For instance, I factor analyzed the attributes of occupations, not workers. Second, I tested claims from one discipline with data from others. Third, I worked to solve nagging puzzles, unravel seeming paradoxes, and discern the deep patterns in superficially chaotic data. These strategies would lead me on a long journey through various disciplines to find evidence on the nature, origins, and societal consequences of human variation in intelligence.

Figure 9.1 schematizes my synthesis of replicated bodies of evidence: a cross-disciplinary theory, or explanation, of *g* in all its manifestations (Gottfredson, 2016). Seven levels of analysis are essential for pinning down what general intelligence is and does. They proceed clockwise from the most molecular processes (Genes) to most macro (Evolution). To be clear, by *g* I mean population variation in general intelligence and its ubiquitous, highly patterned effects in human affairs. The figure also highlights my conviction that we cannot understand this human trait or how it evolved until we know how the mundane tasks in daily life activate latent differences in *g*, make them visible, and magnify the practical advantages of having higher *g*. I will use Figure 9.1 to help answer the six questions to follow.

What Is Intelligence?

"Intelligence" is no longer a scientifically useful concept, in part because scholars have applied the word to ever more numerous and varied forms of

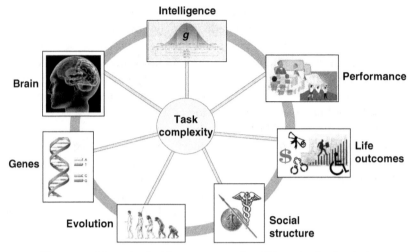

Figure 9.1   Network of evidence on *g* spanning different levels of analysis
(Gottfredson, 2016).
© Elsevier. Reproduced by permission of Elsevier. Permission to reuse must be obtained
from the rights holder.

aptness. No longer informative either are the long-standing debates over
how best "to define" intelligence, as if a natural phenomenon could be
formed or banished by expert consensus. The phenomenon in question is
now best identified as *g*. It is a *trait*, a recurring dimension of human variation, and is best described by evidence converging from different levels of
analysis.

The Problem with Intelligence

Carroll's (1993) empirically derived hierarchical model of human cognitive
abilities helps illustrate why intelligence is no longer a useful theoretical
construct. The three strata in his model order abilities by their observed
generality of application, from highly general (Stratum III) to content
specific (Stratum I). Carroll's laborious reanalysis of hundreds of factor-
analytic studies confirmed there is only one domain-general (Stratum III)
ability factor, *g*. Many intelligence researchers now prefer to focus on this
more precisely specified and measured construct. They sometimes refer to
it as *general* intelligence, by its more technical name (the general mental
ability factor), or with an acronym less likely to provoke sensitivities over
intelligence, such as GMA (general mental ability). Carroll identified eight
broad abilities at the Stratum II level: fluid and crystallized *g* (G*f*, G*c*),

memory and retrieval (G*y*, G*r*), visual and auditory processing *(Gv, Gu)*, and two kinds of speed (G*s*, G*t*). All correlate highly with *g*, which means that each is basically *g* plus some domain-specific additive (e.g., memory, spatial visualization, speed of processing).

Other scholars use the unmodified noun "intelligence" more inclusively. Some include the entire set of human cognitive abilities, general and specific. For them, all the strata in Carroll's model collectively represent intelligence. Others extend the concept to abilities outside the cognitive realm, such as physical coordination (kinesthetic intelligence) and emotion perception and regulation (emotional intelligence). Yet others suggest that the term "intelligence" properly includes all traits and behaviors that contribute to effective performance (adaptive intelligence), or even life outcomes too (successful intelligence) – respectively Performance and Life Outcomes in Figure 9.1. All are important phenomena in their own right, but labeling some unspecified set of them as intelligence is more likely to confuse than inform research and theory.

The Meaning of g, *a Latent Construct*

As Figure 9.1 suggests, *g* can be described at different levels of analysis. Psychometrically, it is the first principal factor derived from factor-analyzing scores on professionally developed batteries of mental tests. *g* manifests itself in test and task performance as variation in a domain-general capacity for processing information. In lay terms it is

> a very general capacity that, among other things, involves the ability to reason, plan, solve problems, think abstractly, comprehend complex ideas, learn quickly and learn from experience. It is not merely book learning, a narrow academic skill, or test-taking smarts. Rather, it reflects a broader and deeper capability for comprehending our surroundings – "catching on," "making sense" of things, or "figuring out what to do." (Gottfredson, 1997a, p. 13)

This description of *g* mirrors Horn and Cattell's construct of fluid intelligence (G*f*). In fact, factor analyses often find that the two *g*'s – Stratum III *g* and Stratum II G*f* – are essentially identical.

No mere chimera of factor analysis, *g* also manifests itself at the Gene and Brain levels of analysis (Gottfredson, 2016). For instance, the genetic structure of (covariation among) cognitive abilities mirrors its phenotypic structure, and the heritability of Stratum III *g* accounts for all but a fraction of the heritability of individual differences in Carroll's Stratum II abilities. Individual differences in *g* are radically polygenic, and no one allele (single nucleotide polymorphism, SNP) has more than a minuscule influence on phenotypic differences in g. Not only that, the heritability of g rises with age, meaning that phenotypes increasingly reflect differences in genotype (they correlate 0.9 by late middle age).

Virtually all differences in brain structure and function correlate to some extent with general cognitive ability measured in some fashion. Thus, far from being located in some particular part or process in the brain, the neural fundaments of g are radically dispersed throughout it. This fits with g's radically polygenic origins. Psychometric g observed at the Intelligence level of analysis is an emergent property of the brain operating as a whole.

All human populations show a wide dispersion in general intelligence that replicates across generations. That this variation is so regular and recurring suggests that it is a biological fact, an evolved feature of our species. It is also a feature with wide and deep influence on human culture. The advantages of higher intelligence operate like a tailwind in virtually all life domains, weak in some but strong in others. It is a strictly cognitive trait, not affective, social, or physical. Data on test, school, and job performance all tell the same story: having higher g gives individuals a bigger edge in performing tasks well when the tasks (a) are instrumental (getting something done, correctly), (b) require more complex information processing, and (c) must be carried out independently. Conversely, low levels of g can create severe disadvantages for individuals, a stiff headwind, as they attempt to navigate our highly complex, bureaucratic, technological modern world.

The Auxiliary Role of Broad Stratum II Abilities

The broad Stratum II abilities seem specific either to content domains, such as language and spatial perception, or to different aspects of mental processing, such as speed, storage, and retrieval. Some are associated with particular Brodmann areas in the brain and some to the neural networks connecting them. Certain domain-specific Stratum II abilities, especially spatial perception, add to the prediction of performance (beyond g) in corresponding content domains, such as the visual arts and hard sciences. Yet, unless samples are highly restricted in range on g (e.g., students at elite colleges or in graduate programs), g always carries the freight of prediction in broad test batteries when predictors and outcomes are assessed reliably and objectively. The extent to which Stratum II or I abilities predict performance is owed primarily to their g component.

How Is Intelligence Best Measured?

It depends on your purpose.

Professional Practice

When the stakes are high for an assessed individual, standards call for a professionally developed, individually administered test of intelligence such as (in the United States) the Wechsler, Stanford-Binet, or Woodcock-Johnson. High-stakes assessment includes diagnosing the cognitive status of individuals referred for forensic or clinical evaluation, determining eligibility of children and adults for services, helping design individualized education programs (IEPs) for eligible students, and recommending treatment for individuals with cognitive impairments. IQ tests may be required, but are rarely sufficient for such purposes.

Group-administered assessments of general intelligence are more feasible and efficient when screening large numbers of individuals for jobs and training programs, especially the more cognitively demanding ones. Examples in the United States include the SAT and ACT college entrance exams, the Armed Services Vocational Aptitude Test Battery (ASVAB) for selecting and placing military recruits, and the Wonderlic Personnel Test (WPT) for screening job applicants (and major league football players). All these tests correlate highly with *g*, so function like an IQ test for ranking applicants. Only the 12-minute Wonderlic, however, is ever referred to as a test of intelligence. Again, scores on these tests are seldom the only factor in accepting or rejecting applicants. Intelligence tests have been designed to discriminate best in the range of IQ 70–130, so other assessments are required to assess the intellectual capabilities of individuals at the two extremes. For example, the SAT (normally administered for college entrance) is effective for identifying extremely gifted children.

Research

Researchers may not be able to use these highly vetted tests of intelligence in their work, perhaps for lack of access, resources, or participant time. Or the datasets they acquire do not include any of them. But Arthur Jensen dramatically increased our options (Gottfredson, 1998) when he reintroduced the concept of *g* and, more importantly, the insight that tests themselves can be assessed for how well they capture individual differences in *g* (their *g* loadedness). When empirical and theoretical precision is essential, say, in determining the neural architecture of general intelligence, the measure should be highly g loaded or at least its g loading should be known.

Standardized tests of academic achievement provide a close surrogate for IQ tests among native speakers of the same age, as do the U. S. Department of Education's national assessments of adult functional literacy (Gottfredson, 1997b). Other social indicators do not measure g directly, but help us view it operating unobtrusively in different life domains. When they differ in g loading, those differences can be exploited to test competing hypotheses about g. To illustrate, if personal health depends more on informed self-care than on wealth, then group disparities in health should line up closest with the most g-loaded indicators of socioeconomic inequality (education level, then occupational status, then income), but in reverse order if the "wealth-is-health" hypothesis is true (it is not; Gottfredson, 2004).

How Is Intelligence Best Developed?

Intelligence is a maximal trait – what a person *can* do when circumstances are favorable. That is what IQ tests are intended to measure, one's best. Developing intelligence can refer to raising one's maximum, working to one's maximum to develop specific skills and knowledge, or protecting it from preventable decline (Gottfredson, 2008). I see no compelling evidence that any educational, brain training, nutritional, or pharmacological intervention has yet been able to raise a person's maximal level of intelligence (g), either absolutely or relative to others their age. The apparent increases produced by education and training programs either do not generalize or they fade away. Nutritional interventions have produced mental and physical growth, but only among individuals with a nutritional (e.g., vitamin) deficiency; it is termed "catch-up growth."

Fully Exploiting Maximal Capacity

Many, perhaps most, individuals routinely function below their maximum. Thinking is hard work. If my students are any guide, many have never experienced working to their maximum (except on standardized tests) so do not even know what they are capable of until pushed. Exploiting one's intelligence more fully is a form of developing it: taking greater advantage of one's existing capacities to learn and accomplish more. Like other forms of capital, human capital is wasted if not invested.

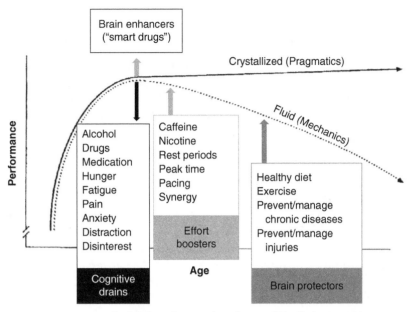

Figure 9.2   The fragility of maximal intelligence (Gottfredson, 2008).

The prospect of boosting maximal intelligence is enticing but remains remote. The closest we have come to smart pills are drugs that temporarily sustain effort and attention, such as Modafinil (for narcolepsy) or Ritalin (for attention deficit disorder). More widely used aids, listed in Figure 9.2, include caffeine and periodic rest periods. More consequential, in my view, are the many ways we unthinkingly squander the intellectual powers we already have. Alcohol, sleep deprivation, and distraction are some of the many ways we waste our available cognitive resources. They dull information processing.

Preventing Needless Decline in Maximal Capacity
Yet more insidious is our frequent failure to prevent needless cognitive damage and decline. Injury and chronic disease can damage the brain. Both are preventable with vigilance and effective self-care. Consider diabetes Type 2. It is epidemic but preventable, as are its debilitating complications. They include not just peripheral neuropathy, blindness, heart disease, and limb amputation, but also accelerated cognitive decline and increased risk of dementia.

What Are Some of the Most Interesting Empirical Results from Your
Own Research and Why Are They Important to the Field?

My most novel work examines the interplay between the structure of human abilities (Intelligence in Figure 9.1) and a society's structure and inner workings (Social Structure). This work was essential for creating a more comprehensive theory of *g*, one that ties together all levels of analysis.

How Did Human Populations Evolve such a Finely Graded,
g-ordered Hierarchy of Occupations?

When I got my PhD, sociologists had just developed a finely graded scale to quantify the standing of occupations according to perceived overall desirability or prestige. Not only did these ratings generalize across social groups in the United States, but across nations as well. The prestige of occupations correlates highly with their incumbents' mean levels of education, income, and IQ, as well as with U.S. Department of Labor ratings of work complexity. The occupational prestige scale provided a more tractable measure of occupational attainment than had broad categories of work (professional, semi-professional, and such). But no one asked how this astonishing regularity in human societies, or *social structure*, ever arose. Once upon a time there were only two occupations, hunter and gatherer.

If I was correct that the occupational hierarchy serves a functional purpose, not just the interests of a powerful elite, I needed to explain how it emerged from serving a society's needs. I also needed to answer reasonable objections, for instance, "If intelligence really is important on the job, why do years of education predict an individual's occupational level better than does IQ?"

Now, occupations are just recurring constellations of work tasks. They often split, disappear, or shift composition as technologies, industries, and cultures change. The evolution of these constellations is constrained, however, by a fixed feature of every society's labor pool: predictable, wide variation in *g*. My analyses of job attributes demonstrated that the core distinction among job demands (cognitive complexity, or *g* loadedness) mirrored the core distinction among human cognitive abilities (*g*). So, how might the constraints and opportunities created by recurring variation in *g* generate a cross-population *g*-ordered set of task constellations? The answer lay in the commonplace processes by which individuals become sorted, and sort themselves, to the different work tasks a society needs doing (Gottfredson, 1985).

When brighter individuals increasingly flow into a particular occupation, the tasks comprising it can re-assort, by *g* loading, to other jobs. We can observe in our own work settings how easier tasks migrate to easier jobs or less capable workers, while brighter workers are assigned or take on more cognitively demanding assignments. Thus do the two populations – occupations and workers – gradually align themselves along parallel continua: occupations by *g* loading and their incumbents by mean IQ/*g*. The hierarchy itself will expand or contract as workers become sorted more vs. less reliably by *g* to the occupational hierarchy. Other things obviously influence how occupations get structured and workers end up in them, but differences in *g* appear to be the most consistent factor. Stratum II abilities appear to distinguish among occupations only at the same cognitive level (Gottfredson, 1986).

What Makes Some Life Tasks and Outcomes More g Loaded than Others?
As noted earlier, the fact that IQ tests predict meaningful outcomes does not prove that whatever they measure actually caused those differences in outcomes. Moreover, IQ tests lack face validity; their items don't resemble anything familiar to the average person. Further, IQ scores are norm-referenced (calculated relative to a group average), so do not describe what people at different IQ levels can actually do in the real world. In this sense, mental test results are opaque, which limits their utility and fuels public doubt about what they really measure.

I did two things to enhance their interpretability. First, I collected what little information there was about individuals' trainability and life chances at different ranges of IQ in early adulthood. That information is summarized in the upper part of Figure 9.3. To explain this pattern, however, requires showing why *g* matters. So, second, I compiled data on jobs to see how the inherent demands of work might differ across tasks and jobs. What aspect of tasks would most strongly call forth the latent trait *g*, and to accomplish what?

Consider the definition of ability, as used to describe an attribute of individuals.

> [A]bility refers to the possible variations over individuals in the ... levels of task difficulty ... at which, on any given occasion in which all conditions appear favorable, individuals perform successfully on a *defined class of tasks*. (Carroll, 1993, p. 8, emphasis added)

Tasks define abilities. Task difficulty signifies ability level, that is, what a person *can* do. Carroll goes on to define *task* as an activity in which a

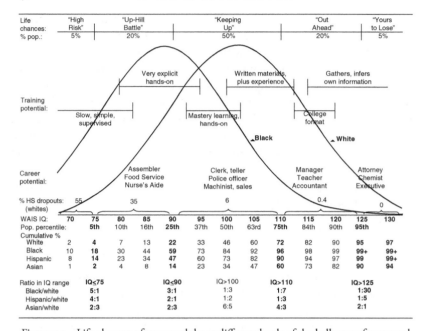

Figure 9.3   Life chances of young adults at different levels of the bell curve for general intelligence, by race (Gottfredson, 2005a, figure 18.2).
Adapted from Gottfredson (1997b, figure 3, p. 117) © Elsevier. Reproduced by permission of Elsevier. Permission to reuse must be obtained from the rights holder.

person engages to achieve specific objectives. It is purposeful work, be it using a map to reach a designated location or repairing a laptop.

Psychometricians, especially Arthur Jensen, had already pointed to the complexity of required information processing as the active ingredient, so to speak, in tests of intelligence. And so it is too in the world of work. As just noted, factor analyses of mental test scores revealed a general mental ability dimension, and factor analyses of job attributes demonstrated a corresponding distinction among jobs, namely, a complexity-of-work factor.

Factor loadings on the work complexity dimension indicate which particular mental processes and structural features of work contribute to a job's overall complexity. Starting with cognitive-processing tasks, loadings on the complexity dimension (essentially, their g loading) reflect the distinction between productive and reproductive thinking: higher for the importance of compiling (0.90), combining (0.88), and analyzing (0.83) information and lower for the importance of coding (0.68), transcribing

(0.51), remembering (0.40), and recognizing (0.36) it. Factor loadings of structural features reflected the importance of independent judgment and the ability to juggle more numerous and varied activities: importance of self-direction (0.88), lack of structure (0.77), lack of supervision (0.73), variety and change (0.41), and negatively with repetitive activities (-0.49; Gottfredson, 1997b).

Analyses of responses on national assessments of functional literacy also determined that item difficulty on scales of supposedly different constructs (Prose, Document, Quantitative, and Health literacies) rested on the same "processing complexity." At this item level of analysis, complexity is associated with more bits of information to integrate, more abstract concepts, more distant inferences, more irrelevant distracting information, and the need to select (not just implement) the correct arithmetic operation. Other findings reflected Spearman's "indifference of the indicator": neither the superficial content nor the readability (word length, sentence length) of task materials contributed to processing complexity. By design, literacy tests simulate everyday tasks, so have good face validity. Table 9.1 gives a gut-level feel for why differences in cognitive capacity matter in real life. I provide a specific example under Question 6.

How Could such a Highly General Information-Processing Ability, g, *Have Evolved so High so Fast in Pretechnological Human Groups?*
General intelligence varies widely within human populations, is dispersed throughout the brain, is a strictly cognitive tool, and has near-universal functional utility. Higher *g* is clearly an advantage for getting ahead and staying healthy in the modern world. But humans evolved their high intelligence in a pretechnological world of small, roving bands, and especially quickly (judging from skull size) beginning 500,000 years ago. No theory of *g* is complete without closing the circle in Figure 9.1, that is, without explaining both the accelerated rise in human intelligence and its sustained variation over the past half million years.

Evidence on *g* contradicted common hypotheses. *g* is strictly cognitive, which falsifies the social-brain hypothesis. The correlates of *g* are widely dispersed throughout the brain, which falsifies theories that intelligence evolved as a single module among many to meet specific adaptive challenges. Yet I struggled to find a plausible alternative. The problem lay in *g*'s most distinctive feature: its universal utility. Something in the human environment of evolutionary adaptation (EEA) had to be equally general and have consistently tilted the odds against less-bright individuals. What could that be?

Table 9.1 *Functional literacy of American adults, by age*

NALS difficulty level	Reading grade level*	%U.S. adults peaking at this level: Prose scale**				Simulated everyday tasks
		Age				Daily self-maintenance in modern literate societies
		16–59	60–69	70–79	80+	
5	16+	4	1	1	0	• Use calculator to determine cost of carpet for a room
4	16	20	8	5	1	• Use table of information to compare two credit cards • Use eligibility pamphlet to calculate SSI benefits • Explain difference between two types of employee benefits
3	12	35	27	19	6	• Calculate miles per gallon from mileage record chart • Write brief letter explaining error on credit card bill
2	7.2	25	33	22	27	• Determine difference in price between two show tickets • Locate intersection on street map
1	2.5	16	30	42	66	• Total bank deposit entry • Locate expiration date on driver's license

* Estimated by Carroll (1987).
** Results and sample items from the National Adult Literacy Survey (Kirsch, I. S., Jungeblut, Jenkins, & Kolstad 1993/2002). Literacy level reflects 80% probability of getting items at that level correct. The Prose, Document, and Quantitative scales on this assessment all correlate >0.9.

I finally realized that the tilt had to be tiny, inconspicuous, and typically affect one person at a time, because humans develop group defenses (such as food sharing) to protect individual members against obvious killers, like starvation. Studies of remaining (mostly) pretechnological human groups, such as the Ache of Paraguay, demonstrated a variety of such group defenses. I had already written about accident prevention being a quintessentially cognitive process (Gottfredson, 2004), and causes of death among the Ache illustrated the sometimes lethal consequences of cognitive error (not noticing poisonous snakes underfoot while hunting prey in the forest canopy, getting lost in the forest without a fire brand for cold nights).

Perhaps beginning with the invention of fire half a million years ago, human innovation began to generate evolutionarily novel hazards (risk of burns). Being novel, man-made hazards (such as falls from bridges, boats, and ladders; bites from domesticated animals) increased the relative risk of injury and death in the lower half of the intelligence distribution, as they still do worldwide. Ever more numerous and dangerous man-made hazards (weapons, poisons, vehicles) can explain humans' suddenly accelerated evolution of high intelligence. The mind's eye became ever more important to spot lurking hazards, imagine consequences, and avoid "accidents waiting to happen." All that evolution required to ratchet up our species' intelligence was for these novel hazards to increase the relative risk of crippling and fatal injuries among individuals of below-average ability, in turn resulting in them leaving relatively fewer genetic descendants behind (Gottfredson, 2007b).

The steady influx of man-made hazards into the human environment created a giant, increasingly g-loaded intelligence test administered to our species over hundreds of generations. No one type of accident or injury correlates noticeably with g. Each is like a barely g-loaded item on an IQ test. Non-g influences generally matter more in precipitating any particular event, but these non-g influences differ across events. However, g – using one's mind's eye to avoid injury – remains a consistent influence. When unintentional injuries are aggregated across all types of injury, over whole populations, and over long stretches of time, like adding items to a mental test, other influences on performance cancel out while the variance due to g grows. As the Spearman-Brown Prophecy Formula for test reliability tells us, even lightly g-loaded test items will, in sufficient number, create a highly g-loaded test when no other source of variance is as consistent as g.

What Do You See as the Most Important Educational or Social Policy
Issue Facing the Field of Intelligence Today?

Public reluctance to entertain human variation in *g*, and the misinforma-
tion and fallacies promulgated to enforce it.

I have written often about this social phenomenon and how it can dis-
tort policy, practice, and science (e.g., Gottfredson, 1994a, 2007a, 2009).
Persisting variation in *g* among a society's members creates the *democratic
dilemma* (Gottfredson, 1996c). Free and democratic societies cannot simultaneously satisfy two guiding principles that intelligence differences put in
conflict: equal opportunity and equal results. Politicians, academics, and
pundits tend to firmly deny any such conflict or trade-off, often by denying the variation itself.

Denying a Consequential Biological Fact Does More Harm than Good
Some argue that to openly acknowledge intelligence differences, especially
by race, would harm the body politic. They overlook the fact that denying
human variation in intelligence does nothing to neutralize its inexorable,
pervasive, observable effects in human affairs. Social policies and practices
that deny it often create more problems, rancor, and suspicion of institutional discrimination than they dispel. Despite good intentions and high
hopes, *g*-oblivious policies invariably disappoint and confound when *g*
actually matters. Worse, interventions that aim to reduce social disparities
in education and health usually increase them instead (Gottfredson, 2004).

Using Knowledge of g *to Predict Policies that Will Fail, and How*
The No Child Left Behind (NCLB) Act of 2001 exemplifies the waste
and futility of *g*-denying social policy, especially in public education. In
no other realm of public life is *g* so tightly linked to differences in performance. The NCLB required all public schools to make "adequate yearly
progress" in getting all their students (including disadvantaged and special
education students) leveled up by 2014 to the same state proficiency standards in reading and mathematics.

Data in the lower part of Figure 9.3 show why many schools were doomed
to fail unless they gamed the system, as many did. Racial groups differ in
their distribution of IQ. Based on their means and standard deviations in
IQ test standardization samples in the United States, I estimated that the
percentages of black, Hispanic, white, and Asian American students scoring below IQ 100 would be, respectively, 84, 73, 46, and 34. Group differences are even more striking at the two tails of the distribution.

Educationists had long argued that all students can learn equally well if their teachers are competent and their schools well funded. But now educators were protesting that some students are harder to teach than others. The states sought and the federal government began granting more waivers (may now exclude results of students in special education), learning opportunities withered for brighter students (whose good performance can widen performance gaps), schools creatively reclassified students (dropouts) to avoid reporting all low scores, and states dumbed down their proficiency tests to demonstrate progress in leveling up proficiency.

Spotting and Confronting the Use of Deceptive Science
There was tremendous political and legal pressure on employers in the 1980s and 1990s to use "nondiscriminatory" tests, meaning ones having no disparate impact (different pass rates by race or gender; Gottfredson & Sharf, 1988). Efforts to increase test reliability and validity had boomeranged because they tended to increase, not reduce, disparate impact by race by better measuring *g*. Adding personality tests to a selection battery hardly dented the disparate impact. The temptation to "psychomagic" grew.

Some selection professionals began advocating testing practices that reduced disparate impact by, in effect, reducing the reliability and validity of tests. The U.S. Employment Service (USES) began race-norming the General Aptitude Test Battery (GATB), which it used to refer better-qualified job applicants to employers. Race-norming calculates an individual's score relative to the average for his or her own race, which eliminates the normally large mean racial differences in test results. This in turn allowed USES to refer equal proportions of each race to participating employers. It had adopted the practice because setting different standards for different races did less damage to the validity of its referrals than being prohibited from using the test at all.

The National Research Council (NRC) created a blue-ribbon committee to assess the appropriateness of this practice. Although race-norming is an outright racial quota, the NRC committee gave a convoluted rationale for endorsing it in 1988 as "scientifically justified." Psychometrician Lloyd Humphreys described it in *Science* (1989, July 7, p. 14) as "statistical legerdemain."

In 1990, I received over-the-transom documents on the draft civil rights bill then under consideration in the U.S. Congress. The NRC's language had been slipped into the bill, which would have legally required employers to race-norm their selection tests. In addition, government agencies had already started threatening major companies if they failed to race-norm. Once these efforts to mandate race-norming were revealed (Blits & Gottfredson, 1990; Gottfredson, 1990, 1994b), Congress banned it instead. Now unable to race-norm the GATB, USES stopped using it.

Using Knowledge of g to Identify and Explain Successes too Good to Be True

No longer able to promote race-norming, the U.S. Department of Justice (DOJ) teamed up with nine eminent industrial-organizational psychologists to achieve the impossible: create a valid police selection test for Nassau County, NY, that had virtually no disparate impact – this despite the team documenting that police work is cognitively demanding. The DOJ immediately began forcing the team's "state-of-the-art," "innovative" test on police jurisdictions nationwide. I learned of the test only after receiving an author-blinded copy of the team's technical report, as did two other experts. Close examination of the foot-high report revealed that the test development team had dropped all subtests showing disparate impact *after* they had administered their large experimental battery to 25,000 applicants in Madison Square Garden.

This elite team had gerrymandered test battery content, post hoc, to eliminate all cognitive demands except reading above the first percentile (Gottfredson, 1996a, 1996b). Its technical report provided a labyrinth of questionable statistical procedures to claim, implausibly, that the new test was *more* valid than previous ones. But denuding a test of cognitive demands, ones actually experienced on the job, guts mental standards for all applicants. It leads to high rates of failure in training and subpar policing in all racial groups, as was observed.

DOJ scrapped the test in the ensuing scandal, but other consultants stood by eager to satisfy it.

What Are the Most Important Questions about Intelligence that Future Research on Intelligence Should Address?

If we take the journal *Intelligence* as our guide, basic research on intelligence falls mostly into two categories.

1. *Individual differences in phenotypic and genotypic intelligence:* for instance, how their expression changes from birth to old age; how both covary with observed individual differences in brain, cognitive processing, achievements, beliefs, attitudes, social behavior, cumulative life outcomes; and whether these relations generalize across all levels of *g* (Genes through Life Outcomes levels of analysis in Figure 9.1).

2. *Group differences in mean phenotypic intelligence (genetic differences by group are still taboo):* including, race and sex differences in the distribution and structure of intelligence; possible origins of intergenerational shifts in IQ scores (Flynn effect); how the mean IQ (or IQ surrogate) of geographic units (counties, states, nations) covaries with societal-level indicators of health, wealth, and social organization (Intelligence through Societal levels of analysis).

In contrast, virtually no intelligence research looks at how task environments activate this latent trait, *g*, to produce the observable differences in behavior that intelligence researchers study. Yet we cannot understand *g*'s remarkably pervasive and systemic, but varied, influence across the social landscape until we know how task environments are distributed, by complexity, across that landscape. Knowing the distribution of task environments by *g* also has practical value, especially as the distribution of *g*-loaded tasks shifts over time.

Modernity and technology have clearly made life more complex, even as they have made it better. The side effect, however, has been to put lower-*g* individuals at increasing disadvantage. For instance, treatment regimens for diabetes and other chronic diseases (now 7 of the 10 major causes of death in the United States) are becoming steadily more complex and hence more difficult for patients of all abilities levels to implement, but especially those in the lower reaches of IQ. Nonadherence to treatment is a huge problem. Patient errors are common, especially among low-literacy and older patients. Both groups have high rates of emergency room care and hospitalization.

Taking the sociological perspective, policy makers assume that "disparities" in health result from social inequality. Their solution is therefore to equalize financial, cultural, and physical access to medical care. As past experience and *g* theory predict, however, equalizing access to resources only increases the disparities it would eradicate. Disparities increase because higher-*g* individuals are better able to exploit newly available resources. This solution leaves less able individuals behind because it does nothing to increase their *cognitive* access of care.

Table 9.1 helps explain why cognitive access is crucial. It gives the percentage of adults who score at each of five levels of functional literacy, separately for four age groups. In health settings, Levels 1 and 2 are designated low literacy. The percentage of adults who can function no higher than Level 2 ranges from 41% at ages 16–59 to 93% among individuals age 80 and above. As Table 9.1 shows, these individuals cannot routinely perform tasks more difficult than "determine the difference in price between two show tickets" listed on a card. However, critical self-care tasks for patients with chronic diseases are often at Levels 3–5.

Consider diabetes self-management. The patient's job, all day every day, is to keep his or her blood glucose levels within safe limits and avoid health-damaging complications. This requires a lot of independent learning and judgment, planning and foresight, quickly spotting problems and taking corrective action, and adjusting self-care as circumstances change. All are attributes of complex occupations. And, worse, diabetes patients get little training, feedback, or supervision in performing this job.

Using insulin (or oral hypoglycemic) makes a patient's job even more complex. All patients with Type 1 diabetes must use insulin, and many with Type 2 do too as their condition worsens. Many need to adjust how much insulin they inject before each meal depending on the meal's carbohydrate content, their current blood glucose level, and the level of physical activity they anticipate. Insulin and oral hypoglycemics also make the patient's job more hazardous, because they form one of three classes of prescription medications with high rates of adverse drug events (the others being anticoagulants and opioids/benzodiazepines; U.S. Department of Health and Human Services, 2014). If patients miscalculate their insulin dose, administer it incorrectly, or fail to eat soon enough after they inject, they risk an insulin reaction (plunging blood glucose). Dangerously low blood glucose levels (severe hypoglycemia) can send patients to the emergency room or to their graves. This risk grows as age- and disease-related comorbidities, functional decline, and dysregulation of homeostatic mechanisms make self-care more difficult while reducing a patient's ability to self-manage.

It is not feasible, fair, or prudent to prescribe lower-ability and older patients such a complex, hazard-laden job. Error rates for individuals peaking at literacy Levels 1–2 range from 50% to 90% when carrying out tasks at complexity Levels 3–5 (Gottfredson & Stroh, 2016). Physicians are starting to recognize that treatment plans should be simplified and made safer for elderly patients and others at risk of adverse events (Mathur, Zammitt, & Frier, 2015; Munshi et al., 2016). Intelligence researchers can help healthcare providers accomplish this.

To illustrate, I am collaborating with certified diabetes educators and other health professionals to assay the complexity of self-care tasks and how they invite patient error among patients having low literacy or experiencing cognitive decline. We aim to develop two strategies. One, for paring back a patient's regimen to the tasks most essential for meeting his or her particular medical needs, while not overtaxing his or her functional capabilities. The second, for sequencing and pacing instruction to bring mastery of these tasks within the patient's cognitive reach.

Physicians and other healthcare professionals apparently receive no instruction in individual differences, so they tend to overestimate what less able individuals can do. They do not realize that what is obvious to them may not be obvious to their patients. Instruction must therefore assure that patients master basic facts (the meaning and relevance of carbohydrates, that "g" on a nutrition label means grams, that time-release pills work differently, not all "insulin" works the same way) before they are taught how to act on those facts: for instance, use a nutrition label to count grams of carbohydrate (*not* g of sugars or serving size), do not chew time-release pills, do not mix up your long- and short-acting insulins or use someone else's.

This is how *g* theory and research on task complexity can be used to improve health outcomes among our most vulnerable citizens and help contain the ballooning costs of health care. As Kurt Lewin (1943) said, there is nothing so practical as a good theory.

References

Blits, J. H., & Gottfredson, L. S. (1990). Employment testing and job performance. *The Public Interest*, Winter, 98, 18–25.

Carroll, J. B. (1987). The national assessments in reading: Are we misreading the findings? *Phi Delta Kappan*, 424–430.

(1993). *Human cognitive abilities: A factor-analytic study*. Cambridge: Cambridge University Press.

Gottfredson, L. S. (1985). Education as a valid but fallible signal of worker quality: Reorienting an old debate about the functional basis of the occupational hierarchy. In A. C. Kerckhoff (Ed.) *Research in sociology of education and socialization, Vol. 5* (pp. 119–165). Greenwich, CT: JAI Press.

(1986). Occupational aptitude patterns map: Development and implications for a theory of job aptitude requirements (Monograph). *Journal of Vocational Behavior*, 29, 254–291.

(1990, December 6). When job-testing "fairness" is nothing but a quota. *Wall Street Journal*, p. A18.

(1994a). Egalitarian fiction and collective fraud. *Society*, 31(3), 53–59.

(1994b). The science and politics of race-norming. *American Psychologist*, 49(11), 955–963.

(1996a). Racially gerrymandering the content of police tests to satisfy the U.S. Justice Department: A case study. *Psychology, Public Policy, and Law*, 2(3/4), 418–446.

(1996b, October 24). Racially gerrymandered police tests. *Wall Street Journal*, p. A16.

(1996c). What do we know about intelligence? *The American Scholar*, Winter, 15–30.

(1997a). Mainstream science on intelligence: An editorial with 52 signatories, history, and bibliography. *Intelligence*, 24(1), 13–23.

(1997b). Why g matters: The complexity of everyday life. *Intelligence*, 24(1), 79–132.

(1998). Jensen, Jensenism, and the sociology of intelligence. *Intelligence*, 26(3), 291–299.

(2004). Intelligence: Is it the epidemiologists' elusive "fundamental cause" of social class inequalities in health? *Journal of Personality and Social Psychology*, 86(1), 174–199.

(2005a). Implications of cognitive differences for schooling within diverse societies. In C. L. Frisby & C. R. Reynolds (Eds.) *Comprehensive handbook of multicultural school psychology* (pp. 517–554). New York: Wiley.

(2005b). Using Gottfredson's theory of circumscription and compromise in career guidance and counseling. In S. D. Brown & R. W. Lent (Eds.) *Career development and counseling: Putting theory and research to work* (pp. 71–100). New York: Wiley.

(2007a). Applying double standards to "divisive" ideas. *Perspectives on Psychological Science*, 2(2), 216–220.

(2007b). Innovation, fatal accidents, and the evolution of general intelligence. In M. J. Roberts (Ed.), *Integrating the mind: Domain general versus domain specific processes in higher cognition* (pp. 387–425). Hove, UK: Psychology Press.

(2008). The fragility of maximal performance. Presented at the conference, "How can we improve our brains?" The Banbury Center, Cold Spring Harbor, NY, September 16. Retrieved from www1.udel.edu/educ/gottfredson/reprints/2008fragility.pdf.

(2009). Logical fallacies used to dismiss the evidence on intelligence testing. In R. Phelps (Ed.), *Correcting fallacies about educational and psychological testing* (pp. 11–65). Washington, DC: American Psychological Association.

(2016). Hans Eysenck's theory of intelligence, and what it reveals about him. *Personality and Individual Differences*, 103, 116–127. doi:10.1016/j.paid.2016.04.036.

Gottfredson, L. S., & Sharf, J. C. (Eds.) (Special Issue) (1988). Fairness in employment testing. *Journal of Vocational Behavior*, 33 (3).

Gottfredson, L. S., & Stroh, K. (2016). How to select or create materials your patients will actually understand. Pre-conference workshop conducted at the annual meeting of the American Association of Diabetes Educators, San Diego, August 11.

Kirsch, I. S., Jungeblut, A., Jenkins, L., & Kolstad, A. (1993/2002). *Adult literacy in America: A first look at the findings of the National Adult Literacy Survey*. U.S. Department of Education, National Center for Education Statistics, Washington, DC. Retrieved from http://nces.ed.gov/pubs93/93275.pdf.

Lewin, K. (1943). Psychology and the process of group living. *Journal of Social Psychology*, 17, 113–131.

Mathur, S., Zammitt, N. N., & Frier, B. M. (2015). Optimal glycaemic control in elderly people with Type 2 diabetes: What does the evidence say? *Drug Safety*, 38, 17–32. doi:10.1007/s40264-014-0247-7.

Munshi, M. N., Slyne, C., Segal, A. R., Saul, N., Lyons, C., & Weinger, K. (2016). Simplification of insulin regimen in older adults and risk of hypoglycemia. *JAMA Internal Medicine*, 176(7), 1023–1025. doi:10.1001/jamainternmed.2016.2288.

U.S. Department of Health and Human Services. (2014). *National action plan for adverse drug event prevention*. Washington, DC: Office of Disease Prevention and Health Promotion. Retrieved from https://health.gov/hcq/pdfs/ade-action-plan-508c.pdf.

CHAPTER 10

Puzzled Intelligence
Looking for Missing Pieces

Elena L. Grigorenko

This chapter attempts to juxtapose the field of intelligence with the bour-geoning field of epigenetics, to shed light on their mutually beneficial potential cross-fertilization. To do so, I first briefly discuss two features of the concept and theories of intelligence that appear to be particularly suitable for this cross-fertilization; both concern the temporal dynamics of intelligence, as they are enacted both across developmental stages and within individuals. Then I briefly summarize the work of our laboratory that is embedded in the larger field of epigenetics to illustrate how epi-genetic processes might be the biological bases of the temporal features of intelligence. Finally, I acknowledge that our understanding of this poten-tial merger is only just being glimpsed and needs to be substantiated by empirical research.

Prelude: Is There Still Anything about Intelligence That We Do Not Know?

Were the role of the concept and its corresponding theories to be judged by the sheer number of both, intelligence and its theories would likely be within the 10 or so most investigated and most contested. Definitions of intelligence are numerous and often associated with different specific theo-ries of intelligence. Usually, researchers working in the field of intelligence (1) adopt an existing definition; (2) modify an existing definition to their liking; or (3) develop a new one. Here yet a different strategy is used: I highlight three facets of intelligence that are shared by most theories of intelligence and proceed with a general understanding, but not precise def-inition, of intelligence. So, however defined, the facets of intelligence that are relevant to this chapter are as follows. First, structurally, intelligence is complex; it is a system reflecting contributions of multiple cognitive pro-cesses, that changes its characteristics by adjusting the weights from these different processes as contextualized by different contexts (e.g., environments and tasks). Second, functionally, intelligence is dynamic; it demonstrates temporal dependence by exercising both stability and change on different time scales (e.g., years of development across the life span and minutes of engagement with a task). Third, etiologically, intelligence is a permutation of genetic and environmental contributions (e.g., a result of compound endogenous and exogenous causes, involved in reciprocal relationships). It is these three facets of intelligence, however defined, that are relevant to this discussion.

Two of these facets are directly relevant to the measurement of intelligence. Given the structural features of intelligence, it is clear that no single "measure" of any kind can do full justice to intelligence. Yet it does not mean that there are no good "measures" of intelligence; it just means that all "measures" of intelligence have limitations that should be considered when any particular one is used. To explain, as the first facet of intelligence assumes a dependence on context, it is clear that intelligence is shaped by such contextual factors as culture, language, religion, type of settlement (rural vs. urban), socioeconomic status, schooling, and so forth. This dependence poses the barrier of incomparability, as different items, subtests, and even tests can behave differently across different contexts. Similarly, as the second facet of intelligence assumes dependence on time, both linear and nonlinear, any "measure" of intelligence, as well as any interpretation of the results of that measurement, should be conditioned on this temporal dependence.

Interestingly, despite the vast number of relevant publications, there are multiple unresolved questions surrounding both the concept and the theories of intelligence. The two featured in this chapter are why intelligence varies across developmental stages and why it shows variability within an individual across different contexts. Regarding the former, across the life span, there is the rapid rise of intelligence from infancy through childhood and the slow fall during adulthood (McArdle et al., 2002). Regarding the latter, there is a remarkable amount of variation in the rank-order stability of an individual across development (Bayley, 1949): lacking in infancy, it stabilizes in middle childhood and plateaus by early adulthood (Larsen, Hartmann, & Nyborg, 2008). Both of these features have been studied extensively in the field of intelligence. There is a spectrum of views on the nature of the first feature, but the dominant concept today is plasticity in its brain-based correlates (Salthouse, 2011). Dominating the landscape of the literature addressing the second feature, that is, that of developmental continuity and change, is the balance between context- and genome-based hypotheses. As is rather obvious from the terms used, context-based theories of stability and change capitalize on the environment as the source of the repeated exposures shaping intelligence (Sameroff et al., 1993), whereas the genome-based hypotheses point to the genome as the source of the repeated action of its various products, which determine the specific characteristics of intelligence and their corresponding constraints (Dickens & Flynn, 2001). An excellent treatment of the dynamic tension between these two hypotheses has been recently offered by Tucker-Drob and Briley (2014), who concluded, perhaps not surprisingly, that stability is substantiated by both genetic and shared environment factors whose cross-time correlations are lower in early childhood and gain magnitude later in development.

This chapter capitalizes on work that has advanced the search for the answers to these questions. Rephrased, the questions are: (1) How does the apparently unstable and malleable intelligence system of a newborn grow into the stable intelligence system of a young adult which, in turn, when exercised (von Stumm & Ackerman, 2013) serves as a predictor of numerous life-span outcomes; and (2) how do individual differences in intelligence crystallize from a fluid (in early childhood) to stable (in early adulthood) intelligence-based rank-order. The ideas provided in what follows implicate the epigenome – a multitude of biochemical compounds that instruct the genome on what to do when – as the possible material substrate that may substantiate the dynamic characteristics of intelligence captured in these two questions.

Interlude: The Epigenome and How It Can Aid the Understanding of Intelligence

As the field of behavioral epigenomics – the study of the epigenome – is very new, there is no massive relevant literature to reference just yet. Whatever the literature is, our laboratory has contributed to it (Bick et al., 2012; Grigorenko, Kornilov, & Naumova, 2016; Naumova et al., 2012; Naumova, Dozier, et al., 2017; Naumova, Hein, et al., 2016; Naumova, Odintsova, et al., 2016; Naumova, Rychkov, et al., 2016; Thompson et al., 2013). The arguments that follow are based on our thinking as we continue to develop this line of our research, but they are rooted in basic, animal models and the current clinical literature on epigenetics.

Epigenetic variation (i.e., variation in the expression of the genome that cannot be attributed to the genome's structural variation) is generated via a variety of different mechanisms (Bird, 2007; Richards, 2006), one of which is DNA methylation (i.e., the attachment of a particular molecular structure to the DNA at a strategic location allowing for an epigenetic signaling mechanism used by cells to control gene expression). Epigenetic marks signify the local adaptations undergone by a genome structure in response to a stimulus in order to alter, facilitate, or stabilize the genome's activity state (Illingworth et al., 2015; Youngson & Whitelaw, 2008). Its importance for brain activity is illustrated by its essential role in normal brain development (Fan et al., 2001), its dysfunction in neurodevelopmental disorders such as Rett (Amir et al., 1999) and Fragile X (Verkerk et al., 1991) syndromes, and its involvement with a host of brain functions, ranging from general neuronal activity (Guo et al., 2011; Ma et al., 2009; Riccio, 2010) to specific actions of learning and memory (Day & Sweatt, 2010; Tong et al., 2015). Specifically, within the brain, DNA methylation is involved in the regulation of multiple aspects of neuronal development, function, and plasticity (Akbarian, Beeri, & Haroutunian, 2013; Feng, Fouse, & Fan, 2007; Ma et al., 2010; Meaney & Ferguson-Smith, 2010). It also has been demonstrated to be a key regulator of memory and learning (Day & Sweatt, 2010, 2011). Three features of DNA methylation make it a particularly interesting aspect of studying the bases of human learning in general and the development of intelligence in particular. First, DNA methylation patterns and their corresponding gene-expression programs can change on rapid timescales (minutes to hours) within the brain (Day et al., 2013; Guo et al., 2011; Kaas et al., 2013; Ma et al., 2009; C. A. Miller & Sweatt, 2007). Second, unique epigenetic profiles are thought to characterize specific cell types, cross-sectionally and developmentally, contributing to brain phenotypic (and therefore functional) divergence and specialization (Lister et al., 2013). Third, there is a small but growing literature on epigenetic pharmacology, that is, therapeutics targeting specific elements of the DNA methylation mechanisms (e.g., 5-methylcytocine), highlighting the possibility that dysfunction of the normal epigenetic status of the genome can have dramatic consequences for typical cognitive functioning, and that therapeutic correction of this dysfunction may have substantial treatment value (Coppieters et al., 2013; Sanchez-Mut et al., 2013).

The epigenome (or, if focusing only on DNA methylation, the methylome) is a source of individual differences that correlates with indicators of learning in general and intelligence in particular, both cross-sectionally and longitudinally. Etiologically, this variability has been correlated, through epigenome-wide studies, with environmental stimuli (Baccarelli et al., 2009; Bollati et al., 2007), diet, and medication use (Dominguez-Salas et al., 2014; Sinclair et al., 2007; Smith et al., 2012), psychosocial factors (Klengel et al., 2013; McGowan et al., 2009; Oberlander et al., 2008), and physiological changes (Barres et al., 2013; Guénard et al., 2013). Although it is well known that both DNA methylation and gene expression have partially stochastic kinetics (Elowitz et al., 2002; Raj & van Oudenaarden, 2008; Singer et al., 2014), there is growing evidence that changes in the methylome may be both comparatively stable and comparatively dynamic. Therefore, DNA methylation profiles may be indicative of past environmental and developmental circumstances (Horvath, 2013; Nestor et al., 2014) as well as of ongoing processes of learning. Metaphorically speaking, the epigenome in general and the methylome in particular play a dual role as historian of the past and fortune-teller of the future.

Two characteristics of the genome substantiate its role as a historian. The *epigenetic clock* is an indicator of DNA methylation age, DNAm (or the epigenetic age), which is viewed as an alternative biomarker of aging and is highly correlated with chronological age across a wide variety of tissues and cell types, including blood, brain, breast, kidney, liver, lung, saliva, and other tissues (Horvath, 2013). Derivable initially only for specific single tissues such as saliva (Bocklandt et al., 2011) or blood (Hannum et al., 2013), DNAm age can now be estimated by methods applicable to all human tissue and cell types that contain DNA, with the exception of sperm (Zannas & West, 2014). It can be estimated from sorted cell types, for example, neurons, glial cells, monocytes, helper T cells, cytotoxic T cells, and complex tissues, such as blood, brain, and saliva (Horvath et al., 2014; Horvath et al., 2015; Zannas & West, 2014). The utility of the epigenetic clock is substantiated by a growing number of studies that use this indicator for both forward and reverse prediction. In forward-prediction models, the older epigenetic age of blood is predictive of mortality (Christiansen et al., 2016; Marioni, Shah, McRae, Chen, et al., 2015), and younger epigenetic age relates to cognitive and physical fitness in the elderly (Marioni, Shah, McRae, Ritchie, et al., 2015). In reverse predictive models, accelerated epigenetic aging has been found to be associated with lifetime stress (Zannas et al., 2015), low SES (G. E. Miller et al., 2015), and psychological trauma (Boks et al., 2015). *Metastable epialleles* are alleles demonstrating variable expressivity in the absence of genetic heterogeneity (Rakyan et al., 2002) due to epigenetic modifications established during early development (Dolinoy et al., 2007). The term "epiallele" refers to their potential to maintain epigenetic marks transgenerationally (Morgan & Whitelaw, 2008; Youngson & Whitelaw, 2008); the term "metastable" refers to the labile nature of their epigenetic state, as their epigenetic patterning is subjected to only small disturbances, if at all, and is stable throughout development (Rakyan et al., 2002). There is growing evidence that epigenetic marks at metastable epialleles can be altered environmentally, for example, through gestational exposure to nutritional agents and other environmental factors (Waterland & Jirtle, 2003). The lability or dynamic nature of the epigenetic states of epialleles results in phenotypic mosaicism between cells (variegation) and also between individuals (variable expressivity). In other words, methylation patterns of specific epialleles is a source of variation that differentiates cells as well as individuals. At present, little is known about the frequency and/or the dynamics of gain/loss rates of epialleles. In fact, models of metastable epialleles remain controversial (Gluckman et al., 2009). Yet, there is a growing literature underscoring their importance, especially in the context of linking environmental exposures during gestation, prenatally, and postnatally to the development of disease in adulthood (Allred et al., 2001; Waterland & Jirtle, 2004). Moreover, there have been some simulation studies investigating whether inherited epigenetic changes can account for either missing heritability or missing causality (Slatkin, 2009), which are characteristic of complex behavior traits, including intelligence.

In addition to the literature referring to DNA methylation as a "molecular reflector of the past," there is a growing literature describing DNA methylation in the context of the nervous system as both receiving and exerting concurrent influences, triggered by behavior experiences (Clark & Nelson, 2015) and behavior change (Yu et al., 2015). Specifically, the past decade of studies of epigenetics/epigenomics has been marked by the emergence of a new field, *neuroepigenetics*, whose primary objective is to research the role of epigenetic mechanisms in general and DNA methylation in particular in learning and memory. Within neuroepigenetics, there is accumulating evidence stressing the future-oriented role of DNA methylation, namely, its role in the control of multiple types of neural plasticity crucial to memory formation (i.e., learning) – the enabling of memory, its maintenance and protection (Sweatt, 2016). Specifically, memory-enabling mechanisms are thought to be substantiated by epigenetic processes through either (a) manifesting the phenomenon of metaplasticity – that is, establishing within each cell a global threshold for local, synapse-specific types of plasticity (Sweatt, 2016); or (b) directly controlling the synapse-specific enhancement of the synaptic strength required for the initial establishment of the memory engram, that is, a hypothetical permanent change in the brain to substantiate memory (Levenson et al., 2006). Memory-maintaining mechanisms ascribe DNA methylation the role of an explicit and tenacious molecular constituent of the engram per se, such that DNA methylation is an essential holistic or componential process of information encoding at the molecular level in the neuron (Sweatt, 2016). Thus, to illustrate, it has been hypothesized that site-specific DNA methylation might contribute to synaptic tagging by identifying specific gene subregions that may trigger the construction of a specific splice variant to result in an alternative version of the gene being transcribed. This alternative transcript controls the production of the gene's specific RNA or protein and targets it to specific synapses or neuronal subregions (Sweatt, 2016). Finally, memory-protective roles of DNA methylation are directly related to the role of DNA methylation in controlling homeostatic synaptic scaling by means of regulating the cell-wide plasticity crucial for the stabilization of synaptic machinery over time and enabling memory storage (Guzman-Karlsson et al., 2014; Halder et al., 2016; C. A. Miller et al., 2010). Importantly, there is substantial evidence that memory formation (i.e., learning) is supported both by increased methylation at memory suppressor genes, that is, hypermethylation, and decreased methylation at memory promoting genes, that is, hypomethylation (Heyward & Sweatt, 2015). In general, although the specific role of DNA methylation in learning (especially human learning) is still an open question, there is a critical mass of animal-model and basic-science literature that allows the formulation of specific hypotheses concerning how transient changes in DNA methylation manifest themselves in altered neuronal function, and how they warrant plasticity and malleability.

Currently, there is no published human work substantiating the hypothesis that both across development and within individuals, fluctuations in intelligence can be attributed to individual differences in the epigenome in general and in the methylome in particular. We have carried out relevant preliminary work and established the presence of statistically significant associations between patterns of methylation in two genes, whose structural variation has been previously associated with variation in cognition: *COMT*, catechol-O-methyltransferase, one of numerous enzymes that degrade catecholamines, including dopamine, epinephrine, and norepinephrine; and *BDNF*, brain-derived neurotrophic factor, a protein that is a member of the neurotrophin family of growth factors.

Postlude: The Only Thing Left to Do

The realization that early-life environment, in particular, repeated exposure to specific environmental stimuli, including dietary, endocrinological, and pharmacological interventions (Gluckman et al., 2007; Lillycrop et al., 2005; Vickers et al., 2005), can cause measurable and stable changes in the epigenome that contribute to and parallel human learning, in general, and maturation in intelligence, in particular, has numerous implications. First, although structural genomic information has added little to the field's understanding of the source of individual differences in intelligence, epigenetic markers such as DNA methylation throughout the genome or at particular locations in the genome (e.g., specific gene promoters) may prove much more useful. Second, epigenetic modifiability itself might be an indicator of behavior modifiability and/or skill acquisition.

How does the assumption that the epigenome correlates with intelligence translate into efforts pertaining to the enhancement of the development of intelligence? In an ideal world, it would be important to try to align and maximize all factors that are known to be influential for the emergence of a "healthy" epigenome, assuming that it will result in the maximized development of intelligence. As these factors are many and their nature is probabilistic, this maximization is based on an equation (or a system of equations). The first term of this equation requires arranging for an optimized nutritional environment at conception, so that the mother is adequately nourished at conception, throughout the pregnancy, and during breastfeeding. The second term calls for the optimization of the stress environment for the mother (and the father) from conception throughout early childhood. The third term focuses on the family, indicating the importance, to a degree, of the variation in SES. This variation is not linear and can be viewed as a threshold function. The fourth, fifth, and six terms are focused on the child. These are nutrition, safety and attachment, and developmentally appropriate stimulation. The seventh is adequate schooling. And the eighth is repeated investment by a self-regulated adult in intellectual activities. From the point of view of social policy, generating a "healthy epigenome" will mean eliminating poverty and abuse and strengthening development opportunities, first and foremost, for lifelong learning.

The only thing left to do is to actually demonstrate that there are associations between intelligence and the epigenome, both concurrently and longitudinally. And this is what the field should attempt to do. This is its important challenge, which has the potential to contribute to the understanding of the biological bases of dynamic features of intelligence and, perhaps, even find the missing pieces of the heritability dilemma in intelligence.

Author Note

The work on this chapter was supported by the U.S. National Institutes of Health grant P50 HD5212 (to R. Wagner) and the Government of the Russian Federation grant 14.Z50.31.0027 (to the author). Grantees undertaking such projects are encouraged to freely express their professional judgment. Therefore, this chapter does not necessarily reflect the position or policies of the aforementioned agencies, and no official endorsement should be inferred. The author is grateful to Ms. Mei Tan for her editorial assistance.

References

Akbarian, S., Beeri, M., & Haroutunian, V. (2013). Epigenetic determinants of healthy and diseased brain aging and cognition. *JAMA Neurology*, 70, 711–718. doi:10.1001/jamaneurol.2013.1459

Allred, C. D., Allred, K. F., Ju, Y. H., Virant, S. M., & Helferich, W. G. (2001). Soy diets containing varying amounts of genistein stimulate growth of estrogen-dependent (MCF-7) tumors in a dose-dependent manner. *Cancer Res*, 61, 5045–5050.

Amir, R. E., Van den Veyver, I. B., Wan, M., Tran, C. Q., Francke, U., & Zoghbi, H. Y. (1999). Rett syndrome is caused by mutations in X-linked MECP2, encoding methyl-CpG-binding protein 2. *Nature Genetics*, 23, 185–188.

Baccarelli, A., Wright, R. O., Bollati, V., Tarantini, L., Litonjua, A. A., Suh, H. H., & et al. (2009). Rapid DNA methylation changes after exposure to traffic particles. *Am J Respir Crit Care Med*, 179, 572–578. doi:10.1164/rccm.200807-1097OC PMID: 19136372

Barres, R., Kirchner, H., Rasmussen, M., Yan, J., Kantor, F. R., Krook, A., & et al. (2013). Weight loss after gastric bypass surgery in human obesity remodels promoter methylation. *Cell Rep*, 3, 1020–1027. doi:10.1016/j.celrep.2013.03.018 PMID: 23583180

Bayley, N. (1949). Consistency and variability in the growth of intelligence from birth to eighteen years. *The Pedagogical Seminary and Journal of Genetic Psychology*, 75, 165–196. doi:10.1080/08856559.1949.10533516

Bick, J., Naumova, O. Y., Hunter, S., Barbot, B., Lee, M., Luthar, S. S., … Grigorenko, E. L. (2012). Childhood adversity and DNA methylation of genes involved in the hypothalamus–pituitary–adrenal axis and immune system: Whole-genome and candidate-gene associations. *Development and Psychopathology*, 24, 1417–1425. doi:10.1017/S0954579412000806

Bird, A. P. (2007). Perceptions of epigenetics. *Nature*, 447, 396–398.

Bocklandt, S., Lin, W., Sehl, M. E., Sánchez, F. J., Sinsheimer, J. S., Horvath, S., & Vilain, E. (2011). Epigenetic predictor of age. *PLoS One*, 6, e14821. doi:10.1371/journal.pone.0014821

Boks, M. P., Mierlo, H. C. v., Rutten, B. P. F., Radstake, T. R. D. J., De Witte, L., Geuze, E., ... Vermetten, E. (2015). Longitudinal changes of telomere length and epigenetic age related to traumatic stress and post-traumatic stress disorder. *Psychoneuroendocrinology,* 51, 506–512. doi:http://dx.doi.org/10.1016/j.psyneuen.2014.07.011

Bollati, V., Baccarelli, A., Hou, L., Bonzini, M., Fustinoni, S., Cavallo, D., & et al. (2007). Changes in DNA methylation patterns in subjects exposed to low-dose benzene. *Cancer Res,* 876–880. doi:PMID:17283117

Christiansen, L., Lenart, A., Tan, Q., Vaupel, J. W., Aviv, A., McGue, M., & Christensen, K. (2016). DNA methylation age is associated with mortality in a longitudinal Danish twin study. *Aging Cell,* 15, 149–154. doi:10.1111/acel.12421

Clark, E. A., & Nelson, S. B. (2015). Synapse and genome: An elusive tête-à-tête. *Science Signaling,* 8, pe2. doi:10.1126/scisignal.aad2441

Coppieters, N., Dieriks, B. V., Lill, C., Faull, R. L. M., Curtis, M. A., & Dragunow, M. (2013). Global changes in DNA methylation and hydroxymethylation in Alzheimer's disease human brain. *Neurobiology of Aging,* 35, 1334–1344.

Day, J. J., Childs, D., Guzman-Karlsson, M. C., Kibe, M., & Moulden, J. (2013). DNA methylation regulates associative reward learning. *Nature Neuroscience,* 16, 1445–1452.

Day, J. J., & Sweatt, J. D. (2010). DNA methylation and memory formation. *Nature Neuroscience,* 13, 1319.

(2011). Epigenetic mechanisms in cognition. *Neuron,* 70, 813–829.

Dickens, W. T., & Flynn, J. R. (2001). Heritability estimates versus large environmental effects: The IQ paradox resolved. *Psychological Review,* 108, 346–369. doi:10.1037/0033-295X.108.2.346

Dolinoy, D. C., Das, R., Weidman, J. R., & Jirtle, R. L. (2007). Metastable epialleles, imprinting, and the fetal origins of adult diseases. *Pediatric Research,* 61, 30R–37R.

Dominguez-Salas, P., Moore, S. E., Baker, M. S., Bergen, A. W., Cox, S. E., Dyer, R. A., ... Hennig, B. J. (2014). Maternal nutrition at conception modulates DNA methylation of human metastable epialleles. *Nature Communications,* 5, 3746. doi:10.1038/ncomms4746 www.nature.com/articles/ncomms4746#supplementary-information

Elowitz, M. B., Levine, A. J., Siggia, E. D., & Swain, P. S. (2002). Stochastic gene expression in a single cell. *Science,* 297, 1183–1186. doi:PMID: 12183631

Fan, G., Beard, C., Chen, R. Z., Csankovszki, G., Sun, Y., Siniaia, M., ... Jaenisch, R. (2001). DNA hypomethylation perturbs the function and survival of CNS neurons in postnatal animals. *Journal of Neuroscience,* 21, 788–797.

Feng, J., Fouse, S. D., & Fan, G. (2007). Epigenetic regulation of neural gene expression and neuronal function. *Pediatric Research,* 61, 58R–63R.

Gluckman, P. D., Hanson, M. A., Buklijas, T., Low, F. M., & Beedle, A. S. (2009). Epigenetic mechanisms that underpin metabolic and cardiovascular diseases. *Nature Reviews Endocrinology,* 5, 401–408.

Gluckman, P. D., Lillycrop, K. A., Vickers, M. H., Pleasants, A. B., Phillips, E. S., Beedle, A. S., … Hanson, M. A. (2007). Metabolic plasticity during mammalian development is directionally dependent on early nutritional status. *Proceedings of the National Academy of Sciences of the United States of America*, 104, 12796–12800. doi:10.1073/pnas.0705667104

Grigorenko, E. L., Kornilov, S. A., & Naumova, O. Y. (2016). Epigenetic regulation of cognition: A circumscribed review of the field. *Development and Psychopathology*. doi:10.1017/S0954579416000857

Guénard, F., Deshaies, Y., Cianflone, K., Kral, J. G., Marceau, P., & Vohl, M.-C. (2013). Differential methylation in glucoregulatory genes of offspring born before vs. after maternal gastrointestinal bypass surgery. *Proceedings of the National Academy of Sciences*, 110, 11439–11444. doi:10.1073/pnas.1216959110

Guo, J. U., Ma, D. K., Mo, H., Ball, M. P., & Jang, M. H. (2011). Neuronal activity modifies the DNA methylation landscape in the adult brain. *Nature Neuroscience*, 14, 1345–1351.

Guzman-Karlsson, M. C., Meadows, J. P., Gavin, C. F., Hablitz, J. J., & Sweatt, J. D. (2014). Transcriptional and epigenetic regulation of Hebbian and non-Hebbian plasticity. *Neuropharmacology*, 80, 3–17. doi:http://dx.doi.org/10.1016/j.neuropharm.2014.01.001

Halder, R., Hennion, M., Vidal, R. O., Shomroni, O., Rahman, R.-U., Rajput, A., … Bonn, S. (2016). DNA methylation changes in plasticity genes accompany the formation and maintenance of memory. *Nature Neuroscience*, 19, 102–110. doi:10.1038/nn.4194 www.nature.com/neuro/journal/v19/n1/abs/nn.4194.html#supplementary-information

Hannum, G., Guinney, J., Zhao, L., Zhang, L., Hughes, G., Sadda, S., … Zhang, K. (2013). Genome-wide methylation profiles reveal quantitative views of human aging rates. *Molecular Cell*, 49, 359–367. doi:http://dx.doi.org/10.1016/j.molcel.2012.10.016

Heyward, F. D., & Sweatt, J. D. (2015). DNA methylation in memory formation: Emerging insights. *The Neuroscientist*. doi:10.1177/1073858415579635

Horvath, S. (2013). DNA methylation age of human tissues and cell types. *Genome Biology*, 14, R115. doi:10.1186/gb-2013-14-10-r115

Horvath, S., Erhart, W., Brosch, M., Ammerpohl, O., von Schönfels, W., Ahrens, M., … Hampe, J. (2014). Obesity accelerates epigenetic aging of human liver. *Proceedings of the National Academy of Sciences of the United States of America*, 111, 15538–15543. doi:10.1073/pnas.1412759111

Horvath, S., Mah, V., Lu, A. T., Woo, J. S., Choi, O.-W., Jasinska, A. J., … Coles, L. S. (2015). The cerebellum ages slowly according to the epigenetic clock. *Aging*, 7, 294–306.

Illingworth, R. S., Gruenewald-Schneider, U., De Sousa, D., Webb, S., Merusi, C., Kerr, A. R. W., … Bird, A. P. (2015). Inter-individual variability contrasts with regional homogeneity in the human brain DNA methylome. *Nucleic Acids Research*, 43, 732–744. doi:10.1093/nar/gku1305

Kaas, G. A., Zhong, C., Eason, D. E., Ross, D. L., Vachhani, R. V., Ming, G. L., … Sweatt, J. D. (2013). TET1 controls CNS 5-methylcytosine hydroxylation, active DNA demethylation, gene transcription, and memory formation. *Neuron, 79*, 1086–1093.

Klengel, T., Mehta, D., Anacker, C., Rex-Haffner, M., Pruessner, J. C., Pariante, C. M., & et al. (2013). Allele-specific FKBP5 DNA demethylation mediates gene-childhood trauma interactions. *Nature Neuroscience, 16*, 33–41. doi:10.1038/nn.3275 PMID: 23201972

Larsen, L., Hartmann, P., & Nyborg, H. (2008). The stability of general intelligence from early adulthood to middle-age. *Intelligence, 36*, 29–34. doi:http://dx.doi.org/10.1016/j.intell.2007.01.001

Levenson, J. M., Roth, T. L., Lubin, F. D., Miller, C. A., Huang, I.-C., Desai, P., ... Sweatt, J. D. (2006). Evidence that DNA (Cytosine-5) methyltransferase regulates synaptic plasticity in the hippocampus. *Journal of Biological Chemistry, 281*, 15763–15773. doi:10.1074/jbc.M511767200

Lillycrop, K. A., Phillips, E. S., Jackson, A. A., Hanson, M. A., & Burdge, G. C. (2005). Dietary protein restriction of pregnant rats induces and folic acid supplementation prevents epigenetic modification of hepatic gene expression in the offspring. *The Journal of Nutrition, 135*, 1382–1386.

Lister, R., Mukamel, E. A., Nery, J. R., Urich, M., Puddifoot, C. A., Johnson, N. D., ... Ecker, J. R. (2013). Global epigenomic reconfiguration during mammalian brain development. *Science, 341*, 629. doi:10.1126/science.1237905

Ma, D. K., Jang, M.-H., Guo, J. U., Kitabatake, Y., Chang, M.-l., Pow-anpongkul, N., ... Song, H. (2009). Neuronal activity–induced Gadd45b promotes epigenetic DNA demethylation and adult neurogenesis. *Science, 323*, 1074–1077. doi:10.1126/science.1166859

Ma, D. K., Marchetto, M. C., Guo, J. U., Ming, G. L., Gage, F. H., & Song, H. (2010). Epigenetic choreographers of neurogenesis in the adult mammalian brain. *Nature Neuroscience, 13*, 1338–1344.

Marioni, R. E., Shah, S., McRae, A. F., Chen, B. H., Colicino, E., Harris, S. E., ... Deary, I. J. (2015). DNA methylation age of blood predicts all-cause mortality in later life. *Genome Biology, 16*, 25. doi:10.1186/s13059-015-0584-6

Marioni, R. E., Shah, S., McRae, A. F., Ritchie, S. J., Muniz-Terrera, G., Harris, S. E., ... Deary, I. J. (2015). The epigenetic clock is correlated with physical and cognitive fitness in the Lothian Birth Cohort 1936. *International Journal of Epidemiology, 44*, 1388–1396. doi:10.1093/ije/dyu277

McArdle, J. J., Ferrer-Caja, E., Hamagami, F., & Woodcock, R. W. (2002). Comparative longitudinal structural analyses of the growth and decline of multiple intellectual abilities over the life span. *Developmental Psychology, 38*, 115–142. doi:10.1037/0012-1649.38.1.115

McGowan, P. O., Sasaki, A., D'Alessio, A. C., Dymov, S., Labonte, B., Szyf, M., ... Meaney, M. J. (2009). Epigenetic regulation of the glucocorticoid receptor in human brain associates with childhood abuse. *Nature Neuroscience, 12*, 342–348.

Meaney, M. J., & Ferguson-Smith, A. C. (2010). Epigenetic regulation of the neural transcriptome: The meaning of the marks. *Nature Neuroscience, 13*, 1313–1318.

Miller, C. A., Gavin, C. F., White, J. A., Parrish, R. R., Honasoge, A., Yancey, C. R., ... Sweatt, J. D. (2010). Cortical DNA methylation maintains remote memory. *Nature Neuroscience*, 13, 664–666. doi:10.1038/nn.2560

Miller, C. A., & Sweatt, J. D. (2007). Covalent modification of DNA regulates memory formation. *Neuron*, 53, 857–869. doi:http://dx.doi.org/10.1016/j.neuron.2007.02.022

Miller, G. E., Yu, T., Chen, E., & Brody, G. H. (2015). Self-control forecasts better psychosocial outcomes but faster epigenetic aging in low-SES youth. *Proceedings of the National Academy of Sciences*, 112, 10325–10330. doi:10.1073/pnas.1505063112

Morgan, D. K., & Whitelaw, E. (2008). The case for transgenerational epigenetic inheritance in humans. *Mammalian Genome*, 19, 394–397.

Naumova, O. Yu, Dozier, M., Dobrynin, P. V., Grigorev, K., Wallin, A., Jeltova, I., Lee, M., Raefski, A., & Grigorenko, E. L. (2017). *Developmental Dynamics of the Epigenome: a Longitudinal Study of Three Toddlers*. Neurotoxicology and Teratology.

Naumova, O. Y., Hein, S., Suderman, M., Barbot, B., Lee, M., Raefski, A., ... Grigorenko, E. L. (2016). Epigenetic patterns modulate the connection between developmental dynamics of parenting and offspring psychosocial adjustment. *Child Development*, 87, 98–110. doi: 10.1111/cdev.12485

Naumova, O. Y., Lee, M., Koposov, R., Szyf, M., Dozier, M., & Grigorenko, E. L. (2012). Differential patterns of whole-genome DNA methylation in institutionalized children and children raised by their biological parents. *Development and Psychopathology*, 24, 143–155.

Naumova, O. Y., Odintsova, V., Arinzina, I., Muhamedrahimov, R., Grigorenko, E. L., & Tsvetkova, L. (2016). Health, development and epigenetic characteristics of institutionalized children: A preliminary study based on a small cohort. *Procedia Social and Behavioral Sciences*, 233, 225–230. DOI:10.1016/j.sbspro.2016.10.208

Naumova, O. Y., Rychkov, S., Odintsova, V., V., K. T., Shabalina, K., Antziferova, D., ... L., G. E. (2016). *DNA methylation alterations in Down Syndrome*.

Nestor, C. E., Barrenas, F., Wang, H., Lentini, A., Zhang, H., Bruhn, S., & et al. (2014). DNA methylation changes separate allergic patients from healthy controls and may reflect altered CD4(+) T-cell population structure. *Plos Genetics*, 10, e1004059. doi:10.1371/journal.pgen.1004059 PMID: 24391521

Oberlander, T. F., Weinberg, J., Papsdorf, M., Grunau, R., Misri, S., & Devlin, A. M. (2008). Prenatal exposure to maternal depression, neonatal methylation of human glucocorticoid receptor gene (NR3C1) and infant cortisol stress responses. *Epigenetics*, 2, 97–106.

Raj, A., & van Oudenaarden, A. (2008). Nature, nurture, or chance: Stochastic gene expression and its consequences. *Cell*, 135, 216–226. doi:10.1016/j.cell.2008.09.050 PMID: 18957198

Rakyan, V. K., Blewitt, M. E., Druker, R., Preis, J. I., & Whitelaw, E. (2002). Metastable epialleles in mammals. *Trends in Genetics*, 18, 348–351. doi:http://dx.doi.org/10.1016/S0168-9525(02)02709-9

Riccio, A. (2010). Dynamic epigenetic regulation in neurons: enzymes, stimuli and signaling pathways. *Nature Neuroscience*, 13, 1330–1337.

Richards, E. J. (2006). Inherited epigenetic variation – revisiting soft inheritance. *Nature Review Genetics*, 7, 395–401.

Salthouse, T. A. (2011). Neuroanatomical substrates of age-related cognitive decline. *Psychological Bulletin*, 137, 753–784.

Sameroff, A. J., Seifer, R., Baldwin, A., & Baldwin, C. (1993). Stability of intelligence from preschool to adolescence: The influence of social and family risk factors. *Child Development*, 64, 80–97. doi:10.2307/1131438

Sanchez-Mut, J. V., Aso, E., Panayotis, N., Lott, I., & Dierssen, M. (2013). DNA methylation map of mouse and human brain identifies target genes in Alzheimer's disease. *Brain: A Journal of Neurology*, 136, 3018–3027.

Sinclair, K. D., Allegrucci, C., Singh, R., Gardner, D. S., Sebastian, S., Bispham, J., & et al. (2007). DNA methylation, insulin resistance, and blood pressure in offspring determined by maternal periconceptional B vitamin and methionine status. *Proceedings of the National Academy of Sciences*, 104, 19351–19356. doi:18042717

Singer, Z. S., Yong, J., Tischler, J., Hackett, J. A., Altinok, A., Surani, M. A., & al., e. (2014). Dynamic heterogeneity and DNA methylation in embryonic stem cells. *Mol Cell.*, 55, 319–331. doi:10.1016/j.molcel.2014.06.029 PMID: 25038413

Slatkin, M. (2009). Epigenetic inheritance and the missing heritability problem. *Genetics*, 182, 845–850. doi:10.1534/genetics.109.102798

Smith, A. K., Conneely, K. N., Newport, D. J., Kilaru, V., Schroeder, J. W., Pennell, P. B., et al. (2012). Prenatal antiepileptic exposure associates with neonatal DNA methylation differences. *Epigenetics*, 7, 458–463. doi:10.4161/epi.19617 PMID: 22419127

Sweatt, J. D. (2016). Dynamic DNA methylation controls glutamate receptor trafficking and synaptic scaling. *Journal of Neurochemistry*, 137, 312–330. doi:10.1111/jnc.13564

Thompson, T. M., Sharfi, D., Lee, M., Yrigollen, C. M., Naumova, O. Y., & Grigorenko, E. L. (2013). Comparison of whole-genome DNA methylation patterns in whole blood, saliva, and lymphoblastoid cell lines. *Behavior Genetics*, 43, 168–176. doi:10.1007/s10519-012-9579-1

Tong, Z., Han, C., Qiang, M., Wang, W., Lv, J., Zhang, S., ... He, R. (2015). Age-related formaldehyde interferes with DNA methyltransferase function, causing memory loss in Alzheimer's disease. *Neurobiology of Aging*, 36, 100–110. doi:http://dx.doi.org/10.1016/j.neurobiolaging.2014.07.018

Tucker-Drob, E. M., & Briley, D. A. (2014). Continuity of genetic and environmental influences on cognition across the life span: A meta-analysis of longitudinal twin and adoption studies. *Psychological Bulletin*, 140, 949–979.

Verkerk, A. J. M. H., Pieretti, M., Sutcliffe, J. S., Fu, Y.-H., Kuhl, D. P. A., Pizzuti, A., ... Warren, S. T. (1991). Identification of a gene (FMR-1) containing a CGG repeat coincident with a breakpoint cluster region exhibiting length variation in fragile X syndrome. *Cell*, 65, 905–914. doi:http://dx.doi.org/10.1016/0092-8674(91)90397-H

Vickers, M. H., Gluckman, P. D., Coveny, A. H., Hofman, P. L., Cutfield, W. S., Gertler, A., ... Harris, M. (2005). Neonatal leptin treatment reverses developmental programming. *Endocrinology*, 146, 4211–4216. doi:doi:10.1210/en.2005-0581

Von Stumm, S., & Ackerman, P. L. (2013). Investment and intellect: A review and meta-analysis. *Psychological Bulletin*, 139, 841–869.

Waterland, R. A., & Jirtle, R. L. (2003). Transposable elements: Targets for early nutritional effects on epigenetic gene regulation. *Mol Cell Biol*, 23, 5293–5300.

(2004). Early nutrition, epigenetic changes at transposons and imprinted genes, and enhanced susceptibility to adult chronic diseases. *Nutrition*, 20, 63–68.

Youngson, N. A., & Whitelaw, E. (2008). Transgenerational epigenetic effects. *Annual Review of Genetics*, 9, 233–257.

Yu, H., Su, Y., Shin, J., Zhong, C., Guo, J. U., Weng, Y.-L., ... Song, H. (2015). Tet3 regulates synaptic transmission and homeostatic plasticity via DNA oxidation and repair. *Nature Neuroscience*, 18, 836–843. doi:10.1038/nn.4008

Zannas, A. S., Arloth, J., Carrillo-Roa, T., Iurato, S., Röh, S., Ressler, K. J., ... Mehta, D. (2015). Lifetime stress accelerates epigenetic aging in an urban, African American cohort: Relevance of glucocorticoid signaling. *Genome Biology*, 16(1), 266. doi:10.1186/s13059-015-0828-5

Zannas, A. S., & West, A. E. (2014). Epigenetics and the regulation of stress vulnerability and resilience. *Neuroscience*, 264(0), 157–170. doi:http://dx.doi.org/10.1016/j.neuroscience.2013.12.003

CHAPTER 11

A View from the Brain

Richard J. Haier

Primitive Beginnings

When I was in graduate school between 1971 and 1975, few researchers interested in the nature of human intelligence were studying the brain. There was no neuroimaging as we know it today. At that time the primary technology for making measurements of the brain was the electroencephalogram (EEG). Early EEG brain-wave characteristics were correlated to IQ tests and other tests of mental ability, but these techniques did not interest most psychologists. There were two basic reasons for this. First, the technology was arcane to most psychologists. Moreover, different EEG research groups used different methods with no agreement on standard procedures. Not surprisingly, replication of EEG findings was limited, especially with respect to correlates of mental test scores. Second, the predominant view about intelligence was based on the Blank Slate idea that environmental stimuli and conditions determined individual differences in mental abilities, including reasoning and problem solving, especially during child development. This belief caused many researchers to favor investigations of environmental correlates of intelligence test scores rather than brain correlates derived from underappreciated and non-standardized EEG technology.

But a third, darker factor was keeping brain research at arm's length. By the early 1970s, there was intense debate about the origins of average IQ score differences among racial groups. This debate had been brought to a head in 1969 with a publication by Berkeley Professor Arthur Jensen entitled, "How much can we boost IQ and scholastic achievement?" This article, perhaps the most infamous in psychology, detailed the failure of compensatory-education programs to reduce achievements gaps between African American and Caucasian students (Jensen, 1969). The article questioned why such environmental interventions had no appreciable effect on mental test scores. It suggested a partial reason might be that intelligence has a strong genetic component. This suggestion was met with fierce opposition. The intense emotions around this issue still permeate perceptions of intelligence research. In fact, for nearly four decades after the publication of this article, research on intelligence became largely un-fundable and a blind alley for academic advancement.

Contributing to the inability to resolve this controversy with additional research was the simple fact that measuring intelligence depended on psychometric tests. Despite the fact that such tests predict academic and life success better than any other single variable (Deary, Penke, & Johnson, 2010; Gottfredson, 1997; Hunt, 2011), although hardly perfectly, they have a fundamental limitation. IQ and other mental test scores have meaning only in relation to other people (Haier, 2014). These scores are not like units of distance or weight. The test scores are on an *interval scale*, not a *ratio scale*. Ten feet is literally twice as long as 5 feet and an object weighing 20 pounds is twice as heavy as an object weighing 10 pounds. Standard measures of feet and pounds have little error variance of measurement. This is not the case for mental test scores. An IQ point is not the same as a unit of distance or weight. A person with an IQ of 140 is not literally twice as smart as a person with an IQ of 70. It is really the rank order of people on an IQ test that predicts academic and life success. This is why IQ scores are best discussed as percentiles assuming a normal distribution. In short, we have no measure of intelligence comparable to a unit of distance or weight. This is an inherent limitation for all studies of intelligence, but it is not a fatal limitation, as a vast number of reliability and validity studies show (Hunt, 2011; Jensen, 1998). Nonetheless, the uncertainties and complexities of psychometric measurement provided fuel for debates about the scientific meaning of intelligence test scores.

Similarly, the definition of intelligence varies, although the most common feature of definitions used by researchers is that intelligence involves a *general* ability common to most if not all mental tests. This common factor was first described by Spearman in the early 1900s as the *g*-factor (Spearman, 1904). Most intelligence researchers agree that *g* is a good estimate of general intelligence, but not all researchers agree that it is the most important factor (Gardner, 1987; Sternberg, 1999, 2000). Other factors derived from psychometric techniques include verbal, numerical, and visual-spatial factors. These can be studied independently of the *g*-factor. Most intelligence tests estimate *g* to varying degrees and the ones with high *g*-loadings are the ones typically used in most scientific studies.

Turning Points

In this historical context, the brain and its relationship to intelligence received little attention. This began to change with two developments. First, large-scale behavioral-genetic studies reported compelling results about intelligence test scores from investigations with sophisticated research designs based on twins, including twins separated at birth and raised in different environments by different families. Second, the ability to quantify brain characteristics improved dramatically with the imaging technologies of positron emission tomography (PET) and subsequently, magnetic resonance imaging (MRI). Both genetic and the neuroimaging developments related to intelligence are detailed in *The Neuroscience of Intelligence* (Haier, 2017), but here is a short review.

At the time Jensen wrote his 1969 article, the data were suggestive but not compelling that genetics plays some role in IQ score differences among individuals. Today, the data are overwhelming and leave no doubt that genetics plays a powerful role. The tide began to turn with a major study of identical twins reared apart (Bouchard, 1999, 2009; Bouchard et al., 1998). There are many detailed descriptions of this research. Briefly, the researchers, based in Minnesota, identified 139 pairs of identical twins adopted at or shortly after birth to different families. It took 21 years to identify this rare sample. Reunited for the research, these adult twins completed a battery of physical and psychological measures, including IQ tests. Among all the measures, the correlation between twin pairs on IQ was among the strongest, suggesting about 70% of the variance in IQ differences had a genetic origin. Because the twins in each pair did not share the same environment as they did in studies of twins reared together, this research design was powerful enough to rekindle attention to the role of genetics in intelligence.

About the same time, a research group in the Netherlands published a series of reports based on twins reared apart and other twins and siblings reared together (Posthuma, Baare, et al., 2003; Posthuma, De Geus, & Boomsma, 2003; Posthuma et al., 2002). These studies were able to statistically separate variance in IQ scores into three components: genetic, shared environment (e.g., family, neighborhood, schools), and unique environment (e.g., different friends, different teachers, different experiences). Although there is not complete agreement about how to calculate heritability and apportion variance (Hunt, 2011), an important feature of this work was that the results were computed separately according to the age when the twins were tested. With increasing age, the amount of variance in measured intelligence attributable to genetics increased to about 80% while the variance attributable to shared environment decreased to nearly zero; unique environment made up the remaining 20% or so (Posthuma, De Geus, et al., 2003).

These genetic studies were not the first to demonstrate that genes play a role, but they were instrumental in changing the view from strictly environmental-centric to a new appreciation of the importance of genetics. Today, another decade of behavioral- and molecular-genetic studies has replicated and extended these findings (see Haier, 2017). Early studies failed to identify and independently replicate specific genes relevant for intelligence. This failure has led to new thinking. The accumulated data indicate that many genes will be involved, perhaps hundreds, with each individual gene likely accounting for a limited portion of variance. Finding these genes of small effect requires much larger samples than used in previous studies. New consortia are solving this problem and the hunt for genes related to intelligence is gaining momentum (Benyamin et al., 2014; Davies et al., 2015; Okbay et al., 2016; Rietveld et al., 2014). Although much remains to be learned, here is the key point: Because genes work through biological mechanisms, there must be some biological basis to intelligence. The genetic findings (Deary et al., 2010; Plomin & Deary, 2015; Plomin et al., 2013), therefore, provide a powerful justification for biological research on the nature of intelligence. Even if environmental factors influence some gene expression, a concept referred to as epigenetics, the interactions either take place in the brain or impact the neurobiology of the brain and its development. That's why the revolution in neuroimaging technology is now central to biological studies of intelligence.

From Personality to Positrons

When I was an undergraduate, I chose psychology as my major. I found most of the topics in the introductory lectures fascinating. It was clear that if I wanted a career in psychology, graduate school was required, but my focus for a PhD was not so clear. In my first year of graduate school, I began studying personality research with Robert Hogan. However, the year I started, Professor Julian Stanley began the Hopkins Study of Mathematically and Scientifically Precocious Youth. The project focused on 12- and 13-year-olds with high SAT-Math scores. I worked on this project too and my interest in individual differences in mental abilities and intelligence really began to heat up with this experience. After Hopkins, my first job was at the National Institute of Mental Health (NIMH) in Bethesda, Maryland. I was hired by David Rosenthal to work in the NIMH Intramural Research Program in the Laboratory of Psychology and Psychopathology. Dr. Rosenthal, a wonderful mentor, was the key researcher in the Denmark Adoption Studies of Schizophrenia. These studies were instrumental in changing the focus of research on mental illnesses from psychoanalytic/family perspectives to a genetic/biological perspective. This transition subsequently informed my research on intelligence. It was at NIMH that I learned about behavioral-genetic research and published personality-test data from the Denmark studies (Haier, Rosenthal, & Wender, 1978). I also met Monte Buchsbaum, who was working down the hall with EEG and evoked-potential studies in psychiatric patients.

After four years, I left NIMH to join the medical school faculty in the Department of Psychiatry at Brown University with Dr. Nate Epstein, another wonderful mentor. I started my own EEG/EP laboratory there to study psychiatric patients, but also to study intelligence (Haier et al., 1983; Robinson et al., 1984). Subsequently, Buchsbaum moved to the University of California, Irvine (UCI), where he had negotiated the acquisition of the newly available technology of positron emission tomography (PET) to image the brain. PET requires multimillion-dollar equipment, including a cyclotron facility to manufacture short-lived radioisotopes. The first scanners became available on a limited basis about 1980. Recognizing the potential for this powerful technology for understanding the nature of intelligence, I moved to UCI in 1985. In 1988, I published my first imaging paper on intelligence (Haier et al., 1988), long before brain imaging became routine for studies of cognition and other areas of psychology.

Early Contributions of Neuroimaging Studies

Where in the brain is intelligence? This was the simple question I intended to address in that first 1988 study. PET measures brain function. It works by injecting a radioactive tracer that accumulates in the brain while the person performs a mental task. The harder any area of the brain is working during the task, the more tracer accumulates. We used a tracer based on glucose, the energy supply for brain function. The PET scanner detects the positrons emitted from the head that originate from the tracer. The more tracer in a brain area, the more positrons emitted from that area. This emission reflects a higher glucose metabolic rate. The PET scan is color-coded to show where different amounts of tracer went during the task. In our study, we had the participants work on abstract-reasoning problems from a test used to estimate levels of the *g*-factor (the Raven's Advanced

Progressive Matrices). We expected to see the parts of the brain that were involved in this kind of reasoning "light up," that is, show the highest glucose metabolic rate. The group performing the reasoning test had eight people (PET scans were quite expensive at $2,500 each), and they were compared to other people performing control tasks of attention. Happily, we did find several unique brain areas that were working harder during the reasoning test. But there were two surprising aspects of the results.

First, there had been an expectation that the main brain areas related to intelligence would be in the frontal lobes. We found frontal but also other areas were related to test performance. This suggested a distributed network rather than a focus on frontal areas alone. Second, within the brain areas of greater activity, there was an inverse relationship between level of activity and scores on the reasoning test. That is, the *more* the brain was active, the *worse* the person did on the reasoning test. We interpreted this unforeseen result as the basis for a brain-efficiency hypothesis about what makes a smart brain. In other words, it is not how hard your brain works, but rather how efficiently it works that contributes to why some people solve problems faster and better than other people.

We continued these explorations with additional PET studies and subsequently we turned as well to MRI studies. In 1992, we published one of the first PET studies of learning to test whether learning a complex task resulted in more efficient brain function. The task we chose was Tetris (Haier, Siegel, MacLachlan, et al., 1992). After 50 days of practice, glucose metabolic rate decreased while playing Tetris, even though practice resulted in the game being harder and faster. These results supported the brain-efficiency hypothesis and this paper achieved cult-like status. It was noted in the book of *Guinness World Records, Gamer's Edition, 2008*. There was also an early suggestion that the participants in the Tetris study with the highest scores on the Raven's test of abstract reasoning were the ones who showed the greatest increase in efficiency after practice (Haier, Siegel, Tang, Abel, & Buchsbaum, 1992).

Following up on my experience with the Hopkins study, we conducted a PET study to see whether participants selected for high SAT-Math scores (over 700) had lower glucose metabolic rate while solving math-reasoning problems than participants selected for average SAT-Math scores (Haier & Benbow, 1995). This work was another test of the brain-efficiency hypothesis and, to make it more interesting, we selected college men and women for comparison to see if either group was more brain-efficient than the other. The results in men showed higher math reasoning scores were correlated to higher glucose metabolic rate in several brain areas – the opposite of the efficiency hypothesis. It may be that brain efficiency is related to general mental ability, but good performance on more specific abilities like math reasoning is related to brain areas working harder (Neubauer & Fink, 2003, 2009a, 2009b). In any case, in this study no pattern of correlations was found in the women, although they performed just as well as the men. Here was a clear sex difference and an early indication that equal performance on mental tests could come about from the use of different brain networks. This 1995 paper was the basis of our longtime advocacy of computing separate analyses for men and women whenever sample sizes allow.

It is important to note that correlating individual differences in task performance with brain characteristics was a novel approach when we first used it in 1988. The standard image analysis in early studies compared group averages, which hid and ignored any individual differences. The correlation approach was standard for us and we used it repeatedly in our other early PET studies, with important results beyond group comparisons, especially for sex differences (Cahill et al., 1996; Cahill et al., 2001; Haier, White, & Alkire, 2003; Mansour, Haier, & Buchsbaum, 1996).

Around the year 2000, MRI machines started to become available at many university hospitals. Cognitive psychologists began using them in earnest, especially given their nascent capability to measure regional blood flow in the brain. This technique is known as functional MRI (fMRI). This technology is based on magnetic fields and radio waves. It does not require any injections of radioactive tracers and it is far less expensive than PET. For these reasons, fMRI rapidly became the neuroimaging method of choice for many investigators. Today these expensive machines can be found in many departments of psychology, independently of clinical uses in hospitals.

While the use of fMRI was expanding rapidly, we used the less exciting capability of MRI to investigate individual differences in brain structures and how they might relate to mental test score differences. Using a method called voxel-based morphometry (VBM), we found the amounts of gray and white matter in various areas across the brain were correlated with IQ scores, supporting the distributed nature of intelligence in the brain (Haier et al., 2004). Moreover, separate analyses in the same sample showed the pattern of brain-area correlates with IQ differed for men and women matched for IQ. The women's IQ scores showed more correlations in frontal areas and the men showed more in parietal areas (Haier et al., 2005). These findings supported our earlier view that not all brains work the same way to achieve equivalent performance on intelligence tests. Using two different approaches, we also reported that the amount of gray matter in different areas distributed across the brain was positively correlated with scores on the subtests of the WAIS IQ test. The subtests with the highest g-loadings showed more brain areas with gray matter correlates than low g-loaded subtests (Colom, Jung, & Haier, 2006a, 2006b).

Our publications between 1988 and 2006 helped define neuroimaging approaches to the study of intelligence and mental abilities, especially with the focus on individual differences. The results of these studies led to four fundamental positions and a number of subsequent research investigations of them by other investigators:

1. The existence of correlations with quantified brain characteristics provided a new kind of compelling construct validity for psychometric tests. If the g-factor was merely a statistical artifact, why would g-scores have any brain correlates?

2. Models that localized intelligence mostly or solely in the frontal lobes became questionable, as the data indicated a distributed network of many areas across the entire brain was involved.

3. The brain-efficiency hypothesis suggested that "activation" studies needed to consider brain areas where decreased function might be important for mental performance.

4. Separate analyses for men and women and for young and older participants had the potential to reveal alternative brain pathways for comparable mental performance. This was a departure from the more customary use of age and sex as covariates to remove any influences they might have from a combined group effect.

By 2006, a number of structural and functional MRI studies reported brain areas related to intelligence and reasoning (although some researchers were shy about using the word "intelligence" for reasons noted in the introduction to this chapter). My colleague Rex Jung and I undertook to review all the available neuroimaging studies to see how the field was progressing.

The Parieto-Frontal Integration Theory (P-FIT) of Intelligence

We first identified 37 studies that related neuroimaging assessments to intelligence/reasoning test scores (Jung & Haier, 2007). There were a number of challenges in reviewing this literature. Different imaging technologies have different strengths and weaknesses and there are a variety of methods for analyzing imaging data. The anatomical location of significant findings was often reported in nonstandard ways and the standard ways were not terribly precise. Moreover, a variety of tests were used; most often only a single test score served as the measure of intelligence. All this made direct apples-to-apples comparisons impossible. Add in a range of sample sizes from eight to hundreds and the value of a formal meta-analysis becomes quite limited. We chose to use a mostly qualitative method, based on a similar review of imaging studies of cognition (Naghavi & Nyberg, 2005). We simply listed the main findings of each study separately for structural MRI, functional MRI, and PET using Brodmann areas (BA) or estimated BAs for localization. Then for all possible BAs, we graphed how many studies had a finding in each area. Some areas never turned up in any studies and some areas were reported in more than 50% of the studies. We focused on the latter and listed these most common areas across studies, irrespective of imaging modality, method of analysis, and intelligence test used. In our view, there was some surprising consistency. The 14 most common areas were distributed across the brain, but mostly in the parietal and frontal regions, hence the Parieto-frontal nomenclature (see richardhaier. com for a figure and reprints).

The P-FIT model divided these areas into stages of information processing. We noted that individual differences in intelligence might be related to efficient flow of information among the brain networks defined by the P-FIT areas and the white matter connections among them. We also speculated that individuals differ in the pattern of P-FIT areas so that subsets of the networks would be more relevant for some people than for others. This could account for the different patterns of cognitive strengths and weaknesses every person has. It could also account for people attaining the same IQ scores by different brain pathways. The P-FIT states and implies a number of testable hypotheses that have helped guide many subsequent imaging studies of intelligence.

Our original P-FIT article was accompanied by 19 commentaries from other researchers, who made mostly favorable and constructive comments, along with our responses. Subsequently, the P-FIT has been cited hundreds of times and remains a focus of numerous new investigations. In our view, the 2007 P-FIT review marked the end of the first phase of neuroimaging studies of intelligence that started in 1988. The second phase is now under way and generally is based on considerably advanced methods of image acquisition and analysis, much larger samples, and tied to more specific hypothesis testing (Haier, 2009). We are also now seeing studies in multicenter collaborations that combine imaging and genetic assessments along with batteries of cognitive tests in large samples. Altogether, the pace of advancement is quickening and the emerging results are exciting. We must be cautious, however, not to go beyond the data. It is useful to keep Haier's three laws in mind: 1) no story about the brain is simple, 2) no one study is definitive, and 3) it takes many years to sort out conflicting and inconsistent findings and establish a compelling weight of evidence (from Haier, 2017).

Phase Two of Neuroimaging/Intelligence Studies

With these laws in mind, here are some examples of studies in the new phase regarding the P-FIT (see Haier, 2017 for a detailed review). A German group reconsidered the P-FIT using some of the same papers and adding some new ones in a meta-analysis (Basten, Hilger, & Fiebach, 2015). They limited the 28 papers in their review to those that included analyses of individual differences in the intelligence measures. They excluded papers showing only average group differences (Jung and Haier had included both kinds of designs). These researchers than compared all the studies quantitatively voxel by voxel. This identified common brain areas related to intelligence (irrespective of the test used) across the 28 studies totaling more than 1,000 participants. They concluded that the results generally supported the P-FIT and they suggested adding some additional areas. Several other studies of patients with brain lesions also supported key elements of the P-FIT (Barbey et al., 2012; Barbey et al., 2014; Glascher et al., 2010). In addition, studies using new methods of structural and functional connectivity analysis support the role of communication and information processing among P-FIT areas and networks (Penke et al., 2012; Santarnecchi et al., 2014; Shehzad et al., 2014; Song et al., 2009; Vakhtin et al., 2014; Van den Heuvel et al., 2009).

Showing correlations between neuroimaging measures and scores on mental ability tests has now become routine. A major goal of this work that would advance progress is to predict IQ scores from brain images. There is a long history of trying to do so and, despite some claims of success, this goal has not been achieved with robust, independently replicated results. A new study, however, shows considerable potential (Finn et al., 2015). This study comes from a multisite consortium, the Human Connectome Project, which ultimately aims to map all the connections in the human brain and determine what they do. Based on 126 participants who completed structural and functional MRIs, connectivity patterns among 268 brain areas were computed. These patterns, based on the strength of correlations between all pairs of areas, were reported to be so stable and unique to each person that the researchers described them as brain fingerprints.

The stability and uniqueness are key findings, but the really eye-catching finding was that IQ scores could be predicted from the connectivity fingerprints. This would be consistent with predictions made by the P-FIT. Although the 2015 report included a replication in an independent sample, so far other researchers have yet to replicate this result. At this writing, we do not yet know whether the goal of predicting IQ from brain images has been achieved beyond reasonable doubt, but we may be close.

Other new studies combine neuroimaging and genetic analyses. One study, for example, found heritability of white matter integrity was highest in frontal and parietal areas, the same areas where IQ scores show high heritability, suggesting common genes for both (Chiang et al., 2009). This same group has used DNA analyses in 472 twins and their non-twin siblings to identify putative genes that may be relevant to intelligence (Chiang et al., 2012). A large multinational collaborative project named ENIGMA and another European Union consortium named IMAGEN have studied the genetics of cortical thickness and its relationship to IQ in 1,583 adolescents (Desrivieres et al., 2015). These are only a few of the worldwide efforts to understand not only where in the brain is intelligence, but also how gene function in the brain influences intelligence. The *where* and the *how* are keys to the ultimate question: *Can we enhance intelligence by manipulating brain mechanisms?* Today, the answer is we do not know how to do so. In fact, despite periodic news reports, there is no proven way to increase IQ (see Haier, 2017, for a detailed review). However, I am optimistic that neuroscience may provide a roadmap to enhancing intelligence. It is not too early to discuss the implications. Consider the following example.

Turning Education Policies Upside Down

Here are two observations about debates about education in the United States: (1) they are typically contentious and (2) they never include any consideration of the relationship between learning and intelligence. A student's level of intelligence (i.e., IQ) is the single best predictor of academic and life success we know. Other factors are undoubtedly important, but it is an empirical fact that intelligence is the single strongest predictor. Why do policy makers ignore this fact? There are many issues here, but consider the widely recognized school achievement gaps among different groups of students. These gaps have persisted virtually unchanged for decades despite all kinds of environmental interventions to close them. To the extent that these gaps are rooted at least in part in intelligence differences among individuals, we should consider what we know about intelligence when discussing how to ameliorate the gaps. Since a large portion of variance in intelligence among people is genetic, how can this information benefit education? Here I will only focus on one point: To the extent that intelligence has a major genetic component, as research demonstrates, it is a positive and optimistic opportunity to understand the neurobiological mechanisms involved so that we can develop ways to influence these mechanisms in ways that could enhance intelligence. This is not science fiction. It is quite possible in the same way that medical science is trying to turn negative genetic influences that cause diseases into positive ways to change gene expression and treat or cure those diseases. In the 21st century, it is realistic to think about genes as probabilistic instead of deterministic. Once we understand how genes work, there is every reason to believe that sooner or later, we can change the output, including intelligence. Imagine having the capability to increase anyone's IQ by 15 points (a full standard deviation). Wouldn't we have a moral obligation to offer this if we knew how to do it? This knowledge would dramatically change education and other social policies. It could change the world. As a first step, it is time to add what we already know about the biological basis of intelligence to discussions that will challenge education reform. That is my optimistic view from the brain about intelligence and the relentless advances in neuroscience that might afford new approaches to old problems.

References

Barbey, A. K., Colom, R., Paul, E. J., & Grafman, J. (2014). Architecture of fluid intelligence and working memory revealed by lesion mapping. *Brain Struct Funct*, 219(2), 485–494.

Barbey, A. K., Colom, R., Solomon, J., Krueger, F., Forbes, C., & Grafman, J. (2012). An integrative architecture for general intelligence and executive function revealed by lesion mapping. *Brain*, 135(Pt 4), 1154–1164. doi:10.1093/brain/aws021

Basten, U., Hilger, K., & Fiebach, C. J. (2015). Where smart brains are different: A quantitative meta-analysis of functional and structural brain imaging studies on intelligence. *Intelligence*, 51(0), 10–27. doi:http://dx.doi.org/10.1016/j.intell.2015.04.009

Benyamin, B., Pourcain, B., Davis, O. S., Davies, G., Hansell, N. K., Brion, M. J., ... Visscher, P. M. (2014). Childhood intelligence is heritable, highly polygenic and associated with FNBP1L. *Mol Psychiatry*, 19(2), 253–258. doi:10.1038/mp.2012.184

Bouchard, T. J. (1999). IQ and human intelligence. *Science*, 284(5416), 922–923.

(2009). Genetic influence on human intelligence (Spearman's g): How much? *Annals of Human Biology*, 36(5), 527–544.

Bouchard, T. J., McGue, M., Hur, Y. M., & Horn, J. M. (1998). A genetic and environmental analysis of the California psychological inventory using adult twins reared apart and together. *European Journal of Personality*, 12(5), 307–320.

Cahill, L., Haier, R. J., Fallon, J., Alkire, M. T., Tang, C., Keator, D., … McGaugh, J. L. (1996). Amygdala activity at encoding correlated with long-term, free recall of emotional information. *Proc Natl Acad Sci U S A*, 93(15), 8016–8021.

Cahill, L., Haier, R. J., White, N. S., Fallon, J., Kilpatrick, L., Lawrence, C., … Alkire, M. T. (2001). Sex-related difference in amygdala activity during emotionally influenced memory storage. *Neurobiol Learn Mem*, 75(1), 1–9.

Chiang, M. C., Barysheva, M., McMahon, K. L., de Zubicaray, G. I., Johnson, K., Montgomery, G. W., … Thompson, P. M. (2012). Gene network effects on brain microstructure and intellectual performance identified in 472 twins. *J Neurosci*, 32(25), 8732–8745. doi:10.1523/JNEUROSCI.5993-11.2012

Chiang, M. C., Barysheva, M., Shattuck, D. W., Lee, A. D., Madsen, S. K., Avedissian, C., … Thompson, P. M. (2009). Genetics of brain fiber architecture and intellectual performance. *Journal of Neuroscience*, 29(7), 2212–2224. doi:Doi 10.1523/Jneurosci.4184-08.2009

Colom, R., Jung, R. E., & Haier, R. J. (2006a). Distributed brain sites for the g-factor of intelligence. *Neuroimage*, 31(3), 1359–1365.

(2006b). Finding the g-factor in brain structure using the method of correlated vectors. *Intelligence*, 34(6), 561–570.

Davies, G., Armstrong, N., Bis, J. C., Bressler, J., Chouraki, V., Giddaluru, S., … Deary, I. J. (2015). Genetic contributions to variation in general cognitive function: A meta-analysis of genome-wide association studies in the CHARGE consortium (N=53949). *Mol Psychiatry*, 20(2), 183–192. doi:10.1038/mp.2014.188

Deary, I. J., Penke, L., & Johnson, W. (2010). The neuroscience of human intelligence differences. *Nature Reviews Neuroscience*, 11(3), 201–211. doi:Doi 10.1038/Nrn2793

Desrivieres, S., Lourdusamy, A., Tao, C., Toro, R., Jia, T., Loth, E., … Consortium, I. (2015). Single nucleotide polymorphism in the neuroplastin locus associates with cortical thickness and intellectual ability in adolescents. *Mol Psychiatry*, 20(2), 263–274. doi:10.1038/mp.2013.197

Finn, E. S., Shen, X., Scheinost, D., Rosenberg, M. D., Huang, J., Chun, M. M., … Constable, R. T. (2015). Functional connectome fingerprinting: Identifying individuals using patterns of brain connectivity. *Nat Neurosci*, 18(11), 1664–1671. doi:10.1038/nn.4135 www.nature.com/neuro/journal/v18/n11/abs/nn.4135.html – supplementary-information

Gardner, H. (1987). The theory of multiple intelligences. *Annals of Dyslexia*, 37, 19–35.

Glascher, J., Rudrauf, D., Colom, R., Paul, L. K., Tranel, D., Damasio, H., & Adolphs, R. (2010). Distributed neural system for general intelligence revealed by lesion mapping. *Proceedings of the National Academy of Sciences of the United States of America*, 107(10), 4705–4709. doi:D10.1073/Pnas.0910397107

Gottfredson, L. S. (1997). Why g matters: The complexity of everyday life. *Intelligence*, 24(1), 79–132.

Haier, R. J. (2009). Neuro-intelligence, neuro-metrics and the next phase of brain imaging studies. *Intelligence*, 37(2), 121–123.

(2014). Increased intelligence is a myth (so far). *Front Syst Neurosci*, 8, 34. doi:10.3389/fnsys.2014.00034

(2017). *The neuroscience of intelligence.* Cambridge: Cambridge University Press.

Haier, R. J., & Benbow, C. P. (1995). Sex differences and lateralization in temporal lobe glucose metabolism during mathematical reasoning. *Developmental Neuropsychology*, 11(4), 405–414.

Haier, R. J., Jung, R. E., Yeo, R. A., Head, K., & Alkire, M. T. (2004). Structural brain variation and general intelligence. *Neuroimage*, 23(1), 425–433.

(2005). The neuroanatomy of general intelligence: sex matters. *Neuroimage*, 25(1), 320–327.

Haier, R. J., Robinson, D. L., Braden, W., & Williams, D. (1983). Electrical potentials of the cerebral cortex and psychometric intelligence. *Personality & Individual Differences*, 4(6), 591–599.

Haier, R. J., Rosenthal, D., & Wender, P. H. (1978). MMPI assessment of psychopathology in the adopted-away offspring of schizophrenics. *Arch Gen Psychiatry*, 35(2), 171–175.

Haier, R. J., Siegel, B., Tang, C., Abel, L., & Buchsbaum, M. S. (1992). Intelligence and changes in regional cerebral glucose metabolic-rate following learning. *Intelligence*, 16(3–4), 415–426.

Haier, R. J., Siegel, B. V., Jr., MacLachlan, A., Soderling, E., Lottenberg, S., & Buchsbaum, M. S. (1992). Regional glucose metabolic changes after learning a complex visuospatial/motor task: A positron emission tomographic study. *Brain Res*, 570(1–2), 134–143.

Haier, R. J., Siegel, B. V., Nuechterlein, K. H., Hazlett, E., Wu, J. C., Paek, J., … Buchsbaum, M. S. (1988). Cortical glucose metabolic-rate correlates of abstract reasoning and attention studied with positron emission tomography. *Intelligence*, 12(2), 199–217.

Haier, R. J., White, N. S., & Alkire, M. T. (2003). Individual differences in general intelligence correlate with brain function during nonreasoning tasks. *Intelligence*, 31(5), 429–441.

Hunt, E. B. (2011). *Human intelligence.* Cambridge; New York: Cambridge University Press.

Jensen, A. R. (1969). How much can we boost IQ and scholastic achievement. *Harvard Educational Review*, 39(1), 1–123.

(1998). *The g factor: The science of mental ability.* Westport, CT: Praeger.

Jung, R. E., & Haier, R. J. (2007). The Parieto-Frontal Integration Theory (P-FIT) of intelligence: Converging neuroimaging evidence. *Behavioral and Brain Sciences*, 30(02), 135–154.

Mansour, C. S., Haier, R. J., & Buchsbaum, M. S. (1996). Gender comparisons of cerebral glucose metabolic rate in healthy adults during a cognitive task. *Personality & Individual Differences*, 20(2), 183–191.

Naghavi, H. R., & Nyberg, L. (2005). Common fronto-parietal activity in attention, memory, and consciousness: Shared demands on integration? *Consciousness and Cognition*, 14(2), 390–425.

Neubauer, A. C., & Fink, A. (2003). Fluid intelligence and neural efficiency: effects of task complexity and sex. *Personality and Individual Differences*, 35(4), 811–827.

(2009a). Intelligence and neural efficiency. *Neuroscience and Biobehavioral Reviews*, 33(7), 1004–1023.

(2009b). Intelligence and neural efficiency: Measures of brain activation versus measures of functional connectivity in the brain. *Intelligence*, 37(2), 223–229.

Okbay, A., Beauchamp, J. P., Fontana, M. A., Lee, J. J., Pers, T. H., Rietveld, C. A., … Benjamin, D. J. (2016). Genome-wide association study identifies 74 loci associated with educational attainment. *Nature*, 533(7604), 539–542. doi:10.1038/nature17671

Penke, L., Maniega, S. M., Bastin, M. E., Hernandez, M. C. V., Murray, C., Royle, N. A., … Deary, I. J. (2012). Brain white matter tract integrity as a neural foundation for general intelligence. *Molecular Psychiatry*, 17(10), 1026–1030. doi:Doi 10.1038/Mp.2012.66

Plomin, R., & Deary, I. J. (2015). Genetics and intelligence differences: Five special findings. *Mol Psychiatry*, 20(1), 98–108. doi:10.1038/mp.2014.105

Plomin, R., Haworth, C. M. A., Meaburn, E. L., Price, T. S., Davis, O. S. P., & Control, W. T. C. (2013). Common DNA markers can account for more than half of the genetic influence on cognitive abilities. *Psychological Science*, 24(4), 562–568.

Posthuma, D., Baare, W. F. C., Pol, H. E. H., Kahn, R. S., Boomsma, D. I., & De Geus, E. J. C. (2003). Genetic correlations between brain volumes and the WAIS-III dimensions of verbal comprehension, working memory, perceptual organization, and processing speed. *Twin Research*, 6(2), 131–139.

Posthuma, D., De Geus, E. J., Baare, W. F., Hulshoff Pol, H. E., Kahn, R. S., & Boomsma, D. I. (2002). The association between brain volume and intelligence is of genetic origin. *Nat Neurosci*, 5(2), 83–84.

Posthuma, D., De Geus, E., & Boomsma, D. (2003). Genetic contributions to anatomical, behavioral, and neurophysiological indices of cognition. In R. Plomin, J. DeFries, I. W. Craig, & P. McGuffin (Eds.), *Behavioral genetics in the postgenomic era* (pp. 141–161). Washington, DC: American Psychological Association.

Rietveld, C. A., Esko, T., Davies, G., Pers, T. H., Turley, P., Benyamin, B., … Koellinger, P. D. (2014). Common genetic variants associated with cognitive performance identified using the proxy-phenotype method. *Proc Natl Acad Sci U S A*, 111(38), 13790–13794. doi:10.1073/pnas.1404623111

Robinson, D. L., Haier, R. J., Braden, W., & Krengel, M. (1984). Psychometric intelligence and visual evoked potentials: A replication. *Personality & Individual Differences*, 5(4), 487–489.

Santarnecchi, E., Galli, G., Polizzotto, N. R., Rossi, A., & Rossi, S. (2014). Efficiency of weak brain connections support general cognitive functioning. *Hum Brain Mapp*, 35(9), 4566–4582. doi:10.1002/hbm.22495

Shehzad, Z., Kelly, C., Reiss, P. T., Cameron Craddock, R., Emerson, J. W., McMahon, K., ... Milham, M. P. (2014). A multivariate distance-based analytic framework for connectome-wide association studies. *Neuroimage*, 93 Pt 1, 74–94. doi:10.1016/j.neuroimage.2014.02.024

Song, M., Liu, Y., Zhou, Y., Wang, K., Yu, C., & Jiang, T. (2009). Default network and intelligence difference. *Conf Proc IEEE Eng Med Biol Soc, 2009*, 2212–2215. doi:10.1109/IEMBS.2009.5334874

Spearman, C. (1904). General intelligence objectively determined and measured. *American Journal of Psychology*, 15, 201–293.

Sternberg, R. J. (1999). Successful intelligence: Finding a balance. *Trends Cogn Sci*, 3(11), 436–442.

(2000). *Practical intelligence in everyday life*. Cambridge; New York: Cambridge University Press.

Vakhtin, A. A., Ryman, S. G., Flores, R. A., & Jung, R. E. (2014). Functional brain networks contributing to the Parieto-Frontal Integration Theory of Intelligence. *Neuroimage*, 103, 349–354. doi:10.1016/j.neuroimage.2014.09.055

Van den Heuvel, M. P., Stam, C. J., Kahn, R. S., & Pol, H. E. H. (2009). Efficiency of functional brain networks and intellectual performance. *Journal of Neuroscience*, 29(23), 7619–7624. doi:10.1523/Jneurosci.1443-09.2009

CHAPTER 12

Is Critical Thinking a Better Model of Intelligence?

Diane F. Halpern & Heather A. Butler

As professors, we spend much of our time watching students learn, so not surprisingly, our definition of what it means to have high intelligence centers on the ability to learn complex information quickly and to be able to apply what is learned to novel situations. These ideas are not original; they are derived from Vygotsky's zone of proximal development and the need for far transfer in learning (Barnett & Ceci, 2002). Students who come to us with high levels of knowledge are not necessarily the most intelligent. Even though they may be a compendium of complex knowledge about a topic, we cannot conclude that they are intelligent because we do not know their learning histories. They may have large amounts of knowledge available for recall, but we do not know if they can use that knowledge effectively when it is needed. Some people are fortunate to have had excellent schooling or out-of-school environments that support learning, such as coming from homes where learning is encouraged and where books, trips to museums, quality videos, insightful discussions, and other opportunities for learning are plentiful.

University classrooms are one type of highly specialized learning environment. In our conception of what it means to be intelligent, a person with high intelligence adapts well to the demands of her or his environment, regardless of the nature of the demands. Given this assumption, students who are intelligent in a contemporary classroom would have done comparatively well if born during a different time period where they may have had to kill animals, forage for food, build safe places to live, make clothing that protects against the elements, avoid poisonous plants, and elude the host of hazards that were common to life in different time periods.

A common element to succeeding in all environments is the ability to find novel ways to solve problems. The nature of the problems will differ, but regardless of their nature, a person with high intelligence will be a problem-solver. Another common trait that cuts across all environments is the ability to learn from mistakes, both those that are made by the individual and ones that are made by others. In contemporary society, high intelligence would be expected to be positively and imperfectly correlated with education. In general, people who are recognized as being high in intelligence have a better chance of having excellent learning experiences, thus creating a circle of high intelligence leading to quality educational experiences. These experiences would, in turn, increase levels of intelligence. With increased education, a person with high intelligence will use data when making decisions and avoid many of the thinking biases that often cause decision-making errors such as generalizing from a small sample, arguing with hindsight bias, confusing correlation with cause, being misled with persuasive language, and many others.

Construct Validity: The Gold Standard in Assessment

Every student of assessment knows that there are several types of validity, all of which are important, but first among equals is construct validity. Is your assessment measuring the construct you want to quantify? Obvious examples where there is mismatch between what is assessed and what the assessor wants to assess are easy to identify. No one would measure intelligence with the size of someone's big toe. But more subtle examples are less obvious to spot. Consider common standardized measures of intelligence, which assess short-term memory, vocabulary, analogies, and spatial skills using puzzle-like components. These assessments have little in common with the definition of intelligence that we are advocating. In fact, there is so little overlap between standardized assessment and our definition of what it means to be intelligent that we prefer to use the term "critical thinking" for our definition of what it means to be intelligent to avoid confusing these two terms.

Critical thinking involves understanding information at a deep, meaningful level, and using thinking skills to overcome fallacies and biases. Both of these components are missing from standardized IQ tests. We agree with Stanovich (2010), who wrote that critical thinking is "What intelligence tests miss." He argues that a critical piece is missing from the traditional conceptualization of intelligence or IQ, namely a rationality quotient (RQ). Stanovich and his colleagues question why seemingly smart, accomplished people do blatantly foolish things. They argue, and we agree, that IQ and rational thinking are different constructs. Rationality, as they see it, involves adaptive reasoning, good judgment, and good decision making, which standard IQ tests fail to measure (Stanovich, West, & Toplak,

2016). Thus, their use of the term "rational intelligence" is virtually identical with the usual definitions of critical thinking.

Sternberg and his colleagues (e.g., Cianciolo et al., 2006) also suggested a definition and assessment of intelligence that differs from IQ scores computed from standardized intelligence tests. They suggested that *Practical Intelligence*, which they defined as "an ability to perform successfully in naturalistic settings in a way that is consistent with one's goals" (p. 236), was a useful way of conceptualizing the variables that predict success. Practical Intelligence is distinct from general IQ measures and fluid intelligence. Thus, it can also be used to predict behavior in real-world settings.

IQ scores computed from standardized intelligence tests predict many important variables, including job performance (individuals who score higher on intelligence tests learn job-related skills more quickly and learn more of them; Hunter & Schmidt, 1996), academic performance in universities and other postsecondary institutions (Kretzschmar et al., 2016: Kuncel, Ones, & Sackett, 2010), and reduced rates of crime (Burhan et al., 2014). For people with very high scores, IQ also predicts some kinds of exceptional achievements such as holding a patent, publishing scholarly articles, and achieving a doctorate (Lubinski, 2009). Thus, IQ scores clearly tap some of the same constructs that predict success in a variety of real-life settings. Of course, such predictions are imperfect and leave considerable variance unexplained when applied to real-life settings.

In this chapter, we assert that scores on a critical thinking assessment have real-world validity and when used along with IQ scores they can increase predictive validity for real-life events that require good thinking.

Critical Thinking: What It Is, How to Get It and How to Get It to Transfer

We think of critical thinking as good or clear thinking. It is rational and goal-directed, such as deciding whom to vote for, how to invest or save money, what career plans to pursue, and most everything else that would benefit from good thinking. The questions of whether or not intelligence can be increased, and if it can, how and how much, are major controversies among the intelligentsia (pun is definitely intended). Although a few doubters still question whether critical thinking abilities can and should be improved, there is a large research literature on this topic, providing extensive evidence that critical thinking can be improved with appropriate educational experiences. We focus here on some of our own work (along with many colleagues) because we were asked to highlight our own contributions, with the acknowledgments that many other researchers have made important contributions to this field.

We define critical thinking as the habitual use of cognitive skills that increase the probability of a desirable outcome as well as the disposition to use those skills (Halpern, 2014). It is the kind of thinking involved in solving problems, formulating inferences, calculating likelihoods, and making decisions. The underlying assumption for instruction designed to enhance critical thinking is that there are identifiable thinking skills that students can learn to recognize and use in different situations and when they do, they become better critical thinkers. There is a long list of skills in Halpern's (2014) textbook, *Thought and Knowledge*. Here are some examples that follow from our definition of what it means to be intelligent: generalizing from samples that are adequately large, giving reasons to support a conclusion, using analogies to solve problems, recognizing and criticizing assumptions, using basic properties of likelihood and uncertainty, understanding the limits of extrapolation, recognizing regression to the mean and adjusting predictions to take this into account, judging the credibility of an information source, considering cost:benefit ratios when making a decision, using multiple forms of representation when solving a problem, and many more. These skills are useful across diverse situations and domains of knowledge. These are important skills regardless of whether one is an investment banker, clinical psychologist, scientist, medical professional, teacher, plumber, parent, student, or in training or assisting in these and virtually every other field. It is difficult to find any job or aspect of life where critical thinking skills would not be useful.

The dispositional aspect of critical thinking is as essential as the skills. Critical thinkers are self-regulated, open-minded in their approach to new information, and persist in doing the hard work of critical thinking. Critical thinking is often contrasted with its polar opposite, rote recall, but it is important to keep in mind that deep learning and comprehension often begin with rote recall. Critical thinkers need knowledge about a content area and the skills of critical thinking. Here are some examples. No one can think deeply about curing cancer without a solid knowledge of the parts of the cell and mitosis. Similarly, no one can understand the relations among nations in the European Union (EU) without knowledge of the history of the countries that now comprise the EU. Although recall may be a good start when learning about a new topic, it is not enough. Deep engagement in a complex topic will benefit from the critical thinking skill of argumentation (Jonassen & Kim, 2010). When we teach in ways that enhance critical thinking, we are promoting the development of deep learning (Franco, Butler, & Halpern, 2015).

The primary goal of education is to get what is learned in school and other educational settings to transfer across time and place (Halpern & Hakel, 2003). The entire reason that we have schools is the belief that whatever is learned in school will be applied in some other context at some other time in the future. It would be meaningless if students were able to learn and demonstrate critical thinking skills while at school or with their instructor, but not when they are at work, at home, or acting as informed citizens. The best way to enhance transfer is with the use of multiple, diverse examples where a particular skill is relevant and where it is not relevant, so learners can apply the appropriate thinking skills when they are needed.

In the past several decades for the first author, and more recently for the second author, along with many colleagues, we have engaged in multiple programs designed to improve the critical thinking skills of students, ranging in age from upper-level high school students to older adults. We provide a few examples of what works when enhancing critical thinking.

In two studies with high school seniors and juniors at a low-performing, largely minority enrollment high school near Los Angeles, Marin and Halpern (2011) compared different ways of developing critical thinking skills, with a primary focus on determining which strategy was most conducive to transfer. We rejected the idea that critical thinking could be managed only by the intellectually elite. High IQ scores are not a prerequisite for critical thinking. All students, regardless of their intellectual level, need to be able to think beyond the formal learning that happens in school. They need to make ethical choices, engage in healthy behaviors, vote rationally, succeed at an ever-changing workplace, and manage the proliferation of information that floods the Internet. Earlier reviews of the research literature showed that explicit instruction of critical thinking skills where students were guided through the practice of thinking critically and programs that were intensive and continuously emphasized specific skills yielded reasonable gains in critical thinking (ds = 0.4 to 0.5; Bangert-Drowns & Bankert, 1990). The least successful programs targeted measures on traditional tests of intelligence. In designing these programs, we used principles from studies that found that simulating real-world experiences and providing opportunities to discuss the challenges that were presented in scenarios were most beneficial for engagement and learning gains (e.g., Staib, 2003). In our high school studies, we developed a curriculum based on four broad areas of critical thinking skills.

These were analyzing arguments (recognizing reasons, conclusions, and persuasive appeals), correlations and causal claims, confirmation bias, and decision making. In one study, we randomly assigned volunteer participants to one of two different treatments (with a wait-list control group), and in a second study we randomly assigned entire classes to different treatment conditions. In both studies, we compared embedded instruction (skills were embedded in traditional domain knowledge classes) with explicit instruction in critical thinking (the enhancement of specific critical thinking skills was the main content). Learning outcomes were assessed with numerous measures related to academic success and critical thinking, using the Halpern Critical Thinking Assessment (HCTA, described later; Halpern, 2012). Students in the explicit instruction classes showed the greatest gain in critical thinking, with generally small effects for the embedded model. The skills that were learned with explicit instruction transferred to the novel scenarios that were used in the HCTA. Results made abundantly clear that high school students in a low-performing, largely minority public school can show gains in critical thinking when we explicitly teach them the skills of critical thinking. We believe that these results provide empirical evidence that instruction in critical thinking can "bridge the considerable divide that separates those who are advantaged from those whose life histories compromise their exposure to the skills associated with critical thought" (Marin & Halpern, 2011, p. 12).

A second set of studies was conducted using a computerized learning game, named OperationARIES! (Acquiring Research and Investigative Skills), with a later name change to OperationARA! (Acquiring Research Acumen). We had numerous incredible coauthors on these studies, which included development and programming of the game (e.g., Forsyth et al., 2012; Forsyth et al., 2013). The goal of the game was to teach the critical thinking skills that are commonly used in understanding research and are used more generally in inductive reasoning. In this game, students interacted using natural language (English) with the characters. There was a storyline in which aliens were invading the earth and potentially ruining it by turning humans into mindless consumers with the use of faulty research and poor reasoning. Students completed three learning modules – using an e-book supposedly written by an alien as a way of creating basic-level knowledge, then competing with an avatar in a Jeopardy-like game, and finally identifying flaws in research and thinking in order to determine if an avatar was a human or an alien. The critical thinking skills included operational definitions, experimental control, experimenter bias, causal claims, and sample size, among others.

All of these topics are useful when evaluating information, whether it is gathered from formal research or everyday interactions. We found that compared to control groups, students who played OperationARA! showed better learning both immediately after playing the game and after a delay (Halpern et al., 2012) and substantial gains were made by students in open-admissions community colleges, state universities, and at a private elite liberal arts college.

These two sets of studies, and many more that are described in the following section, provide empirical evidence that critical thinking skills can be enhanced when students are provided with explicit instruction that uses the best of what we know about how students learn, including active engagement, relevant and engrossing materials, active responding, and instruction explicitly focused on the development and transfer of critical thinking skills. Though no empirical data exist as to whether critical thinking instruction should be explicitly taught in a single course or spread out across the curriculum, based on the cognitive principle of distributed practice, we strongly encourage educators to explicitly teach critical thinking first as a separate course and then with follow-up of specific skills in all of their courses, so that explicit critical thinking instruction is practiced across the curriculum.

Assessment of Critical Thinking

Employers list critical thinking as one of the most highly valued skills they want from current and prospective employees (Hart Research Associates, 2015, para 4). Ninety-one percent of all employers say that "a demonstrated capacity to think critically, communicate clearly, and solve complex problems is more important than [a candidate's] undergraduate major." Universities claim that they develop it (e.g., Rutgers University Learning Goals, The University of Edinburgh, Hong Kong University, and countless others). Although there is a long list of institutions that claim to develop critical thinking or hire individuals with good critical thinking skills, few have taken the necessary steps to assess it using sound psychometric measures. Adelman, an expert in higher education at the Institute for Higher Education Policy, called these goals without adequate assessment "a wish list of things, like 'graduates will have critical thinking skills'" (Jaschik, 2008). Some institutions use self-reports of whether or not students have developed critical thinking skills and others have faculty make global judgments of critical thinking skills that are reflected in these and other student products that the faculty have already graded and found satisfactory.

The international educational community is also focusing on critical thinking. The Assessment of Higher Education Learning Outcomes sponsored by the Organization for Economic and Cooperative Development (OECD; Tremblay, Lalancette, & Roseveare, 2012) has begun examining international measures of critical thinking as a potential index for seeing how well different types of learning institutions measure up on this essential educational component and for allowing between-country comparisons. The Bologna Process (European Association for International Education, 2007), a joint endeavor for collaboration in higher education among the countries in Europe, also notes the emphasis placed on critical thinking in the United States and makes recommendations for a greater emphasis among the members of the European Union. Similar efforts are emerging in the African Union, Latin American Union, and Caribbean Higher Education Associations. This interest from international organizations reflects global trends in education that are now demanding quality instruction in higher education.

The reason for the surge of interest in assessing critical thinking is the need for quality assurance across institutions and the realization that there is a growing need for a thinking workforce in what has been called the "knowledge economy." Our personal contributions (we were asked to focus on our own work for this chapter) is in the assessment of critical thinking skills for adults from 18 years of age and older. The Halpern Critical Thinking Assessment (HCTA) has been in development for more than 30 years. It was developed in response to the need to determine if students really are improving in their critical thinking abilities after specific educational experiences and to allow employers to ascertain the level of critical thinking in their employees. Although there are other assessments of critical thinking, the HCTA is unique in several ways. First, specific thinking skills were targeted for assessment (e.g., not confusing correlation and cause, understanding regression to the mean, slippery slope fallacy). Numerous common everyday scenarios were written where these skills were required. Due to issues of test confidentiality, we cannot provide an actual test item here, but we can provide a similar example scenario. Participants who take the assessment first read a short scenario and then answer a specific question in one or two sentences. Imagine that respondents read about a newspaper article summarizing recent research that found children who attended preschool were better readers by the end of first grade. Respondents would be asked whether preschool should be mandatory for all children and to consider only the information provided in this scenario when responding. The ideal answer would suggest that because the data were correlational another factor could be causing the increase in reading skills other than attending preschool (i.e., families who can afford to send their children to preschool may also be able to provide other academic opportunities to their children). Immediately following this, the same scenario appears a second time and the respondents would now indicate the answer by using a forced choice format – which of the alternatives is the best answer, or which of a following set of statement is relevant to the scenario, or rank order a set of responses. In the given scenario, the respondents might be given a set of facts (e.g., children from wealthy homes who did not attend preschool also tended to be excellent readers in first grade) and asked to rate whether that fact would help them make an informed decision about whether or not to make preschool mandatory. Thus, the HCTA uses two response formats: constructed responses – how people first respond to a situation (in their own words) – and recognition responses, which is a measure of how well they can recognize a correct or optimal alternative among a list of possible answers. It is the only test of critical thinking that uses a dual-response format.

Even though most scholars agree that constructed responses are the best measure of what people actually think and do, most critical thinking assessments use multiple-choice responses because they can be graded quickly and easily. Another reason why some test developers stay away from constructed-response formats is that it can be difficult to get adequate inter-rater reliabilities. Despite these difficulties, most of the high-stakes examinations (College Board SAT for college admissions, admission to the judicial bar, medical licensing examinations, graduate school admissions tests, and many more) use constructed-response formats because of the added validity. The HCTA uses both forced-choice and constructed responses and has a unique computerized grading system that makes the grading of the constructed-response questions faster and more reliable. Graders are presented with a series of questions as they grade and scores on the constructed responses are calculated based on the graders responses to those questions. Inter-rater reliability, using the grading system, is good (ranging from 0.83 to 0.96; Halpern, 2012).

The use of scenarios that embed the skill in a realistic context is similar to "situational judgment tests," which are commonly used in selection. There is a massive literature on their use (Jansen et al., 2013). As expected, there are alternative forms to guard against exposure of test items and to prevent any recall of a specific scenario with pre- and post-intervention testing. The HCTA was written to assess five broad categories of critical thinking skills: verbal reasoning, argument analysis, thinking as hypothesis testing, likelihood and uncertainty, and decision making and problem solving. Confirmatory factor analyses have confirmed these five factors (Halpern, 2012). Separate factors were also confirmed for constructed-response and forced-choice modes of responding. We had expected this result, which is why we use both types of response modes. Additionally, scores on the HCTA showed low, but positive correlations with the Need for Cognition Scale and no correlation with the Conscientiousness Scale of the Big 5 Personality Dimensions, so it is not assessing a personality trait (Halpern, 2012). Most importantly, the HCTA has shown validity in predicting behavior in real-world problems.

Can Critical Thinking Assessments Tell Us What People Do in Real Life?

The short answer is, yes! Our recent research explored exactly that question and found that those who scored higher on the critical thinking assessment made fewer choices that resulted in negative life events (Butler, 2012; Butler et al., 2012; Butler, Pentoney, & Bong, in press). In the initial study, college students and community adults took the HCTA and completed a decision-making inventory that included negative life events. The inventory was originally developed by De Bruin, Parker, and Fischhoff (2007) as a measure of decision-making competence. New items were added to the original inventory to make it more relevant to college students. The inventory included life events that ranged from mild (e.g., had to pay late fees on a movie rental) to severe (e.g., contracted a sexually transmitted disease because you didn't use a condom) and inquired about life events from many domains of life, including education (e.g., failed an exam), finance (e.g., charged a late fee for not paying a bill on time), interpersonal (e.g., cheated on significant other), health (e.g., had or was responsible for an unplanned pregnancy), and legal (e.g., arrested for driving under the influence of alcohol or drugs) domains. Most of the inventory items appeared in sets, which allowed us to control for the proportion of decisions that the individuals made for themselves. The first question in the set would ask about a neutral decision (e.g., I did my own laundry) that would precede the negative life event (e.g., I ruined my laundry). The proportion of negative life events reported was quantified and compared to scores on the HCTA. For both college students and community adults, those who scored higher on the HCTA reported experiencing fewer negative life events than those who scored lower on the HCTA, but the relationship was stronger for community adults than college students.

The research just described was conducted in the United States, but the pattern of results was found in Ireland also (Butler et al., 2012). However, our colleagues in the Netherlands did not find such a relationship (De Bie, Pascal, & Van der Meij, 2015). Both the inventory of negative life events and the HCTA were translated into Dutch so that it could be administered to college students in the Netherlands. Although the Dutch-language version of the HCTA yielded good reliability and two separate factors (one for constructed responses and one for forced-choice responses), the relationship between scores on the HCTA and scores on the inventory of negative life events was not statistically significant. It is difficult to know whether the lack of relationship is due to cultural or language differences (recall that the HCTA and inventory were translated into Dutch) or, as the authors suggested, due to the young age of the college students from the Netherlands sample. The authors suggested, and we agree, that college students may have a limited range of negative life events that they have experienced (e.g., been kicked out of an apartment before the lease was up).

At the very heart of this chapter is the idea that intelligence should incorporate some aspect of good thinking in order to be a valid predictor of human behavior. We put this idea to the test recently when we asked whether intelligence or critical thinking was a better predictor of human behavior (Butler et al., in press). We hypothesized that both intelligence and critical thinking would predict behavior in the real world, but that critical thinking would be the stronger predictor. We administered the HCTA and an intelligence test (the Intelligenz-Struktur-Batterie, INSBAT; Arendasy et al., 2012), along with an inventory of negative life events to a new sample of college students and community adults in the United States. As predicted, those with high scores on the critical thinking assessment and those with high IQ scores experienced fewer negative life events, and critical thinking was a stronger predictor than intelligence. Perhaps most important though, critical thinking contributed unique incremental validity to the relationship between intelligence and negative life events. That is, when critical thinking was added to the predictive model (in the second step), it contributed uniquely to our ability to predict human behavior. This supports the main point of this chapter. Critical thinking is important and it is time that we update our traditional conceptualization of intelligence, so that we can better understand and predict human behavior.

We believe that we can create a better future by enhancing critical thinking skills of citizens around the world. This optimism is tempered with the reality that so far, we only have data showing that individuals make fewer negative decisions in their personal lives when they are better thinkers, but we can optimistically imagine the impact of a worldwide increase in better thinking. We have nothing to lose by trying.

References

Arendasy, M., Hornke, L. F., Sommer, M., Wagner-Menghin, M., Gittler, G., Häusler, J., Bognar, B., & Wenzl,. M. (2012). *Intelligenz-Struktur-Batterie (Intelligence Structure Battery*; INSBAT).

Bangert-Drowns, R. L., & Bankert, E. (1990). Meta-analysis of effects of explicit instruction for critical thinking. *ERIC, Collection of Educational Resources*. Retrieved from http://eric.ed.gov/?id=ED328614.

Barnett, S. M., & Ceci, S. J. (2002). When and where do we apply what we learn?: A taxonomy for far transfer. *Psychological Bulletin*, 128(4), 612–637. doi:10.1037/0033-2909.128.4.612

Burhan, K. A., Kurniawan, Y., Sidek, A. H., & Mohamad, M. R. (2014). Crimes and the Bell curve: The role of people with high, average, and low intelligence. *Intelligence*, 47, 12–22. doi:http://dx.doi.org/10.1016/j.intell.2014.08.005

Butler, H. A. (2012). Halpern Critical Thinking Assessment predicts real-world outcomes of critical thinking. *Applied Cognitive Psychology*, 26, 721–729. doi:10.1002/acp.2851

Butler, H. A., Dwyer, C. P., Hogan, M. J., Franco, A., Rivas, S. F., Saiz, C., & Almeida, L. F. (2012). Halpern Critical Thinking Assessment and real-world outcomes: Cross-national applications. *Thinking Skills and Creativity*, 7, 112–121. doi:10.1016/j.tsc.2012.04.001

Butler, H. A., Pentoney, C., & Bong, M. (in press). Predicting Real-World Outcomes: Critical Thinking Ability is a Better Predictor of Life Decisions than Intelligence. *Thinking Skills and Creativity*.

Cianciolo, A. T., Grigorenko, E. L., Jrvin, L., Gil, G.,Drebot, M. E., & Sternberg, R. J. (2006). Practical intelligence and tacit knowledge: Advancements in the measurement of developing expertise. *Learning and Individual Differences*, 16, 235–253. doi:10.1016/j.lindif.2006.04.002

De Bie, H., Wilhelm, P., & van der Meij, H. (2015). The Halpern Critical Thinking Assessment: Toward a Dutch appraisal of critical thinking. *Thinking Skills and Creativity*, 1733–44. doi:10.1016/j.tsc.2015.04.001

De Bruin, W. B., Parker, A. M., & Fischhoff, B. (2007). Individual differences in adult decision-making competence. *Journal of Personality and Social Psychology*, 92, 938–956.

European Association for International Education. (2007, March 22–23). *The Bologna Process: Advancing trans-Atlantic collaboration in a changing higher education landscape*. www.eua.be/fileadmin/user_upload/files/Publications/EUA_Bologna_brochure_novo6_v2l.pdf.

Forsyth, C. M., Graesser, A. C., Walker, B., Millis K. Pavlik, P., & Halpern, D. F. (2013). Didactic galactic: Acquiring knowledge learned in a serious game.

In H. C. Lane, K. Yacef, J. Mostow, & P. Pavlik (Eds.). *Proceedings of the International Conference on Artificial Intelligence in Education: 16th International Conference* (AIED 2013) (pp. 832–835). Berlin Heidelberg: Springer Verlag.

Forsyth, C. M., Pavlik, P., Graesser, A. C. Cai, Z., Germany, M., Millis, K., Butler, H., Halpern, D. F., & Dolan, R. (2012). Learning gains for core concepts in a serious game on scientific reasoning. In K. Yacef, O. Zaïane, H. Hershkovitz, M. Yudelson, & J. Stamper (Eds.) *Proceedings of the 5th International Conference on Educational Data Mining* (pp 172–175). Chania, Greece: International Educational Data Mining Society.

Franco, A. H. R., Butler, H. A., & Halpern, D. F. (2015). Teaching critical thinking to promote learning. In D. S. Dunn (Ed.), *The Oxford handbook of psychology education* (pp. 65–74). New York: Oxford University Press. doi:0.1093/oxfordhb/9780199933815.013.007

Halpern, D. F. (2012). *Halpern Critical Thinking Assessment.* Publisher: SCHUHFRIED (Vienna Test System). www.schuhfried.com/vienna-test-system-vts/all-tests-from-a-z/test/hcta-halpern-critical-thinking-assessment-1/.

(2014). *Thought and knowledge: An introduction to critical thinking* (5th Edition). New York: Routledge Publishers.

Halpern, D. F., & Hakel, M. D. (2003). Applying the science of learning to the university and beyond: Teaching for long-term retention and transfer. *Change,* July/August, 2–13.

Halpern, D. F., Millis, K., Graesser. A., Butler, H., Forsyth, C. & Cai, Z. (2012). Operation ARA: A computerized learning game that teaches critical thinking and scientific reasoning. *Thinking Skills and Creativity,* 7, 93–100.

Hart Research Associates. (2015, January 20). *Employers judge recent graduates ill-prepared for today's workplace, endorse broad and project-based learning as best preparation for career opportunity and long-term success.* Retrieved from www.aacu.org/press/press-releases/2015employerstudentsurveys.

Hunter, J. E. & Schmidt, F. L. (1996). Intelligence and job performance: Economic and social implications. *Psychology, Public Policy, and Law,* 2, 447–472.

Jansen, A., Melchers, K. G., Lievens, F., Kleinmann, M., Brändli, M., Fraefel, L., & König, C. J. (2013). Situation assessment as an ignored factor in the behavioral consistency paradigm underlying the validity of personnel selection procedures. *Journal of Applied Psychology,* 98, 326–341. doi:10.1037/a0031257}

Jaschik. S. (2008, May 21). Wake-up call for American higher ed. *Inside Higher Ed,* Retrieved from www.insidehighered.com/news/2008/05/21/bologna.

Jonassen, D. H., & Kim, B. (2010). Arguing to learn and learning to argue: Design justifications and guidelines. *Educational Technology Research and Development,* 58, 439–457. doi:10.1007/s11423-009-9143-8

Kretzschmar, A., Neubert, J. C., Wusternberg, S., & Greiff, S. (2016). Construct validity of complex problem-solving: A comprehensive view on different facts of intelligence and school grades. *Intelligence,* 54, 55–69. http://dx.doi.org/10.1016/j.inell.2015.11,004.

Kuncel, N. R., Ones, D. S., & Sackett, P. R. (2010). Individual differences as predictors of work, educational, and broad life outcomes. *Personality and Individual Differences, 49,* 331–336.

Lubinski, D. (2009). Exceptional cognitive ability: The phenotype. *Behavior Genetics, 39,* 350–358.

Marin, L., & Halpern, D. F. (2011). Pedagogy for developing critical thinking in adolescents: Explicit instruction produces greatest gains. *Thinking Skills and Creativity, 6,* 1–13. doi:10.1016/j.tsc.2010.08

Stanovich, K. E. (2010). *What intelligence test miss: The psychology of rational thought.* New Haven, CT: Yale University Press.

Stanovich, K. E., West, R. F., & Toplak, M. E. (2016). *The Rationality Quotient: Toward a test of rational thinking.* Cambridge, MA: MIT Press

Staib, S. (2003). Teaching and measuring critical thinking. *Journal of Nursing Education, 42,* 498–508.

Tremblay, K., Lalancette, D., & Roseveare, D. (2012). *Assessment of higher education learning outcomes.* OECD. Retrieved from www.oecd.org/education/skills-beyond-school/AHELOFSReportVolume1.pdf.

CHAPTER 13

Many Pathways, One Destination
IQ Tests, Intelligent Testing, and the Continual Push for More Equitable Assessments

Alan S. Kaufman[1]

I am a bit of an outlier in this book, given that my contributions to the field of intelligence have primarily been through the development and interpretation of IQ tests. IQ tests are often seen as a bastard stepfather of the intelligence field, despite the indisputable fact that if we do not measure intelligence, we cannot study it. First attempts at testing intellectual abilities predate psychology (and even Western civilization) itself (A. S. Kaufman, 2009). Yet early leaders like Francis Galton and Henry Goddard were steeped in eugenics; the field has often started and sputtered and stopped and started again, often driven by a publisher's wallet instead of scientific progress or societal benefit. It is in such an area I have spent my entire career, nearly a half-century's worth. I entered the field at a time when IQ tests were largely unchallenged and enjoyed wide acceptance – yet conversely were at a nadir of creativity and growth. I exit the field at a time when IQ tests have the potential to build off of a supernova of new ideas, research, theory, and technological capability – yet may be slowly sinking into irrelevance.

Looking Backward: Measuring Intelligence

A decade before I received my PhD (in 1970), IQ tests were remnants from the 1890s and World War I and filled with anachronisms. Only the thin line of Spearman's (1904) *g* theory kept them from being little more than a haphazard collection of laboratory tasks. In 1961, J. McV. Hunt (1961) was the first to try to introduce cognitive theory (Hebb, 1949; Piaget, 1930) into IQ testing; his work was an early strong influence that first sparked my life-long passion for integrating theory into measurement. My first published paper, in fact, was an outgrowth of Hunt's work (A. S. Kaufman, 1971).

There were many early multiple ability theorists whose works could have impacted IQ tests, such as L. L. Thurstone (1938), Raymond Cattell (1941), and J. P. Guilford (1956). Unfortunately, IQ remained blissfully ignorant and isolated from mainstream research on learning and intelligence, especially the cognitive and behavioral theories that emerged from these investigations.

For more than a half-century after Lewis Terman (1916) brought Alfred Binet's groundbreaking Binet-Simon measure (Binet & Simon, 1905) to America, IQ test development occurred in a theoretical vacuum. David Wechsler's (1939) Wechsler-Bellevue Intelligence Scale departed from the Binet-Terman *verbal* approach by adding a nonverbal (*performance*) piece to the IQ equation. Wechsler was my mentor and taught me immeasurably about measurement and life, but I can still recognize his limitations. He was guided by practicality, not a need for theory or innovation. Wechsler borrowed liberally from tests developed at the onset of America's entrance into World War I – namely the Army Alpha, a group-administered version of the Stanford-Binet developed by Arthur Otis, Terman's doctoral student at Stanford; the Army Beta, a nonverbal group test designed for illiterate and non-English-speaking draftees; and the Army Individual Performance Scale (Yoakum & Yerkes, 1920). The Alpha and Beta were used to label draftees ("Superior," "Very Inferior," etc.) and to select officers, whereas the individual test was used primarily to detect malingerers.

Ultimately, the tasks that Wechsler used to measure IQ were an aggregation of other people's tests. He took subtests (often exact items) from the Binet and Alpha to form his Verbal Scale and from the Beta and Individual Performance Scale to create his Performance Scale. Aside from the rare exception (Block Design, for example, was borrowed from Kohs, 1923), about a dozen tests developed in the early 1900s remained the bread-and-butter measures of the IQs of children, adolescents, and adults well into the 1990s.

I was project director of the WISC-R and worked directly with Wechsler. He taught me that tests were clinical instruments that told you about the entire person. As for my part, I ostensibly was there to offer the psychometric insights I learned from Robert Thorndike (my PhD advisor). Even more than that, however, I tried to make sure that children understood as much of the testing process as possible. By making the test directions as transparent as possible (e.g., telling a child to "try to work quickly" if a test awarded bonus points for quick, perfect performance), I hoped to make each child have the same opportunity as the next child.

Despite these improvements, the litter of tests (Wechsler, 1949, 1974, 1981) spawned by the original Wechsler-Bellevue resembled their predecessor and its ancestors as closely as the carbon copies of the original studies mirrored the first typed manuscript. The third editions of the WISC and

WAIS developed in the 1990s added a few "new" tests, such as Matrix Reasoning, a copy of the venerated task John Raven developed for his 1936 master's thesis. Status quo often gets rewarded; the Wechsler scales never lost their immense popularity despite its publisher's minimal concern with innovation and theory. Not until the publication of the WAIS-IV (Wechsler, 2008) and WISC-V (Wechsler, 2014) did Wechsler's tests embrace the future instead of the past (Kaufman, Raiford, & Coalson, 2016).

The conservatism in revising Wechsler's tests has led many critics to assume that the entire field remained stagnant. That was not the case. In the 1970s, I was among the handful of psychologists who tried to bring theory and sound measurement practices to the forefront of IQ test interpretation (A. S. Kaufman, 1979b; see also Matarazzo, 1972; Sattler, 1974). Such a battle began uphill. Wechsler's scales were not built from a theoretical foundation. If the clinicians who administered the tests even gave theory a passing thought, they were more likely to rely on Freud's psychoanalytic theory than on any cognitive or learning model. They would interpret any of the dozen subtests as if each one measured a specific skill (e.g., Picture Completion was notorious for measuring the ability to distinguish essential from nonessential detail). Further, clinicians rarely bothered to discern whether the person's pattern of so-called strengths and weaknesses painted a consistent picture of an individual's mental abilities, let alone if there might be an underlying theoretical explanation for the pattern.

When they did settle on a theory-based reason for a test result, it was often embarrassing (A. S. Kaufman et al., 2016). If a person failed an easy Comprehension item, the clinician might diagnose her or him as schizophrenic or psychotically depressed. A high score on Picture Completion might indicate paranoia (Mayman, Schafer, & Rapaport, 1951; Rapaport, Gill, & Schafer, 1945–1946). Such nonsense did not stop in the 1950s. Just one example: Allison, Blatt, and Zimet (1968) argued that someone with high Digit Symbol (Coding) and low Digit Span represented a sublimation of intense anxiety through extensive activity.

I entered the field of IQ testing at a time when the WISC and WAIS were assumed to measure a bagful of unimportant "splinter" abilities. My initial goal was to replace that mythology with an emphasis on the three factors that formed the foundation of Wechsler's scales: Verbal Comprehension, Perceptual Organization, and the ridiculously named Freedom from Distractibility factor. Cohen (1952, 1959) came up with the distractibility label, and I perpetuated the absurdity (A. S. Kaufman, 1975) at a time when I was a practicing and devout coward, unwilling to go against the crowd. One turning point was when I heard people at APA symposia refer to "Kaufman's Freedom from Distractibility factor." This silly nontheoretical interpretation that I simply didn't bother to rename or redefine was suddenly considered my creation. I had learned my lesson; complacency was easy but dangerous.

Battling over-interpretations of scatter (peaks and valleys in a person's profile of test scores), literal-mindedness, and being the unwanted namesake of an atheoretical factor, I gathered my courage and challenged a previous generation of "WISC Masters" in *Intelligent Testing with the WISC-R* (A. S. Kaufman, 1979b). Using a term borrowed from my former boss and mentor, Alexander Wesman (1968), I developed the intelligent testing approach. This approach was more than simply squashing simplistic psychoanalytical analysis of tiny differences or trying to infuse some cognitive theory into a test's interpretation.

In the intelligent testing philosophy, I urged practitioners to apply theoretical constructs to explain strengths or weaknesses on any of these factors. I focused on a few theories available at this time, such as Guilford's (1956) Structure of Intellect Model, Sperry's (1968) cerebral specialization theory, Luria's (1973) neuropsychological processing approach, and Osgood's (1952) theory of communication. As I continued to revise the intelligent testing approach and began my own journey of test development, new theories would become part of the approach. Throughout it all, I retained the term "intelligent testing" because stupid test interpretation remained so prevalent. It was front and center in the clinical case reports I often read and in the leading interpretive texts of the day. My main goal in promoting the intelligent testing philosophy was to bridge gaps: between theory and practice; between psychometrics and school psychology; and between psychology and special education.

Intelligent Testing was a slim volume, more akin to a brief "how to" book than the type of thick tome that usually causes a commotion. It offered psychologists a step-by-step method for using sensible, data-based procedures to interpret patterns of strengths and weaknesses on WISC-R profiles from the vantage point of diverse theories and within the context of how the child behaved during the evaluation (Anxious? Bored? Attentive? Impulsive? Oppositional? Immature?). It was reasonable to interpret low scores on the third factor as reflecting distractibility, poor attention span, or anxiety – but *only* if the intelligent tester observed these behaviors during the clinical evaluation. This approach asked examiners to conduct a research study with $N = 1$ every time a child or adult is evaluated.

Like many, I think, I shy away from self-praise, but the approach both changed the field and shaped my own career as a test developer. It is crucial to my conception of intelligence. I will let others I respect sing my praises as I slightly redden: *Intelligent Testing* "became the gold standard for psychometric test interpretation and clinical assessment" (Fletcher-Janzen, 2009, p. 15), "is at the core of our teaching, writing, research, and practice" (Flanagan, McGrew, & Ortiz, 2000, p, xviii), and "has saved a generation of psychologists from doing bad work" (Alm, 2009, p. 192). It "helped to clarify, refine, and substantiate, the most efficacious ways intelligence tests can and should be used with individuals having or suspected of having SLD [Specific Learning Disabilities]" (Mather, 2009, p. 30) and "offered the first glimpses of how to apply concepts from cognitive psychology and neuropsychology to the clinical practice of neuropsychology" (McCloskey & Perkins, 2013, p. 11).

It is important to note the dates of the glowing quotes. Praise did not come immediately. The blend of psychometrics and clinical observations to interpret fluctuations in a test profile was soundly criticized by some researchers (e.g., McDermott et al., 1992). The controversy persists to this day (Floyd & Kranzler, 2012), particularly among advocates of *g*, the whole *g*, and nothing but the *g* (Canivez & Kush, 2013). I have consistently tried to revise the method in response to such criticisms (A. S. Kaufman, 1994; A. S. Kaufman & Lichtenberger, 2006), with the occasional overhaul (A. S. Kaufman et al., 2016).

In its simplest structure, across 40 years the intelligent testing approach emphasizes three broad concepts. It urges examiners to interpret profiles of test scores from the vantage point of diverse theoretical perspectives. It asks them to integrate theory with clinical observations of test behaviors, relevant background information, state-of-the art research, and test scores on related neuropsychological and noncognitive constructs. And it urges the examiner to feature the person's *relative* strengths and weaknesses even if the test-taker scores well below the norms.

My colleagues, students, and I taught clinicians to interpret existing tests from theory in the 1970s, but we did not actually develop theory-based tests. I talked the talk (A. S. Kaufman, 1979a, 1979b), but it wasn't until the 1980s that I walked the walk. That decade witnessed the publication of three influential theory-based intelligence tests: our own Kaufman Assessment Battery for Children (K-ABC; A. S. Kaufman & Kaufman, 1983), along with the Stanford-Binet Intelligence Scale – 4th edition (Thorndike, Hagen, & Sattler, 1986), and the Woodcock-Johnson Psycho-Educational Battery – Revised (Woodcock & Johnson, 1989).

The K-ABC was built on an amalgam of Luria's neuropsychological processing theory and Sperry's psychobiological cerebral specialization theory. It was the first individually administered test of intelligence founded on theory.

The K-ABC spawned a second edition (KABC-II; A. S. Kaufman & Kaufman, 2004), with a digital version (KABC-D) on the horizon. Adaptations and translations of K-ABC and now KABC-II are popular worldwide, used often in countries like Germany, Japan, France, and Korea. Yet with a handful of international exceptions, no one has come close to giving Wechsler a serious challenge. The WISC-V "discovered" some aspects of contemporary theory (Wechsler, 2014), so perhaps a minor victory can be claimed for theoretical vs. atheoretical tests, but it is a hollow one.

Defining Intelligence So It Is Measurable

I have said at the outset that I am an outlier. Indeed, I have spent the first part of this chapter primarily discussing IQ tests, not intelligence. I find it hard to separate defining intelligence from outlining how I would best measure it, perhaps an occupational hazard. To me, a theory of intelligence must be operational. It must be clear how one could build a test that measures every dimension specified. I grant that this requirement is my own – but it is how I approach the field. I often agree philosophically with many of my sharpest critics, but I also believe in the real world. As much as I may want to measure a shadowy or elusive quality, if I cannot see how to test it, I cannot in good conscience include it in any official definition I would offer. Indeed, "[I]f a thing exists, it can be measured" (Reynolds, 2010, p. 1).

Given this preamble, I think of intelligence as the ability to solve new problems, process information, learn new material, and (for those with equal opportunity) assimilate knowledge from school, family, peers, and society. I think the distinction between "intelligence" and "achievement" is essential and was an underlying factor in how Nadeen and I first developed the K-ABC. Back then, we defined intelligence as problem-solving ability, akin to fluid reasoning, but made the mistake of not including enough strong measures of *Gf*. We defined achievement as a blend of conventional academic achievement (like reading comprehension) and traditional Binet-Wechsler tests of verbal intelligence (like vocabulary). We revised our approach with the KABC-II, which is built on the dual theoretical foundations of the CHC multiple abilities model (Schneider & McGrew, 2012) and Luria's (1973) neuropsychological processing approach.

We continue to revise our approach to measuring intelligence to the current day. If fortune and our publisher allow, the KABC-D will merge these models with Vygotsky's (1978) zones of proximal development. Intelligence will not just be measured statically, but also dynamically to identify those who are quick learners.

My conception of intelligence varies based on situation, though in no way am I a *g* theorist. If children and adults are referred to psychologists, usually for the purpose of solving actual, real-life problems, patterns of strong and weak abilities are needed to answer referral questions intelligently. Indeed, throughout the development of our tests, we have always given clinicians the option of excluding language and factual tasks for children who come from a non-mainstream cultural background that might impact either knowledge acquisition or verbal development (A. S. Kaufman & Kaufman, 2004).

The continued evolution of the various Kaufman tests and my own definition of intelligence have come, in part, from response to critics and our own research and experience. We have been criticized, sometimes correctly, for being too narrow in our approach to intelligence. The editor of this volume once argued the original K-ABC was "based on an inadequate conception of intelligence, and as a result, it is not a good measure of intelligence" (Sternberg, 1984, p. 277). Robert Sternberg's (1985, 2009), own theories, which also encompass traditionally ignored components such as creativity and practical intelligence, offer alternate perspectives.

Interestingly enough, it has been two of my children who have convinced me that even if IQ tests are unable (at present time and with current resources) to measure aspects beyond analytic intelligence, both creativity and practical intelligence are worthy constructs that will ideally be included in future tests. My son James has done seminal work on creativity (initially under Sternberg's mentorship), advancing new approaches to creativity theory and assessment (J. C. Kaufman, 2016). Like Sternberg, he has noted creativity's poor representation on IQ tests (J. C. Kaufman, 2015), even though including creativity measures in the IQ mix could help issues of equity (J. C. Kaufman, 2010). My daughter Jennie is a psychologist and professor of criminal justice who has studied both people with strong tacit knowledge of dangerous worlds (Singer, 2010) and those without the practical intelligence to function in the real world (Singer, Maguire, & Hurtz, 2013).

Measuring Intelligence So It Is Equitable

How should one best measure intelligence? In a word, "intelligently." Not with a single number. Not based on a single theory. Not in a group-administered format when people are referred for evaluation and life-changing decisions may rest on their scores. Not solely by a computer. Not in a vacuum that ignores the person's affect, effort, attitude, motivation, and problem-solving style. Assessments should be conducted by a care-fully trained professional, regardless of that person's title, who is a keen observer of behavior, steeped in cutting-edge research and theory, and who brings more to the table than just a well-developed test kit or carefully programmed iPad. The scores are less important than the interpretation given to them. The tester means more than the test.

Best measurement practices reflect how you believe a child intellectually develops. I have long been an advocate for teaching concepts, not facts. The world is oriented toward factual knowledge. People win money on game shows and get good grades for memorizing and retrieving minutiae. I am a strong believer in the parent's role in teaching concepts and cat-egorical thinking to infants and toddlers, virtually from day one. Actual teaching is not feasible for a week-old infant, but providing a stimulating visual, auditory, and kinesthetic environment is easy and essential. Over the past three decades, I have walked and talked with my nine grandchil-dren. In casual (often one-sided) conversation, I informally teach soft vs. hard; high vs. low; and plants vs. animals. I discuss the differences between colors, shapes, sizes, textures, and emotions. The stimuli are plentiful and young children's eagerness to learn is eternal and often contagious.

Behavioral genetic and epigenetic research suggests that heredity accounts for about 50% of the variance in the IQs of American children and adults (A. S. Kaufman, 2009; Plomin & Petrill, 1997) and that there is a dynamic interaction between the DNA we inherit and the environ-ment in which we are nurtured (Haggerty et al., 2010). The results of an array of genetic and epigenetic research studies converge on the notion that environment is instrumental in determining the intellectual heights children can reach. Early parental support has been shown in at least one longitudinal study to have a direct impact on brain development (Luby et al., 2012). It is the 50% that is *not* accounted for by heredity, I believe, that determines the intellectual heights children can reach. We have a respon-sibility as parents and grandparents (not to mention as teachers, mentors, or simply members of society) to create the optimal environment to help children develop their intellect. Merely providing cultural and educational opportunities is not sufficient. We need to interact directly and foster concept learning with methods that evoke curiosity and imagination. I want our children to score high not only on IQ tests of today, but on creativity or practical intelligence tests of tomorrow.

During my career I have attempted to apply my philosophy on how intelligence is best defined, developed, and measured to the research I have conducted, the tests I have developed with Nadeen, and the books I have written on intelligent interpretation of IQ tests. One of the driving forces throughout my life – something that coalesced more than I might have guessed before writing this chapter – has been the fervent need to reduce any type of bias. I want to level the playing field as much as possible. I have already mentioned my work with Wechsler to make the WISC-R as nonmysterious and straightforward as possible. My goal was to have no child penalized on timed tasks for not knowing to look up at the examiner at the end of every item. The pathways to success should be well marked. If two separate "ideas" are required for perfect scores on social comprehension items, then the examiner should press on: "Tell me another reason why…"

My determination to stop people from getting haphazardly punished first began with my research on how much scatter was normal in an individual's test profile. Scatter refers to variability in a person's profile of scores on ability tests. On a more global level, it might refer to the size of the difference between a person's Verbal IQ (V-IQ) and Performance IQ (P-IQ). Clinicians loved to interpret discrepancies between V-IQ and P-IQ as diagnostic of everything from early infantile autism to juvenile delinquency to brain damage (e.g., Black, 1976). For more specific abilities, scatter also refers to the amount of variability in a person's subtest profile. Someone consistently good (or mediocre) across all areas would have low scatter. In contrast, someone with high scatter might be good at solving visual-spatial problems but bad at verbal reasoning or visual-motor coordination. It was expected that children with learning disabilities would show notable scatter (Clements, 1966). Such diagnostic assertions about scatter begged two simple questions: (a) How much scatter is normal?; and (b) How can clinicians diagnose an *abnormality* without knowing what is *normal?*

To answer these questions, I investigated data for the 2,200 children and adolescents in the WISC-R standardization sample and discovered that it is normal to have scatter. The average child had a V-P discrepancy (in either direction) of 10 points (Kaufman, 1976b). One in four children had IQ discrepancies of more than 15 points, supposedly conclusive proof of brain damage. And subtest scatter? The WISC-R was comprised of 10 subtests whose scaled scores (standard scores with mean = 10 and SD = 3) could range from 1 to 19. Thus, one's scaled-score range (highest scaled score minus lowest scaled score) could potentially be as high as 18. The average person had a scaled-score range of 7 ± 2 points; a range of nine was entirely within normal range (Kaufman, 1976a). Based on common clinical practice at the time, children were often diagnosed with SLD (specific learning disability) because they had "scatter-filled" profiles with scores that ranged, for example, from 7–14 or 5–11.

In other words, subtest scatter did not necessarily mean that a child was learning disabled. High variability could be perfectly normal. A spate of research ensued on a variety of exceptional populations; in nearly every study, subtest scatter and V-P discrepancies did not indicate the presence of a neuropsychiatric disorder. The basic 7 ± 2 rule was confirmed for nearly every age range, demographic, and ability level (A. S. Kaufman, 1994). Data on V-P IQ discrepancies had been available a generation earlier (Seashore, 1950), but they had been ignored. When coupled with the new data on subtest scatter, clinicians paid attention and diagnostic practices changed. Children and adults were no longer saddled with inaccurate and unhelpful labels.

From my initial work on scatter to the *Intelligent Testing* approach, I tried to guide the interpretation of IQ tests to help children from getting lost in the riptides of ritual, rigidity, and adherence to mathematical formulas. When Nadeen and I developed the K-ABC from 1978 to 1983, we wanted to focus on process (sequential versus simultaneous processing) rather than content (verbal versus nonverbal). We aimed to develop a new set of child-oriented tasks beyond a reshaping of the same century-old mental tasks. Consistent with the *Intelligent Testing* philosophy, every child should understand the directions given by the examiner. We decided to separate intelligence (problem solving) from academic achievement and language ability. We included dozens of validity studies directly in the test manual, *prior* to the K-ABC's publication; previous IQ tests left the key question of construct validity for researchers to evaluate *after* the test was published. The most important goal, however, was to reduce the ethnic differences that have plagued (and continue to plague) conventional IQ tests into the present day.

We searched the literature for new tasks that would be both interesting and equitable (e.g., Kagan & Klein, 1973). Sometimes, testing the same information in a new format matters. The K-ABC subtest "Faces and Places" taps into a child's knowledge of basic information using photos and images instead of Wechsler's school-like verbal questions; by doing so, a task that produced large ethnic differences on Wechsler's tests produced small differences on ours (Kaufman, 1994).

We wanted to ensure that each task could be completely understood, so we introduced teaching items in which examiners could improvise. They could use their own words (in any language) to convey what was expected of each child on each subtest. Some critics balked at much of what we did, arguing that such items violated the whole nature of standardized assessment. Yet, we argued, if *every* child gets the teaching items, then the procedure *is* standardized for all. Most importantly, though, how can it be good to earn a low scaled score on Wechsler's Similarities subtest (i.e., How are RED and GREEN the same?) simply because a child did not understand the underlying conceptual meaning of "same"?

As for the goal of reducing ethnic differences, the empirical research showed we were at least partially successful. The traditional 15–16-point ethnicity gap was cut in half such that African Americans averaged 95 on the K-ABC and Hispanic Americans averaged 99 (A. S. Kaufman & Kaufman, 1983, tables 4.36 and 4.37). The test became popular for use with children from diverse ethnic groups, thereby helping reduce the disproportion of minority children in special education classes. Controversy, nonetheless, abounded. Was the reduction in ethnic differences due to our inclusion of too many memory tasks and too few reasoning tasks, as Herrnstein and Murray (1994) argued in *The Bell Curve?* Was it because our theory of intelligence was inadequate? Was it due to the language tasks being placed on a separate Achievement Scale? Or because we went out of our way to include tasks in the K-ABC that had already been identified in the research literature as "culture fair"?

We addressed these issues when we developed the KABC-II. We enhanced the theoretical foundation, added new tests of reasoning, and offered two global indexes (one with language and factual tasks, one without; the examiner could choose). We held our collective breath until the standardization data were analyzed. The results stayed the same: ethnic differences were still cut in half, even on the global scale (the Fluid-Crystallized Index or FCI) that includes measures of verbal knowledge and language abilities (A. S. Kaufman & Kaufman, 2004, tables 8.6 and 8.7). An additional validity study conducted by Elaine Fletcher-Janzen found that 30 Native American children scored about eight points higher on the KABC-II than the WISC-IV (A. S. Kaufman & Kaufman, 2004, pp. 97–98).

The original K-ABC had flaws both in theory and in content, but it led to change in the world of clinicians and in the conservative test-publishing industry (A. S. Kaufman, 2009). Even as the Wechsler tests remained dominant, many clinicians shifted their focus from content to process. At our urging, a school psychologist served as project director of the K-ABC instead of the traditional pure psychometricians without hands-on experience. More than 40 research studies were conducted before publication to appear in the manual to document the test's validity. These innovations, along with the teaching items and the development of novel subtests, are now standard protocol.

The development of the K-ABC began at the University of Georgia (1974–1979), and I believe another legacy will be the amazing constellation of doctoral students who worked with us in the research and development of the K-ABC – Bruce Bracken, Jack Cummings, Patti Harrison, Randy Kamphaus, Steve McCallum, Jack Naglieri, and Cecil Reynolds. This unbelievable array of talent converged in Athens, Georgia, at the same time. They went from working with us on the K-ABC to being leaders in school psychology. Collectively, they have won prestigious awards, founded and edited journals, published an array of widely read books and articles, and authored blockbuster clinical tests (e.g., Bracken & McCallum, 2016; Harrison & Oakland, 2015; Naglieri, Das, & Goldstein, 2014; Reynolds & Kamphaus, 2015a, 2015b). I am honored for whatever part Nadeen and I (and the K-ABC) played in the eventual success of our outrageously talented students, including Toshinori Ishikuma, who brought school psychology to Japan.

What I ultimately believe and hope the legacy of the K-ABC will be is that ethnic differences in IQ can be reduced if fairness is a priority. Indeed, I think that the equity of IQ tests for diverse groups remains the key educational and social policy issue of our time. IQ tests are still used to identify children and adolescents as intellectually disabled or gifted. They inform high-stakes decisions, such as whether a criminal should live or die in capital punishment cases. (Based on *Atkins* v. *Virginia*, 2002, it is unconstitutional to execute a person with an intellectual disability.) As long as IQ continues to play a key role in educational and societal decisions – and there is no evidence that policy change is on the horizon – the development and widespread utilization of fair measures must be a priority. The K-ABC and KABC-II have made progress in providing more equal opportunities, but further innovations are still needed.

Looking Forward: Measuring Intelligence

The field of IQ testing has always been slow to embrace new ideas. It took 70 years after the Stanford-Binet was published (Terman, 1916) for theory to weave its way into IQ tests, and the snail's pace has continued regarding technology. Based on advances in nearly every segment of society, computerized IQ tests should have been a done deal by now; indeed, it probably should have happened a decade ago. We began developing the KABC-D nearly 10 years ago as an iPad-to-iPad test designed to keep the clinician in the loop but also to take advantage of the latest in computer technology and cutting-edge neuroscience research on brain development. For five years we went full steam ahead on the KABC-D, but then the project was dropped for a couple of years; it was apparently too expensive to hire programmers at the same level as those who design video games, mobile applications, or interactive websites. The project has been revived again, replete with its integration of conventional IQ test theory (Luria, CHC) with Vygotsky's dynamic assessment and the inclusion of an fMRI validity study. But if and when the KABC-D will see the light of day is unknown.

There has been some progress in applying computer technology to IQ assessment, primarily by Pearson's Q-interactive technique, but this approach uses iPads to administer and score the same old tests. Innovation and risk-taking is lacking, and these tests do not come close to taking advantage of the potential of the sophisticated software that abounds elsewhere in the high-tech world. The future will come. Stealth assessment of intellectual abilities via video games is already in progress, just not with test developers (Shute & Ventura, 2013). Similarly, exciting brain research studies (e.g., Chavarria-Siles, Fernández, & Posthuma, 2014) will be integrated into intellectual assessment, even if not by mainstream publishers.

Q-interactive administrations of tests like the WISC-V and KTEA-3 continue to make headway despite the protests of clinicians and educators (especially in large school systems) slow to give up on the old ways. Many practitioners prefer the clinical administration of "paper-and-pencil" tests; I understand this resistance. I don't want to see the clinician removed from the IQ equation either. Behavioral observations and clinical inferences should remain an aspect of the clinical assessment of intelligence. I believe clinicians can hold on to a key role if the computer is allowed to do what it does best: stay behind the scenes. Technology can help ease the examiner's burden and keep track of every examinee mistake, reaction time, and each time the examinee's attention wavers. Computers can teach material to children using standardized techniques, compare their growth using standardized procedures, and quickly identify students who respond effectively to intervention.

The latest batch of revised tests published in 2014 (CAS2, WISC-V, and the WJ IV) has not made much progress on the computerization front. Until the technology can be successfully integrated into theory, however, it does not particularly matter. Right now the theories being applied to the Q-interactive are those that happen to lend themselves to one-on-one administration.

The revolution will come when an IQ test is developed that is rooted in a comprehensive, multifaceted theory of intelligence. It will use advances in AI, programming, and online capabilities that might right now only be imaginable to a handful of people. It will use these capabilities to measure aspects of intelligence that may seem impossible to currently capture. I would like to see the KABC-D take the field a step forward by blending existing theory with Vygotsky's zones of proximal development.

In closing, it is an honor to have been invited to contribute to this volume on intelligence. As I have mentioned, the editor of this book was one of the strongest critics of the original K-ABC (Sternberg, 1985). But he also paid me the highest compliment I have ever received (Sternberg, 2009):

> If one were to ask who are the people who most have influenced and impacted ability testing, almost certainly Alfred Binet would be #1. David Wechsler would probably be #2. In my mind, Alan Kaufman would be #3. And in terms of productivity, he surpassed Binet and Wechsler relatively early in his career. (p. 113)

I am not sure I agree with his last statement, flattering as it is. For one, Wechsler (2008, 2014) continues to publish tests at a frenetic pace despite his death in 1981; he even published a brand-new achievement test a decade after he died (Wechsler, 1992)! More seriously, however, his influence is seen throughout my own work. His mentorship shaped my own thinking on intelligence, just as I hope I have mentored future generations. And – like Binet, like Wechsler – I hope my efforts to move IQ testing as far as possible from its early elitist roots and toward its use as a tool to help all children, regardless of background, will be my own legacy for the future.

Note

1 I am indebted to James Kaufman for his insightful overhaul of the first draft of this chapter and to Nadeen Kaufman, Cecil Reynolds, and Jennie Singer for their valuable input.

References

Allison, J., Blatt, S. J., & Zimet, C. N. (1968). *The interpretation of psychological tests*. New York: Harper & Row.

Alm, J. (2009). Alan Kaufman's deep influence in Sweden. In J. C. Kaufman (Ed.), *Intelligent testing*. (pp. 191–192). New York: Cambridge.

Bannatyne, A. (1971). *Language, reading, and learning disabilities*. Springfield, IL: Charles C Thomas.

Binet, A., & Simon, T. (1905). Methodes nouvelles pour le diagnostic du niveau intellectuel des anormaux. *L'Annee Psychologique, 11*, 191–244.

Black, F. W. (1976). Cognitive, academic, and behavioral findings in children with suspected and documented neurological dysfunction. *Journal of Learning Disabilities, 9*, 182–187.

Bracken, B. A., & McCallum, R. S. (2016). *Universal nonverbal intelligence test, second edition (UNIT2)*. Austin, TX: PRO-ED.

Canivez, G. L., & Kush, J. C. (2013). WISC–IV and WAIS–IV structural validity: Alternate methods, alternate results. Commentary on Weiss et al. (2013a) and Weiss et al. (2013b). *Journal of Psychoeducational Assessment, 31*, 157–169.

Cattell, R. B. (1941). Some theoretical issues in adult intelligence testing. *Psychological Bulletin, 38*, 592.

Chavarría-Siles, I., Fernández, G., & Posthuma, D. (2014). Brain imaging and cognition. In D. Finkel & C. A. Reynolds (Eds.). *Behavior genetics of cognition throughout the lifespan* (pp. 235–256). New York: Springer.

Clements, S. D. (1966). *Minimal brain dysfunction in children: Terminology and identification – Phase I (NINDB Monograph #3, U. S. Public Service Publication No. 1415)*. Washington, DC: Department of Health, Education, and Welfare.

Cohen, J. (1952). A factor-analytically based rationale for the Wechsler-Bellevue. *Journal of Consulting Psychology, 16*, 272–277.

(1959). The factorial structure of the WISC at ages 7–6, 10–6, and 13–6. *Journal of Consulting Psychology, 23*, 285–299.

Flanagan, D. P., McGrew, K. S., & Ortiz, S. O. (2000). *The Wechsler intelligence scales and CHC theory*. Boston: Allyn & Bacon.

Fletcher-Janzen, E. (2009). Intelligent testing: Bridging the gap between classical and romantic science in assessment. In J. C. Kaufman (Ed.), *Intelligent testing* (pp. 15–29). New York: Cambridge.

Floyd, R. G., & Kranzler, J. H. (2012). Processing approaches to interpretation of information from cognitive ability tests. In D. P. Flanagan & P. L. Harrison (Eds.), *Contemporary intellectual assessment* (3rd edn., pp. 497–525). New York: Guilford Press.

Guilford, J. P. (1956). The structure of intellect. *Psychological Bulletin, 53*, 267–293.

Haggerty, P., Hoad, G., Harris, S. E., Starr, J. M., Fox, H. C., Deary, I. J., & Whalley, L. J. (2010). Human intelligence and polymorphisms in the DNA methyltransferase genes Involved in epigenetic marking. PLoS One, 5, e11329. Published online 2010 Jun 25. doi: 10.1371/journal.pone.0011329.

Harrison, P. L., & Oakland, T. (2015) *Adaptive behavior assessment system, third edition (ABAS-3)*. Torrance, CA: Western Psychological Services.

Hebb, D. O. (1949). *The organization of behavior*. New York: Wiley.

Herrnstein, R. J., & Murray, C. A. (1994). *The bell curve*. New York: Free Press.

Hunt, J McV. (1961). *Intelligence and experience*. New York: Ronald Press.

Kagan, J., & Klein, R. E. (1973). Cross-cultural perspectives on early development. *American Psychologist, 28*, 947–961.

Kaufman, A. S. (1971). Piaget and Gesell: A psychometric analysis of tests built from their tasks. *Child Development*, 42, 1341–1360.

(1975). Factor analysis of the WISC-R at eleven age levels between 6-1/2 and 16-1/2 years. *Journal of Consulting and Clinical Psychology*, 43, 135–147.

(1976a). A new approach to the interpretation of test scatter on the WISC-R. *Journal of Learning Disabilities*, 9, 160–168.

(1976b). Verbal-performance IQ discrepancies on the WISC-R. *Journal of Consulting and Clinical Psychology*, 44, 739–744.

(1979a). Cerebral specialization and intelligence testing. *Journal of Research and Development in Education*, 12, 96–107.

(1979b). *Intelligent testing with the WISC-R*. New York: Wiley.

(1994). *Intelligent testing with the WISC-III*. New York: Wiley.

(2009). *IQ testing 101*. New York: Springer.

Kaufman, A. S., & Kaufman, N. L. (1983). *K-ABC interpretive manual*. Circle Pines, MN: American Guidance Service.

(2004). *Kaufman Assessment Battery for Children – Second Edition (KABC-II)*. Circle Pines, MN: American Guidance Service.

Kaufman, A. S., & Lichtenberger, E. O. (2006). *Assessing adolescent and adult intelligence* (3rd edn.). New York: Wiley.

Kaufman, A. S., Raiford, S. E., & Coalson, D. L. (2016). *Intelligent testing with the WISC-V*. Hoboken, NJ: Wiley.

Kaufman, J. C. (2010). Using creativity to reduce ethnic bias in college admissions. *Review of General Psychology*, 14, 189–203.

(2015). Why creativity isn't in IQ tests, why it matters, and why it won't change anytime soon ... Probably. *Journal of Intelligence*, 3, 59–72.

(2016). *Creativity 101* (2nd edn.). New York: Springer.

Kohs, S. C. (1923). *Intelligence measurement*. New York: Macmillan.

Luby, J. L., Barch, D. M., Belden, A., Gaffrey, M. S., Tillman, R., Babb, C., Nishino, T., Suzuki, H., & Botteron, K. N. (2012, February). Maternal support in early childhood predicts larger hippocampal volumes at school age. *Proceedings of the National Academy of Science USA*, 109, 2854-2859. doi: 10.1073/pnas.1118003109.

Luria, A. R. (1973). *The working brain: An introduction to neuropsychology* (trans: Haigh, Basil). London: Penguin.

Matarazzo, J. D. (1972). *Wechsler's measurement and appraisal of adult intelligence* (5th edn.). New York: Oxford University Press.

Mather, N. (2009). The intelligent testing of children with specific learning disabilities. In J. C. Kaufman (Ed.), *Intelligent testing* (pp. 30–52). New York: Cambridge.

Mayman, M., Schafer, R., & Rapaport, D. (1951). Interpretation of the WAIS in personality appraisal. In H. H. Anderson & G. L. Anderson (Eds.), *An introduction to projective techniques* (pp. 541–580). New York: Prentice-Hall.

McCloskey, G., & Perkins, L. A. (2013). *Essentials of executive functions assessment*. Hoboken, NJ: Wiley.

McDermott, P. A., Fantuzzo, J. W., Glutting, J. J., Watkins, M. W., & Baggaley, A. R. (1992). Illusions of meaning in the ipsative assessment of children's ability. *Journal of Special Education, 25,* 504–526. doi:10.1177/0022466992025000407

Naglieri, J. A., Das, J. P., & Goldstein, S. (2014). *Cognitive assessment system – CAS2* (2nd edn.). Austin, TX: PRO-ED.

Osgood, C. E. (1952). The nature and measurement of meaning. *Psychological Bulletin, 49,* 197–237.

Piaget, J. (1930). *The child's conception of physical causality.* London: Kegan Paul.

Plomin, R., & Petrill, S. A. (1997). Genetics and intelligence: What's new? *Intelligence, 24,* 53–77.

Rapaport, D., Gill, M. M., & Schafer, R. (1945–1946). *Diagnostic psychological testing.* Chicago, IL: Year Book Publishers.

Raven, J. C. (1936). Mental tests used in genetic studies: The performance of related individuals on tests mainly educative and mainly reproductive. Unpublished master's thesis, University of London.

Reynolds, C. R. (2010). Measurement and assessment: An editorial view. *Psychological Assessment, 22,* 1–4.

Reynolds, C. R., & Kamphaus, R. W. (2015a). *Behavior assessment system for children, third edition (BASC-3).* Bloomington, MN: Pearson Clinical Assessment.

(2015b). *Reynolds intellectual assessment scales, third edition (RIAS-2).* Odessa, FL: Psychological Assessment Resources.

Sattler, J. M. (1974). *Assessment of children's intelligence* (Rev. edn.). Philadelphia, PA: Saunders.

Schneider, W. J., & McGrew, K. S. (2012). The Cattell-Horn-Carroll model of intelligence. In D. P. Flanagan & P. L. Harrison (Eds.), *Contemporary intellectual assessment* (3rd edn., pp. 99–144). New York: Guilford Press.

Seashore, H. G. (1950). Differences between verbal and performance IQs on the Wechsler intelligence scale for children. *Journal of Consulting Psychology, 15,* 62–67.

Shute, V. J., & Ventura, M. (2013). *Measuring and supporting learning in games: Stealth assessment.* Cambridge, MA: MIT Press.

Singer, J. K. (2010). Creativity in confinement. In D. H. Cropley, A. J. Cropley, J. C. Kaufman & M. A. Runco (Eds.), *Dark side of creativity* (pp. 177–203). New York: Cambridge.

Singer, J. K., Maguire, M., & Hurtz, G. M. (2013). The prevalence of mental illness in California sex offenders on parole: A comparison of those who recidivated with a new sex crime versus those who did not. *Victim and Offender, 8,* 253–277.

Spearman, C. E. (1904). "General intelligence": Objectively determined and measured. *American Journal of Psychology, 15,* 201–293.

Sperry, R. W. (1968). Hemisphere deconnection and unity in conscious awareness. *American Psychologist, 23,* 723–733.

Sternberg, R. J. (1984). Evaluation of the Kaufman Assessment Battery for Children from an information-processing perspective. *Journal of Special Education*, 18, 269–279.

Sternberg, R. J. (2009). The theory of successful intelligence as a basis for new forms of ability testing at the high school, college, and graduate school levels. In J. C. Kaufman (Ed.), *Intelligent testing* (pp. 113–147). New York: Cambridge.

Terman, L. M. (1916). *The measurement of intelligence*. Boston: Houghton Mifflin.

Thorndike, R. L., Hagen, E. P., & Sattler, J. M. (1986). *Stanford-Binet Intelligence Scale* (4th edn.). Chicago, IL: Riverside.

Thurstone, L. L. (1938). Primary mental abilities. *Psychometric Monographs*, 1.

Vygotsky, L. (1978). *Mind in society: The development of higher mental functioning*. Cambridge, MA: Harvard University Press.

Wechsler, D. (1939). *The measurement of adult intelligence*. Baltimore, MD: Williams & Wilkins Co.

(1949). *Wechsler Intelligence Scale for Children*. New York: The Psychological Corporation.

(1974). *Manual for the Wechsler Intelligence Scale for Children-Revised (WISC-R)*. New York: The Psychological Corporation.

(1981). *Manual for the Wechsler Intelligence Scale for Children-Revised*. San Antonio, TX: The Psychological Corporation.

(1992). *Wechsler Individual Achievement Test (WIAT)*. San Antonio, TX: The Psychological Corporation.

(2008). *Wechsler Adult Intelligence Scale* (4th edn.). San Antonio, TX: Pearson.

(2014). *Wechsler Intelligence Scale for Children* (5th edn.). Bloomington, MN: Pearson.

Wesman, A. G. (1968). Intelligent testing. *American Psychologist*, 23, 261–214.

Woodcock, R. W., & Johnson, M. B. (1989). *Woodcock-Johnson Psycho-Educational Battery – Revised*. Itasca, IL: Riverside Publishing.

Yoakum, C. S., & Yerkes, R. M. (1920). *Army mental tests*. New York: Henry Holt.

CHAPTER 14

My Quest to Understand Human Intelligence

Scott Barry Kaufman

It is truly an honor to contribute to this volume. Many of the contributors have had a significant influence on my interest to go into this field in the first place. In thinking through how to structure this chapter, I decided it would make the most sense to go in chronological order and be as honest as I could be about the development of my thinking on this fascinating topic of human intelligence – a topic that has consumed my mind from as early as I can remember.

The Wonder Years (1979–1998)

My early experiences most certainly shaped my thinking about intelligence. By the age of three, I had 21 ear infections. As a result, I was diagnosed with Central Auditory Processing Disorder (CAPD), a hearing problem that made it difficult for me to process auditory input in real time. It would take me a few extra milliseconds to process new information because I had to replay in my head what was said before I could understand what was being spoken. I repeated third grade, and was placed in special education. I remained in special education until ninth grade, unquestioningly, despite feeling I was capable of more intellectual challenges. Every time I asked to take more challenging courses, I was denied. Also, even though the learning disability no longer posed a challenge to my learning, I was kept in special education because the educators felt as though I was too anxious. Of course, I was anxious because I was not being challenged. So this was a vicious cycle that did nothing to enhance my learning.

Respite came in ninth grade, when a special-education teacher who was covering class one day took me aside and asked why I was still there. I realized I had no good answer to that question, and also realized I had been waiting for just this moment when someone would believe in a higher potential for me. While my parents were certainly well meaning by wanting to ease any burden on me in school, they did not challenge the authorities. So I knew I would have to take myself out of special education, which I did. Once I was in regular classes, I learned a lot about myself – my strengths and weaknesses. I was grateful for the opportunity to fully explore the depths of my being.

Why tell this story? Perhaps it seems out of place in such an academic volume. But I believe my personal experience, and the other experiences I saw firsthand, are very relevant to the discussion of the nature of human intelligence. As I went through these early years, I very much wondered about the nature of human intelligence and potential. I knew that my friends in special education weren't disabled just because they had specific difficulties in learning. I witnessed the negative expectations from teachers, and became sure that such expectations were being signaled loud and clear to all of us.

So, long before I started to scientifically investigate intelligence, I had intuitions, based on personal experiences, that our dominant paradigm of intelligence was practically limiting the potential of students. I could plainly see it all around me. Even those on the "other side" – the students who did well on standardized tests and received accolades from teachers – yearned to be valued for something more than their test performance. It would take me awhile before I was able to formulate my thoughts into a formal scientific theory, but a major impetus along this path was my encounter as an undergraduate with cognitive psychology.

Introduction to Intelligence Research (1998–2003)

While I didn't initially get accepted as a psychology major at Carnegie Mellon University, I transferred into the department soon after I entered as an opera major. During a course in cognitive psychology taught by Anne Fay, I discovered the science of intelligence. I remember very clearly the crystallizing experience (Walters & Gardner, 1998).

I was sitting on the sofa in my dorm reading the chapter on intelligence that was in the cognitive psychology textbook we were assigned. I remember becoming so overwhelmingly excited by this material that I flipped to the inside cover to see who wrote the book. It said, "Robert J. Sternberg, Yale University." I made a commitment in that moment that *one day, no matter what*, I would study the science of human intelligence with Sternberg. In fact, if you told my 20-year-old self that I would not only study with Sternberg, but I would end up coediting a handbook on intelligence with him (Sternberg & Kaufman, 2011), and even be a contributor to this very volume that is in your hands, I would have probably fainted! So with the help of Professor Fay, I read voraciously on the topic, virtually reading every single book in the CMU library on the topic of human intelligence. In addition to Sternberg's work, I was also exposed to the ideas of Howard Gardner on multiple intelligences, and Ellen Winner's work on gifted children. I also took Herbert Simon's graduate course on cognition and learned about the role of expertise in skill development.

Nevertheless, I knew that if I ever were to go beyond the traditional view of intelligence, I would have to go into the lion's den and learn as much as I could about IQ. So I reached out to University of Cambridge professor Nicholas J. Mackintosh, author of *IQ and Human Intelligence* (Mackintosh, 2011). To my great surprise and excitement, he accepted me as an intern for a semester study abroad. So I took a semester off of CMU, and attempted to learn as much as I could about IQ from one of the most sensible and thoughtful scientists in the field. It was to be the start of a fascinating journey to understand the nature of IQ and its boundary conditions.

Dual-Process Theory of Human Intelligence (2003–2009)

After interning for both Robert J. Sternberg and Nicholas J. Mackintosh as an undergraduate, I was accepted to continue my studies with both of them – Sternberg at Yale for my PhD, and Mackintosh at Cambridge for my M. Phil under a Gates Cambridge Scholarship. Once embarking on this adventure, I made two commitments to myself: (1) I would keep my personal story a secret, fearful that I would be perceived as not objective in my science, and (2) I would take my own personal feelings out of the equation, and work as hard as possible to understand human intelligence, regardless of where the search led.

One of the first questions I had was whether the field was missing any lower-order factors. After all, Carroll (1993) did such a wonderful job cataloging the many subcomponents of general intelligence (*g*). But were we missing anything?

Through working with Mackintosh, I was exposed to his seminal work on associative learning (Mackintosh, 1974). While more rudimentary forms of associative learning were included in Carroll's model, Mackintosh and I were interested in looking at the unique contribution of more sophisticated forms of associative learning, such as the forms that Mackintosh and his colleagues had investigated in other animals. Evolution has endowed animals (including humans!) with quite sophisticated mental structures for associative learning.

So we adopted the three-term contingency learning task from Williams and Pearlberg (2006), which, over the course of four learning blocks, requires participants to learn word associations that are contingent on a particular key press. For example, one trial the word "LAB" might be shown with the letters "A," "B," and "C" shown underneath. When participants selected one letter (e.g., "A"), they would see one association (e.g., PUN), when they selected another letter (e.g., "B"), they would see a second association (e.g., "TRY"), and so on. During the test blocks, participants were required to type in the outcome word corresponding to a particular stimulus-response pair.

We found that this more complex form of associative learning showed stronger correlations with g than paired-associates learning, a form of associative learning not dependent on contingencies (Kaufman et al., 2009). What's more, an overarching associative learning factor predicted g above and beyond the effects of two other well-known contributors to g: working memory and processing speed. We concluded that these findings added to a growing literature on the existence of multiple cognitive mechanisms supporting g (see Conway & Kovacs, Chapter 4, this volume), and that the ability to explicitly learn complex associations between stimuli was one of those important mechanisms.

Was that it? Were there other forms of associative learning that made a contribution to intelligence? As I continued to study with Mackintosh, I became fascinated with a form of learning called *implicit learning*, which involves the learning of information without conscious intent or awareness of what has been learned (Stadler & Frensch, 1997). What fascinated me so much about this form of learning is that it seemed to be independent of general intelligence (Gebauer & Mackintosh, 2007; Reber, Walkenfeld, & Hernstadt, 1991). This was quite remarkable to me since in my reading of the intelligence literature it seemed that every form of cognition under the sun loaded onto g.

So when I returned to Yale to complete my PhD, I rounded up as many implicit learning tasks as I could from the cognitive science literature, and adapted them for the individual-differences paradigm. With the assistance of Luis Jiménez, a leading researcher on attention and implicit learning, we found that the ability to *implicitly* detect complex and noisy regularities in the environment (by learning complex probabilities in a sequence) showed a weak correlation with g (Kaufman et al., 2010). Nevertheless, individual differences in implicit learning independently predicted verbal analogical reasoning, processing speed, and academic performance on two foreign-language exams. What's more, implicit-learning ability was correlated with self-reported intuition, openness to experience, and impulsivity – three variables that have also been linked to increased creativity (see Kaufman & Gregoire, 2015).

These findings excited me greatly, because it suggested a boundary condition for *g: implicit cognition*. For me, this opened up a whole new universe of investigation from an individual-differences perspective (Kaufman, 2011)! The field of human intelligence had been so focused on the ability to explicitly learn, but what about the ability to *implicitly* learn? These findings dovetailed nicely with extant dual-process theories of cognition, which posited two forms of information processing: a slower mode that was more dependent on working memory, and a faster mode that was relatively independent from executive functioning, but nevertheless quite cognitively complex (see Kaufman, 2011, for a review).

However, despite the various dual-process theories of cognition that existed, there wasn't explicitly a dual-process theory of human intelligence. What's more, the dual-process theories that existed tended to devalue the importance of the implicit route. Rationality and explicit reasoning were held up as the most important contributor to adaptive cognition. Not only was there such a preponderant focus on the foibles of implicit cognition, but individual differences in implicit cognition were thought to be minimal and unimportant.

So I was inspired to propose the Dual-Process Theory of Human Intelligence for my doctoral dissertation (Kaufman, 2009) that attempted to overcome these limitations. Arguing that all human intelligent behaviors are the result of a mix of both goal-directed and spontaneous cognitive processes (in varying degrees depending on the task), I argued that there are adaptive individual differences along both dimensions. What's more, I argued that neither mode of information processing is more universally "intelligent" than any other, but that intelligence is better thought of as the ability to *flexibly* switch mode of thought depending on the situation. Finally, and foretelling the work that would yet to come, I argued that there are a variety of paths to the same intelligent behavior, with different people drawing on a different mix of cognitive traits to reach the same intelligent outcome.

In addition to my dissertation data, I also drew on other collaborations I was having at the time (e.g., Brown et al., 2010, Pretz et al., 2010). For example, Jaimie Brown and I found that the ability to implicitly learn a variety of information was not impaired in those with autism-spectrum conditions, and this was not a consequence of compensation by explicit-learning ability or IQ. A major implication of this finding was that a sole focus on explicit cognition would underestimate the intellectual capabilities of this population, and, I suspected, many other populations as well.

Coming out Ungifted and the Theory of Personal Intelligence (2009–2013)

After I completed my PhD, I moved to New York City. While the academic journey I had been on to understand intelligence was enriching, I ultimately was left unsatisfied. I certainly had learned a lot about the nature of human intelligence, but *how was it actually helping children?* What about all of those classmates of mine who clearly had so much potential: how would knowing the structure of *g* impact their lives in any concrete way? I was ready to go beyond the science of the structure and correlates of cognitive ability and contemplate the implications for creating an education system that gives opportunities for everyone to intellectually and creatively flourish.

Something that became clear is that psychologists – whether we like it or not – have a real impact on the lives of children, however indirect that effect may seem. For instance, school psychologists in training learn about the latest IQ tests, and are taught how to use that information to inform a custom-tailored intervention for the child. Conceptualizations of intelligence coming from scientists do trickle down to the students via the educators. As much as scientists may wish to operate in a vacuum and do "pure science," the stakes are too high when it comes to the study of human intelligence. The scientists' conceptualization of what intelligence means, how it is measured, and what it foretells about a person's future prospects in life is often taken at face value by educators in training, who make high-stakes decisions on a daily basis about what a child is and is not capable of achieving in life. So I wanted to really think through how all of the latest research on human intelligence, talent, creativity, and potential could inform an education system that brings out the best in *all* children.

To my delight, Giles Anderson – a literary agent in New York City – was interested in having me develop my ideas about intelligence into a book. Thus began the period of writing *Ungifted: Intelligence Defined.* In this book, I decided to "come out" as ungifted, and reveal my personal story, in the hopes that it would inspire others to overcome their own learning difficulties. Weaving my personal story with the latest science of IQ testing, general intelligence, talent, and creativity, I proposed the Theory of Personal Intelligence, which was informed by my Dual-Process Theory, but went beyond it so it could have more of a direct impact on the real lives of children.

Surveying 13 widely used definitions of intelligence, I noticed a serious mismatch between conceptualizations of intelligence in the literature and its operationalization. One common theme across various definitions of intelligence was adaptation to the environment: not just dealing with the school environment, but also the capacity for flexibility, resiliency, tenacity, motivation, and coping strategies for dealing with the inevitable daily stressors and unknowns of life. These skills clearly go beyond what is measured on an IQ test, or what could possibly *ever* be captured by a single snapshot of intelligence.

Indeed, David Wechsler, creator of one of the most widely used intelligence tests, the *Wechsler Adult Intelligence Scale* and the *Wechsler Intelligence Scale for Children*, explicitly noted:

> One need not be afraid or ashamed to acknowledge impulse, instinct, and temperament as basic factors in general intelligence. My point has always been that general intelligence cannot be equated with intellectual ability, but must be regarded as a manifestation of the personality as a whole.

Similarly, Richard Snow made a call to take into account a broader range of personal characteristics (or as he put it, "aptitudes"), and to conceptualize potential as "degree of readiness" to perform in a particular situation or domain. Critically, he believed in the importance of multiple paths to the same outcome, and helping students figure out for themselves the best path to develop their expertise given their unique set of aptitudes. In his 1980 paper "Intelligence for the Year 2001," Snow writes:

> It is not unreasonable to hypothesize that both conative and affective aspects of persons and situations influence the details of cognitive processing … A theoretical account of intelligent behavior in the real world requires a synthesis of cognition, conation and affect. We have not really begun to envision this synthesis.

Certainly, my goal was never to lambaste IQ tests. As I recognized in the book, IQ tests can be useful for scientifically investigating the mind and brain. What's more, by adopting an intelligent testing approach (see A. S. Kaufman, 1979; A. S. Kaufman, Raiford, & Coalson, 2016), the pattern of strengths and weaknesses identified by a comprehensive IQ test battery can usefully inform educational interventions. So I fully acknowledged the existence of general cognitive ability. But from a real, practical perspective, I felt the need to propose a much more personal form of intelligence, which I referred to as Personal Intelligence and defined as "the dynamic interplay of engagement and abilities in pursuit of personal goals."

I argued that this form of personal intelligence is not well captured by IQ tests, for a number of reasons. For one, IQ tests are so reliant on working memory, and these tests will under-predict the intellectual potential of many children with different kinds of minds (e.g., children with dyslexia, autism, etc.) who may have working memory deficits, but still have immense capability and drive to master the rules of a domain (for my definition of talent, see Kaufman, 2013b). Second, engagement and skill development feed off each other. Engaging in an IQ session is not an inherently motivating task for most people! However, I reviewed examples throughout the book of what people are capable of achieving once they are fully engaged in something that they have an inclination for and are passionate about. Ability and engagement dynamically shape each other over time. I'd like to emphasize that last point: *intelligence develops over time, in a particular context* (see Ceci, 1996; Sternberg & Grigorenko, 2001; Vygotsky, 1978). While IQ tests may be able to reliably measure abstract reasoning ability and working memory, let's not underestimate what a person is capable of accomplishing intellectually or creatively given a long period of active engagement. There are many cases of children with learning disabilities who have been written off, only to far surpass expectations once engaged in a particular area of interest.

To achieve this perspective on intelligence, I found it necessary to shift from the individual-differences level to the *personal* level. I was particularly inspired by the work of developmental psychologists who are developing exciting new techniques to study variation *within* the person (e.g., Blair & Diamond, 2008; Kaufman & Duckworth, 2015; Molenaar et al., 2004, 2009; Sternberg & Grigorenko, 2001). Instead of selecting a few fixed time points, a select range of cognitive skills, and aggregating the results across subjects, the new "person-specific paradigm" focuses on a single person, selects a range of time points, and considers the trajectory of a dynamic system of cognitive, emotional, and personality processes as they unfold over time.

It's becoming clear that not all results from the individual differences paradigm necessarily apply at the person-specific level (see Molenaar, 2009). When we select a single variable (e.g., IQ) and compare people on that variable, we can rank relative differences in performance. But within a person, any single variable is *inseparable* from the rest of the system. You can't just strip out reasoning ability from a single individual, as their reasoning performance is undoubtedly affected by a whole host of variables, including motivation, history of expectations from teachers and parents, and levels of anxiety.

Therefore, consistent with a long line of thinkers on the development of intelligence (e.g., Snow, 1980; Sternberg & Grigorenko, 2001; Vygotsky, 1978), I preferred to think of potential as *readiness for engagement*. So instead of any single test score representing a person's lifelong potential, it is merely viewed as a person's readiness to handle more enriched resources at that particular time (Vygotsky, 1978). In this view, potential is a moving target dependent on a variety of factors, including engagement. Therefore, when we apply arbitrary thresholds without taking into account personal goals, engagement, and other within-person variables, we limit possibility. The Theory of Personal Intelligence is a call to be open to the incredible transformations people can undergo when they are allowed to engage in a domain that is aligned with their self-identity. After all, creativity researcher E. Paul Torrance found that a love for the domain was the single best predictor of lifelong creative achievement – both societal and personal – long after the effects of IQ and divergent thinking faded away (e.g., Torrance, 1983).

Of course, the Theory of Personal Intelligence was influenced by many different perspectives, and I really view it as a synthesis rather than a completely new theory. According to Sternberg (1997, 2011), successful intelligence is defined as the ability to achieve one's goals in life (in terms of one's own personal standards), within one's sociocultural context, by capitalizing on strengths and correcting or compensating for weaknesses, in order to adapt to, shape, and select environments, through a combination of analytical, creative, and practical abilities. Many elements of this theory have inspired the Theory of Personal Intelligence, including the personal definition of success, the importance of context and building on strengths, and the inclusion of abilities that go beyond IQ. The Theory of Personal Intelligence goes beyond ability, however, including engagement, character strengths, and other "noncognitive" traits in the model (Heckman, 2000; Peterson & Seligman, 1994). Additionally, the Theory of Personal Intelligence is also more explicitly a developmental model of intelligence. Likewise, while Gardner's (1983, 1999) theory of multiple intelligences expands the repertoire of abilities that fall within the domain of intelligence, the theory doesn't highlight the deeply intertwined nature of engagement and ability during the course of intellectual and creative development.

Within the social domain, Gardner's (1983) intrapersonal and interpersonal intelligence, Kihlstrom and Cantor's (2011) social intelligence, Mayer and Salovey's (1993) emotional intelligence, and Mayer's (2008) personal intelligence all certainly elucidate the nature of the capacities for understanding and adaptively employing emotion, social cognition, and one's own personality. Even though my theory shares a similar name (and in one case, is the same exact name, which was a pure coincidence!), my Theory of Personal Intelligence has a broader focus, considering the whole person as a dynamic system as he or she works toward reaching personal goals and adapting to inevitable setbacks along the way. Social and emotional processes certainly play a role, but they are only part of a whole suite of traits that are unique to each individual, and that can be mixed and matched in unique ways to develop one's own unique style of adaptive intellectual and creative functioning.

This broader focus of the Theory of Personal Intelligence really resonated with teachers and parents, especially those who work with kids on the margins (e.g., children with learning difficulties, children in gifted and talented programs, and even those students who simultaneously have learning difficulties *and* qualify for gifted and talented education). I was pleased to make some sort of practical impact. Even within the academic world, however, I was pleased to read Earl Hunt's positive review of *Ungifted* in the journal *Intelligence* (Hunt, 2013). Nevertheless, I still felt as though I had partially left a world of academic scientific inquiry that had once captivated me so much.

As it would so happen, I would enter a whole new world of scientific inquiry that aligned very much with my thinking about intelligence: positive psychology.

Positive Psychology, Imagination, and Character (2014–2017)

When Martin Seligman, one of the founders of the field of positive psychology, asked me if I would be interested in moving to Philadelphia and becoming scientific director of the Imagination Institute, of course I said yes! Seligman and his graduate student Marie Forgeard (who is now a postdoc at McLean Hospital) had received a large grant from the Templeton Foundation to advance the measurement and development of imagination across all sectors of society. About $3 million went toward a grants competition, in which we selected 16 research projects aimed at the development of better ways of assessing and developing imagination and creativity. The rest of the grant went toward a series of "Imagination Retreats," which consisted of a few days of discussion with some of the world's most imaginative thinkers across a wide range of fields – from psychology to comedy to physics to spirituality – about how imagination operates within their specific domains, and how we can cultivate that form of imagination in young people in the field.

At the time of this writing, the findings from all of these endeavors are still coming in, but some research I've conducted on creativity made clear to me the importance of going beyond abstract cognitive ability, to other aspects of the person's cognition and personality that may lead to high accomplishment and fulfillment. For instance, in a series of papers, I showed that not only can intellectual curiosity, the drive for imaginative thinking, and appreciation of beauty predict creative achievement above and beyond the *g*-factor, but these aspects of personality are even a *better* predictor of creative achievement than knowing one's ranking on the *g*-factor (see Kaufman, 2013a; Kaufman & Gregoire, 2016; Kaufman et al., 2015).

Similarly, in a series of neuroscience studies led by Roger Beaty, we found that these personality drives – which form the personality domain "openness to experience" – are associated with the structure of the "default mode network" (Beaty et al., 2015a). This is interesting considering that this is *not* the network that has received the most attention in the intelligence field: the executive attention network (e.g., Barbey et al., 2012, see Conway & Kovacs, Chapter 4, this volume). To be sure, executive attention is important, and does significantly influence performance on IQ tests, but this research suggests that IQ tests are missing out on some really importance slices of human cognition, namely, curiosity and imagination.

Indeed, in another study, we found that divergent-thinking ability – the ability to generate a number of different solutions to a problem – involved the interaction of both the executive attention network *and* the default mode network (Beaty et al., 2015b). IQ tests are more known to tap into convergent thinking than divergent thinking (see Guilford, 1967). But life, and the ability to adapt to an ever-changing environment (which has been a common definition of intelligence by the test constructors themselves), requires much more than convergent thinking.

However, it's not just that IQ tests miss out on divergent thinking. In my view, these findings suggest that IQ tests miss out on the very heart of *human existence* (see Maslow, 1968; May, Angel, & Ellenberger, 1958). The cognitive processes that have been associated with the default mode network in recent years – such as daydreaming, mental simulation, personal future planning, reflective compassion, and the construction of our sense of self (see Gottlieb et al., 2016) – are the processes that make us each unique in this world.

Through my time at the Positive Psychology Center at the University of Pennsylvania, I learned a lot about the field of positive psychology and realized how much it dovetailed with the strengths-based approach to intelligence that resonated so strongly with me (also see Sternberg, 1997). However, stepping into the world of positive psychology felt like stepping into a different universe than the traditional field of human intelligence. Instead of scholars intensely debating which model of cognitive ability was the best fit to the data, psychologists were intensely debating which model of *the good life* was the best fit to the data.

Keeping my intelligence hat from my prior life closely by the bed-side table, I could see how the kind of constructs studied in positive psychology – for example, positive emotions, life satisfaction, engagement, purpose, meaning, relationships, character, and achievement – fit into the realm of human intelligence. As Wechsler himself argued, general intelligence is broader than sheer intellectual ability, but involves the *whole person*. Indeed, this idea was a major impetus for the proposal of the Theory of Personal Intelligence. I certainly could have attempted to redefine general intelligence, but I thought that would be a harder sell. The term "general intelligence" is used so synonymously with the *g*-factor (the common variance across a diverse battery of tests of cognitive ability) that it would be quite the uphill battle to tell an entire field – which has been using a particular term in a particular way for more than 100 years (e.g., Spearman, 1904) – to just think about the term differently.

Instead, I decided to adopt a different strategy. I have immense respect for the hard-working and rigorous scientists who have advanced our knowledge of the structure of cognitive ability. I really do think that line of research can exist peacefully alongside a different program of intelligence research, one that is no less important. This line of research, which is the direction I've been moving toward, conceptualizes and operationalizes intelligence in the way in which it has actually been defined over the past century, as adaptation to the environment. However, I go further and define (personal) intelligence as the ability to adapt to the environment *in pursuit of personal goals*.

What I want to do is put the *whole person* back into the intelligence picture. For too long, intelligence researchers have focused on abstract on-the-spot reasoning divorced from the unique personal journey of the individual. While important, this work has not been fully integrated with the emerging literature on what it means to live a full life of purpose, passion, meaning, and fulfillment. It is my belief that a new science of intelligence that explicitly aims to help individuals achieve their own personal goals must integrate the latest findings across these various fields to come to a more complete picture of what it means to be an intelligent human being.

References

Barbey, A. K., Colom, R., Solomon, J., Krueger, F., Forbes, C., & Grafman, J. (2012). An integrative architecture for general intelligence and executive function revealed by lesion mapping. *Brain*, 135, 1154–1164.

Beaty, R. E., Benedek, M., Kaufman, S. B., & Silvia, P. J. (2015b). Default and executive network coupling supports creative idea production. *Nature Scientific Reports*.

Beaty, R. E., Kaufman, S. B., Bender, M., Jung, R. E., Kenett, Y. N., Jauk, E., Neubauer, A. C., & Silvia, P. J. (2015a). Personality and complex brain networks: The role of openness to experience in default network efficiency. *Human Brain Mapping*.

Blair, C., & Diamond, A. (2008). Biological processes in prevention and intervention: The promotion of self-regulation as a means of preventing school failure. *Developmental Psychopathology*, 20, 899–911.

Brown, J. B., Aczel, B., Jimenez, L., Kaufman, S. B., Mackintosh, N., & Plaisted, K. (2010). Intact implicit learning in autism spectrum conditions. *Quarterly Journal of Experimental Psychology*, 1, 1–24.

Carroll, J. B. (1993). *Human cognitive abilities: A survey of factor-analytic studies.* Cambridge: Cambridge University Press.

Ceci, S. (1996). *On intelligence … more or less: A biological treatise on intellectual development.* Cambridge, MA: Harvard University Press.

Gardner, H. (1983). *Frames of mind: The theory of multiple intelligences.* New York: Basic Books.

(1999). *Intelligence reframed: Multiple intelligences for the 21st century.* New York: Basic Books.

Gebauer, G. F., & Mackintosh, N. J. (2007). Psychometric intelligence dissociates implicit and explicit learning. *Journal of Experimental Psychology: Learning, Memory, and Cognition*, 33, 34–54.

Gottlieb, R., Hyde, E., Immordino-Yang, M. H., & Kaufman, S. B. (2016). Cultivating the social-emotional imagination in gifted education: Insights from educational neuroscience. *Annals of the New York Academy of Sciences*.

Guilford, J. P. (1967). *The nature of human intelligence.* New York: McGraw-Hill.

Heckman, J. J. (2000). Policies to foster human capital. *Research in Economics*, 54, 3–56.

Hunt, E. (2013). Book review: A gifted discussion of misclassification. *Intelligence*.

Kaufman, A. S. (1979). *Intelligent testing with the WISC-R.* New York: Wiley.

Kaufman, A. S., Raiford, S. E., & Coalson, D. L. (2016). *Intelligent testing with the WISC-V.* New York: Wiley.

Kaufman, S. B. (2009). *Beyond general intelligence: The dual-process theory of human intelligence (Unpublished Ph.D. dissertation).* Yale University, New Haven, CT. Kaufman, S. B. (2011).

Kaufman, S. B. (2011). Intelligence and the cognitive unconscious. In R. J. Sternberg & S. B. Kaufman (Eds.), *The Cambridge handbook of intelligence* (pp. 442–467). New York: Cambridge University Press.

Kaufman, S. B. (2013a). Opening up openness to experience: A four-factor model and relations to creative achievement in the arts and sciences. *Journal of Creative Behavior*, 47, 233–255.

(2013b). *Ungifted: Redefining intelligence.* New York: Basic Books.

Kaufman, S. B., DeYoung, C. G., Gray, J. R., Brown, J., & Mackintosh, N. (2009). Associative learning predicts intelligence above and beyond working memory and processing speed. *Intelligence*, 37, 374–382.

Kaufman, S. B., DeYoung, C. G., Gray, J. R., Jimenez, L., Brown, J. B., & Mackintosh, N. (2010). Implicit learning as an ability. *Cognition*, 116, 321–340.

Kaufman, S. B., & Duckworth, A. L. (2015). World-class expertise: A developmental model. *Wiley Interdisciplinary Reviews: Cognitive Science.*

Kaufman, S. B., & Gregoire, C. (2015). *Wired to create: Unraveling the mysteries of the creative mind.* New York: Penguin.

Kaufman, S. B., & Gregoire, C. (2016). *Wired to create: Unraveling the mysteries of the creative mind.* New York: Perigee Books.

Kaufman, S. B., Quilty, L. C., Grazioplene, R. G., Hirsh, J. B., Gray, J. R., Peterson, J. B., & DeYoung, C. G. (2015). Openness to experience and intellect differentially predict creative achievement in the arts and sciences. *Journal of Personality*, doi: 10.1111/jopy.12156.

Kihlstrom, J. F., & Cantor, N. (2011). Social intelligence. In R. J. Sternberg & S. B. Kaufman (Eds.), *The Cambridge handbook of intelligence* (pp. 564–581). New York: Cambridge University Press.

Mackintosh, N. J. (1974). *The psychology of animal learning.* London: Academic Press.

(2011). (2nd edn.) *IQ and human intelligence.* Oxford: Oxford University Press.

Maslow, A. H. (1968). *Toward a psychology of being* (2nd edn.). New York: Van Nostrand.

May, R., Angel, E., & Ellenberger, H. F. (Eds.) (1958). *Existence: A new dimension in psychiatry and psychology.* New York: Simon & Schuster.

Mayer, J. D. (2008). Personal intelligence. *Imagination, Cognition, and Personality*, 27, 209–232.

Mayer, J. D., & Salovey, P. (1993). The intelligence of emotional intelligence. *Intelligence*, 17, 433–442.

Molenaar, P. C. M. (2004). A manifesto on psychology as idiographic science: Bringing the person back into scientific psychology, this time forever. *Measurement*, 2, 201–218.

Molenaar, P. C. M., & Campbell, C. G. (2009). The new person-specific paradigm in psychology. *Current Directions in Psychological Science*, 18, 112–117.

Peterson, C., & Seligman, M. E. P. (1994). *Character strengths and virtues.* Washington, DC/New York: American Psychological Association/Oxford University Press.

Pretz, J. E., Totz, K. S., & Kaufman, S. B. (2010). The effects of mood, cognitive style, and cognitive ability on implicit learning. *Learning and Individual Differences*, 20, 215–219.

Reber, A. S., Walkenfeld, F. F., & Hernstadt, R. (1991). Implicit and explicit learning: Individual differences and IQ. *Journal of Experimental Psychology: Learning, Memory, and Cognition*, 17, 888–896.

Snow, R. E. (1980). Intelligence for the year 2001. *Intelligence*, 4, 185–199.

Spearman, C. (1904). "General intelligence," objectively determined and measured. *American Journal of Psychology*, 15, 201–293.

Stadler, M. A., & Frensch, P. A. (1997). *Handbook of implicit learning*. Thousand Oaks, CA: SAGE Publications.

Sternberg, R. J. (1997). *Successful intelligence: How practical and creative intelligence determine success in life*. New York: Plume.

Sternberg, R. J. (2011). The theory of successful intelligence. In R. J. Sternberg & S. B. Kaufman (Eds.), *The Cambridge handbook of intelligence* (pp. 504–527). New York: Cambridge University Press.

Sternberg, R. J., & Grigorenko, E. L. (2001). *Dynamic testing*. New York: Cambridge University Press.

Sternberg, R. J., & Kaufman, S. B. (Eds.) (2011). *The Cambridge handbook of intelligence*. New York: Cambridge University Press.

Torrance, E. P. (1983). The importance of falling in love with "something." *Creative Child & Adult Quarterly*, 8, 72–78.

Vygotsky, L. S. (1978). *Mind in society: The development of higher psychological processes*. Boston, MA: Harvard University Press.

Walters, J., & Gardner, H. (1998). The crystallizing experience: Discovering an intellectual gift. In R. S. Albert (Ed.), *Genius and eminence* (pp. 135–155). New York: Psychology Press.

Williams, B. A., & Pearlberg, S. L. (2006). Learning of three-term contingencies correlates with Raven scores, but not with measures of cognitive processing. *Intelligence*, 34, 177–191.

CHAPTER 15

Individual Differences at the Top
Mapping the Outer Envelope of Intelligence

David Lubinski

In his 1998 James McKeen Cattell Award Address at the American Psychological Society (now the Association for Psychological Sciences), "The Power of Quantitative Thinking," Paul E. Meehl observed:

> Verbal definitions of intelligence have never been adequate or commanded consensus. Carroll's (1993) *Human Cognitive Abilities* and Jensen's (1998) *The g Factor* (books which will be definitive treatises on the subject for many years to come) essentially solve the problem. Development of more sophisticated factor analytic methods than Spearman and Thurstone had makes it clear that there is a *g* factor, that it is manifested in either omnibus IQ tests or elementary cognitive tasks, that it is strongly hereditary, and that its influence permeates all areas of competence in human life. What remains is to find out what microanatomic or biochemical features of the brain are involved in the heritable component of *g*. A century of research – more than that if we start with Galton – has resulted in a triumph of scientific psychology, the foot-draggers being either uninformed, deficient in quantitative reasoning, or impaired by political correctness. (Meehl, 2006, p. 435)

Those tomes will indeed remain on the bookshelves of scholars for decades. Carroll (1993) focused on the highly replicated internal structure of psychometric tools developed over the previous century, whereas Jensen (1998) explicated how the central dimension of this hierarchy connects with important biosocial phenomena. Hunt's subsequent (2011) volume, *Human Intelligence*, deeply enriches these two. Collectively, this psychometric triptych provides a comprehensive depiction of the nature and real-world significance of intellectual abilities.

Essentially, general intelligence denotes individual differences in abstract/conceptual reasoning. This dimension accounts for around half of the common variance found in measures of intellectual functioning. Fifty-two experts (including Meehl) provided an excellent working definition: "[A] very general capacity that, among other things, involves the ability to reason, plan, solve problems, think abstractly, comprehend complex ideas, learn quickly and learn from experience. It is not merely book learning, a narrow academic skill, or test-taking smarts. Rather, it reflects a broader and deeper capability for comprehending our surroundings – 'catching on,' 'making sense' of things, or 'figuring out what to do'" (Gottfredson, 1997, p. 13).

Precisely because it is general, this dimension can be measured in multiple ways. For example, by "aptitude items" that require processing complex relationships, often, but not exclusively, across quantitative/numerical, spatial/mechanical, verbal/linguistic media, or, less efficiently, with varying and widely sampled "achievement items" of cultural content or knowledge (Lubinski & Humphreys, 1997; Roznowski, 1987). As Thurstone (1924, p. 247) pointed out, the former "type" of assessment concentrates on intelligence at work during the test (processing), the latter on the product of intelligence (knowledge). But often, when these assessments are broad, they engender equivalent correlates and are functionally interchangeable (Terman, 1925, pp. 289–306). In this vein, when introducing the "jangle fallacy," Kelley (1927) warned that attaching different labels to experimentally independent measures of the same attribute (e.g., academic aptitude, developmental level, fluid reasoning, general mental ability, general intelligence, *g*, IQ) does not mean that they measure different things.

> [C]ontaminating to clear thinking is the use of two separate words or expressions covering in fact the same basic situation, but sounding different, as though they were in truth different. The doing of this … the writer would call the "jangle" fallacy. "Achievement" and "intelligence" … We can mentally conceive of individuals differing in these two traits, and we can occasionally actually find such by using the best of our instruments of mental measurement, but to classify all members of a single school grade upon the basis of their difference in these two traits is sheer absurdity. (p. 64)[1]

Five decades later, an APA Task Force (Cleary et al., 1975) explicated the four dimensions involved in distinguishing "achievement" (specific knowledge) from "aptitude" (IQ) tests: breadth of sampling, recency of learning, the extent to which items are tied to an educational program, and purpose of assessment (current status versus potential for development). Achievement and aptitude tests do not differ in kind; they differ in degree. Cronbach (1976) echoed these considerations in responding to critics of psychological testing:

> *In public controversies about tests, disputants have failed to recognize that virtually every bit of evidence obtained with IQs would be approximately duplicated if the same study were carried out with a comprehensive measure of achievement.* (p. 211, italics original)

These highly replicated empirical generalizations are refreshing in the context of contemporary discourse on the "replication crisis" (Open Science Collaboration, 2015). It is critical to begin with and assimilate these well-established facts about the central parameter of intellectual functioning (Carroll, 1993; Hunt, 2011; Jensen, 1998) before we can evaluate any claim to have moved beyond them. An intellectual dimension provides value beyond general intelligence only if it truly gives us something more than general intelligence. As Messick noted (1992, p. 379),[2] "Because IQ is merely a way of scaling general intelligence [g], the burden of proof in claiming to move beyond IQ is to demonstrate empirically that ... test scores tap something more than or different from general intelligence by, for example, demonstrating differential correlates with other variables (which is the external aspect of construct validity)." Longitudinal studies of intellectually precocious children, as described in what follows, have done just that.

The Organization of Intellectual Abilities

Important intellectual dimensions beyond the general factor have been mapped in multiple ways and different labels applied (many with attendant "jangle"), yet they all possess differential value in the prediction of educational, occupational, and creative outcomes: fluid versus crystalized abilities (Cattell, 1971), verbal-educational-numerical versus mechanical-practical-spatial (Humphreys, 1962; Vernon, 1961), Wechsler's performance IQ versus verbal IQ (Matarazzo, 1972), and mathematical, spatial, and verbal reasoning (Corno, Cronbach et al., 2002; Gustafsson, 2002; Guttman, 1954; Snow et al., 1996). Because specific-ability measures focus on one particular type of content (e.g., verbal/linguistic, mathematical/quantitative, or spatial/pictorial), the individual differences they index constitute an amalgam of the general factor and the content-focused specific ability (Corno, Cronbach et al., 2002; Gustafsson, 2002). Conversely, when these indicators are systematically combined (Lubinski, 2004, p. 99), a distillate is formed that primarily indexes general intelligence (overall level of sophistication of the intellectual repertoire). Both levels of analysis – general and specific – are important (Wai et al., 2009). The radex model of intellectual functioning consists of a general dimension of abstract/symbolic processing or reasoning capability, surrounded by three specific abilities indexing degrees of competence with distinct symbolic systems: quantitative/numerical, spatial/figural, and verbal/linguistic (Wai et al., 2009, p. 821). The radex affords a global outline of the intellectual hierarchy (Lubinski & Dawis, 1992), and is as good as any framework for succinctly organizing the structure of human intelligence (Corno, Cronbach et al., 2002; Gustafsson, 2002; Guttman, 1954; Snow et al., 1996; Snow & Lohman, 1989).

Empirical Findings

That mathematical, spatial, and verbal reasoning abilities each add unique value to the prediction of important outcomes is well established for the general population and college-bound high school students (Humphreys, 1962; Humphreys et al., 1993; Kell & Lubinski, 2015; Lubinski, 2010, 2016; Wai et al., 2009). Following the editor's directive that authors focus here on their specific contributions to the field of intelligence, I will now describe how these intellective dimensions operate among intellectually precocious populations, specifically, the populations yielding empirical findings from the Study of Mathematically Precocious Youth (SMPY).

Study of Mathematically Precocious Youth (SMPY)

SMPY is a planned 50-year longitudinal study currently in its fourth decade (Clynes, 2016; Lubinski & Benbow, 2006). Launched by Julian C. Stanley in 1971, it was designed to identify mathematically precocious youth and uncover ways to facilitate their educational development. Shortly after its beginning, equal emphasis was placed on exceptional verbal ability. SMPY identified young adolescents ages 12 to 13 in the top 3% on conventional achievement tests routinely given in their schools, and gave them the opportunity to take college entrance exams, specifically, the SAT. These above-level assessments produce the same score distributions as they do for college-bound high school students. For decades (Assouline et al., 2015; Benbow & Stanley, 1996; Colangelo et al., 2004), young adolescents scoring at or above the mean for college-bound high school seniors have routinely enjoyed assimilating a full high school course in three weeks at summer residential programs for talented youth. Today, approximately 200,000 young adolescents are assessed annually with above-level instruments for such opportunities (Lubinski, 2016).

Currently co-directed by Camilla P. Benbow and David Lubinski at Vanderbilt University, SMPY is tracking five cohorts consisting of more than 5,000 intellectually talented participants identified in 1972–1997. Moreover, SMPY has evolved, from studying educational development to occupational and personal development as well as eminence and

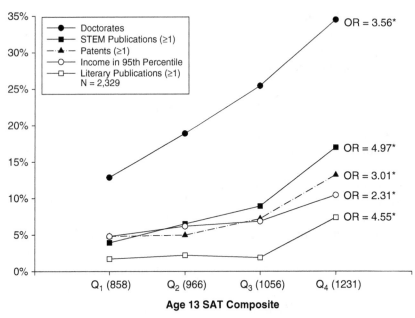

Figure 15.1   Participants are separated into quartiles based on their age 13 SAT-M +
SAT-V Composite. The mean age 13 SAT composite scores for each quartile are displayed
in parentheses along the x-axis. Odds ratios (ORs) comparing the likelihood of each
outcome in the top (Q4) and bottom (Q1) SAT quartiles are displayed at the end of every
respective criterion line. An asterisk indicates that the 95% confidence interval for the
odds ratio did not include 1.0, meaning that the likelihood of the outcome in Q4 was
significantly greater than in Q1. These SAT assessments by age 13 were conducted before
the re-centering of the SAT in the mid-1990s (i.e., during the 1970s and early 1980s); at
that time, cutting scores for the top 1 in 200 were SAT-M ≥ 500, SAT-V ≥ 430; for the top
1 in 10,000, cutting scores were SAT-M ≥ 700, SAT-V ≥ 630 by age 13.
Adapted from Lubinski (2009).

leadership. For present purposes, SMPY's unique empirical contributions
highlight the psychological and social implications of assessing individual
differences *within* the top 1% of ability.

Ability Level

Figure 15.1 contains data from 2,329 SMPY participants (Lubinski, 2009).
By age 13, all met the top 1% cut score on either the SAT-Math or SAT-
Verbal for their age group. Frey and Detterman (2004) documented that
the SAT-M plus SAT-V composite constitutes an excellent measure of

general intelligence (for above-average populations). First, their age-13 SAT composite (M + V) was divided into quartiles. Then, longitudinal criteria secured 25 years later were regressed onto the four quartiles. These criteria reflect valued accomplishments in education, the world of work, and creative expression (e.g., securing a patent, publishing a novel or major literary work, or publishing a refereed scientific article). Finally, odds ratios (ORs) were computed comparing the top and the bottom quartiles for each attainment. Figure 15.1 shows that individual differences within the top 1% of general intellectual ability, even when assessed at age 13, ultimately result in a set of achievement functions. More ability enhances the likelihood of many important accomplishments.

While the base rate for patents in the United States is 1% for the general population, the first quartile of this group achieves almost five times that. Further, the difference between the top and bottom quartiles, 13.2% versus 4.8%, respectively, is statistically and substantively significant. The same is true for the difference between the top and bottom quartiles in having an income at or above the 95th percentile (10.5% versus 4.8%). Note that these participants are in their mid-30s and such incomes are typically earned only much later in life. Thus, there is neither an ability threshold nor any sign of diminished returns within the top 1% of ability. But does the uniqueness of the specific abilities, each focused on a distinct symbolic modality, have additional psychological significance for intellectually talented youth?

Ability Pattern

Park and colleagues (2007) analyzed a group of 2,409 SMPY participants tracked for more than 25 years. Figure 15.2 organizes their findings into four Tukey plots: specifically, participants' SAT composites were plotted on the y-axis and their SAT-M minus SAT-V scores were plotted on the x-axis. These plots result in two independent dimensions, concurrently assessing overall ability level (i.e., the common variance these two measures share – "g", on the y-axis), versus ability-pattern (i.e., the unique psychological import of each measure's specific ability – on the x-axis). For the latter, positive scores on the x-axis denote greater mathematical relative to verbal reasoning ability (M > V), whereas the opposite is true for scores to the left (M < V). Finally, bivariate means for educational, occupational, and creative attainments were plotted. These were then surrounded by ellipses, defined by +/- one standard deviation on x and y, respectively, for members in each group.

(a) Terminal Four-Year and Masters Degrees in the Humanities and STEM

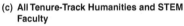

X STEM (518)
• Humanities (136)

◄—— Verbal | Quant ——►
Ability Tilt

(b) PhDs in Humanities and STEM

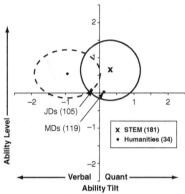

JDs (105)

MDs (119)

X STEM (181)
• Humanities (34)

◄—— Verbal | Quant ——►
Ability Tilt

(c) All Tenure-Track Humanities and STEM Faculty

X STEM Top 50 (18)
• Humanities Top 50 (7)
+ STEM > Top 50 (24)
✦ Humanities >Top 50 (13)

◄—— Verbal | Quant ——►
Ability Tilt

(d) Literary Publications and Patents

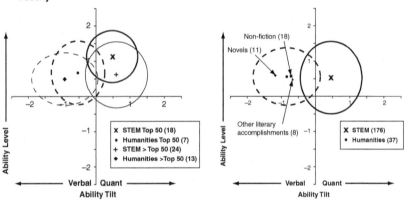

Non-fiction (18)

Novels (11)

Other literary accomplishments (8)

X STEM (176)
• Humanities (37)

◄—— Verbal | Quant ——►
Ability Tilt

Figure 15.2   Participants' achievements as a function of ability tilt (SAT-Math score minus SAT-Verbal score) and ability level (sum of both SAT scores), in standard deviation units. Achievement categories were (a) completing a terminal four-year or master's degree, (b) completing a Ph.D. (means for MDs and JDs are also shown), (c) securing a tenure-track faculty position, and (d) publishing a literary work or securing a patent. In each graph, bivariate means are shown for achievements in humanities and in science, technology, engineering, and mathematics (STEM), respectively; the ellipse surrounding each mean indicates the space within one standard deviation on each dimension. The *n* for each group is indicated in parentheses. Mean SAT-Math and SAT-V scores, respectively, for each criterion group were: four-year and master's STEM degree – 575, 450; four-year and master's humanities degree – 551, 497; STEM Ph.D. – 642, 499; humanities Ph.D. – 553, 572; tenure-track STEM position in a top-50 university – 697, 534; tenure-track humanities position in a top-50 university – 591, 557; tenure track STEM position in a non-top-50 university – 659, 478; tenure-track humanities position in a non-top-50 university – 550, 566; patents (i.e., STEM creative achievements) – 626, 471; and publications (i.e., humanities creative achievements) – 561, 567. From Park et al. (2007).

In all four panels, outcomes in the humanities and STEM were featured because they had the largest sample sizes to justify statistically stable results. However, bivariate points for other outcomes (e.g., MDs, JDs, novelists, and nonfiction writers) are also plotted to provide an even wider picture. Moving from four-year and master's degrees (panel A) to doctorates (panel B), we see increases in ability level (y-axis), as well as ability pattern (x-axis) becoming more distinctive. Tenured faculty at major universities in the humanities versus STEM (panel C) are distinct, as are those who secured refereed publications and patents (panel D). Participants achieving these qualitatively different attainments occupy different regions of the intellectual space defined by these dimensions. Importantly, these differences are detectable during early adolescence. However, they routinely pass unnoticed because of the ceiling problem. The vast majority of these participants will earn close to top possible scores on conventional college entrance examinations well before graduating from high school (when SAT assessments are typically conducted). At that point, for this population, such assessments are no longer capable of distinguishing the exceptionally able from the able. They are insensitive to their individuality, and especially so among the profoundly gifted.

Profoundly Gifted

The differential attainments observed earlier continue to be found at ever-higher points on these ability dimensions. Two scatter plots in Figure 15.3 illustrate the breadth of intellectual diversity typically unseen due to measurement limitations but routinely uncovered through above-level assessments. The bottom plot is based on a group of 320 SMPY participants scoring in the top 1 in 10,000 in either mathematical or verbal reasoning ability (Kell et al., 2013a); the top plot consists of 259 equally able participants identified by Duke University's Talent Identification Program (TIP), used for replication (Makel et al., 2016). Both groups were identified by age 13 and tracked for 25 years. As the diagonal line on each scatter plot reveals, a large majority in each group had estimated IQs > 160, yet the psychological diversity displayed by these profoundly gifted participants is stunning: some participants who scored in the top 1 in 10,000 for mathematical reasoning ability have verbal reasoning abilities that are more impressive than their mathematical prowess, while the verbal reasoning ability of others is "merely" around the cutting score for the top 1% (an age 13 SAT-V score just under 400). The same breadth of differential talent is observed among those scoring in the top 1 in 10,000 in verbal reasoning

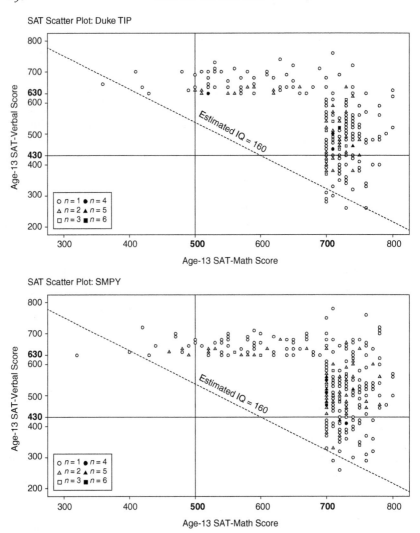

Figure 15.3   Scatterplot of age-13 SAT-Math (X) and SAT-Verbal (Y) scores for Duke TIP participants (top panel) and SMPY participants (bottom panel). Circles, triangles, and squares are used to denote bivariate points with more than one participant. The diagonal line in each scatterplot denotes where estimated IQs of 160 fall; bivariate values above these diagonals correspond to estimated IQs above 160. On the axes, the boldface numbers on the x-axis (**500, 700**) and the y-axis (**430, 630**) indicate cutoffs for the top 1 in 200 and the top 1 in 10,000 for this age group. TIP = Talent Identification Program; SMPY = Study of Mathematically Precocious Youth.

From Makel et al. (2016).

ability. High-ceiling assessments such as these are needed to capture the differential potentialities of profound intellectual talent. To validate the psychological significance of these assessments compellingly, however, data are needed on criterion outcomes such as their ultimate educational, career, and creative attainments as well as other longitudinally remote indices of their occupational stature.

Figure 15.4 presents a sampling of the creative outcomes of these two groups as a function of their ability pattern. Critically, all participants possess more mathematical and verbal reasoning ability than the typical PhD in any discipline, yet they tend to invest in those pursuits that draw on their greater strength. Participants whose intellectual profile was more distinguished by verbal relative to mathematical reasoning generally focused on the humanities and literary pursuits (the northwest quadrant of this graph), whereas participants whose mathematical acumen was more impressive than their verbal reasoning ability concentrated more on STEM pursuits (the southeast quadrant). The same patterns of investments were found at earlier stages in their educational-occupational development (Makel et al., 2016).

The preceding analysis characterizes the *nature* of accomplishment among profoundly gifted youth. Tables 15.1 and 15.2 assess its *magnitude*. Table 15.1 organizes a sampling of accomplishments prior to age 40 for the TIP and SMPY groups, which may be benchmarked normatively (e.g., the base rate for earning a doctorate in the United States is just under 2%). Table 15.2 lists some individual accomplishments (each listing representing a unique individual), which affords an idiographic qualitative appraisal of their consequential accomplishments. While any one of these individual accomplishments, if viewed in isolation, might be dismissed as a noteworthy anecdote, taken together, and replicated across both samples, the data aggregate to tell a compelling, systematic story. These normative and idiographic findings reveal, quantitatively and qualitatively, the magnitude of human capital predictable from above-level assessments prior to age 13. There appears to be nothing categorically different regarding the profoundly gifted. Rather, the data document a continuous gradation of extraordinary capability and its accompanying accomplishments.

Just as qualitatively different outcomes are observed as a function of contrasting ability patterns among college students (Humphreys et al., 1993; Lubinski, 2010; Wai et al., 2009), the gifted (Park et al., 2007), and the profoundly gifted (Kell et al., 2013a, Makel et al., 2016), so too does the magnitude of accomplishment vary across ability-levels of three, four, and

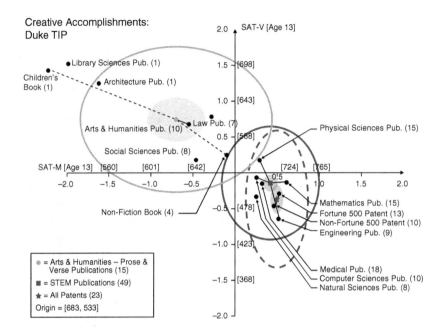

Creative Accomplishments:
Duke TIP

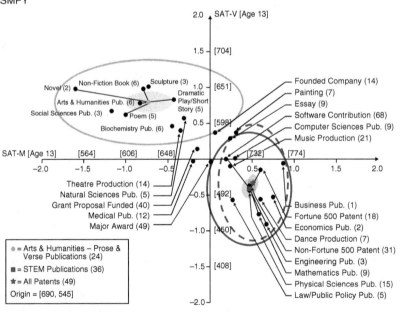

Creative Accomplishments:
SMPY

Figure 15.4 Bivariate means for age-13 SAT-Math (SAT-M; *x*) and SAT-Verbal (SAT-V; *y*) scores within categories of creative accomplishments for Duke University's

Table 15.1   *Selected Educational, Occupational, and Creative Accomplishments of the Talent Identification Program (TIP) and the Study of Mathematically Precocious Youth (SMPY) Participants*

Accomplishment	TIP	SMPY
Doctoral degree	37%	44%
Doctoral degree from top 10 university[a]	16.3%	22.5%
Tenure at the college level	7.5%	11.3%
Tenure at research-intensive university[b]	4.3%	7.5%
Peer-reviewed publication (≥ 1)	39%	24%
Patent (≥ 1)	9%	15%
Fortune 500 patent (≥ 1)	5%	6%
Book (≥ 1)	2%	3%
NSF grant (≥ 1)	4% (mean award = $63,700)	6% (mean award = $91,600)
NIH grant (≥ 1)	1% (mean award = $10,700)	3% (mean award = $18,900)

Note: Standard errors for the percentages reported in this table are as follows: 1% for percentages < 9%; 2% for percentages from 9% through 25%; and 3% for percentages greater than 25%. The one exception is that the standard error for the percentage of tenured professors among TIP participants is 2%. NIH = National Institutes of Health; NSF = National Science Foundation.
[a] Identification of the top 10 doctoral programs was based on the National Research Council's (1995) ratings. [b]Universities were classified as research-intensive by the Carnegie Foundation (2010) if they were deemed to have "very high research productivity."
Taken from Makel et al. (2016).

Figure 15.4 *(cont.)*

Talent Identification Program (TIP) participants (top panel) and the Study of Mathematically Precocious Youth (SMPY) participants (bottom panel). Bivariate means for individual categories are represented by black circles; the sample sizes for these categories are in parentheses. Three rationally derived outcome clusters are highlighted in this two-dimensional space: Arts & Humanities (NW quadrant in green) and two STEM outcomes (SE quadrant in purple): solid line = STEM publications, dotted line = patents. The dashed lines emanating from the centroids denote the constituents of those clusters. Each centroid is surrounded by two elliptical tiers: an inner ellipse defined by the standard errors of the SAT-M and SAT-V means for individuals within that centroid (i.e., width and height = ±1 *SEM* for SAT-M and SAT-V, respectively) and an outer ellipse formed by the standard deviations of the SAT scores for these individuals (i.e., width and height = ±1 *SD* for SAT-M and SAT-V, respectively). Along the axes, un-bracketed values are SAT-M and SAT-V scores in *z*-score units, and bracketed values are raw SAT scores.
Adapted from Makel et al. (2016).

Table 15.2   *Outlying Accomplishments of the Talent Identification Program (TIP) and the Study of Mathematically Precocious Youth (SMPY) Participants*

TIP	SMPY
Named as one of "America's Top Physicians" (Consumers' Research Council of America)	Co-director of hospital organ-transplant center serving more than 3 million people
Holder of 43 patents	
President of chamber of commerce of one of the 100 richest cities in the United States, by per capita income	Produced 100 software contributions
	Raised more than $65 million in private equity investment to fund own company
Associate chief counsel for a U.S. federal agency	
Member of the Council on Foreign Relations	Vice president of Fortune 500 company
Deputy director of the Office of the Assistant Secretary for a U.S. federal agency	Deputy assistant to a president of the United States (national policy adviser)
Argued more than 10 cases before the U.S. Supreme Court	Founder of three companies
Professional poker player with annual earnings > $100,000	Producer of 500 musical productions
	Marshall Scholar
Rhodes Scholar	Recipient of eight grants from the National Science Foundation (total funding > $5.5 million)
Recipient of nine grants from the National Science Foundation (total funding > $6.5 million)	
Recipient of six grants from the National Institutes of Health (total funding > $1.4 million)	Recipient of six grants from the National Institutes of Health (total funding > $1.6 million)

Note: The accomplishments listed in this table are non-overlapping, and each refers to the achievement of a single individual.
Taken from Makel et al. (2016).

five standard deviations above the normative mean (see Figure 15.1). There is a continuous progression in real-world accomplishment, impact, and creativity within the top 1% of ability (over one-third of ability range). In addition, the relationship between occupational and creative output and individual differences within the top 1% of ability continues to be meaningful even after advanced educational credentials and the caliber of the university attended for graduate study are controlled (Park et al., 2008).

Assessing individual differences within the top 1% of ability has even further implications. For decades, empirical evidence has revealed that college entrance examinations in the United States are suboptimal for reasons beyond their ceiling limitation. They are also suboptimal qualitatively (Humphreys et al., 1993; Wai et al., 2009). Intellectual dimensions beyond general-, mathematical-, and verbal-reasoning ability add important value for the gifted and the profoundly gifted, just as they do for typical college students.

Spatial Ability: The "Orphan Ability"

Spatial ability has been called the "orphan ability." Relative to general, mathematical, and verbal abilities (cf. Gohm et al., 1998; Humphreys et al., 1993; Kell et al., 2013b; Wai et al., 2009), spatial ability has been sorely neglected. Years ago, arguably the leading authority on the educational and occupational significance of spatial ability remarked,

> There is good evidence that [visual-spatial reasoning] relates to specialized achievements in fields such as architecture, dentistry, engineering, and medicine ... Given this plus the longstanding anecdotal evidence on the role of visualization in scientific discovery, ... it is incredible that there has been so little programmatic research on admissions testing in this domain. (Snow, 1999, p. 136)

Two years later, Shea and colleagues (2001) published educational and occupational outcomes for 563 SMPY participants recorded at ages 18 (after high school), 23 (after college), and 33 (early career). The three-dimensional plots in Figure 15.5 graph outcomes over a 20-year period for favorite and least favorite high school class, four-year college degree, and occupation. In standard deviation units, mathematical reasoning ability is scaled on the x-axis, verbal reasoning ability on the y-axis; the base of each arrow marks the location of these two abilities on the x- and y-axes. Spatial ability was also assessed during early adolescence and scaled here in standard deviation units using arrows: arrows to the right represent positive values; to the left, negative values. Now, imagine that the (right-pointing) positive arrows have rotated upward from the plane of the page, and the (left-pointing) negative arrows downward, so as to form 90-degree angles with the x- and y-axes. The arrowheads will then mark the locations in three-dimensional space of the trivariate points occupied by each labeled group. It is apparent that at all three lifetime stages, each of the abilities add independent predictive value for understanding the various life choices and preferences representing the outcomes.

Thus, for this gifted sample, those who find the humanities to be their favorite high school courses tend to have an intellectual repertoire dominated by verbal ability relative to mathematical and spatial ability, whereas the inverse is true for students who prefer STEM domains. This is not only true for preferences in learning environments, but also for work environments. A different specific ability configuration anticipates affinity for and accomplishments in STEM: salient mathematical and spatial abilities, relative to verbal ability. Dotted rectangles are used in each or the four panels of Figure 15.5 to isolate the location of the STEM outcomes. Neglecting any one of these specific abilities misses a critical component. None of the three specific abilities can be ignored without compromising our understanding of the outcomes.

This conclusion was reinforced 15 years later, when the creative accomplishments of the Shea and colleagues (2001) participants were followed up at age 48 by Kell and colleagues (2013b). For purposes of analysis, the creative criteria were placed in four mutually exclusive and exhaustive content groups, consisting of three types of refereed publications, Art-Humanities-Law-Social-Sciences (n = 27), Biology-Medicine (n = 35), STEM (n = 65), and fourth, patents (n = 33). Individuals who both held patents and published were retained in the relevant publication category, as that was considered more informative. Hence, the 33 in the patent category had no publications by age 48.

A discriminant function analysis employed the age 13 mathematical, spatial, and verbal ability assessments to predict the four types of creative outcomes described previously 35 years later. Mathematical and verbal ability scores jointly accounted for 10.5% of the variance in creative group outcomes. The inclusion of spatial ability – the "orphan ability" – added another 7.5% to that variance.

Although it was known for years that the level and pattern of mathematical and verbal ability are important in forecasting both the likelihood and nature of creative life outcomes among intellectually precocious youth (Lubinski, 2016; Park et al., 2007), Kell and colleagues' (2013b) was the first demonstration that spatial ability adds substantially to such predictions.

Figure 15.6 displays three different rotations of these findings when plotted in three mathematical, spatial, and verbal dimensions. Each trivariate point is surrounded by the orthogonal orbits of the three standard errors of each ability to form ellipsoids, which reveals their distinctiveness. It is clear that the creative outcomes under analysis are supported by different configurations of intellectual talent. For example, among participants who secure patents, their spatial ability is commensurate

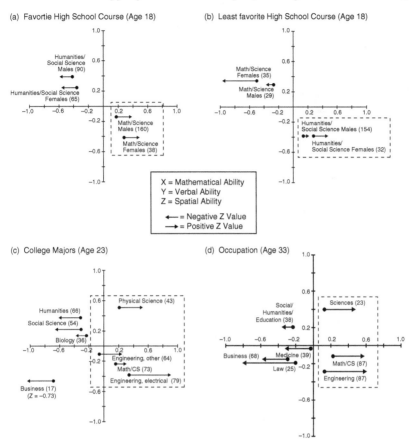

Figure 15.5   Shown are trivariate (X/Y/Z = Mathematical/Verbal/Spatial) means for (Panel A) favorite and (B) least favorite high school course at age 18, (C) college majors at age 23, and (D) occupation at age 33. Mathematical, verbal, and spatial ability are on the x-, y-, and z-axes, respectively (arrows to the right indicate a positive z value; arrows to the left indicate a negative z value). Panels A and B are standardized within sex; Panels C and D are standardized across sexes. For Business in Panel C, note that the length of the arrow is actually z = 0.73. Dotted rectangles surround the STEM preferences, degrees, and occupations to underscore that they occupy similar intellectual spaces at different time points.
Adapted from Shea et al. (2001). CS = computer science.

with those who publish in STEM, but the latter are more impressive in mathematical and verbal reasoning. Participants who publish in Art-Humanities-Law-Social Sciences are the lowest in spatial ability of all four groups. This informative graph maps the intellectual design

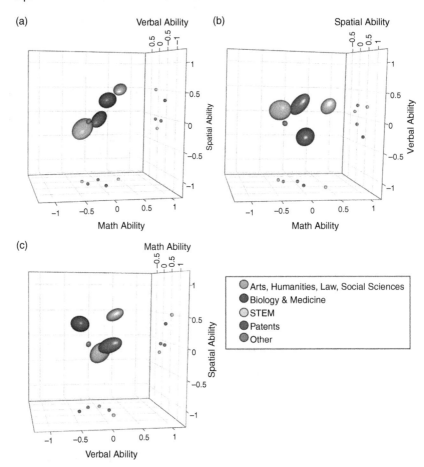

Figure 15.6   Confidence ellipsoids showing the locations of the four criterion groups in the three-dimensional space defined by scores for mathematical, verbal, and spatial reasoning ability. The data are rotated such that the graph in (a) shows mathematical ability on the x-axis, spatial ability on the y-axis, and verbal ability on the z-axis; the graph in (b) shows mathematical ability on the x-axis, verbal ability on the y-axis, and spatial ability on the z-axis; and the graph in (c) shows verbal ability on the x-axis, spatial ability on the y-axis, and mathematical ability on the z-axis. The ellipsoids are scaled so that each semi-principal axis is approximately equal in length to the standard error of the corresponding principal component. Each ellipsoid is centered on the trivariate mean (centroid), and bivariate means are plotted on the bordering grids. The criterion groups were defined as participants with a refereed publication in the arts, humanities, law, or social sciences; a refereed publication in biology or medicine; a refereed publication in science, technology, engineering, or mathematics (STEM); or a patent. In addition, an ellipsoid is shown for participants with none of these creative accomplishments ("other"). From Kell et al. (2013b).

space of much of what is considered important creative thought in modern cultures, especially the two subcultures that C. P. Snow (1967) famously labeled "science intellectuals" and "literary intellectuals."

Discussion

Decades of longitudinal research have documented that the hierarchical organization of human intellectual abilities has scientific significance. When researchers use developmentally appropriate measures and collect rare and highly valued outcome criteria from sufficiently large samples over protracted intervals, differential developmental trajectories of exceptional intellectual talent are consistently revealed.[3]

An important new insight comes from the configural relationships involving spatial ability. *They demonstrate that key intellectual attributes operate in learning and work settings whether or not participants consider them, practitioners or theorists assess them, or selection occurs on them.* The intellectually talented young adolescents in the studies reviewed here understood the importance of doing well on mathematical and verbal reasoning tests for their eventual college placement. However, the significance of spatial ability was never considered, nor was it ever used in selecting them for educational or occupational opportunities. Nonetheless, spatial ability played a critical role in structuring their educational, occupational, and creative pursuits and ultimate accomplishments. Abilities affect outcomes, like all natural causes, whether recognized or unrecognized.

Unfortunately, approximately half of young adolescents in the top 1% in spatial ability are missed by modern talent searches restricted exclusively to mathematical and verbal reasoning ability (Wai et al., 2009; Wai & Worrell, 2016). This omission not only neglects an underserved population – and a critical source of human capital for technical professions – it also constitutes a lost opportunity for the kind of refinements seen in Figures 15.5 and 15.6 for all individuals. Individuals may be highly similar on any two specific abilities (mathematical/spatial/verbal), but if they differ markedly on the third, differential development can be anticipated. They will differentially select contrasting opportunities, and they will experience markedly different degrees of satisfaction and display different degrees of competence across these areas. The challenge for educators and career counselors is to find the optimal niche for each student, so that he or she can maximize the positive aspects of his or her individuality (Lubinski, 1996, 2016; Lubinski & Benbow, 2000). This is best done by knowing and treating each student as an individual.

Nurturing Exceptional Talent

Ninety-five years ago, Carl Emil Seashore (1922) pointed out that among a random sample of college freshmen, the top 5% can learn five times more academic material than the bottom 5% (per unit time), and that there are successive gradations in between these levels. An analysis of level and pattern of general and specific abilities underscores the environmental diversity needed to optimally meet the needs of each student. Both the rate at which each student learns abstract/complex material and the nature and pace of the curriculum need to be aligned with students' specific level and pattern of ability (Assouline et al., 2015; Benbow & Stanley, 1996; Colangelo et al., 2004; Stanley, 2000). Young adolescents scoring in the top 1 in 10,000 have different educational needs relative to those scoring in the top 1 in 200, and both of these groups have different educational needs from typically developing students (Lubinski, 2016).

Once basic fundamental needs are met (e.g., health, nourishment, safety), the best way to develop intelligence is to draw on the salient positive features of each person's individuality (Lubinski & Benbow, 2000). Just as there are unique strengths and relative weaknesses in each person's intellectual profile, there are huge individual differences in each person's aversions and passions for contrasting opportunities. There are also huge differences in how much each individual is willing to invest in his or her intellectual development (Ferriman et al., 2009; Lubinski et al., 2014). Taking a multidimensional view of the personal attributes each person brings to learning and work settings is critical. That has always been a central feature of applied and theoretical research in the study of individual differences because that tradition eschews "truncated appraisals of human individuality" (Lubinski, 1996, 2010). When opportunity is available, abilities, commitment, energy, interests, and personality all matter. Drawing on the psychological fabric upon which interventions and opportunities act maximizes the motivation for sustaining positive development.

Benbow and Stanley (1996) entitled their compelling analysis "Inequity in equity: How 'equity' can lead to inequity for high-potential students" because one size will never fit all. This is readily accepted for students with developmental delays and, thankfully, in the United States, important legislation ensures that appropriate accommodations are made for students with special needs (Lubinski, 2016). Intellectually precocious students have special needs as well.[4] For that very reason, Stanley (2000) developed an instructional philosophy for intellectually precocious students that is generalizable to all students: "teach students only what they don't already know." Managing the vast differences in student readiness for learning and the knowledge they possess, which is routinely observed even among siblings reared in the same home (Murray, 1998, 2002; Waller, 1971), is sometimes challenging but imperative for achieving optimal learning for each child. This challenge is likely to intensify – there is evidence that it already has (Tyre, 2016) – as increased opportunities become available for students to self-select their learning environments and personally manage their rate of growth (e.g., receiving instruction over the Internet, selecting like-minded peers with similar interests and competence, and taking college courses in high school, among others).

Horizontal and Vertical Levels of Analysis

Just as McNemar (1964) and Schmidt and Hunter (1998) showed that for certain performances in school and work environments, respectively, general intelligence is sufficient to account for the criterion variance that the hierarchical organization of intellectual abilities offers, this chapter shows that for other outcomes, specific abilities do add value to general intellectual appraisals. Depending on the purpose of assessment, predictor sets and criterion outcomes can and should vary. When assessments of the quantitative and qualitative scope of intellectual abilities are conducted at exceptional levels of talent, meaningful research designs require commensurate measurement of qualitatively different and rare criterion outcomes to validate assessment procedures.

Finally, Meehl (2006) was correct that what remains "is to find out what microanatomic or biochemical features of the brain are involved" (p. 435). Undoubtedly, such advances will extend beyond general intellectual functioning (Asbury & Plomin, 2014). The patterns of intellectual talent found in Figures 15.3 through 15.6 offer distinct phenotypes for behavioral genetics and neuroscience inquiry. Examining the biological phenomena underpinning general intellectual ability has produced meaningful findings (and more remains to be learned), but additional clarity is likely if specific abilities are examined using biologically based procedures (Lubinski, 2016; Rimfeld et al., 2017). Just as additional insight into lifespan development is achieved by assessing ability level and pattern in its full scope, so too is it likely to occur for underlying biological phenomena.

Conclusion

More than 60 years ago, Lewis Terman (1954) reflected on his multiple-decade longitudinal study by affirming the importance of initially using general intelligence to identify participants when the gifted field was young and his groundbreaking work had just begun. Nevertheless, he then added: "[s]uch tests do not, however, enable us to predict what direction the achievement will take, ... both interest patterns and special aptitudes play important roles in the making of a gifted scientist, mathematician, mechanic, artist, poet, or musical composer, ..." (p. 224). Clear and consistent empirical findings reveal the wisdom of his remarks. Modern empirical findings have established the unique psychological significance of mathematical, spatial, and verbal abilities. Other studies have shown the added value of educational/occupational interests, personality, and the huge range of lifestyle preferences displayed when each individual has the opportunity to choose freely (Ferriman et al., 2009; Lubinski, 2016; Lubinski et al., 2014). Individuals embrace opportunities for development with different degrees of enthusiasm. Future studies of intellectual development and human accomplishment need to take into account personal attributes beyond individual differences in rates of learning and the extent to which a person can efficiently develop expertise. Individual differences in mathematical, spatial, and verbal reasoning ability, however, will always be part of the story. Their psychological significance can be seen most clearly when measured simultaneously and in their full scope.

Acknowledgment

Support for this chapter was provided by a research and training grant from the Templeton Foundation (Grant 55996) and by the Vanderbilt Kennedy Center for Research on Human Development. Invaluable suggestions for this article were provided by Brian O. Bernstein, Robert A. Gordon, Kira O. McCabe, Frank Miele, and Leslie J. Yonce.

Notes

1 As Kelley (1927) observes, under some circumstances, tools that focus on abstract reasoning versus specific content acquired in schools can be differentially informative. Assessments too tied to an educational curriculum rather than abstract problem solving can particularly disadvantage children who have experienced poor schooling. The early focus on the SAT was on reasoning, rather than knowledge per se, to facilitate uncovering exceptional intellectual talent in rare places.

2 It has been repeatedly shown that the predictive validity of innovative measures of competence such as "health literacy," "moral reasoning," and many others is largely driven by the general intelligence dimension that cuts across all measures of cognitive functioning (e.g., Gottfredson, 2002; Messick, 1992;

Sanders et al., 1995). When novel measures are purported to assess broad forms of competence in specific areas, the importance of determining whether they add any incremental validity to general intelligence has long been emphasized by measurement experts (Corno, Cronbach et al., 2002; Humphreys, 1962; McNemar, 1964), but their advice repeatedly goes unheeded (cf. Judge et al., 2007; Lubinski, 2004, 2010) as researchers strive for innovative originality.

3 The Graduate Record Examination (GRE), with which applicants for advanced degrees are routinely assessed in the United States, provides an interesting illustration of the extent to which upper ranges of intellectual talent may be undervalued. Scores on the verbal (V) and quantitative (Q) subtests of this instrument are reported on a scale with 600 points of range, from 200 to 800. A mid-range score of 500 on GRE-V denotes the 59th percentile, whereas 500 on GRE-Q represents only the 18th percentile! Thus, half of the score range on GRE-Q is expended on the bottom 18% of the distribution. GRE-Q scores of 700 or more, falling in only a sixth of the range, are obtained by 40% of test takers. A perfect score of 800 lies only at the 92nd percentile. See www.ets.org/s/gre/pdf/concordance_information.pdf. Contrast this with selection procedures used by Bill Gates in developing Research Institute-Beijing or at the Indian Institute of Technology. These two cross-cultural examples reflect procedures corresponding to selecting within the top 1 in 10,000 in ability (Kell et al., 2013a, p. 648).

4 Intellectual dimensions of central relevance for intellectually precocious youth may be viewed as reflections or mirror images of dimensions of central importance for meeting the learning needs of students with developmental delays. "Interventions designed to facilitate learning in students with developmental delays essentially reduce to delays in either general abstract reasoning and/or those concerning numerical/quantitative, spatial/pictorial, or verbal/linguistic media" (Lubinski, 2016, footnote 3, p. 935).

References

Asbury, K., & Plomin, R. (2014). *G is for genes: The impact of genetics on educational achievement*. New York: Wiley.

Assouline, S. G., Colangelo, N., & Vantassel-Baska, J. (2015). *A nation empowered* (volume I). Iowa City, IA: Belin-Blank Center.

Assouline, S. G., Colangelo, N., Vantassel-Baska, J., & Lupkowski-Shoplik, A. (2015). *A nation empowered* (volume II). Iowa City, IA: Belin-Blank Center.

Benbow, C. P., & Stanley, J. C. (1996). Inequity in equity: How "equity" can lead to inequity for high-potential students. *Psychology, Public Policy, & Law*, 2, 249–292.

Carroll, J. B. (1993). *Human cognitive abilities: A survey of factor-analytic studies*. Cambridge: Cambridge University Press.

Cattell, R. B. (1971). *Abilities: Their structure and growth*. Boston: Houghton Mifflin.

Cleary, T. A., Humphreys, L. G., Kendrick, S. A., & Wesman, A. (1975). Educational uses of tests with disadvantaged students. *American Psychologist*, 30, 15–41.

Clynes, T. (2016). How to raise a genius: A long-running study of exceptional children reveals what it takes to produce the scientists who will lead the twenty-first century. *Nature*, 573, 152–155.

Colangelo, N., Assouline, S. G., & Gross, M. U. M. (Eds.) (2004). *A nation deceived: How schools hold back America's brightest students.* Iowa City, IA: University of Iowa.

Corno, L., Cronbach, L. J., et al. (Eds.) (2002). *Remaking the concept of aptitude: Extending the legacy of Richard E. Snow.* Mahwah, NJ: Erlbaum.

Cronbach, L. J. (1976). Measured mental abilities: Lingering questions and loose ends. In B. D. David & P. Flaherty (Eds.). *Human diversity: Its causes and social significance* (pp. 207–222). Cambridge, MA: Ballinger.

Ferriman, K., Lubinski, D., & Benbow, C. P. (2009). Work preferences, life values, and personal views of top math/science graduate students and the profoundly gifted: Developmental changes and sex differences during emerging adulthood and parenthood. *Journal of Personality and Social Psychology*, 97, 517–532.

Frey, M. C., & Detterman, D. K. (2004). Scholastic assessment or *g*? The relationship between the scholastic assessment test and general cognitive ability. *Psychological Science*, 15, 373–378.

Gohm, C. L., Humphreys, L. G., & Yao, G. (1998). Underachievement among spatially gifted students. *American Educational Research Journal*, 35, 515–531.

Gottfredson, L. S. (1997). Special issue on intelligence and social policy. *Intelligence*, 24.

Gottfredson, L. S. (2002). *g*: Highly general and highly practical. In R. J. Sternberg & E. L. Grigorenko (Eds.). *The general factor of intelligence: How general is it?* (pp. 331–380). Mahwah, NJ: Erlbaum.

Gustafsson, J. E. (2002). Measurement from a hierarchical point of view. In H. L. Braun, D. G. Jackson, & D. E. Wiley (Eds.). (2002). *The role of constructs in psychological and educational measurement* (pp. 73–95). Mahwah, NJ: Erlbaum.

Guttman, L. (1954). A new approach to factor analysis: The radex. In P. Lazarsfeld (Ed.). *Mathematical thinking in the social sciences* (pp. 258–348). Glencoe. IL: Free Press.

Humphreys, L. G. (1962). Organization of human abilities. *American Psychologist*, 17, 475–483.

Humphreys, L. G., Lubinski, D., & Yao, G. (1993). Utility of predicting group membership and the role of spatial visualization in becoming an engineer, physical scientist, or artist. *Journal of Applied Psychology*, 78, 250–261.

Hunt, E. B. (2011). *Human intelligence.* New York: Cambridge University Press.

Jensen, A. R. (1998). *The g factor: The science of mental ability.* Westport, CT: Praeger.

Judge, T. A., Jackson, C. L., Shaw, J. C., Scott, B. A., & Rich, B. L. (2007). Self-efficacy and work-related performance: The integral role of individual differences. *Journal of Applied Psychology*, 92, 107–127.

Kell, H. J., & Lubinski, D. (2015). Intellectual abilities for counseling interventions, practice, and theory: Dismissing their significance for learning and work constitutes malpractice. In P. J. Hartung, M. L. Savickas, & W. B. Walsh (Eds.). *APA handbook of career intervention* (pp. 303–326). Washington, DC: APA.

Kell, H. J., Lubinski, D., & Benbow, C. P. (2013a). Who rises to the top? Early indicators. *Psychological Science*, 24, 648–658.

Kell, H. J., Lubinski, D., Benbow, C. P., & Steiger, J. H. (2013b). Creativity and technical innovation: Spatial ability's unique role. *Psychological Science*, 24, 1831–1836.

Kelley, T. L. (1927). *Interpretation of educational measurements*. New York: World Book.

Lubinski, D. (1996). Applied individual difference research and its quantitative methods. *Psychology, Public Policy, and Law*, 2, 187–203.

(2004). Introduction to the special section on cognitive abilities: 100 years after Spearman's (1904) " 'General intelligence,' objectively determined and measured." *Journal of Personality and Social Psychology*, 86, 96–111.

(2009). Exceptional cognitive ability: The phenotype. *Behavior Genetics*, 39, 350–358.

(2010). Neglected aspects and truncated appraisals in vocational counseling: Interpreting the interest-efficacy association from a broader perspective. *Journal of Counseling Psychology*, 57, 226–238.

(2016). From Terman to today: A century of findings on intellectual precocity. *Review of Educational Research*, 86, 900–944.

Lubinski, D., & Benbow, C. P. (2000). States of excellence. *American Psychologist*, 55, 137–150.

(2006). Study of Mathematically Precocious Youth after 35 years: Uncovering antecedents for the development of math-science expertise. *Perspectives on Psychological Science*, 1, 316–345.

Lubinski, D., Benbow, C. P., & Kell, H. J. (2014). Life paths and accomplishments of mathematically precocious males and females four decades later. *Psychological Science*, 25, 2217–2232.

Lubinski, D., & Dawis, R. V. (1992). Aptitudes, skills, and proficiencies. In M. D. Dunnette & L. M. Hough (Eds.). *Handbook of I/O psychology*, 2nd edn., Vol. 3 (pp. 1–59). Palo Alto, CA: Consulting Psychology Press.

Lubinski, D., & Humphreys, L. G. (1997). Incorporating general intelligence into epidemiology and the social sciences. *Intelligence*, 24, 159–201.

Makel, M., Kell, H. J., Lubinski, D., Putallaz, M., & Benbow, C. P. (2016). When lightning strikes twice: Profoundly gifted, profoundly accomplished. *Psychological Science*, 27, 1004–1018.

Matarazzo, J., D. (1972). *Wechsler's measurement and appraisals of adult intelligence (5th edition)*. Baltimore, MD: Williams & Wilkins.

McNemar, Q. (1964). Lost: Our intelligence? Why? *American Psychologist*, 19, 871–882.

Meehl, P. E. (2006). The power of quantitative thinking. In N. G. Waller, L. J. Yonce, W. M. Grove, D. Faust, & M. F. Lenzenweger (Eds.). *A Paul Meehl*

Reader: Essays on the practice of scientific psychology (pp. 433–444). Mahwah, NJ: Erlbaum.

Messick, S. (1992). Multiple intelligences or multilevel intelligence? Selective emphasis on distinctive properties of hierarchy: On Gardner's *Frames of Mind* and Sternberg's *Beyond IQ* in the context of theory and research on the structure of human abilities. *Psychological Inquiry*, 3, 365–384.

Murray, C. (1998). *Income, inequality, and IQ*. Washington, DC: American Enterprise Institute.

—— (2002). IQ and income inequality in a sample of sibling pairs from advantaged family backgrounds. *American Economic Review*, 339–343.

Open Science Collaboration. (2015). Estimating the reproducibility of psychological science. *Science*, 349, 4716.

Park, G., Lubinski, D., & Benbow, C. P. (2007). Contrasting intellectual patterns for creativity in the arts and sciences: Tracking intellectually precocious youth over 25 years. *Psychological Science*, 18, 948–952.

—— (2008). Ability differences among people who have commensurate degrees matter for scientific creativity. *Psychological Science*, 19, 957–961.

Rimfeld, K., Shakeshaft, N. G., Malanchini, M., Rodic, M. et al. (2017). Phenotypic and genetic evidence for a unifactorial structure of spatial abilities. *Proceedings of the National Academy of Sciences, Early Edition Online*, 1–6. PNAS 2017 doi: 10.1073/pnas.1607883114

Roznowski, M. (1987). The use of tests manifesting sex differences as measures of intelligence: Implications for measurement bias. *Journal of Applied Psychology*, 72, 480–483.

Sanders, C. E., Lubinski, D., & Benbow, C. P. (1995). Does the Defining Issues Test measure psychological phenomena distinct from verbal ability?: An examination of Lykken's query. *Journal of Personality and Social Psychology*, 69, 498–504.

Schmidt, F. L., & Hunter, J. E. (1998). The validity and utility of selection methods in personnel psychology: Practical and theoretical implications of 85 years of research findings. *Psychological Bulletin*, 124, 262–274.

Seashore, C. E. (1922). The gifted student and research. *Science*, 56, 641–648.

Shea, D. L., Lubinski, D., & Benbow, C. P. (2001). Importance of assessing spatial ability in intellectually talented young adolescents: A 20-year longitudinal study. *Journal of Educational Psychology*, 93, 604–614.

Snow, C. P. (1967). *The two cultures and a second look*. London: Cambridge University Press.

Snow, R. E. (1999). Commentary: Expanding the breadth and depth of admissions testing. In S. Messick (Ed.). *Assessment in higher education* (pp. 133–140). Hillsdale, NJ: Erlbaum.

Snow, R. E., Corno, L., & Jackson, D., III. (1996). Individual differences in affective and conative functions. In D. C. Berliner & R. C. Calfee (Eds.). *Handbook of educational psychology* (pp. 243–310). New York: Macmillan.

Snow, R. E., & Lohman, D. F. (1989). Implications of cognitive psychology for educational measurement. In R. L. Linn (Eds.). *Educational measurement* (3rd edn.) (pp. 263–331). New York: Collier.

Stanley, J. C. (2000). Helping students learn only what they don't already know. *Psychology, Public Policy, and Law*, 6, 216–222.

Terman, L. M. (1925). *Genetic studies of genius*. Stanford, CA: Stanford University Press.

(1954). The discovery and encouragement of exceptional talent. *American Psychologist*, 9, 221–230.

Thurstone, L. L. (1924). The nature of intelligence and ability (III). *British Journal of Psychology*, 14, 243–247.

Tyre, P. (2016). The math revolution. *Atlantic*, 3, 50–57.

Vernon, P. E. (1961). *The structure of human abilities* (2nd edn.). London: Methuen.

Wai, J., Lubinski, D., & Benbow, C. P. (2009). Spatial ability for STEM domains: Aligning over fifty years of cumulative psychological knowledge solidifies its importance. *Journal of Educational Psychology*, 101, 817–835.

Wai, J., & Worrell, F. C. (2016). Helping disadvantaged and spatially talented students fulfill their potential: Related and neglected national resources. *Policy Insights from the Behavioral and Brain Sciences*, 3, 122–128.

Waller, J. H. (1971). Achievement and social mobility: Relationships among IQ score, education, and occupation in two generations. *Social Biology*, 18, 252–259.

CHAPTER 16

The Intelligence of Nations

Richard Lynn

Our publication of IQs for all nations in the world (Lynn & Vanhanen, 2002) has generated a research program that has established substantial correlations between national IQs and a wide range of economic, educational, cognitive, political, epidemiological, demographic, and sociological variables. The major results of this research are reviewed in this chapter. I began to collect the IQs of nations in the 1970s stimulated by the rapid economic development of Japan, Singapore, and other free market countries in East Asia in the years following the end of World War Two. By the 1970s, these had achieved approaching the same per capita income as that of Western Europe, Australia, New Zealand, Canada, and the United States, in contrast with the countries of South Asia, Africa, Latin America, and most of the rest of the world where living standards remained much lower. These differences prompted me to wonder whether there might be differences in intelligence between nations that might contribute to these differences in economic development.

To investigate this possibility, I looked first for data on the IQ in Japan. I found that the American Wechsler tests for children and adults had been standardized in Japan, from which I calculated that the contemporary Japanese IQ was 104, in relation to an American IQ of 100 (Lynn, 1977a). I was also able to find data for the standardization of the Standard Progressive Matrices in Singapore, from which I calculated that the IQ was 103, in relation to a British IQ of 100 (Lynn, 1977b). These two results provided some confirmation for my hypothesis that a high IQ might have contributed to the rapid economic development of what had become known as "the tiger economies" of East Asia.

During the 1980s, I collected data for IQs for a number of countries and published a compilation of these in Lynn (1991). This set the British IQ at 100 (standard deviation 15), and documented studies showing that European nations also had an average IQ of 100, Northeast Asian nations had an average IQ of 106, South Asian and North African nations had an average IQ of 84, and the sub-Saharan African nations had an average IQ of 70. Most of these national IQs were calculated from the Progressive Matrices.

In 2000 I began a collaboration with Tatu Vanhanen, a Finnish political scientist, to examine the relation between national IQs and per capita income. There is a large research literature showing the positive effect of intelligence on earnings among individuals. The classical study is Christopher Jencks's *Inequality* (1972), in which he synthesized American research and estimated that the correlation between intelligence and earnings is 0.31. He also estimated that IQ has a heritability of about 50 percent, and therefore that genetic factors contribute to income differences. Jencks's estimate has proved remarkably accurate in the light of later studies reported for a number of countries. For instance, it was shown that in a national sample in Britain intelligence measured at the age of eight years was correlated with income at the age of 43 years at 0.37 for men and at 0.32 for women (Irwing & Lynn, 2006). Nations are aggregates of individuals, so our expectation was that the positive relation of IQ and income for individuals would hold for nations.

We published the results in Lynn and Vanhanen (2002), giving measured IQs for 81 nations and additional IQs for 104 nations estimated from the measured IQs of neighboring nations with similar populations. We showed that measured average national IQs were positively correlated with per capita GDP (Gross Domestic Product, a measure of per capita income) at 0.66. Thus, IQ explained 44 percent of the variance in per capita GDP among nations. For 185 nations, average national IQs were positively correlated with per capita GDP at 0.68. From this result we argued that national IQs are the single most important variable in the determination of national per capita income. We envisioned a positive feedback relation between national IQs and per capita income in which IQ is a determinant of income, and income is a determinant of IQ through its positive effects on nutrition, health, and education. We proposed that the other principal determinants of income are free market economies and the possession of natural resources.

In our last study of the association between national IQs and per capita income we showed that the positive association was present in the year AD 1 for 120 populations corresponding approximately to contemporary nations, although at a lower correlation (0.24) than in subsequent years (Lynn & Vanhanen, 2012). We showed that the positive association was also present in the years 1500 and 1820 at approximately the same magnitude (068 and 0.63) as those reported in our study of contemporary nations. These results have been confirmed in a number of subsequent studies. Cribari-Neto and Souza (2013) have reported a correlation of 0.71 for 124 countries between national IQ and per capita GNI (Gross National Product) and Lv and Xu (2016) have reported a correlation of 0.76 for 93 countries between national IQ and per capita log GDP, 2001–2012.

Economic Growth

Because national IQs are substantially correlated with per capita income, it can be assumed that national IQs must have been associated with economic growth at some time in the past. We showed that this was the case over the 500 years from 1500 to 2000 for which IQs for 109 nations were correlated with rates of economic growth at 0.71 (Lynn & Vanhanen, 2006). A lower correlation of 0.37 for 126 countries for the years 1975–2005 was reported by Meisenberg (2011).

The principal explanation for the lower correlation over the shorter time period is that various shocks such as wars and large increases in the price of oil reduce the growth rate of some countries in the short term. The higher correlation over the long term shows that these have little permanent effect and national IQ emerges as the major determinant of national differences in economic growth. This conclusion may be surprising to economists because theoretically it would be expected that low-IQ countries would have faster economic growth rates than high-IQ countries because of what economists call "the advantage of backwardness." This advantage should be present because of the potential of poor countries to adopt the technologies and management practices of wealthier countries, whereas wealthier countries depend on innovation. However, the studies show that this is not so and that the correlation between national IQs and economic growth over the long period is positive. Meisenberg (2011) discusses this question and suggests that the explanation may be that a high-IQ population is more likely to establish effective economic institutions that favor economic growth.

Income Inequality

Meisenberg (2004) was the first to report a negative correlation of -0.60) for national IQs for 59 countries with income inequality measured with the Gini index, the values of which range from zero (complete equality of incomes) to one (one person earns everything). This result has been confirmed for 127 countries with a correlation of -0.51 by Kanazawa (2009).

The negative correlations show that there is less income inequality in high-IQ countries. The explanation proposed by Meisenberg (2011) is that "a more-or-less equal income distribution leads to the greatest happiness of the greatest number. We can expect that societies whose members are capable of reasoning at this level will develop mechanisms to restrain the exploitation of the weak by the strong and to redistribute wealth from the rich to the poor."

Educational Attainment

Many studies have shown that intelligence predicts subsequent educational attainment among individuals typically at a magnitude of a correlation of around 0.5 to 0.7. For example, Benson (1942) showed that in the United States, intelligence measured at age 12 years predicted educational attainment at age 23 at correlation of 0.57 and Thienpont and Verleye (2003) showed that in Britain, intelligence measured at age 11 years predicted educational attainment at age 21 at correlation of 0.70. It would be expected from these results that the same positive relation should be present across nations. This was confirmed with a correlation of 0.88 for 38 counties between national IQs and scores obtained by school students in math in the 1999 TIMSS (International Math and Science Study) (Lynn & Vanhanen, 2002) and further confirmed by a correlation of 0.97 between national IQs and educational attainment measured by all the PISA (Program for International Student Assessment) studies of the attainment of 15-year-olds in math, science, and reading comprehension and the TIMSS studies, providing strong predictive validity for the national IQs (Rindermann, Woodley, & Stratford, 2012).

Educational Input

National IQs are highly correlated with educational input measured as the quantity of education. Meisenberg (2004) reported the first study showing this with a correlation for 78 countries of 0.77 for the average number of years of schooling with the percentage of the population that was literate. This was confirmed by Rindermann (2008a) with a correlation of 0.78 for 173 countries.

The high correlations between national IQ and years of education are best understood as arising from a positive feed loop in which national IQ is a determinant of per capita income, and higher per capita income is used to raise the quantity of schooling, which feeds back to increase intelligence and literacy. The explanation of the association between national IQ and adult literacy has been discussed by Barber (2005, p. 280). He suggests that adult literacy is not simply a function of the proportion of children enrolled in secondary education because "illiteracy had strong and consistent negative effects on IQ, even with schooling controlled" (p. 280). He suggests that "perhaps a high level of illiteracy in a society impoverishes the overall level of intellectual stimulation with a depressing effect on IQ scores." This explanation is consistent with studies showing that greater secondary education is a determinant of IQ among individuals (Ceci, 1991).

Cognitive Achievement

A high IQ is a necessary although not a sufficient condition for high cognitive achievement, so it would be expected that this would be found in countries with high IQs. This has been confirmed by Morse (2008), who gives a correlation for 139 countries of 0.87 between national IQs and the numbers of papers per capita published in academic journals. Gelade (2008, p. 712) gives a correlation for 112 countries of 0.51 between national IQs and the patent index measured as the number of patents granted in the United States per million population. Gelade adopts the patent index as a measure of a nation's technological achievement, and "technological achievement mediates the relationship between IQ and wealth; in other words, high IQ nations generate more technical knowledge, which in turn leads to more wealth." Rindermann, Sailer, and Thompson (2009) give the correlations for 97 countries between national IQs and Nobel prizes awarded per capita (1901–2004) for literature (0.13 not statistically significant), peace (0.21), and science (0.34).

Rindermann (2011) gives a correlation for 108 countries of 0.68 between national IQs and performance in the International Mathematical Olympiad (IMO), a competition for young people below age 20 years. Countries select six individuals to participate in the IMO, which consists of mathematical problems in geometry, number theory, and functional equations. The study gives national IMO scores, relative to the population size, in the IMO from 1991 to 2010. The proposed explanation is that national IQs are a significant determinant of high mathematical ability.

Political Institutions

Studies of national IQ and political institutions have shown that high IQ is positively associated with democracy. A correlation of 0.53 for 192 nations assessed in 2002 was given in Lynn and Vanhanen (2006) and confirmed for democracy assessed at various times by Rindermann (2008a, 2008b), Meisenberg (2009, 2011), and Lv and Xu (2016). The major exception to this positive association is China, which has a high IQ but is not a democracy.

Positive correlations have also been reported for institutions normally associated with democracy, including the rule of law at 0.64 for 131 nations (Rindermann, 2008a); political freedom at 0.49 for 170 nations (Meisenberg, 2009); property rights for 116 nations at 0.63 (Jones & Potrafke, 2014); freedom of expression at 0.68 for 71 nations (Van de Vliert, 2013); the ease of conducting business transactions measured by the Doing Business Index for 21 Asian countries at 0.72 (Jones, 2011); the efficiency of bureaucracy measured as the quality and speed of decisions made by public officials for 140 nations at 0.64 (Rindermann, 2008a); the absence of corruption measured by the Corruption Perception Index first shown for 126 nations at 0.54 by Meisenberg (2004) and confirmed in numerous studies reporting correlations of 0.59 for 132 countries (Lynn & Vanhanen, 2006), 0.55 for 134 countries (Meisenberg, 2012), 0.56 for 129 countries (Kanyama, 2014) and 0.63 for 125 countries (Potrafke, 2012), who proposes that populations with higher IQs have longer time horizons that enable them to resist corruption.

Voracek (2013) has reported a correlation for 117 of -0.71 between national IQs and the Failed State Index, a measure of vulnerability to political breakdown and measured as a compound of 12 social, economic, and political indicators. The negative correlation with national IQ shows higher national intelligence is associated with lower vulnerability to political breakdown. Meisenberg (2012) has reported a correlation for 134 countries of 0.22 between national IQs and "big government" defined as government expenditure as a percentage of GDP, 1980–1989, showing a small tendency for high-IQ nations to have more government expenditure. Meisenberg (2004) has reported a positive correlation for 59 countries of 0.76 for national IQs with economic freedom defined and measured as the extent of personal choice, voluntary exchange, freedom of economic competition, and the rule of law providing legal protection for the person and property. This result was confirmed for 125 countries at a correlation 0.61 with economic freedom measured as the EFR (Economic Freedom in the World) index calculated from the size of government, legal security of property rights, sound money, free trade across countries, and regulation of credit, labor, and business (Meisenberg, 2011).

Personality

The relation between national IQ and the "big five" personality traits has been reported for 51 nations by Stolarski, Zajenkowski, and Meisenberg (2013) with nonsignificant correlations of -0.01 for Neuroticism and 0.16 for Conscientiousness, and significant correlations of 0.30 for Extraversion, 0.34 for Openness, and 0.33 for Agreeableness. The authors note that the positive correlation between national IQ and openness confirms this relationship found in studies of individuals.

Lv and Xu (2016) report a positive correlation of 0.56 for 93 countries between national IQ and individualism as contrasted with collectivism showing that high-IQ nations are generally more individualistic. Rindermann (2008a) reports a positive correlation of 0.49 for 41 nations between national IQ and "interpersonal trust," defined as the extent to which people trust each other to behave honestly in transactions.

Meisenberg (2004) reports correlations for 45 countries of 0.74 and 0.43 between national IQs and "Modernism" and "Post-modernism." "Modernism" consists of a liberal set of values such as support for abortion and euthanasia, lack of respect for authority, and lack of belief in religion. "Post-modernism" also consists of a liberal set of values, including sympathy for and acceptance of homosexuality and prostitution, criminals, immigrants, alcoholics, people with AIDS, and others with different views. The positive correlation shows that countries with higher IQs have stronger Modernist and Post-modernist values. Kanazawa (2009) confirms this, reporting a positive correlation of 0.51 for 127 countries between national IQ and liberalism. Dama (2013) reports a low but statistically significant negative correlation for 119 countries of -0.18 between national IQ and son preference possibly consistent with more liberal values in higher-IQ countries.

Rindermann (2008a) reports a positive correlation for 31 countries of 0.59 between national IQ and the speed of life measured as the speed of service at post offices, walking speed, and the accuracy of clocks. The positive correlation suggests that the populations of high-IQ countries are more energetic.

Jones and Podemska (2010) report a correlation for 129 countries of 0.48 between national IQs and the savings rate calculated from the ratio of the holdings of U.S. treasury bonds to nominal GDP over the years 1980–2005. They argue that this is predictable from the positive association of IQ with a lower time preference and a greater propensity to postpone immediate gratification for future benefits among individuals. Jones (2011) provides further evidence for this theory by giving a significant correlation for 10 Asian countries of 0.70 between national IQ and low time preference measured by responses to the question "Would you prefer $3,400 this month or $3,800 next month?" Choosing the second option indicates low time preference or in psychological terms, a capacity to delay gratification. The author argues that high-IQ countries with low average rates of time preference have higher savings rates and stocks of financial capital, which contribute to economic growth. Hafer (2016) confirms the positive correlation between national IQs and the savings rate with a correlation of 0.76 for 80 countries.

Happiness and Life Satisfaction

Studies of happiness and life satisfaction correlates of national IQ have reported positive correlations of 0.64 for 148 countries and 0.63 for 136 countries (Lynn & Vanhanen, 2012). These results have been confirmed for life satisfaction with a correlation of 0.62 by Burhan, Mohamad, Kurniawan and Sidek (2014). These studies show that the populations of higher-IQ nations tend to be happier than those of low-IQ nations.

As the populations of high-IQ countries tend to be happier than those of low-IQ countries, it might be expected that they would have lower rates of suicide. Contrary to this expectation, Voracek (2008, 2009) has shown that for 85 countries, the correlation with national IQ is positive at 0.54. He suggests that a certain level of intelligence is required to understand that a person's kin would benefit from one's death, and therefore that suicide can increase a person's inclusive fitness.

Health

Studies at the individual level have shown that intelligence is positively associated with health indexed by life expectancy, e.g., Deary, Whalley, and Starr (2009). The same positive relation has been reported for nations for which a correlation for 197 countries of 0.76 between national IQ and life expectancy at birth in 2008 is reported in Lynn and Vanhanen (2012). The national IQ-life expectancy association has been confirmed for 99 countries at a correlation of 0.82 (Belasen & Hafer, 2013) and for 93 countries at a correlation of 0.81 (Lv & Xu, 2016). One explanation for this is the positive correlation of 0.33 for 46 countries between national IQs and the quality of nutrition assessed by energy consumption in Kcal per day 2003–2005 reported by Rindermann, Woodley, and Stratford (2012). Another factor is the positive correlation of 0.35 for 93 countries between national IQ and expenditure on health as a percentage of GDP reported by Lv and Xu (2016), suggesting that high national IQ contributes to good health through greater expenditure.

The studies reporting positive correlations between national IQ and health have been confirmed by many studies reporting negative correlations between national IQ and poor health and disease. Barber (2005) has reported a correlation for 81 countries of -0.48 between national IQ and low birth weight defined as below 2,500 gr., showing that the incidence of babies with low birth weight is greater in low-IQ countries. He suggested the likely explanation is that the incidence of low birth weight is determined largely by malnutrition and diseases, and that these are partly determined by national IQ.

Negative correlations of -0.48 for the percentage prevalence of HIV infection in 2001–2003 in 165 counties have been reported by Rindermann (2008a) and of -0.88 between national IQs and the prevalence of sexually transmitted diseases for 97 countries has been reported by Meisenberg and Woodley (2013).

A negative correlation of -0.89 between national IQ and the prevalence of infectious diseases for 184 countries has been reported by Eppig, Fincher, and Thornhill (2010). This negative correlation has been confirmed at -0.85 between national IQs and the disease burden for 137 countries reported by Hassall and Sherratt (2011), showing that high-IQ countries have a lower prevalence of disease. A correlation of -0.57 for the prevalence of tuberculosis infection in 2008 in 154 counties was reported by Lynn and Vanhanen (2012).

A number of studies have reported that mortality is higher in low-IQ countries. This was first shown by Barber (2005), who reported a negative correlation for 81 countries of -0.34 for infant mortality rates averaged for 1978–1980 and suggested that this arises because "infant mortality is affected by the prevalence of infection as well as infant nutritional status and is considered a sensitive indicator of infant health for a population" (p. 278). The negative association between rates of infant mortality and national IQ has been confirmed for 149 countries at -0.77 by Lynn and Vanhanen (2006) and for 191 countries at -0.76 by Reeve (2009). Christainsen (2013) has reported a negative correlation for 130 countries of -0.65 between national IQ and child mortality, the death rate of children under age five. Negative correlations between national IQ and maternal mortality for 140 countries of -0.73 have been reported by Lynn and

Vanhanen (2006) and confirmed for 131 countries at -0.65 by Reeve (2009). The negative correlations of national IQs with infant and child mortality are predictable from the negative relationship among individuals reviewed by Cvorovic, Rushton, and Tenjevic (2008).

Crime

A number of studies have reported that crime tends to be more prevalent in low-IQ countries. Rushton and Templer (2009) reported negative correlations for 116 countries between national IQ and homicide at -0.25, rape at -0.29, and assault at -0.21. These results have been confirmed by a correlation of -0.51 for all crime for 97 countries reported by Meisenberg and Woodley (2013). The negative correlations of IQ and crime rates across countries are consistent with numerous studies reporting that crime is negatively related to IQ among individuals, e.g., Herrnstein and Murray (1994).

Fertility

A negative correlation of -0.85 between national IQ and birth rates has been reported for 129 countries by Templer (2008) and has been confirmed by several studies reporting negative correlations between national IQ and fertility, e.g., at -0.71 for 111 countries reported by Shatz (2008) and at -0.73 for 192 countries reported by Reeve (2009). Shatz (2008, p. 111) suggests as a possible explanation that (1) "the IQ fertility relationship is mediated by economics ... it is possible that countries that are poorer have lower quality educational systems, lower quality health care, and more difficult access to birth control, all of which may contribute to higher fertility rates"; (2) "differential K theory ... it is possible that countries with higher IQ scores and lower fertility rates have larger aggregates of high K selected individuals with lower IQ scores and higher fertility rates."

The effect of the negative correlation between national IQ and fertility is greater population growth in low-IQ countries, shown by Shatz (2008), who reports a negative correlation of -0.52 between national IQ and population growth rates for 111 countries. The effect of this is a decline in the world's genotypic IQ estimated at --.253 points a decade by Woodley, Piffer, Peñaherrera and Rindermann (2016). Furthermore, all the high-IQ counties have below-replacement fertility, entailing declining populations. This is a major disadvantage of a high national IQ.

Conclusion

These studies showing that national IQs are a significant determinant of a number of socially desirable outcomes raise the question of what could be done to increase intelligence in low-IQ countries. Research suggests that the most promising ways of achieving this are by improvements in nutrition and health (Lynn, 1990) and education (Ceci, 1991). During recent decades, these improvements have been taking place in a number of economically developing countries and have contributed to raising intelligence, while from the mid-1990s IQs have declined in several economically developed countries, including France, Norway, Denmark, Australia, Britain, Sweden, and the Netherlands (Dutton & Lynn, 2015). It is likely that these trends will continue, leading to a reduction of global inequality.

References

Barber, N. (2005). Educational and ecological correlates of IQ: A cross-national investigation. *Intelligence, 33,* 273–284.

Belasen, A. & Hafer, R. W. (2013). IQ and alcohol consumption: International data. *Intelligence, 41,* 615–621.

Benson, V. E. (1942) The intelligence and later scholastic success of sixth grade pupils. *School and Society, 55,* 163–167.

Burhan, N. A. S., Mohamad, M. R., Kurniawan, Y., & Sidek, A. H. (2014). National intelligence, basic human needs, and their effect on economic growth. *Intelligence, 44,* 103–111.

Ceci, S. J. (1991). How much does schooling influence general intelligence and its cognitive components? A reassessment of the evidence. *Developmental Psychology, 27,* 703–722.

Christainsen, G. B. (2013). IQ and the wealth of nations: How much reverse causality? *Intelligence, 41,* 688–698.

Cribari-Neto, F. & Souza, T. C. (2013). Religious belief and intelligence: Worldwide evidence. *Intelligence, 41,* 482–489.

Cvorovic, J., Rushton, J. P., & Tenjevic, L. (2008). Maternal IQ and child mortality in 222 Serbian Roma (Gypsy) women. *Personality and Individual Differences, 44,* 1604–1609.

Dama, M. S. (2013). Cognitive ability, used as an indirect measure of cross-cultural variation in condition, predicts sex ratio at birth. *Naturwissenschaften, 100,* 559–569.

Deary, I. J., Whalley, L. J., & Starr, J.M. (2009). *A lifetime of intelligence.* Washington, DC: American Psychological Association.

Dutton, E. & Lynn, R. (2015). A negative Flynn effect in France, 1999 to 2008–9. *Intelligence, 51,* 57–66.

Eppig, C., Fincher, C. L., & Thornhill, R. (2010). Parasite prevalence and the worldwide distribution of cognitive ability. *Proceedings of the Royal Society B*, 277, 3801–3808.

Gelade, G. A. (2008). IQ, cultural values, and the technological achievements of nations. *Intelligence*, 36, 711–718.

Hafer, R. W. (2016). Cross-country evidence on the link between IQ and financial development. *Intelligence*, 55, 7–13.

Hassall, C. & Sherratt, T. N. (2011). Statistical inference and spatial patterns in correlates of IQ. *Intelligence*, 39, 303–310.

Herrnstein, R. J. & Murray, C. (1994). *The bell curve: Intelligence and class structure in American life*. New York: The Free Press.

Irwing, P. & Lynn, R. (2006). The relation between childhood IQ and income in middle age. *Journal of Social, Political and Economic Studies*, 31, 191–196.

Jencks, C. (1972). *Inequality*. New York: Basic Books.

Jones, G. (2011). National IQ and national productivity: The Hive Mind across Asia. *Asian Development Review*, 28, 51–71.

Jones, G. & Podemska, M. (2010). IQ in the utility function: Cognitive skills, time preferences, and cross-country differences in savings rates. Retrieved 17 Dec. 2010 from http://mason.gmu.edu/-gjonesb/IQsavings.pdf.

Jones, G. & Potrafke, N. (2014). Human capital and national institutional quality: Are TIMSS, PISA, and national average robust predictors? *Intelligence*, 46, 148–155.

Kanazawa, S. (2009). IQ and the values of nations. *Journal of Biosocial Science*, 41, 537–556.

Kanyama, I. K. (2014). Quality of institutions: Does intelligence matter? *Intelligence*, 42, 44–52.

Lv, Z. & Xu, T. (2016). The impact of national IQ on longevity: New evidence from quantile regression. *Personality and Individual Differences*, 101, 282–287.

Lynn, R. (1977a). The intelligence of the Japanese. *Bulletin of the British Psychological Society*, 30, 69–72.

(1977b). The intelligence of the Chinese and Malays in Singapore. *Mankind Quarterly*, 18, 125–128.

(1990). The role of nutrition in secular increases of intelligence. *Personality and Individual Differences*, 11, 273–285.

(1991). Race differences in intelligence: A global perspective. *Mankind Quarterly*, 31, 254–296.

Lynn, R. & Vanhanen, T. (2002). *IQ and the wealth of nations*. Westport, CT: Praeger.

(2006). *IQ and global inequality*. Augusta, GA: Washington Summit Books.

(2012). *Intelligence: A unifying construct for the social sciences*. London: Ulster Institute for Social Research.

Meisenberg, G. (2004). Talent, character and the dimensions of national culture. *Mankind Quarterly*, 45, 123–169.

(2009). Wealth, intelligence, politics and global fertility differentials. *Journal of Biosocial Science*, 41, 519–536.

(2011). Secularization and desecularization in our time. *Journal of Social, Political & Economic Studies*, 36, 316–356.

(2012). National IQ and economic outcomes. *Personality and Individual Differences*, 53, 103–107.

Meisenberg, G. & Woodley, M. A. (2013). Global behavioural variation: A test of differential-K. *Personality and Individual Differences*, 55, 273–278.

Morse, S. (2008). The geography of tyranny and despair: Development indicators and the hypothesis of genetic inevitability of national inequality. *The Geographical Journal*, 174, 195–206.

Potrafke, N. (2012). Intelligence and corruption. *Economics Letters*, 114, 109–112.

Reeve, C. I. (2009). Expanding the g-nexus: Further evidence regarding the relations among IQ, religiosity, and national health outcomes. *Intelligence*, 37, 495–505.

Rindermann, H. (2008a). Relevance of education and intelligence at the national level for the economic welfare of people. *Intelligence*, 36, 127–142.

(2008b). Relevance of education and intelligence for the political development of nations: Democracy, rule of law and political liberty. *Intelligence*, 36, 306–322.

(2011). Results in the International Mathematical Olympiad (IMO) as indicators of the intellectual classes' cognitive-ability level. In A. Ziegler & Ch. Perleth (Eds.). *Excellence. Essays in honour of Kurt. A. Heller* (pp. 303–321). Münster: Lit.

Rindermann, H., Sailer, S., & Thompson, J. (2009). The impact of smart fractions, cognitive ability of politicians and average competence of peoples on social development. *Talent Development & Excellence*, 1, 3–25.

Rindermann, H., Woodley, M. A., & Stratford, J. (2012). Haplo groups as evolutionary markers of cognitive ability. *Intelligence*, 40, 362–375.

Rushton, J. P. & Templer, D. I. (2009). National differences in intelligence, crime, income and skin color. *Intelligence*, 37, 341–346.

Shatz, S. M. (2008). IQ and fertility: A cross national study. *Intelligence*, 36, 109–111.

Stolarski, M., Zajenkowski, M., & Meisenberg, G. (2013). National intelligence and personality: Their relationships and impact on national economic success. *Intelligence*, 41, 94–101.

Templer, D. I. (2008). Correlational and factor analytic support for Rushton's differential K life history theory. *Personality & Individual Differences*, 45, 440–444.

Thienpont, K. & Verleye, G. (2003). Cognitive ability and occupational status in a British birth cohort. *Journal of Biosocial Science*, 36, 333–349.

Van de Vliert, E. (2013). Climato-economic habitats support patterns of human needs, stresses and freedoms. *Behavioral & Brain Sciences*, 36, 465–479.

Voracek, M. (2008). Cross national social ecology of intelligence and suicide prevalence: Integration, refinement and update of studies. *Perceptual & Motor Skills*, 106, 550–556.

(2009). National intelligence, suicide rate and subjective well-being. *Perceptual and Motor Skills*, 109, 718–720.

(2013). National intelligence estimates and the failed state index. *Psychological Reports*, 113, 519–524.

Woodley, M. A., Piffer, D., Peñaherrera, M. A., & Rindermann, H. (2016). Evidence of contemporary polygenic selection on the big G of national cognitive ability: A cross-cultural sociogenetic analysis. *Personality and Individual Differences*, 102, 90–97.

CHAPTER 17

Intelligences about Things and Intelligences about People

John D. Mayer[¹]

In 1994, Linda Gottfredson, a professor at the University of Delaware, authored an editorial directed toward the educated public entitled "Mainstream science in intelligence," which was cosigned by 52 eminent intelligence researchers. Gottfredson sought to describe the current status of the field; this would help address what she and others regarded as mischaracterizations of intelligence research that had appeared in media accounts. Her piece appeared in the *Wall Street Journal*, and was subsequently reprinted in the journal *Intelligence* (Gottfredson, 1997). What is of particular interest here are not any missteps of the media at that time, but, given the consensual nature of the document, the opening definition of intelligence. Intelligence is, Gottfredson explained:

> a very general mental capability that, among other things, involves the ability to reason, plan, solve problems, think abstractly, comprehend complex ideas, learn quickly and learn from experience ... [I]t reflects a ... capability for comprehending our surroundings – "catching on," "making sense" of things, or "figuring out" what to do. (Gottfredson, 1997, p. 13)

This already very good definition can be further sharpened, I believe, by acknowledging that intelligence has evolved to help people adapt to and survive in their environments. This evolutionary perspective encourages our consideration of intelligence's role in people's understanding of their surrounding world. Shaped that way, I would describe intelligence as:

> A person's mental capacity to solve problems that concern the inner self and surrounding world. The capabilities include the ability to represent information relevant to specific topics and contexts accurately in memory and to manipulate that information systematically. The ability further involves identifying the similarities and differences among concepts and contexts, "getting the point," and drawing upon appropriate generalizations so as to relate existing information to new problems; it involves "figuring things out," with the purpose of finding effective solutions.

Gottfredson's definition employs the opening phrase, "a very general mental capability … ," placing an emphasis on general intelligence. Although I agree people possess a general capacity to problem solve, I also believe they specialize in particular areas of problem solving – especially by adulthood (Ackerman, 2014). For that reason, I have added the idea that the information relates to "particular topics and contexts" relevant to the person – a modification designed to allow for more than one area of intelligence.

Although a theoretical model of intelligence that emphasizes general problem solving fits contemporary data adequately, there is increasing consensus that taking account of a group of differentiated "broad intelligences," such as verbal-comprehension intelligence, perceptual-organizational reasoning, mental speed, and other qualities can enhance our representation of human intellectual performance beyond global reasoning alone.

A Note on General Intelligence and Broad Intelligences

Charles Spearman (1904) first observed that people's abilities correlated positively with one another across a diverse group of intellectual problems: as a person's ability on one task rose, so it did on other tasks. This *positive manifold*, as the positive correlations became known, was a ubiquitous finding. If all human intellectual abilities rose and fell together, Spearman argued, perhaps they could be represented as just one overall general intelligence. Spearman's observation that mental abilities all correlated positively was supported by subsequent research. The correlations among abilities, however, were not all at the same level. Without getting too far into the technical details, I'll observe that subsets of tasks existed that correlated more highly with one another than with other subsets of tasks. The positive manifold, in other words, was not equally present across all abilities, and the statistical grey areas provided potential evidence for subgroups of intelligences (multiple intelligences) as well as a general one. The next 70 or so years were marked by a lively debate over whether human intelligence was best regarded as one or multiple in nature (see, for example, Gardner, 1983; Gignac & Weiss, 2015; Jensen, 1998; Sternberg, 1985; Van et al., 2006; Visser, Ashton, & Vernon, 2006).

In the 1970s, mathematical psychologists introduced a new tool called structural equation modeling (SEM) for modeling correlations in the field. SEM allowed for statistical tests of which theoretical representations best fit a set of correlations (e.g., Joreskog, 1969; Kenny, 1976; Thompson, 2004). John Carroll (1993) assembled hundreds of findings from intelligence tests over the 20th century and applied SEM to his combined data set. He concluded that intelligences could be organized into three strata (levels): his three-stratum model (also referred to as the Cattell-Horn-Carroll model) describes a hierarchy of mental abilities in which general intelligence is positioned at the top, rather like the CEO at the top of a corporate organizational chart, beneath which are a series of 10 to 15 broad intelligences, analogous to the corporate chief officers responsible for the financial, information technology, human relations, and other functions of the organization. Examples of these broad intelligences include the perceptual-organizational, spatial, and verbal intelligences (Flanagan, McGrew, & Ortiz, 2000; Schneider & Newman, 2015). Carroll placed still more specific abilities at the third, lowest level of the hierarchy – analogous to the distinct individuals who run smaller departments of the organization. For example, vocabulary knowledge is part of the broader verbal-propositional intelligence (McGrew, 2009).

Many of the broad intelligences relate to specific subject or topic areas: people use their perceptual-organizational intelligence to understand how to fit objects together, such as the parts of an engine. People use their spatial intelligence to recognize objects and understand how they would appear from different angles, and to throw balls, rocks, and spear-like projectiles along particular trajectories. People employ quantitative intelligence to solve mathematical problems. Other broad intelligences concern memory retrieval and working memory and play more basic, foundational roles in thinking.

Today there is considerable evidence that these broad, interrelated intelligences exist subsidiary to general reasoning ability (Flanagan et al., 2013; Schneider & Newman, 2015; Sternberg & Hedlund, 2002; Sternberg & the Rainbow Project, 2009; Visser et al., 2006). I would argue, however, that the Carroll model of 1993 and models since have examined a diverse but nonetheless incomplete set of intelligences.

A Startling Omission

The problem with the Cattell-Horn-Carroll model of 1993 (and other models of the time) was that, integrative as it was, it nonetheless omitted key areas of intelligence. The broad intelligences focused more-or-less exclusively on reasoning about *things*: puzzle pieces (the perceptual-organizational), objects in space (spatial), quantitative (numbers), even the "things" that are the words and sentences we use (verbal), although words and sentences also include thinking about people. This reflected the more general thing-orientation of academic psychology at the time.

A second example of this thing-oriented focus was the classical approach to primate cognition of the mid-20th century: comparative psychologists, who were studying chimpanzees' and bonobos' intellect, chiefly focused on their "understanding of objects and their various spatial, causal, and featural interrelations" (Tomasello & Call, 1997, p. 25). Psychologists viewed chimpanzees and bonobos as mostly preoccupied with foraging for food: mapping the world around them, finding shortcuts to the food, and predicting where food would next appear (Tomasello & Call, 1997). These nonhuman primates could indeed categorize objects, understand the objects as permanent (in the Piagetian sense), rotate objects in their minds, and count small numbers of objects – mental abilities that paralleled such human intelligences as the perceptual-organizational, the spatial, and the quantitative.

Reasoning about Individuals?

Over time, however, comparative psychologists realized that our nearest primate relatives not only reasoned about things, but also about one another, although the researchers were "somewhat slow to recognize this fact" (Tomasello & Call, 1997, p. 187). Nonhuman primates, it turned out, also strove to assess other individuals' intentions, to learn from them, and ultimately to predict other individuals' behaviors as best they could. Tomasello and Call observed:

> Because primates individually recognize many of the members of their social groups, they come to know … the … behavioral tendencies of specific individuals, both toward themselves and toward one another making for a highly complex "social field" in which virtually every decision made must take account of … the social relationships of virtually all the individuals present. (1997, p. 187)

Intelligences about People

Although academic psychologists mostly focused on reasoning about things, there were exceptions: Edward L. Thorndike (1920) had proposed a social intelligence: "an ability to understand and manage men and women, boys and girls, to act wisely in human relations." A first ability-based measure of social intelligence was developed (Hunt, 1928), but sophisticated reviewers regarded its test scores as insufficiently distinct from general IQ to demonstrate the existence of a new mental ability (R. L. Thorndike & Stein, 1937). Twenty-three years later, Lee J. Cronbach concurred that "social intelligence remain[ed] undefined and unmeasured" (Cronbach, 1960, p. 319). And still today, strong evidence for an independent social intelligence remains elusive (e.g., Conzelmann, Weis, & Süß, 2013).

But alternative concepts fared better: in 1990, Peter Salovey and I introduced the idea of an "emotional intelligence" – an ability to reason about emotions (Mayer, DiPaolo, & Salovey, 1990; Salovey & Mayer, 1990), which drew on precursor ideas, including those of social intelligence and Gardner's (1983) theory of multiple intelligences. In 2008, I introduced *personal intelligence*, described as the capacity to understand personality in oneself and others (Mayer, 2008). Personal intelligence drew together areas of reasoning described in such earlier concepts as psychological mindedness (Appelbaum, 1973) and the good judge of people (Funder, 2001), and involved an explicit rationale for the existence of a unitary reasoning process about personality (Mayer, 2009, 2014).

At the time of Carroll's three-stratum model, the idea of any intelligence focused on personality, or on people's emotions, seemed a poor fit with the more thing-focused intelligences of the day. Initially, many psychologists rejected the possibility that an emotional intelligence might exist (Davies, Stankov, & Roberts, 1998; Locke, 2005). Although I will focus on emotional and personal intelligences here, there are other possible members of the group, including practical intelligence (Wagner, 2000; Wagner & Sternberg, 1985), spiritual intelligence (Emmons, 2000), and the aforementioned social intelligence (Conzelmann et al., 2013; Weis & Süß, 2007; Wong et al., 1995).

Measuring People-Centered Intelligences

The Test Development Process

The most direct evidence for intelligences about people comes from empirical research based on the ability-based theories of emotional and personal intelligences: if a reliable measure of a well-defined psychological variable can be developed, and its validity demonstrated, the existence of the variable is supported (Cacioppo, Semin, & Berntson, 2004; Haig, 2005). In our laboratory, we have been involved in a program of test development and improvement around both the emotional and personal intelligences (Mayer, Caruso, & Salovey, 2016).

For both intelligences, we have engaged in a multiple-step process of test development (see Figure 17.1), centered around the principle that

Figure 17.1   Initial processes involved in developing an intelligence test.

these intelligences can be assessed as mental abilities (Mayer et al., 2016). In the first stage of test development, we define the intelligence in part by specifying its problem-solving domain (Figure 17.1, left-hand box). For example, personal intelligence is focused on reasoning about personality-related information; emotional intelligence is concerned with reasoning about emotions and emotion-related information (brief definitions are shown in Table 17.1 (Row 1).

Specifying the relevant areas of problem-solving content helps to define both areas of intelligence and to distinguish them from other similar areas of reasoning. The four areas of reasoning for personal intelligence shown in Table 17.1 involve identifying personality-relevant information, forming models of personality, guiding personal choices, and systematizing personal plans (Table 17.1, Row 2).

We next describe the informational building blocks, termed the conceptual *units*, people reason about in the area (Figure 17.1, second box), as well as the mental processes they apply to those units. For personal intelligence, one type of unit is the "mental trait," including instances such as extraversion and verbal intelligence. Then we consider possible *operators* – clearly specified procedures of reasoning – used with those units (cf., Newell, Shaw, & Simon, 1958, p. 152; Newell & Simon, 1972). For example, one key operator relevant to traits is the "go together" operator: if person X is dutiful, then person X is also likely to be self-disciplined and cautious, according to several models that examine hierarchies of personality traits (DeYoung, Quilty, & Peterson, 2007; Goldberg, 1993).

Dynamic pairs (DPs) are pairs of personality parts or aspects of personality that, relative to society, may cause the personality system conflict, owing to the inner or social conflicts they may elicit. A dynamic pair that leads to social conflict is the trait of *disagreeableness* in social relationships: a person with disagreeableness exerts considerable effort to disagree with others rather than going along with a crowd. In addition, disagreeable people are often shunned, potentially reducing their well-being (Baumeister & Leary, 1995).

Table 17.1   *A Brief Overview of Emotional and Personal Intelligences and their Measurement*

	Emotional Intelligence	Personal Intelligence
Brief definition	The ability to reason validly with emotions and with emotion-related information, and to use emotions to enhance thought*	The ability to reason about personality – both our own and the personalities of others – including about motives and emotions, thoughts and knowledge, plans and styles of action, and awareness and self-control*
Areas of reasoning	(a) Perceiving emotions, (b) using emotion to facilitate thought, (c) understanding emotions, (d) managing emotions	(a) Identifying personality-relevant information, (b) forming models of personality, (c) guiding choices with personality-relevant information, (d) systematizing plans
Ability test description	*Mayer-Salovey-Caruso Emotional Intelligence Test* (Mayer, Salovey, & Caruso, 2002); see also MacCann and Roberts (2008) for an alternative	*Test of Personal Intelligence* (Mayer, Panter, & Caruso, 2012; 2017)
Sample test item	If a person feels more and more frustrated over time, and thinks he has been treated unfairly, the person may become (choose one): a. regretful b. angry c. guilty d. happy	If a person is outgoing and talkative, most likely, she is also inclined to be (choose one): a. self-controlled b. willing to take more risks than average c. anxious and impulsive d. fairly thick-skinned

* from Mayer, Caruso, & Salovey, 2016, p. 7

Dynamic pairs of traits or goals sometimes also may cause inner conflict. A person who is both anxious and sensation-seeking will simultaneously crave risk and be fearful of the consequences his or her daring acts may entail. As a second example, a person whose goals include "being honest all the time" but who also hopes "to appear better in public than I really am" will face some difficult decisions regarding his or her aspirations (Emmons & King, 1988). Dynamic pairs also emerge from misrepresentations of the self, for example, if people's erroneous beliefs as to who they are causes friction with how others see them. A narcissistic individual may believe he is cool whereas others perceive him as exploitative – and this ultimately can lead to negative social consequences for the individual such as impaired work performance (Oltmanns & Turkheimer, 2006).

In the third step of our test development (Figure 17.1, Step 3) we formulate test questions that pertain to the subject area and concern the units and operators described previously. Table 17.1 (Row 3) provides references for the specific tests we and a few others have developed in the area along with some sample test items, for example, the *Test of Personal Intelligence* or *TOPI*. That measure includes items such as the one reproduced in the bottom right of Table 17.1: that asks, "If a person is outgoing and talkative, most likely, she is also inclined to be..."? followed by four alternatives. The correct answer is "b. more assertive than average," because research on the big five personality traits indicate that talkativeness and sociability are more highly correlated with assertiveness than with the other listed alternatives.

Although both personal and emotional intelligences concern people, they are substantially different in their subject areas. It is possible, for example, to write 100 test items in the area of personal intelligence without much mention of emotions. Similarly, it is possible to write 100 questions about emotions without asking anything much about personality traits or other information about personality. In Step 4, we administer test items to people to evaluate whether the intelligence exists, and simultaneously, the quality of our test items and test. Our theory of personal intelligence predicts that people who recognize personality-relevant units and their interactions will score higher on our test of personal intelligence than other people.

Personal and Emotional Intelligences as Broad Intelligences within the Three-Stratum Model

Findings from personal and emotional intelligence tests indicate that each one samples a broad range of problems solving, and each individually assesses a reliable individual-difference variable (reliabilities typically in the $r = 0.80$ to 0.90 range for the overall tests) that is largely unitary. (How each intelligence might be best subdivided remains unsettled).

MacCann and colleagues reported the results from a large-scale study funded by the *United States Army Research Institute* and *Educational Testing Services*. Their findings indicated that emotional intelligence, represented as three factors of the Mayer-Salovey-Caruso Emotional Intelligence Test (MSCEIT), fit well within the broad-intelligence stratum of the Cattell-Horn-Carroll model (MacCann et al., 2014). A reanalysis of the same data by Legree and colleagues reached the same conclusion regarding the MSCEIT's fit within the three-stratum model, but represented all portions of the test as a single factor (Legree et al., 2014). (For a more detailed discussion of the MSCEIT's indeterminate factor structure, see Mayer et al., 2016).

Personal intelligence, the newer construct, has not yet been tested in such a large-scale study, but it exhibits the same positive manifold with other broad intelligences suggestive of a broad intelligence. Personal intelligence may also divide into two subsidiary factors that correlate about $r = 0.80$ with one another (Mayer, Panter, & Caruso, 2017). The first factor involves perceiving consistencies in people's behaviors. The second factor represents reasoning about personality dynamics, such has how goals interrelate, and how multiple observers each may perceive the same person differently.

Thing-Centered versus People-Centered Intellectual Development

People vary in their interest in things versus people beginning as early as the third grade. To ask yourself which you are most interested in, decide whether you most like "to stop to watch a machine working on the street" or "to make the first attempt to meet a new neighbor" (Graziano et al., 2012, p. 468). Intellectual development may be guided by these interests. William Skimmyhorn and I were able to model course performance at the U.S. Military Academy at West Point largely by dividing GPA into course grades for thing-related courses such as engineering, math, and science, on the one hand, and for people-related courses such as literature, philosophy, and environmental and social sciences on the other (Mayer & Skimmyhorn, 2017). Occupations, too, are often distinguished by whether they are thing- or people-oriented: compare accounting, clerical, engineering, and research work, on the one hand, to sales, social services, and interior decorating on the other (Holland, 1966). Interest in the two general areas may in turn encourage a person to develop thing- or person-centered intelligences over adulthood (Von Stumm & Ackerman, 2013).

Specificity of Prediction?

Correlates and Predictions

A number of findings distinguish people- from thing-focused broad intelligences. First, within the generally positive correlations among broad intelligences, the more specifically thing-oriented an intelligence is, the lower its correlation with people-centered intelligences. For example, personal intelligence correlates just $r = 0.17$ and $r = 0.20$ with SAT-Math and spatial intelligence measures, but rises to $r = 0.39$ with verbal intelligence (which presumably is midway between thing- and person-focused), and rises again to $r = 0.53$ with the Reading the Mind in the Eyes scale, a measure of understanding people, and exhibits an $r = 0.69$ with the MSCEIT understanding emotions and managing emotions areas (the latter, managing emotion area, arguably blends somewhat into personal intelligence at a conceptual level).

Second, most intelligences correlate with the openness dimension of the Big Five at about the $r = 0.20$ level, but people-focused intelligences, compared to thing-focused intelligences, exhibit a unique pattern of correlations with the Big Five personality traits beyond that. Individuals who are better able to reason about themselves and others are also able to interact with others more smoothly and their self-understanding may lead to better self-control. Both personal and emotional intelligences, it turns out, also correlate with higher levels of agreeableness and conscientiousness (an index of self-control) than thing-focused intelligences (DeYoung, 2011; Mayer, Panter, & Caruso, 2012; 2017; Mayer & Skimmyhorn, 2017).

Specificity of Course Performance. Mayer and Skimmyhorn (2017) presented evidence that personal intelligence predicted performance in person-centered courses – those in the humanities and social sciences – better than thing-focused courses. Eight pairs of correlations were computed over a main and a replication sample ($Ns = 893$ to 1063) between an intelligence type (e.g., thing- or people-centered) that matched or mismatched grades in a course type (e.g., thing- or people-focused). In each case, when the intelligence and course types matched, the correlation was higher than when they mismatched. For example, personal intelligence correlated more highly with courses in literature and philosophy than did spatial intelligence, also in both samples; spatial intelligence correlated more highly with thing-focused courses than personal intelligence did over both samples.

Specificity of Social Relationships. Both tests also appear to predict better interpersonal relationships with others. People better like and respect individuals who have higher personal and emotional intelligences than those with lower ability levels (Mayer, Roberts, & Barsade, 2008; Mayer & Skimmyhorn, 2017). Emotional intelligence relates to fewer depressive symptoms and greater well-being (Fernádez-Berrocal & Extremera, 2016;

Lopes, 2016; Mayer et al., 2008) and higher personal intelligence may protect against symptoms of personality disorders (Mayer et al., 2012).

Discussion

The Definition of Intelligence Revisited

At the outset of this chapter, I compared two definitions of intelligence – one that emphasized general intelligence and the other that allowed for more consideration of broad, content-focused intelligences. The identification of a group of broad intelligences argues for the importance of content-specialization for at least some broad intelligences (others, such as mental speed, may be more general). I further argued that one key means of organizing such intelligences was into those focused on things, and those focused on people.

Too Many Intelligences? Yes and No

In a pair of influential commentaries, Hedlund and Sternberg (2000) and Austin and Saklofski (2005) raised concerns that there were, perhaps, too many proposed intelligences to accommodate in contemporary research: how, they wondered, would we manage an expansion of the already large number of broad intelligences? One possible solution raised here is to arrange broad intelligences according to key dimensions that distinguish them and help to define their interrelationships.

Thing- and person-centered intelligences. Our focus here was on a person-thing continuum: indeed, people-centered intelligences appear to have predictable and distinct predictions relative to thing-centered intelligences, such as the courses at which students may excel (Mayer & Skimmyhorn, 2017). But there may be other dimensions as well.

Basic versus subject-oriented broad intelligences. A possible second organizing continuum may be a basic, neurocognitive versus subject-focused dimension, in which the neurocognitive side is occupied by mental speed, working memory and memory retrieval, and the subject-focused end contains both the thing- and people-oriented intelligences discussed here. It seems likely that the neurocognitive intelligences may be more *g*- and fluid-intelligence related, whereas the thing- and person-centered intelligences may reflect more crystallized intelligence.

Implications of Person-Centered Intelligences for Education

Although intelligence levels are hard to change, education is highly effective at improving a person's functioning given the intelligence level people do possess. For example, we are unlikely to improve people's *quantitative intelligence* simply by teaching them algebra, but teaching high school students how to organize their thinking about algebra and about the already-worked-out ideas of the field is very effective at improving how well students solve problems in the area. Most people won't come up with the binomial or quadratic equations on their own, but once taught them, can use the equations to solve algebraic problems. Similarly, by guiding people to build and organize their knowledge around personality, we may improve their effectiveness in thinking in the area.

A number of after-school programs seek to promote skills about human relationships by teaching emotional knowledge, social understanding, and self-understanding more generally. Although the curricula of these programs vary widely, and not all might meet the standards of teaching their areas well, meta-analyses of social and emotional learning programs indicate that teaching people about interpersonal relationships allows students to function better interpersonally (and often academically) with substantial effect sizes in the range of 0.21 to 0.41 (Durlak et al., 2011). As we better specify the units and operators of people-centered intelligences, we may be able to teach people these areas of study more effectively.

Concluding Thoughts

Between 1905 to 1990, just a few measures of people-centered intelligences existed, mostly of social intelligence, and research use of them had proven disappointing. As a consequence, the new models of human mental abilities that emerged in the 1990s mostly omitted their consideration. Now we have tests, data, and intriguing findings in the areas of both personal and emotional intelligences. None of the tests in these new areas is perfect, but collectively they indicate that intelligences about people exist and are consequential. The research on people-centered intelligences has been eye-opening as to the importance of reasoning about oneself and others. To succeed in life doesn't depend just on "who you know" or "what you know," but also on "what you know about who you know."

Note

1 The author gratefully acknowledges the assistance of Victoria M. Bryan, who read and commented on an earlier draft of this manuscript.

References

Ackerman, P. L. (2014). Adolescent and adult intellectual development. *Current Directions in Psychological Science*, 23(4), 246–251.

Appelbaum, S. A. (1973). Psychological-mindedness: Word, concept and essence. *The International Journal of Psychoanalysis*, 54(1), 35–46.

Austin, E. J., & Saklofske, D. H. (2005). Far too many intelligences? On the communalities and differences between social, practical, and emotional intelligences. In R. D. Roberts (Ed.), *Emotional intelligence: An international handbook.* (pp. 107–128). Ashland, OH: Hogrefe & Huber Publishers.

Baumeister, R. F., & Leary, M. R. (1995). The need to belong: Desire for inter-personal attachments as a fundamental human motivation. *Psychological Bulletin*, 117(3), 497–529. doi:10.1037/0033-2909.117.3.497

Cacioppo, J. T., Semin, G. R., & Berntson, G. G. (2004). Realism, instrumental-ism, and scientific symbiosis: Psychological theory as a search for truth and the discovery of solutions. *American Psychologist*, 59(4), 214–223. doi:10.1037/0003-066X.59.4.214

Carroll, J. B. (1993). *Human cognitive abilities: A survey of factor-analytic studies.* New York: Cambridge University Press.

Conzelmann, K., Weis, S., & Süß, H. (2013). New findings about social intel-ligence: Development and application of the Magdeburg test of social intel-ligence (MTSI). *Journal of Individual Differences*, 34(3), 119–137. doi:10.1027/1614-0001/a000106

Cronbach, L. J. (1960). *Essentials of psychological testing* (2nd ed.). Oxford: Harper.

Davies, M., Stankov, L., & Roberts, R. D. (1998). Emotional intelligence: In search of an elusive construct. *Journal of Personality and Social Psychology* , 75(4), 989–1015. doi:10.1037/0022-3514.75.4.989

DeYoung, C. G. (2011). Intelligence and personality. In R. J. Sternberg & S. B. Kaufman (Eds.) *The Cambridge handbook of intelligence* (pp. 711–737). New York: Cambridge University Press. doi:10.1017/CBO9780511977244.036

DeYoung, C. G., Quilty, L. C., & Peterson, J. B. (2007). Between facets and domains: 10 aspects of the big five. *Journal of Personality and Social Psychology*, 93(5), 880–896. doi:10.1037/0022-3514.93.5.880

Durlak, J. A., Weissberg, R. P., Dymnicki, A. B., Taylor, R. D., & Schellinger, K. B. (2011). The impact of enhancing students' social and emotional learning: A meta-analysis of school-based universal interventions. *Child Development*, 82(1), 405–432. doi:10.1111/j.1467-8624.2010.01564.x

Emmons, R. A. (2000). Is spirituality an intelligence? Motivation, cognition, and the psychology of ultimate concern. *International Journal for the Psychology of Religion*, 10(1), 3–26. doi:10.1207/S15327582IJPR1001_2

Emmons, R. A., & King, L. A. (1988). Conflict among personal strivings: Immediate and long-term implications for psychological and physical well-being. *Journal of Personality and Social Psychology*, 54(6), 1040–1048. doi:10.1037/0022-3514.54.6.1040

Fernádez-Berrocal, P., & Extremera, N. (2016). Ability emotional intelligence, depression and well-being. *Emotion Review*, 8, 311–315.

Flanagan, D. P., Alfonso, V. C., Ortiz, S. O., & Dynda, A. M. (2013). Cognitive assessment: Progress in psychometric theories of intelligence, the structure of cognitive ability tests, and interpretive approaches to cognitive test performance. In D. H. Saklofske, C. R. Reynolds & V. L. Schwean (Eds.), *The Oxford handbook of child psychological assessment* (pp. 239–285). New York: Oxford University Press.

Flanagan, D. P., McGrew, K. S., & Ortiz, S. O. (2000). *The Wechsler intelligence scales and gf-gc theory: A contemporary approach to interpretation.* Needham Heights, MA: Allyn & Bacon.

Funder, D. C. (2001). Accuracy in personality judgment: Research and theory concerning an obvious question. In R. Hogan (Ed.), *Personality psychology in the workplace.* (pp. 121–140). Washington, DC: American Psychological Association. doi:10.1037/10434-005

Gardner, H. (1983). *Frames of mind: The theory of multiple intelligences.* New York: Basic Books.

Gignac, G. E., & Weiss, L. G. (2015). Digit span is (mostly) related linearly to general intelligence: Every extra bit of span counts. *Psychological Assessment*, 27(4), 1312–1323. doi:10.1037/pas0000105

Goldberg, L. R. (1993). The structure of phenotypic personality traits. *American Psychologist*, 48(1), 26–34. doi:10.1037/0003-066X.48.1.26

Gottfredson, L. S. (1997). Mainstream science on intelligence: An editorial with 52 signatories, history and bibliography. *Intelligence*, 24(1), 13–23. doi:10.1016/S0160-2896(97)90011-8

Graziano, W. G., Habashi, M. M., Evangelou, D., & Ngambeki, I. (2012). Orientations and motivations: Are you a "people person," a "thing person," or both? *Motivation and Emotion*, 36(4), 465–477. doi:10.1007/s11031-011-9273-2

Haig, B. D. (2005). An abductive theory of scientific method. *Psychological Methods*, 10(4), 371–388. doi:10.1037/1082-989X.10.4.371

Hedlund, J., & Sternberg, R. J. (2000). Too many intelligences? Integrating social, emotional, and practical intelligence. In J. D. A. Parker (Ed.), *The handbook of emotional intelligence: Theory, development, assessment, and application at home, school, and in the workplace* (pp. 136–167). San Francisco, CA: Jossey-Bass.

Holland, J. L. (1966). A psychological classification scheme for vocations and major fields. *Journal of Counseling Psychology*, 13(3), 278–288. doi:10.1037/h0023725

Hunt, T. (1928). The measurement of social intelligence. *Journal of Applied Psychology*, 12(3), 317–334. doi:10.1037/h0075832

Jensen, A. R. (1998). *The g factor: The science of mental ability.* Westport, CT: Praeger Publishers/Greenwood Publishing Group.

Joreskog, K. G. (1969). A general approach to confirmatory maximum likelihood factor analysis. *Psychometrika*, 34(2), 183–202. doi:10.1007/BF02289343

Kenny, D. A. (1976). An empirical application of confirmatory factor analysis to the multitrait-multimethod matrix. *Journal of Experimental Social Psychology*, 12(3), 247–252. doi:10.1016/0022-1031(76)90055-X

Legree, P. J., Psotka, J., Robbins, J., Roberts, R. D., Putka, D. J., & Mullins, H. M. (2014). Profile similarity metrics as an alternate framework to score rating-based tests: MSCEIT reanalyses. *Intelligence*, 47, 159–174. doi:10.1016/j.intell.2014.09.005

Locke, E. A. (2005). Why emotional intelligence is an invalid concept. *Journal of Organizational Behavior*, 26(4), 425–431. doi:10.1002/job.318

Lopes, P. N. (2016). Emotional intelligence in organizations: Bridging research and practice. *Emotion Review*, 8.

MacCann, C., Joseph, D. L., Newman, D. A., & Roberts, R. D. (2014). Emotional intelligence is a second-stratum factor of intelligence: Evidence from hierarchical and bifactor models. *Emotion*, 14(2), 358–374.

MacCann, C., & Roberts, R. D. (2008). New paradigms for assessing emotional intelligence: Theory and data. *Emotion*, 8(4), 540–551. doi:10.1037/a0012746; 10.1037/a0012746.supp (Supplemental)

Mayer, J. D. (2008). Personal intelligence. *Imagination, Cognition and Personality*, 27(3), 209–232. doi:10.2190/IC.27.3.b

(2009). Personal intelligence expressed: A theoretical analysis. *Review of General Psychology*, 13(1), 46–58. doi:10.1037/a0014229

(2014). *Personal intelligence: The power of personality and how it shapes our lives.* New York: Scientific American/Farrar Strauss & Giroux.

Mayer, J. D., Caruso, D. R., & Salovey, P. (2016). The ability model of emotional intelligence: Principles and updates. *Emotion Review*, 8, 1–11.

Mayer, J. D., DiPaolo, M., & Salovey, P. (1990). Perceiving affective content in ambiguous visual stimuli: A component of emotional intelligence. *Journal of Personality Assessment*, 54(3), 772.

Mayer, J. D., Panter, A. T., & Caruso, D. R. (2012). Does personal intelligence exist? Evidence from a new ability-based measure. *Journal of Personality Assessment*, 94, 124–140. doi:10.1080/00223891.2011.646108

(2017). A closer look at the *Test of Personal Intelligence (TOPI)*. *Personality and Individual Differences*, 111, 301–311.

Mayer, J. D., Roberts, R. D., & Barsade, S. G. (2008). Human abilities: Emotional intelligence. *Annual Review of Psychology*, 59, 507–536. doi:10.1146/annurev.psych.59.103006.093646

Mayer, J. D., Salovey, P., & Caruso, D (2002). *Mayer-Salovey-Caruso Emotional Intelligence Test (MSCEIT) Users Manual.* Toronto, Ontario: MHS.

Mayer, J. D., & Skimmyhorn, W. (2017). Personality attributes that predict performance of cadets at West Point. *Journal of Research in Personality*, 66, 14–16.

McGrew, K. S. (2009). CHC theory and the human cognitive abilities project: Standing on the shoulders of the giants of psychometric intelligence research. *Intelligence*, 37(1), 1–10. doi:10.1016/j.intell.2008.08.004

Newell, A., Shaw, J. C., & Simon, H. A. (1958). Elements of a theory of human problem solving. *Psychological Review*, 65(3), 151–166. doi:10.1037/h0048495

Newell, A., & Simon, H. A. (1972). *Human problem solving*. Oxford: Prentice-Hall.

Oltmanns, T. F., & Turkheimer, E. (2006). Perceptions of self and others regarding pathological personality traits. In J. L. Tackett (Ed.), *Personality and psychopathology*. (pp. 71–111). New York: Guilford Press.

Salovey, P., & Mayer, J. D. (1990). Emotional intelligence. *Imagination, Cognition and Personality*, 9(3), 185–211.

Schneider, W. J., & Newman, D. A. (2015). Intelligence is multidimensional: Theoretical review and implications of specific cognitive abilities. *Human Resource Management Review*, 25(1), 12–27.

Spearman, C. (1904). "General intelligence," objectively determined and measured. *The American Journal of Psychology*, 15(2), 201–293. doi:10.2307/1412107

Sternberg, R. J. (1985). *Beyond IQ: A triarchic theory of human intelligence*. New York: Cambridge University Press.

Sternberg, R. J., & Hedlund, J. (2002). Practical intelligence, g, and work psychology. *Human Performance*, 15(1–2), 143–160. doi:10.1207/S15327043HUP1501&02_09

Sternberg, R. J., & Project, R. (2009). The rainbow project: Enhancing the SAT through assessments of analytical, practical, and creative skills. In J. C. Kaufman & E. L. Grigorenko (Eds.), *The essential Sternberg: Essays on intelligence, psychology, and education* (pp. 273–319). New York: Springer Publishing Co. Retrieved from http://search.ebscohost.com/login.aspx?direct=true&db=psyh&AN=2009-00687-011&site=ehost-live

Thompson, B. (2004). *Exploratory and confirmatory factor analysis: Understanding concepts and applications*. Washington, DC: American Psychological Association. doi:10.1037/10694-000

Thorndike, E. L. (1920). Intelligence and its uses. *Harper's Magazine*, 140, 227–235.

Thorndike, R. L., & Stein, S. (1937). An evaluation of the attempts to measure social intelligence. *Psychological Bulletin*, 34(5), 275–285. doi:10.1037/h0053850

Tomasello, M., & Call, J. (1997). *Primate cognition*. New York: Oxford University Press.

Van, D. M., Dolan, C. V., Grasman, R. P. P. P., Wicherts, J. M., Huizenga, H. M., & Raijmakers, M. E. J. (2006). A dynamical model of general intelligence: The positive manifold of intelligence by mutualism. *Psychological Review*, 113(4), 842–861. doi:10.1037/0033-295X.113.4.842

Visser, B. A., Ashton, M. C., & Vernon, P. A. (2006). Beyond g: Putting multiple intelligences theory to the test. *Intelligence*, 34(5), 487–502. doi:10.1016/j.intell.2006.02.004

Von Stumm, S., & Ackerman, P. L. (2013). Investment and intellect: A review and meta-analysis. *Psychological Bulletin*, 139(4), 841–869. doi:10.1037/a0030746

Wagner, R. K. (2000). Practical intelligence. In R. J. Sternberg (Ed.), *Handbook of intelligence*. (pp. 380–395). New York: Cambridge University Press.

Wagner, R. K., & Sternberg, R. J. (1985). Practical intelligence in real-world pursuits: The role of tacit knowledge. *Journal of Personality and Social Psychology,* 49(2), 436–458. doi:10.1037/0022-3514.49.2.436

Weis, S., & Süß, H. (2007). Reviving the search for social intelligence – A multitrait-multimethod study of its structure and construct validity. *Personality and Individual Differences,* 42(1), 3–14. doi:10.1016/j.paid.2006.04.027

Wong, C. T., Day, J. D., Maxwell, S. E., & Meara, N. M. (1995). A multitrait-multimethod study of academic and social intelligence in college students. *Journal of Educational Psychology,* 87(1), 117–133. doi:10.1037/0022-0663.87.1.117

CHAPTER 18

Mechanisms of Working Memory Capacity and Fluid Intelligence and Their Common Dependence on Executive Attention

Zach Shipstead & Randall W. Engle

We did not set out to study intelligence. The question at the origin of this line of work was why complex memory span tasks correlate so highly and so consistently (Turner & Engle, 1989) with a huge array of real-world tasks when simple span tasks do so less well and very inconsistently (Dempster, 1981). We attempted to answer this question by a combination of methods taken from both experimental psychology and differential psychology – a response to Cronbach's (1957) complaint that the two approaches to psychology historically have disregarded each other.

Approaching working memory research through a mixture of experimental and correlational techniques eventually led us and others (Engle & Kane, 2004; Engle et al., 1999; Kyllonen & Christal, 1990) to the strikingly strong relationship between a construct formed from complex working memory tasks and the established construct of fluid intelligence. Much of our work since that discovery has been directed at trying to understand why this relationship exists. The use of quasi-experimental techniques using extreme groups in our early work (Conway & Engle, 1994; Rosen & Engle, 1997) led to some conclusions that we now know from large-scale latent variable studies are misleading and sometimes outright wrong. The rest of this chapter describes the state of our search for the psychological mechanisms that are responsible for the relationship between working memory capacity and fluid intelligence.

Fluid Intelligence

The aspects of intelligence that most interest us relate to the Cattel-Horn-Carrol (Carroll, 1993; McGrew, 2005) theory, and specifically to the distinction between fluid and crystalized intelligence. This distinction dates back to the work of Donald Hebb (see Brown, 2016), who distinguished between intelligence A (fluid) and B (crystallized; Hebb, 1942). Beginning with his work on the relation between brain damage and specific intellectual impairments, it has come to be known that damage to the prefrontal cortex can impair fluid intelligence (Duncan, Burgess, & Emslie, 1995), the ability to reason with novel information. Conversely, crystalized intelligence, a person's accumulated knowledge base that can be put to use in routine problem-solving situations, is unaffected by such damage.

From a measurement perspective, fluid intelligence is the more tractable construct. A number of standardized tasks are available for measuring a person's fluid intelligence (e.g., Cattell's Culture Fair Test; Cattell, 1973; Raven's Progressive Matrices; Raven, 1990) that have come to define the construct. This allows for a relatively straightforward perspective of human reasoning, at least from a testing perspective. Crystalized intelligence, conversely, varies from person to person and situation to situation because it is dependent upon a person's learning history.[1]

Despite these differences, fluid and crystalized intelligence likely share a causal link. As proposed by Cattell (1971), the development of crystalized intelligence occurs through investment of fluid intelligence at the time of learning (Thorsen, Gustafsson, & Cliffordson, 2014). From this position, fluid intelligence is not simply the more general construct, but also the more fundamental one.

Fluid Intelligence and Working Memory Capacity

A long-standing issue in fluid intelligence research is the need to define its nature at a deeper level than "novel problem-solving ability." In other words: what are the cognitive mechanisms that account for novel reasoning? In recent years, a chief explanation of differences people show in fluid intelligence has been through appeal to its correlation with working memory capacity. *Working memory* is a cognitive system that allows people to maintain and manipulate information in the service of ongoing cognition. *Capacity* refers to individual differences in the efficacy with which this system functions.

Individual differences in working memory capacity (as it is typically defined) and individual differences in fluid intelligence are strongly predictive of one another. It is well established that these factors share 50–80% of their variance at the latent level (Chuderski, 2013; Kane et al., 2005; Oberauer et al., 2005). Thus, research has been progressing under the assumption that when the working memory system is understood, this knowledge can be applied to a large portion of fluid intelligence.

As the story goes, working memory has a causal influence on reasoning ability. Stable maintenance in working memory allows people to focus on relevant information (Engle, 2002) and integrate disparate concepts (Cowan et al., 2005; Oberauer et al., 2007). These attention and memory processes, in turn, facilitate reasoning processes. More simply, people with high working memory capacity are at a particular advantage when working through novel problems, since they can consider more information at any given moment.

Unfortunately, if one desires to truly understand the nature of human intelligence, the working-memory-as-a-cause explanation is rather limited. All it really states is that memory is a prerequisite to reasoning and that tests of working memory capacity are particularly good measures of this type of memory.

Nonetheless, we do believe that working memory is critical to human reasoning. However, our work has moved in a direction where we now assume that classic tests of working memory capacity provide only a limited view of the working memory system as a whole. In particular, we believe that individual differences in fluid intelligence can provide unique insights into the qualitative interactions between attention and memory. These insights advance both our understanding of the working memory system and its contributions to complex thought.

The System Underlying Tests of Working Memory Capacity and Fluid Intelligence

Working memory capacity tasks are, by their nature, focused on the aspects of working memory that allow a person to maintain access to relevant information (either through active maintenance or through retrieval; Unsworth & Engle, 2007). Yet, in a true "working" memory system, the relevancy of information will be subject to constant change. This system will therefore also require mechanisms of *disengagement* (e.g., inhibition, episodic tagging, unbinding of temporary associations) that allow for the removal of no-longer-relevant information (e.g., updating; Ecker et al., 2010; Miyake et al., 2000).

These disengagement mechanisms (Figure 18.1), however, are not likely to be critical to the performance of most standard measures of working memory, since these tasks require people to retain access to information. Forgetting of information will lead to lower test scores, and thus be deemed an indicator of low working memory capacity. In all likelihood,

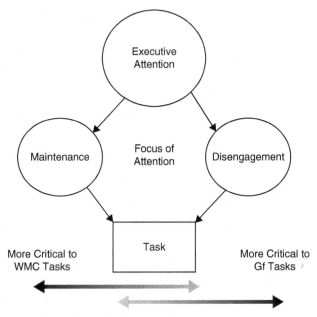

Figure 18.1   Our model of the working memory system and its relation to performance of working memory capacity and fluid intelligence tasks. WMC = working memory capacity; Gf = general fluid intelligence.

the only time these tasks tap into disengagement processes is between trials, when forgetting of outdated information leads to the reduction of proactive interference (May, Hasher, & Kane, 1999; Shipstead & Engle, 2013; Shipstead & Nespozany, 2017). That is to say, it prevents old memories from competing for representation among currently relevant memories.

Our contention is that disengagement is the factor that accounts for the less than perfect correlation between working memory capacity and fluid intelligence. While forgetting is detrimental to performing a working memory task, it is advantageous to tests of fluid intelligence. When reasoning through a problem, people will have mistaken assumptions that can lead to dead-end thinking. Disengagement allows for a fresh perspective and for blocking outdated assumptions.

From this perspective, we do not see the factors underlying working memory capacity and fluid intelligence as representing different cognitive systems (Engle, 2002). Instead, we view both as arising from the working memory system (see bottom of Figure 18.1).

Working memory capacity and fluid intelligence task performance correlate due to the common need to engage executive attention, in order to define and carry out goals. Both maintenance and disengagement generally require executive attention. The less than perfect correlation between working memory capacity and fluid intelligence task performance is attributable to the tests being differentially sensitive to critical working memory functions. That is, executive attention engages different cognitive mechanisms when these tasks are completed.

Evidence for this Perspective

Our perspective makes a simple, straightforward prediction. If tests of fluid intelligence indeed tap into the disengagement-related aspects of working memory, then individual differences in fluid intelligence should reflect the ability to forget outdated information in simple memory tasks (the type that require very little reasoning). Moreover, this aspect of reorganizing the contents of working memory will not be attributable to individual differences in working memory capacity (at least not as they are traditionally defined).

To be clear, our argument is not (working memory capacity = maintenance) and (fluid intelligence = disengagement). It is that tests of working memory capacity place primary demand on the maintenance-related aspects of the working memory system and secondary demand on the disengagement aspects. Fluid intelligence tests place demand in the reverse order. Thus, the observed constructs of working memory capacity and fluid intelligence do not represent separate cognitive abilities, so much as they represent different and sometimes contradictory functions that are necessary for information processing.

These different degrees of reliance lead the constructs to be somewhat unrelated (and even contradictory). But working memory tasks do reflect between-trials disengagement (e.g., Kane & Engle, 2000) and fluid intelligence tasks do require mental representations to be maintained. This leads to a degree of relation. More importantly, maintenance and disengagement processes are organized around goals, and subject to attentional resources, which further strengthens the relation between these varieties of task.

From this perspective, traditional measurement of a person's working memory capacity (using complex span or visual arrays tasks) has provided a limited view of the functions carried out by working memory. This is because the primary goal in these tasks is to remember as much information as possible. Thus, traditional measurement of working memory capacity minimizes the role of functions that allow for intentional forgetting, save for between-trial disengagement.

Indeed, this position that working memory capacity is primarily a measure of maintenance stability, but not flexibility, is apparent in several recent studies. Ecker and colleagues argue that individual differences in working memory capacity predict maintenance and retrieval aspects of updating tasks, but are not related to the actual act of replacing maintained-information (Ecker et al., 2011; Ecker et al., 2014). Harrison and colleagues (2015) argue that high working memory capacity is more strongly correlated with performance of fluid intelligence problems that retain the same rules on a trial-to-trial basis, relative to when rules change (cf. Wiley et al., 2011). Finally, DeCaro and colleagues (2015) argue that high working memory capacity can hinder insight when an established mental set needs to be restructured. In other words, working memory capacity tasks primarily pick up on individual differences in the ability to stabilize information in focal attention so that it will not be forgotten.

The first indication that this may serve as the basis for a dissociation between working memory capacity and fluid intelligence came in a study we performed that used time-based manipulations to increase and decrease the presence of proactive interference (Shipstead & Engle, 2013). An important finding was that individual differences in working memory capacity were most predictive of performance on trials where the presentation of relevant and irrelevant information occurred in a relatively crunched time frame. High working memory capacity allows a person to remember relevant information when proactive interference is high (Unsworth & Engle, 2007).

From a perspective in which working memory capacity is the primary explanation of fluid intelligence (i.e., the more traditional perspective), the most straightforward prediction would be that individual differences in fluid intelligence would be similarly predictive of task performance. This was not the case. Instead, the correlation between fluid intelligence and task performance spiked when relatively long delays were included between trials. That is, fluid intelligence seemed to be predicting the ability to break from outdated information.

Critical to this interpretation, post hoc analyses indicated that only people with higher fluid intelligence benefited from longer delays: their scores on the most recent trial increased when they were given extra time to disengage from the previous trial, relative to cases where the inter-trial interval was short. People with lower fluid intelligence did not show this effect.

The results of Shipstead and Engle (2013) indicated that working memory capacity and fluid intelligence predicted different things. Working memory capacity predicted the ability to remember appropriate information, despite high proactive interference (stable maintenance). Fluid intelligence predicted the ability to reduce proactive interference through disengagement from outdated information. This finding was unexpected and we sought other evidence to support or refute this hypothesis.

A follow-up study (Shipstead, Harrison, & Engle, 2016) focused on performance on the three-back task. In this task, test takers see a list of serially presented items and must indicate when the currently presented item matches the one that was seen three items ago. Our critical dependent variable was tendency to false alarm on lure items. In other words, how likely is a person to indicate that an item was a three-back repetition when in fact it repeated in a different position?

We report composite performance across six tasks. One-third of the tasks used faces as the to-be-recognized stimuli, one-third used words, and one-third used wing-ding characters (e.g., ✌✍✗▤). In half of the tasks, lure items could repeat in the two-, four-, or five-back position. In the other tasks, lure items could repeat in the seven-, eight-, or nine-back position.

In our overall sample d' (defined as three-back accuracy vs. false alarms at a specific position) increased as lure items were presented in more distant positions. This is not particularly surprising. Overall, people were less and less likely to false alarm as lure items moved farther away from the three-back position.

More surprising, d' was most predictive of fluid intelligence and working memory capacity when the lure items were in distant positions. As the task got easier, performance became a better predictor of cognitive ability.

Why would this be? One reason we selected this task was a finding by McCabe and Hartman (2008) in which, relative to younger individuals, older individuals not only have a greater tendency to false alarm on lure items, but this tendency does not diminish across lure positions: age-related cognitive declines are associated with people answering that five-back or six-back items were presented in the three-back position. In other words, familiarity of outdated items was higher for older individuals. In effect, these people have more difficulty disengaging from outdated information.

Returning to our data (Shipstead et al., 2016), a median split analysis of people with high or low fluid intelligence revealed a trend similar to that reported by McCabe and Hartman (2008). People with high fluid intelligence were more accurate at spotting lures than were people with low fluid intelligence. But contrary to intuition, this difference was smallest at the two- and four-back positions and greatest at the nine-back. The specific reason was that, as lure items became more distant, people with high fluid intelligence were less likely to false alarm. People with low fluid intelligence, conversely, did not show much benefit of lure item distance. They basically false alarmed at the same rate, regardless of the position in which an item repeated. It seems that they cannot let go of information once it becomes outdated.

The first point to address is that this conclusion might seem odd from a position in which working memory is a limited capacity storage system. Shipstead, Harrison, and Engle (2016) took a different direction. Building on the work of Oberauer and colleagues (2007), we argued that the measurable storage capacity of working memory is not due to a strict maintenance limit, but to a trade-off between maintaining access to relevant information and disengaging from information once it becomes outdated.

In other words, if a person has a working memory capacity of two, it might be that the person can only maintain two items (e.g., Cowan, 2001). However, it might also be that the person is maintaining access to so many items that the important items lose their distinctiveness. This is reminiscent of the fan effect (Anderson, 1974; Conway & Engle, 1994), in which responding to critical information can be slowed, or made inaccurate, due to an item having a relatively large number of associations in semantic memory. The difference in this case is that activation is distributed across recently relevant elements of episodic memory. People who cannot constrain this spread will need to contend with increased proactive interference.

The second important point is that the disengagement mechanism needs to be attributable to fluid intelligence. Shipstead and Engle (2013) found a clean distinction, but Shipstead and colleagues (2016) found that both fluid intelligence and working memory capacity showed the same trend where low-ability individuals had relative difficulty with long-outdated items.

Given the high correlation between fluid intelligence and working memory capacity, it is understandable that these constructs will occasionally be confounded (sometimes to the point where they become stand-ins for one another). Shipstead and colleagues (2016) resolved this issue using regression analysis. When we controlled for working memory capacity, the magnitude of the correlation between fluid intelligence and false alarms decreased, but did not affect the overall trend of increasing correlations with distance (Figure 18.2a). Conversely, controlling for fluid intelligence effectively wiped out any relation between working memory capacity and

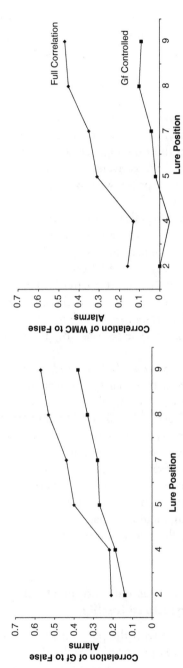

Figure 18.2   (a) Correlation between fluid intelligence and false alarms with and without working memory capacity controlled.
(b) Correlation between working memory capacity and false alarms, with and without fluid intelligence controlled. Gf = General fluid
intelligence; WMC = Working memory capacity.

Adapted from "Working memory capacity and fluid intelligence: Maintenance and disengagement," by Z. Shipstead et al., 2016,
Perspectives on Psychological Science, 11, p. 781.

false alarms (Figure 18.2b). This was completely consistent with our theoretical position that difficulty in disengaging from outdated information could be specifically attributed to a person's fluid intelligence, but not to working memory capacity.

A second regression analysis supported Shipstead and Engle's (2013) argument that working memory capacity is particularly important for maintaining information when proactive interference is high. Looking specifically at three-back accuracy, working memory capacity accounted for the correlation between fluid intelligence and hits in the two-, four-, and five-back lure tasks, but the converse was not true. Individual differences in working memory capacity were particularly important under high-interference conditions.

A more recent study by Nespodzany and Shipstead (2016) examined the roles of working memory capacity and fluid intelligence in stabilizing and reorganizing the contents of memory using an AX-CPT task (adapted from D'Ardenne et al., 2012). In this serial-order task, test takers first see a context letter, either "A" or "B." Next a letter is presented, to which a response must be made, either "X" or "Y." If the context letter was "A," then 1 needs to be pressed in response to "X" and 2 needs to be pressed in response to "Y." If the context letter was "B," then the responses are reversed.

Critical to this study (Nespodzany & Shipstead, 2016), the context letter could stay the same from one trial to the next (A...A), or it could switch from one trial to the next (A...B). On trials in which the context letter stayed the same, accuracy was weakly correlated to individual differences in working memory capacity (0.24), but uncorrelated to fluid intelligence (0.10). Conversely, on trials that involved a change of context (and thus a reorganization of task rules), regression analysis revealed that only fluid intelligence retained a relationship to performance, once variance that was common to maintenance and updating trials was controlled. That is to say, while working memory capacity was critical to maintaining task instructions, fluid intelligence was uniquely related to reorganizing those instructions.

Maintenance, Disengagement, and the Development of Crystalized Intelligence

As previously stated, we agree with the position that investment of fluid intelligence leads to the development of crystalized intelligence (Cattell, 1971; Thorsen et al., 2014). The mechanisms of this process were explored

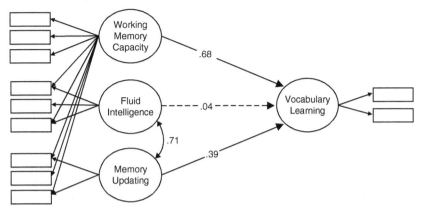

Figure 18.3   An adapted version of a structural equation model by Martin et al. (2017) demonstrating that the strong correlation between fluid intelligence and vocabulary learning (0.77) can be explained by working memory maintenance and updating variance that is independent of working memory capacity.

by Martin and colleagues (2017) in a study involving a delayed (~1.5 hours) surprise recognition test in which participants needed to match auditory Arabic words with their visually presented English equivalent, following an earlier period of learning.

A structural equation model revealed that fluid intelligence had a strong direct relation to vocabulary learning (0.77), and also accounted for any relation that working memory capacity had to the task. Working from the perspective that fluid intelligence reflected both the maintenance and disengagement aspects of learning (for instance, holding the word pairs in memory while blocking interference from previous trials), Martin and colleagues (2017) entered a set of updating tasks into the model (running memory span, n-back, and keeping track).

Common variance from the fluid intelligence, updating tasks, and working memory capacity tasks was assigned to the working memory factor (Figure 18.3), in order to create a maintenance-driven factor. This factor had a strong relation to vocabulary learning (0.68). Critically, any residual relation between fluid intelligence and vocabulary learning was explained by the updating factor, which was independent of any processes shared with working memory capacity. These results also held for an immediate test of reading comprehension.

Consistent with investment theory (Cattell, 1971; Thorsen et al., 2014), fluid intelligence is a strong predictor of the ability to learn verbal information both over long (delayed vocabulary learning) and short (reading comprehension) time intervals. Extending this theory, Martin and colleagues (2017) demonstrated that these correlations could be explained through two factors: maintenance, as traditionally measured by working memory capacity tasks; and disengagement, as uniquely measured by memory updating tasks.

These can be further understood within the knowledge-acquisition account of Sternberg and Powell (1983). In this perspective, acquisition is driven by three processes. The first is selective encoding, which involves distinguishing between relevant and irrelevant information. The second is selective combination, in which information is plausibly integrated. The third is selective comparison, in which new information is related to knowledge. In each of these steps, we see maintenance ability as key to allowing relevant comparisons to be made. But – as with our theory in general – strength of maintenance cannot be confused with accuracy of maintenance. All of these processes will likely require letting go or inappropriate assumptions or comparisons, in order for appropriate combinations to be created and stored.

The Limitations of Extreme-Groups Research

Our line of research has a history of mixing elements of both experimental and correlation research (e.g., Cronbach, 1957), in which differences in task performance between people with high (upper quartile) or low (lower quartile) working memory capacity is examined. This technique has allowed for a better understanding of the range of ways in which people vary in their attentional and memorial capabilities. But certain limitations in these studies have become apparent in light of our new perspective.

Obvious concerns with extreme groups studies are that they ignore people in this middle, and thus assume a linear progression from low to high ability. These studies can also exaggerate the effect size, by cutting out the portion of the distribution that can muddle a correlation. Moreover, quasi-experimentation can introduce confounding third variables that might explain differences in task performance as something other than individual differences in working memory capacity.

This third concern has been a limitation that we have needed to accept, since a person's working memory capacity cannot be experimentally assigned. However, the strong relation between working memory capacity and fluid intelligence means that people who are very high or very low in working memory capacity are likely to be very high or very low in fluid

Table 18.1 *Extreme-groups studies that attributed disengagement to working memory*

Study	Task	Finding
Rosen and Engle (1997)	Verbal Fluency	People with low working memory capacity tend to repeat already-given responses.
Kane and Engle (2000)	Brown Peterson	People with high working memory capacity are less susceptible to buildup of proactive interference.
Rosen and Engle (1998)	Paired Associates	People with high working memory capacity are capable of suppressing outdated associations.
Conway et al. (1999); Long and Prat (2002)	Negative Priming	People with low working memory capacity are deficient in the ability to suppress distractors.

intelligence. This did not seem problematic from a theoretical perspective in which working memory capacity was a causal factor that determined fluid intelligence. However, from a perspective in which working memory capacity and fluid intelligence task performance provides different perspectives of the working memory system, it is problematic.

Several extreme-groups studies concluded that working memory capacity is related to some type of disengagement process, such as cognitive inhibition (Table 18.1). However, from an extreme-groups perspective, working memory capacity can readily serve as a stand-in for fluid intelligence and vice versa. This opens the door to the question: did these studies mistakenly attribute properties of fluid intelligence to working memory capacity?

Shipstead and colleagues (2016) addressed this question when they examined the relation of verbal fluency to both working memory capacity and fluid intelligence, while controlling for general executive function (e.g., executive attention from Figure 18.1). In verbal fluency, a cue is given (e.g., a letter or a profession) and the test taker must produce as many cue-consistent responses as possible within a limited time frame.

Rosen and Engle (1997) found that people with high working memory capacity produce more responses than people with low working memory capacity, but that this trend was not attributable to category knowledge. Instead, people with high working memory capacity are less prone to repeating already-given responses. In other words, once people with low working memory capacity produce a response, they have relatively greater difficulty not returning to it.

Using a full-rage analysis, Shipstead and colleagues (2016) found that, once general executive function was controlled, verbal fluency was not related to working memory capacity, but did retain a significant correlation (0.30) to fluid intelligence. Due to the nature of their data, it could not be demonstrated that this correlation is directly attributable to item repetition, however, this finding nonetheless opens the door to the possibility that the extreme-groups research of Rosen and Engle (1997) confounded working memory capacity with fluid intelligence. As such, Rosen and Engle may have misattributed a mechanism of disengagement (i.e., suppression of outdated information) to working memory capacity, when it rightfully should be attributed to fluid intelligence.

Future studies will need to replicate the studies in Table 18.1, but this time using full-range samples in which both working memory capacity and fluid intelligence are measured. We predict that multiple regression analysis will reveal that these inhibitory or suppressive behaviors (which we interpret as mechanisms of disengagement) will be unrelated to working memory capacity, when individual differences in fluid intelligence are controlled. At the very least, these results will be critical to understanding the boundaries of our current theory.

Developing Working Memory/Intelligence

Our position on modern working memory training interventions is that they are simply ineffective for improving cognitive abilities (Harrison et al., 2013; Redick et al., 2013; Shipstead, Hicks, & Engle, 2012a, 2012b; Shipstead, Redick, & Engle, 2010, 2012). This has led to the repeated question, "Why do you feel working memory capacity cannot be improved?" and to accusations of an outdated perspective of an immutable working memory system (Klingberg, 2012[2]).

This interpretation of our work could not be further from the truth. We have yet to argue that working memory is an immutable system. Instead we have argued that modern interventions are insufficient to change working memory capacity. Part of this is due to questioning the idea that simply making people perform working memory tasks over and over (e.g., Jaeggi et al., 2008; Klingberg et al., 2005) will somehow increase their memory capacity. These tasks were intended to be rulers for measuring psychological space, not mental exercises. And to date, the only solid conclusion that can be drawn from the working memory training literature is that working memory training will make people better at performing working memory tasks (Shipstead et al., 2012a, 2012b).

In effect, the simplest conclusion is that trainees do not increase working memory capacity. They increase their knowledge regarding effective task performance (e.g., Chase & Ericsson, 1982). In order to demonstrate that working memory capacity is improving, one must demonstrate that training transfers to working memory tasks that do not resemble the method of training (see Shipstead et al., 2012a, 2012b). Most researchers do not even attempt this, instead opting for near transfer[3] tasks that resemble the training method. In the rare cases that researchers have attempted to measure broad transfer to working memory tasks, the results have been mixed at best (Harrison et al., 2013) and are often rather disheartening (Dahlin et al., 2008; Jaeggi et al., 2008; Jaeggi et al., 2010; Li et al., 2008).

Our present theory offers a new direction that may be relevant to training researchers. If the goal is to improve fluid intelligence, perhaps the focus should be on training mechanisms of disengagement, instead of mechanisms of maintenance (e.g., memory for long lists, memory for n-back targets at further distances). Yet, while we would like to see such research conducted, we are skeptical of its eventual efficacy.

This point can be summarized in a recent quotation by Elizabeth Stine-Morrow – " 'Does brain training work?': Yes, it's called school" (Yong, 2016). And when one considers that a full year of school is associated with a few points of IQ per year – at best (Winship & Korenman, 1997) – it seems unreasonable to expect that a few hours of working memory task performance will ever affect any meaningful change to cognitive ability.

Proper Measurement of the Working Memory System – A Work in Progress

From our perspective, the root of effective problem-solving ability is the working memory system itself. To be clear, we use the phrase "working memory system" to differentiate our theoretical perspective from historical research on "working memory capacity." The point is that, to date, the operational definition of working memory capacity has focused on maintenance capacity (e.g., Colom et al., 2008; Cowan, 2001) or maintenance stability (e.g., Engle, 2002; Shipstead, Harrison, & Engle, 2015). We now take the position that these studies have been interpreting one property of working memory as representative of working memory overall.

To further explain the model in Figure 18.1, we see working memory as representing two primary mechanisms that are prevalent in the literature: executive attention control (Baddeley, 1986; Engle, 2002), around which behavior is organized; and the focus of attention (Cowan, 1988;

Cowan et al., 2006). However, we see the focus of attention as more nuanced than simply a capacity-bound storage system. Focal attention requires maintenance and disengagement to ensure access is retained to only relevant information (Oberauer et al., 2007; Shipstead et al., 2016). A logical extension of this theory is that our attempts to measure the maintenance capacity of attention, or short-term memory, or working memory are corrupted by the failure to take disengagement into account. If a person can remember four items on a memory test, this might be due to a limitation of maintenance, but it could also be due to an abundance of inappropriate maintenance. The point of maintenance is to reduce proactive interference. However, if a person is not capable of recalling a certain number of items, it is not necessarily a failure of maintenance. It can also be a failure of disengagement. Too much maintenance leads to a new source of proactive interference within focal attention.

In effect, this theory does away with any strict rules regarding storage capacity limitations in favor of a perspective in which measurable limits represent a point at which the trade-off between maintenance and disengagement is appropriately balanced. People with low scores on working memory capacity tasks may be deficient in either mechanism.

At present there is not a task that appropriately measures this function. The closest in the literature is the set of memory-updating tasks, of the kind used by Miyake and colleagues (Miyake & Friedman, 2012). These tasks have a strong working memory component, plus other functions that allow for within-trial disengagement (e.g., Figure 18.3; Shipstead et al., 2014; see also Colom et al., 2008). In order to effectively measure the properties of maintenance and disengagement and their common reliance on attention control, future research will need to focus on memory and reasoning tasks that allow for examining both effective maintenance and disengagement.

On a final note, our work does not seek to reduce intelligence, or working memory, to a single number or mechanism. Although we are interested in individual differences, we are interested in understanding the mechanisms behind individual differences. It is entirely likely that there are additional processes important to the nature of fluid intelligence and its predictive validity for real-world tasks.

Notes

1 Obviously, there are ways of operationalizing crystalized intelligence as an individual differences variable, i.e., the verbal section of an aptitude test. However, the descriptive definition of this concept necessitates that it will be embodied

in different ways on an individual-to-individual basis. For instance, the subject-specific versions of the GRE test may be quite relevant to a specific field, but quite worthless as a society-wide indicator of intelligence.

2 To our knowledge, "immutability" has never been a property of any major theory of working memory capacity.

3 One might argue that "near transfer" simply refers to improvements in tasks that are contextually similar to the method of training (e.g., Barnett & Ceci, 2002). In the case of working memory training, this definition is inappropriate. The goal is to improve a latent ability that drives performance – independent of task context.

References

Anderson, J. R. (1974). Retrieval of propositional information from long-term memory. *Cognitive Psychology*, 6, 451–474.

Baddeley, A. D. (1986). *Working memory*. Oxford: Clarendon Press.

Barnett, S. M., & Ceci, S. J. (2002). When and where do we apply what we learn? A taxonomy for far transfer. *Psychological Bulletin, 128*, 612–637.

Brown, R. E. (2016). Hebb and Cattell: The genesis of the theory of fluid and crystallized intelligence. *Frontiers in Human Neuroscience*, 10, 606. doi:10.3389/fnhum.2016.00606

Carroll, J. B. (1993). *Human cognitive abilities: A survey of factor-analytic studies*. Cambridge: Cambridge University Press.

Cattell, R. B. (1943). The measurement of adult intelligence. *Psychological Bulletin*, 40, 153–193. http://dx.doi.org/10.1037/h0059973

(1971). *Abilities: Their structure, growth and action*. Boston: Houghton-Mifflin.

(1973). *Measuring intelligence with the Culture Fair tests*. Champaign, IL: Institute for Personality and Ability Testing.

Chase, W. G., & Ericsson, K. A. (1982). Skill and working memory. In G. H. Bower (Ed.), *The psychology of learning and motivation*, Vol. 16 (pp. 1–58). New York: Academic Press. doi:10.1016/S0079-7421(08)60546-0

Chuderski, A. (2013). When are fluid intelligence and working memory isomorphic and when are they not? *Intelligence*, 41, 244–262. doi:10.1016/j.intell.2013.04.003

Colom, R., Abad, F. J., Quiroga, M. Á., Shih, P. C., & Flores-Mendoza, C. (2008). Working memory and intelligence are highly related constructs, but why? *Intelligence*, 36, 584–606. doi:10.1016/j.intell.2008.01.002

Conway, A. R. A., & Engle, R. W. (1994). Working memory and retrieval: A resource-dependent inhibition model. *Journal of Experimental Psychology: General*, 123, 354–373.

Conway, A. R. A., Tuholski, S. W., Shisler, R. J., & Engle, R. W. (1999). The effect of memory load on negative priming: An individual differences investigation. *Memory & Cognition*, 27, 1042–1050. doi:10.3758/BF03201233

Cowan, N. (1988). Evolving conceptions of memory storage, selective attention, and their mutual constraints within the human information-processing system. *Psychological Bulletin*, 104, 163–191.

(2001). The magical number 4 in short-term memory: A reconsideration of mental storage capacity. *Behavioral and Brain Sciences*, 24, 87–185. doi:10.1017/S0140525X01003922

Cowan, N., Elliott, E. M., Saults, J. S., Morey, C. C., Mattox, S., Hismjatullina, A., & Conway, A. R. A. (2005). On the capacity of attention: Its estimation and its role in working memory and cognitive aptitudes. *Cognitive Psychology*, 51, 42–100. doi:10.1016/j.cogpsych.2004.12.001

Cowan, N., Fristoe, N. M., Elliot, E. M., Brunner, R. P., & Saults, J. S. (2006). Scope of attention, control of attention, and intelligence in children and adults. *Memory & Cognition*, 34, 1754–1768.

Cronbach, L. J. (1957). The two disciplines of scientific psychology. *American Psychologist*, 12, 671–684.

D'Ardenne, K., Eshel, N., Luka, J., Lenartowicz, A., Nystrom, L. E., & Cohen, J. D. (2012). Role of prefrontal cortex and the midbrain dopamine system in working memory updating. *Proceedings of the National Academy of Science*, 109, 19900–19909.

Dahlin, E., Nyberg, L., Bäckman, L., & Stigsdotter Neely, A. (2008). Plasticity of executive functioning in young and old adults: Immediate training gains, transfer, and long-term maintenance. *Psychology & Aging*, 23, 720–730. doi:10.1037/a0014296

DeCaro, M. S., Van Stockum, C. A. Jr., & Wieth, M. B. (2015). When higher working memory capacity hinders insight. *Journal of Experimental Psychology: Learning, Memory, & Cognition*, 42, 39–49. doi:10.1037/xlm0000152

Dempster, F. N. (1981). Memory span: Sources of individual and developmental differences. *Psychological Bulletin*, 89, 63–100. http://dx.doi.org/10.1037/0033-2909.89.1.63

Duncan, J., Burgess, P., & Emslie, H. (1995). *Fluid intelligence after frontal lobe lesions. Neuropsychologia*, 33, 261–261.

Ecker, U. K. H., Lewandowsky, S., & Oberauer, K. (2014). Removal of information from working memory: A specific updating process. *Journal of Memory and Language*, 74, 77–90. doi:10.1016/j.jml.2014.03.006

Ecker, U. K. H., Lewandowsky, S., Oberauer, K., & Chee, A. E. H. (2010). The components of working memory updating: An experimental decomposition and individual differences. *Journal of Experimental Psychology: Learning, Memory, and Cognition*, 36, 170–189. doi:10.1037/a0017891

Engle, R. W. (2002). Working memory capacity as executive attention. *Current Directions in Psychological Science*, 11, 19–23. doi:10.1111/1467-8721.00160

Engle, R. W. & Kane, M. J. (2004). Executive attention, working memory capacity, and a two-factor theory of cognitive control. In B. Ross (Ed.), *The psychology of learning and motivation*, Vol. 44 (pp. 145–199). New York: Elsevier.

Engle, R. W., Tuholski, S. W., Laughlin, J. E., & Conway, A. R. A. (1999). Working memory, short-term memory and general fluid intelligence: A latent variable approach. *Journal of Experimental Psychology: General*, 128, 309–331.

Harrison, T. L., Shipstead, Z., & Engle, R. W. (2015). Why is working memory capacity related to matrix reasoning tasks? *Memory & Cognition*, 43, 389–396. doi: 10.3758/s13421-014-0473-3.

Harrison, T. L., Shipstead, Z., Hambrick, D. Z., Hicks, K. L., Redick, T. S., & Engle, R. W. (2013). Working memory training may increase working memory capacity but not fluid intelligence. *Psychological Science*, 24, 2409–2419. doi: 10.1177/0956797613492984

Hebb, D. O. (1942). The effect of early and late brain injury upon test scores, and the nature of normal adult intelligence. *Proceedings of the American Philosophical Society*, 85, 275–292.

Jaeggi, S. M., Buschkuehl, M., Jonidas, J., & Perrig, W. J. (2008). Improving fluid intelligence with training on working memory. *Proceedings of the National Academy of Sciences of the United States of America*, 105, 6829–6833. doi:10.1073/pnas.0801268105

Jaeggi, S. M., Studer-Luethi, B., Buschkuehl, M., Su, Y.-F., Jonides, J., & Perrig, W. J. (2010). The relationship between n-back performance and matrix reasoning – Implications for training and transfer. *Intelligence*, 38, 625–635. doi:10.1016/j.intell.2010.09.001

Kane, M., & Engle, R. (2000). Working-memory capacity, proactive interference, and divided attention: Limits on long-term memory retrieval. *Journal of Experimental Psychology: Learning, Memory, & Cognition*, 26, 336. doi:10.1037/0278-7393.26.2.336

Kane, M. J., Hambrick, D. Z., & Conway, A. R. A. (2005). Working memory capacity and fluid intelligence are strongly related constructs: Comment on Ackerman, Beier, and Boyle (2005). *Psychological Bulletin*, 131, 66–71. doi:10.1037/0033-2909.131.1.66

Klingberg, T. (2012). Is working memory capacity fixed? *Journal of Applied Research in Memory and Cognition*, 1, 194–196.

Klingberg, T., Fernell, E., Olesen, P., Johnson, M., Gustafsson, P., Dahlström, K., … Westerberg, H. (2005). Computerized training of working memory in children with ADHD – A randomized, controlled, trial. *Journal of the American Academy of Child and Adolescent Psychiatry*, 44, 177–186. doi:10.1097/00004583-200502000-00010

Kyllonen, P. C., & Christal, R. E. (1990). Reasoning ability is (little more than) working memory capacity? *Intelligence*, 14, 389–433.

Li. S.-C., Schmiedeck, F., Huxhold, O., Röcke, C., Smith, J., & Lindenberger, U. (2008). Working memory plasticity in old age: Practice gain, transfer, and maintenance. *Psychology and Aging*, 23, 731–742. doi:10.1037/a0014343

Long, D. L., & Prat, C. S. (2002). Working memory and Stroop interference: An individual differences investigation. *Memory & Cognition*, 30, 294–301. doi:10.3758/BF03195290

Martin, J. D., Shipstead, Z., Harrison, T. L., Reddick, T. S., Bunting, M., & Engle, R. W. (2017). The role of maintenance and disengagement in predicting reading comprehension and vocabulary learning. *Manuscript submitted for publication.*

May, C. P., Hasher, L., & Kane, M. J. (1999). The role of interference in memory span. *Memory & Cognition, 27*, 759–767.

McCabe, J., & Hartman, M. (2008). Working memory for item and temporal information in younger and older adults. *Aging, Neuropsychology, and Cognition, 15*, 574–600. doi:10.1080/13825580801956217

McGrew, K. S. (2005). The Cattell-Horn-Carroll theory of cognitive abilities: Past, present, and future. In D. P. Flanagan, J. L. Genshaft, & P. L. Harrison (Eds.), *Contemporary intellectual assessment: Theories, tests, and issues* (pp. 151–179). New York: Guilford.

Miyake, A., & Friedman, N. P. (2012). The nature and organization of individual differences in executive functions: Four general conclusions. *Current Directions in Psychological Science, 21*, 8–14.

Miyake, A., Friedman, N. P., Emerson, M. J., Witzki, A. H., Howerter, A., & Wager, T. D. (2000). The unity and diversity of executive functions and their contributions to complex "frontal lobe" tasks: A latent variable analysis. *Cognitive Psychology, 41*, 49–100. doi:10.1006/cogp.1999.0734

Nespodzany, A. L., & Shipstead, Z. (2016). Fluid intelligence as a predictor of memory updating. *Manuscript in preparation for submission.*

Oberauer, K., Schulze, R., Wilhelm, O., & Süß, H. M. (2005). Working memory and intelligence – their correlation and their relation: A comment on Ackerman, Beier, and Boyle (2005). *Psychological Bulletin, 131*, 61–65. doi:10.1037/0033-2909.131.1.61

Oberauer, K., Süß, H.-M., Wilhem, O., & Sander, N. (2007). Individual differences in working memory capacity and reasoning ability. In A. R. A. Conway, C. Jarrold, M. H. Kane, A. Miyake, & J. N. Towse (Eds.), *Variation in working memory* (pp. 49–75). New York: Oxford University Press.

Raven, J. C. (1990). *Advanced progressive matrices.* Oxford: Oxford Psychological Press.

Redick, T. S., Shipstead, Z., Harrison T. L., Hicks, K. L., Fried, D. E., Hambrick, D. Z., Kane, M. J., & Engle, R. W. (2013). No evidence of intelligence improvement after working memory training: A randomized, placebo-controlled study. *Journal of Experimental Psychology, General, 142*, 359–379. doi:10.137/a0029082

Rosen, V. M., & Engle, R. W. (1997). The role of working memory capacity in retrieval. *Journal of Experimental Psychology: General, 126*, 211–227. doi:10.1037/0096-3445.126.3.211

(1998). Working memory capacity and suppression. *Journal of Memory and Language, 39*, 418–436. doi:10.1006/jmla.1998.2590

Shipstead, Z., & Engle, R. W. (2013). Interference within the focus of attention: Working memory tasks reflect more than temporary maintenance. *Journal of Experimental Psychology: Learning, Memory, and Cognition, 39*, 277–289. doi:10.1037/a0028467

Shipstead, Z., Harrison, T. L., & Engle, R. W. (2015). Working memory capacity and the scope and control of attention. *Attention, Perception, & Psychophysics, 77*, 1863–1880.

Shipstead, Z., Harrison, T. L., & Engle, R. W. (2016). Working memory capacity and fluid intelligence: Maintenance and disengagement. *Perspectives on Psychological Science*, 11, 771–799.

Shipstead, Z., Hicks, K. L., & Engle, R. W. (2012a). Cogmed working memory training: Does the evidence support the claims? *Journal of Applied Research in Memory and Cognition*, 1, 185–193. doi.org/10.1016/j.jarmac.2012.06.003

(2012b). Working memory training remains a work in progress. *Journal of Applied Research in Memory and Cognition*, 1, 217–219. doi.org/10.1016/j.jarmac.2012.07.009

Shipstead, Z., Lindsey, R. B., Marshall, R. L., & Engle, R. W. (2014). The contributions of maintenance, retrieval and attention control to working memory capacity. *Journal of Memory and Language*, 72, 116–141.

Shipstead, Z. & Nespodzany, A. (2017). The Contribution of Disengagement to Temporal Discriminability. *Manuscript in press at Memory*.

Shipstead, Z., Redick, T. S., & Engle, R. W. (2010). Does working memory training generalize? *Psychologica Belgica*, 50, 245–276.

(2012). Is working memory training effective? *Psychological Bulletin*. doi:10.1037/a0027473

Sternberg, R. J., & Powell, J. S. (1983). Comprehending verbal comprehension. *American Psychologist*, 38, 878–893.

Thorsen, C., Gustafsson, J.-E., & Cliffordson, C. (2014). The influence of fluid and crystallized intelligence on the development of knowledge and skills. *Educational Psychology*, 84, 556–570.

Turner, M. L., & Engle, R. W. (1989). Is working memory capacity task dependent? *Journal of Memory and Language*, 28, 127–154.

Unsworth, N., & Engle, R. W. (2007). The nature of individual differences in working memory capacity: Active maintenance in primary memory and controlled search from secondary memory. *Psychological Review*, 114, 104–132. doi:10.1037/0033-295X.114.1.104

Wiley, J., Jarosz, A. F., Cushen, P. J., & Colflesh, G. J. H. (2011). New rule use drives the relation between working memory capacity and Raven's Advanced Progressive Matrices. *Journal of Experimental Psychology: Learning, Memory, and Cognition*, 37, 256–263. doi:10.1037/a0021613

Winship, C., & Korenman, S. (1997). Does staying in school make you smarter? In B. Devlin, S. E. Fienberg, D. P. Resnick, & K Roeder (Eds.). *Intelligence, genes and success: Scientists respond to the bell curve* (pp. 215–234). Springer-Verlag.

Yong, E. (2016, October 3). The weak evidence behind brain-training games: Seven psychologists reviewed every single scientific paper put forward to support these products – and found them wanting. *The Atlantic*.

CHAPTER 19

Successful Intelligence in Theory, Research, and Practice

Robert J. Sternberg

What Is Intelligence?

Two symposia on the nature of intelligence ("Intelligence and its measurement, 1921"; Sternberg & Detterman, 1986) each revealed as many definitions of intelligence as there were theorists to define the term. In contrast, Gottfredson (1997) proposed a definition and recruited 52 theorists of intelligence to sign on to it. I prefer to speak of *successful intelligence* (Sternberg, 1997a, 1997b), so as not to get into arguments regarding what intelligence "really is." Intelligence really is nothing in particular, as it is a construct humans have invented, largely to explain why some people are better at performing some classes of tasks than others (Sternberg, 1984a). Many different metaphors can characterize intelligence (Sternberg, 1990), but these too are creations to help us understand our own invention.

Successful intelligence is one's ability to choose, reevaluate, and, to the extent possible, attain one's goals in life, within one's sociocultural context. A successfully intelligent person recognizes his or her strengths and weaknesses and then capitalizes on strengths while compensating for or correcting weaknesses. He or she does so through a combination of analytical, creative, practical, and wisdom-based/ethical skills (Sternberg, 2003).

In the theory, intelligence is realized through a set of information-processing components (Sternberg, 1977b, 1981, 1983; see also Sternberg, 1985b, 1985c). The components are of three kinds (Sternberg, 1984b, 1984c, 1985a). *Metacomponents* plan, monitor, and evaluate information processing; *performance components* execute the plans of the metacomponents; and *knowledge-acquisition components* learn how to perform information-processing tasks in the first place.

Execution of components occurs on a continuum of experience. When the components are applied to abstract but nevertheless fairly conventional kinds of materials, analytical abilities are involved; when they are applied to relatively novel kinds of materials, creative abilities are involved (Sternberg

& Davidson, 1982, 1983); and when they are applied to familiar and concrete materials in order to adapt to, shape, and select environments, practical abilities are involved. Wisdom-based abilities are involved when the components (as well as the knowledge base) are applied to achieve a common good, which balances one's own, others', and larger interests, over the long as well as the short terms, through the infusion of positive ethical values. This view suggests that analytical, creative, practical, and wisdom-based abilities will be at least weakly correlated, because the same components are involved. What differs is the level of experience at which they are applied and the purpose to which they are applied (Sternberg, 1985a).

As an example, consider the writing of this chapter (or any scholarly work). Creative abilities are involved in formulating ideas that are at the same time novel and compelling. Analytical abilities are involved in ascertaining whether the ideas are good ones. Practical abilities are involved in presenting the ideas in an engaging and persuasive way. Wisdom-based abilities are used to try to ensure that the theory presented can help serve a common good, whether to scientists or educators or the public at large. Many if not most of the tasks we encounter in life involve some combination of analytical, creative, and practical skills, and many tasks, at least those involving people, draw on wisdom-based skills as well.

The theory of successful intelligence has evolved over time. It started out as a componential (sub)theory of human intelligence (Sternberg, 1980b). The componential theory basically involved only what later became called the "analytical" aspect of the theory of successful intelligence. Later, the theory expanded and became the triarchic theory of human intelligence, which had the analytical, creative, and practical parts (e.g., Sternberg, 1988a, 1988b). The componential subtheory was melded with an experiential subtheory, which dealt with the different levels on the experiential continuum at which the components could be executed, and a contextual subtheory, which dealt with the practical aspect of the theory. Later, the theory transformed into the theory of successful intelligence (Sternberg, 1997b), which emphasized how intelligence is used to achieve success according to each individual's choice of goals in life. At this point, the theory still had its analytical, creative, and practical aspects, but emphasized the role of capitalization on strengths and compensation for or correction of weaknesses. And later the theory was augmented to include wisdom (Sternberg, 2003) as well as analytical, creative, and practical skills.

The theory of successful intelligence is similar to conventional theories of intelligence (e.g., Carroll, 1993; Johnson & Bouchard, 2005) in some ways but also different from such theories (Sternberg, 1996). Consider several similarities as well as differences.

First, the theory of successful intelligence, like conventional theories, views intelligence as one of many important keys to people's success in their lives. But whereas conventional theories tend to view levels of intelligence as fairly static across the life span, the theory of successful intelligence views intelligence as largely dynamic. People's intelligence in terms of adaptive skills can increase or decrease over the life span (Sternberg, 2014). Some abilities increase, some decrease; abilities that were not very relevant earlier become more relevant later, and vice versa. And patterns of capitalization, on the one hand, and compensation or correction, on the other, change as life tasks change and as skills increase or decrease throughout the life span.

Second, many conventional theories place a general factor of intelligence (g) at the top of a hierarchy of abilities. The theory of successful intelligence also comprises the abilities that constitute g but in the context of the analytical aspect of intelligence. The skills comprising analytical ability – to analyze, infer, map relations, judge, evaluate, critique, compare, and contrast – are central to g and to the theory of successful intelligence.

Third, the theory of successful intelligence, like Carroll's theory, posits multiple kinds of abilities comprising intelligence. But whereas in Carroll's theory, the abilities are hierarchically related, in the theory of successful intelligence, the abilities that are hierarchical in Carroll's theory all fall under the analytical aspect. Creative, practical, and wisdom-based abilities are seen as largely distinct.

Fourth, the theory of successful intelligence, like standard psychometric theories, asserts that the basic units of intelligence (in the theory of successful intelligence, components and mental representations upon which those components act) are the same across different sociocultural contexts. But in the theory of successful intelligence, the ways in which the components are instantiated differ substantially over sociocultural contexts (Sternberg, 2004a, 2014). Although the mental components may not differ, what constitutes intelligent behavior may differ radically from one culture to another in terms of the adaptive requirements of the culture. For example, in a rural Kenyan village, knowledge of natural herbal medicines used to combat parasitic illnesses may be key to adaptation and hence intelligence (Sternberg et al., 2001); in the United States, such knowledge may be useless. In a rural Yup'ik Eskimo village, knowledge of ice fishing may be essential to survival and hence intelligence (Grigorenko et al.,

2004); in much of the rest of the United States, such knowledge would be of much less use.

Moreover, because cultures have different implicit theories of intelligence (Sternberg, 2004a), behavior that is considered intelligent in one culture may be considered unintelligent in another culture. An example is young children who forcefully assert their opinions on matters. In some cultures, as in the United States, such behavior is viewed as characteristic of a bright child. In rural Kenya, such behavior would be viewed as inappropriate and not very intelligent (Grigorenko et al., 2001).

Fifth, the theory of successful intelligence is similar to and different from Gardner's (2011) theory of multiple intelligences. It is similar in its attempt to expand the range of abilities considered within the umbrella of the term "intelligence." Gardner and I agree that conventional theories view intelligence too narrowly. We disagree as to what intelligence means. I do not speak of "multiple intelligences" such as linguistic, logical-mathematical, etc.

Sixth, the theory of successful intelligence, like more conventional theories, has implications for teaching and for assessment. As discussed later, the theory suggests how teaching can be done so as to develop and utilize analytical, creative, practical, and wisdom-based skills, both at the elementary-secondary level (e.g., Sternberg & Grigorenko, 2004, 2007; Sternberg, Jarvin, & Grigorenko, 2009; Sternberg, Reznitskaya, & Jarvin, 2007) and at the university level (Sternberg, 2016). Assessments of intelligence also have been created based on the theory of successful intelligence (see, e.g., Sternberg, 2010). These assessments are not as time-tested and widely validated as conventional assessments of intelligence. We consider assessment next.

How Is Intelligence Best Assessed?

My colleagues and I have sought to create assessments at various levels based on the theory of successful intelligence. Some of our more recent assessments have been at the high school and college levels (Sternberg, 2010; Sternberg & The Rainbow Project Collaborators, 2006); we also have designed measures of achievement based on the theory – that is, measures that assess knowledge analytically, creatively, practically, and, where possible, for wisdom (Stemler et al., 2006, 2009).

We have conducted three fairly large-scale projects assessing successful intelligence in the context of college admissions – Rainbow, Kaleidoscope, and Panorama. Rainbow (Sternberg, 2010; Sternberg & The Rainbow Project Collaborators, 2006), conducted in the final days of my time as a professor at Yale University, was a project done across the United States with high school seniors and college freshmen of widely differing geographic dispersion, ethnicities, and ability levels. Kaleidoscope, initiated when I became dean of arts and sciences at Tufts University and still used today, was an actual admission procedure used to admit tens of thousands of undergraduate students to the university (Sternberg, 2009, 2010). Panorama was initiated for undergraduate admissions when I became provost and senior vice president of Oklahoma State University and also is still used today. I left Oklahoma State before the data were formally analyzed.

The seven main results of these projects (Sternberg, 2010; Sternberg et al., 2010, 2012) were as follows. First, we were able to factorially distinguish creative and practical abilities from each other and from analytical abilities. That said, the assessments did not group factorially as we initially had hypothesized. As it turned out, all multiple-choice tests, regardless of what they were supposed to measure, loaded most highly on an analytical factor. These results suggested why our previous attempts to measure analytical, creative, and practical abilities distinctively through a multiple-choice format were less than fully successful (Sternberg et al., 2001). Second, our assessments improved prediction of academic performance, at least in the first year of college study. The improvement in prediction in the Rainbow Project was striking – prediction of first-year GPA was doubled relative to SAT alone. Third, our assessments decreased ethnic-group differences relative to the SAT/ACT. Again, the difference was striking. In Rainbow, the reduction was by more than 50%, and in Kaleidoscope, it was even greater. Fourth, we were able to predict extracurricular success in a way that the SAT/ACT did not. Fifth, students liked taking our assessments far more than they liked taking traditional standardized tests. Sixth, at both Tufts and Oklahoma State, use of our assessments resulted in the admission of students who otherwise would not have been admitted and who became successful when they enrolled at the universities. Finally, at Tufts (I do not have data for Oklahoma State), average SAT scores actually increased slightly once Kaleidoscope was implemented, presumably because SAT is weakly positively correlated with our measures.

We also have created measures for other admissions situations, including business school (Hedlund et al., 2006). We found that our assessment improved prediction of academic work significantly over the GMAT. It also predicted performance on an independent research project, whereas the GMAT did not.

Most recently, my wife, Karin Sternberg, and I have been investigating how universities might improve graduate admissions in the behavioral and brain sciences, including psychology (Sternberg & Sternberg, 2017). We have devised a test of scientific reasoning (as applied to psychology). In our first study, undergraduate students took tests requiring them to formulate hypotheses, assess the validity of hypotheses to explain experimental outcomes, and formulate experiments. We found that, although our three tests correlated with each other, at least among Cornell students, they showed trivial or even negative correlations with SAT scores. The data suggest that, whatever the SAT measures, it is not scientific reasoning, at least as measured by our assessments.

As mentioned previously, we also have devised assessments where creative and practical assessments were added to knowledge-based and analytical assessments of the kinds found on advanced placement (AP) examinations (Stemler et al., 2006, 2009). We found that our assessments increased the content validity of the tests at the same time that they decreased ethnic-group differences.

Not all of our assessments have been of multiple abilities. During most of my career, most of the assessments have been of one or another aspect of intelligence. These studies, however, like the more recent ones, were designed with the purpose in mind of construct-validating the theory as it has evolved.

Analytical skills are used to analyze, compare and contrast, evaluate, judge, and critique. For example, one might analyze a scientific problem, critique a newspaper article, or compare and contrast two literary characters. My colleagues' and my earliest assessment studies were largely experimental, using mathematical models complemented by psychometric methods. In a typical study, I might seek to analyze the components of a particular analytical task, such as analogies (Sternberg, 1977a), linear syllogisms (Sternberg, 1980a), or verbal comprehension (Sternberg & Powell, 1983). The goal of such research was to isolate the fundamental components of (analytical) intelligence, ascertain the strategies into which they combine, discover the mental representations upon which the components and strategies act, and measure the latencies and error rates of individual components (Sternberg, 1978). This research showed, for example, that in analogical reasoning tasks, some components were executed exhaustively (all possible attributes examined) and others in self-terminating fashion (only some attributes examined). Moreover, strategies develop with age (Sternberg & Rifkin, 1979). In linear-syllogisms tasks, individuals use different strategies – some use a linguistic strategy, some a spatial strategy, and most a mixed linguistic/spatial strategy – and which strategy they use could be ascertained through a combination of experimental and psychometric methods (Sternberg & Weil, 1980).

Creative skills are used to create, invent, design, imagine, discover, explore, and innovate (Sternberg, 2005). For example, one might invent a new type of eating implement, or create an artwork, or design a scientific experiment. My colleagues' and my studies of creative skills started out in a similar experimental fashion. For example, my collaborators and I isolated the components involved in a novel reasoning task (based on the work of Nelson Goodman, 1955), in which objects were green until a certain year and blue thereafter, or vice versa (Sternberg, 1982; Tetewsky & Sternberg, 1986). In another set of studies (Sternberg & Gastel, 1989a, 1989b), we looked at the components of students' abilities to reason factually versus counterfactually (Sternberg & Gastel, 1989a, 1989b). But as time went on, we broadened our approach as we realized that creativity in people's lives involved much more than creative intelligence – that creativity is in large part an attitude toward life of defying the crowd – of buying low and selling high in the world of ideas (Sternberg & Lubart, 1991, 1995, 1996). We then found ourselves using not only experimental methods, but also methods of personality research (looking for individual differences) and of research on motivation (looking at intrinsic as opposed to extrinsic motivation).

Practical skills are used to put ideas into practice, apply, implement, use, utilize, and execute. For example, one might apply a theory of intelligence to design curriculum or a lesson from history to present-day problems. My colleagues' and my research on practical intelligence (see Sternberg & Hedlund, 2002) and social intelligence (see Sternberg & Smith, 1985) eschewed traditional random-assignment experimental methods altogether. Instead, it was based largely on situational-judgment tasks to measure tacit knowledge (Hedlund et al., 2003; Sternberg et al., 2000; Sternberg & Hedlund, 2002). We studied people in a wide variety of life pursuits: students, business executives, professors, public school teachers, salespeople, and more). We found, first, that practical intelligence is largely although not entirely distinct from analytical intelligence. People can be high in analytical intelligence but not necessarily high in practical intelligence (common sense) and vice versa. Second, we found that assessments of practical intelligence improved upon conventional intelligence tests in prediction of job performance. This was not an either-or situation: The best measurement was obtained by combining the two kinds of assessments. Third, we found that different kinds of practical intelligence – understanding of how to manage oneself, how to manage others, and how to manage tasks – are highly correlated with each other. And fourth we found that practical intelligence is even correlated, to some extent, across domains. People who are good at picking up tacit knowledge tend to be good at picking it up in a variety of contexts.

Wisdom-based skills are used to craft solutions to problems by seeking a common good. People can be analytically intelligent but foolish (Sternberg, 2002, 2004b). We see examples in everyday life all the time, especially at election time. Our studies of wisdom (see Sternberg, 1998) have been, for the most part, instructional, and hence are discussed in the next section, on how to develop intelligence.

How Is Intelligence Best Developed?

We have sought to test and implement the theory of successful intelligence in the classroom. In a first set of studies, we explored the question of whether conventional education in school systematically discriminates against children with creative and practical strengths (Sternberg et al., 1999). Motivating this work was the belief that the systems in most schools strongly tend to favor children with strengths in memory and analytical abilities.

We used the Sternberg Triarchic Abilities Test, as described earlier, in some of our instructional work. The test was administered to 326 children around the United States and in some other countries who were identified by their schools as gifted by any standard whatsoever. Children were selected for a summer program in (college-level) psychology if they fell into one of five ability groupings: high analytical, high creative, high practical, high balanced (high in all three abilities), or low balanced (low in all three abilities). Students who came to Yale were then divided into four instructional groups. Students in all four instructional groups used the same introductory psychology textbook and listened to the same psychology lectures. What differed among them was the type of afternoon discussion section to which they were assigned. They were assigned to an instructional condition that emphasized either memory, analytical, creative, or practical instruction.

Students in all four instructional conditions were evaluated in terms of their performance on homework, a midterm exam, a final exam, and an independent project. Each type of work was evaluated for memory, analytical, creative, and practical quality. Thus, all students were evaluated in exactly the same way.

We found that all three ability tests – analytical, creative, and practical – significantly predicted course performance. When multiple-regression analysis was used, at least two of these ability measures contributed significantly to the prediction of each of the measures of achievement. Perhaps as a reflection of the difficulty of deemphasizing the analytical way of teaching, one of the significant predictors was always the analytical score.

Third and most important, there was an aptitude-treatment interaction whereby students who were placed in instructional conditions that better matched their pattern of abilities outperformed students who were mismatched. In other words, when students are taught in a way that fits how they think, they do better in school. Children with creative and practical abilities, who are almost never taught or assessed in a way that matches their pattern of abilities, may be at a disadvantage in course after course, year after year.

A follow-up study (Sternberg, Torff, & Grigorenko, 1998) examined learning of social studies and science by third-graders and eighth-graders. In this study, students were assigned to one of three instructional conditions. In the first condition, they were taught the course that basically they would have learned had there been no intervention. The emphasis in the course was on memory. In a second condition, students were taught in a way that emphasized critical (analytical) thinking. In the third condition, they were taught in a way that emphasized analytical, creative, and practical thinking. All students' performance was assessed for memory learning (through multiple-choice assessments) as well as for analytical, creative, and practical learning (through performance assessments).

As expected, students in the successful-intelligence (analytical, creative, practical) condition outperformed the other students in terms of the performance assessments. One could argue that this result merely reflected the way they were taught. Nevertheless, the result suggested that teaching for these kinds of thinking succeeded. More important, however, was the result that children in the successful-intelligence condition outperformed the other children even on the multiple-choice memory tests. In other words, to the extent that one's goal is just to maximize children's memory for information, teaching for successful intelligence is still superior. It enables children to capitalize on their strengths and to correct or to compensate for their weaknesses, and it allows children to encode material in a variety of interesting ways.

In a third study, we taught reading either triarchically or through the regular curriculum. At the middle school level, reading was taught explicitly. At the high school level, reading was infused into instruction in mathematics, physical sciences, social sciences, English, history, foreign languages, and the arts. In all settings, students who were taught triarchically substantially outperformed students who were taught in standard ways (Grigorenko, Jarvin, & Sternberg, 2002). However, when we attempted to upscale to thousands of students (Sternberg et al., 2014), we found that we lost much of the effect because of difficulty in controlling the fidelity of the training of teachers.

We have also attempted to teach for wisdom (Sternberg, 2001; Sternberg et al., 2007). Students can be taught to think more wisely, but the biggest challenge is teaching the teachers, who are not used to teaching in this way.

Future Agenda

There are four pressing issues, I believe, facing the science and practice of intelligence.

First, the field needs to move beyond studies that show g predicts this, that, and the other thing. Of course, g does predict a lot of things at a lot of different periods of life. But the field knows this now. It's time to move beyond such studies. The work in this volume, I believe, represents many of the promising directions for the future of the field.

Second, we are using assessments, especially in university admissions, that are in the order of a century old. They have changed cosmetically but not conceptually from the assessments used early in the 20th century. Imagine using medical tests based on early 20th-century medicine. We need to use assessments that reflect current knowledge about intelligence. At the very least, we should be experimenting with broader assessments than we are now using.

Third, we need to teach in ways that reflect our current knowledge of best teaching practices. Of course, I would like such teaching to be for successful intelligence (e.g., Sternberg & Grigorenko, 2007). But at the very least, we need to reflect the findings of current cognitive psychology, not the proto-psychology, in many cases, of centuries ago.

Finally, we as a field need to be more transparent with the public. The public still does not fully understand the limitations of the tests we as a field give them. Test manuals or websites may speak of these limitations but often in ways that readers do not understand. The public is owed an explanation of what the tests they take measure, and what those tests do not measure. We need to be honest with our public and we need to be honest with ourselves.

References

Carroll, J. B. (1993). *Human cognitive abilities: A survey of factor-analytic studies.* New York: Cambridge University Press.

Gardner, H. (2011). *Frames of mind: The theory of multiple intelligences.* New York: Basic Books.

Goodman, N. (1955). *Fact, fiction, and forecast.* Cambridge, MA: Harvard University Press.

Gottfredson, L. S. (1997). Mainstream science on intelligence. *Intelligence,* 24, 13–23.

Grigorenko, E. L., Geissler, P. W., Prince, R., Okatcha, F., Nokes, C., Kenny, D. A., Bundy, D. A., & Sternberg, R. J. (2001). The organization of Luo conceptions of intelligence: A study of implicit theories in a Kenyan village. *International Journal of Behavioral Development,* 25(4), 367–378.

Grigorenko, E. L., Jarvin, L., & Sternberg, R. J. (2002). School-based tests of the triarchic theory of intelligence: Three settings, three samples, three syllabi. *Contemporary Educational Psychology,* 27, 167–208.

Grigorenko, E. L., Meier, E., Lipka, J., Mohatt, G., Yanez, E., & Sternberg, R. J. (2004). Academic and practical intelligence: A case study of the Yup'ik in Alaska. *Learning and Individual Differences,* 14, 183–207.

Hedlund, J., Forsythe, G. B., Horvath, J. A., Williams, W. M., Snook, S., & Sternberg, R. J. (2003). Identifying and assessing tacit knowledge: Understanding the practical intelligence of military leaders. *Leadership Quarterly,* 14, 117–140.

Hedlund, J., Wilt, J. M., Nebel, K. R., Ashford, S. J., & Sternberg, R. J. (2006). Assessing practical intelligence in business school admissions: A supplement to the Graduate Management Admissions Test. *Learning and Individual Differences,* 16, 101–127.

Intelligence and its measurement: A symposium. (1921). *Journal of Educational Psychology,* 12, 123–147, 195–216, 271–275.

Johnson, W., & Bouchard, T. J. (2005). The structure of human intelligence: It is verbal, perceptual, and image rotation (VPR), not fluid and crystallized. *Intelligence,* 33(4), 393–416. doi:10.1016/j.intell.2004.12.002

Stemler, S. E., Grigorenko, E. L., Jarvin, L., & Sternberg, R. J. (2006). Using the theory of successful intelligence as a basis for augmenting AP exams in psychology and statistics. *Contemporary Educational Psychology,* 31(2), 344–376.

Stemler, S., Sternberg, R. J., Grigorenko, E. L., Jarvin, L., & Sharpes, D. K. (2009). Using the theory of successful intelligence as a framework for developing assessments in AP Physics. *Contemporary Educational Psychology,* 34, 195–209.

Sternberg, R. J. (1977a). Component processes in analogical reasoning. *Psychological Review,* 84, 353–378.

(1977b). *Intelligence, information processing, and analogical reasoning: The componential analysis of human abilities.* Hillsdale, NJ: Lawrence Erlbaum Associates.

(1978). Isolating the components of intelligence. *Intelligence*, 2, 117–128.

(1980a). Representation and process in linear syllogistic reasoning. *Journal of Experimental Psychology: General*, 109, 119–159.

(1980b). Sketch of a componential subtheory of human intelligence. *Behavioral and Brain Sciences*, 3, 573–584.

(1981). A componential theory of intellectual giftedness. *Gifted Child Quarterly*, 25, 86–93.

(1982). Natural, unnatural, and supernatural concepts. *Cognitive Psychology*, 14, 451–488.

(1983). Components of human intelligence. *Cognition*, 15, 1–48.

(1984a). A contextualist view of the nature of intelligence. *International Journal of Psychology*, 19, 307–334.

(1984b). Toward a triarchic theory of human intelligence. *Behavioral and Brain Sciences*, 7, 269–287.

(1984c). What should intelligence tests test? Implications of a triarchic theory of intelligence for intelligence testing. *Educational Researcher*, 13, 5–15.

(1985a). *Beyond IQ: A triarchic theory of human intelligence*. New York: Cambridge University Press.

(Ed.). (1985b). *Human abilities: An information-processing approach*. San Francisco: Freeman.

(1985c). Teaching critical thinking, Part 1: Are we making critical mistakes? *Phi Delta Kappan*, 67, 194–198.

(Ed.). (1988a). *Advances in the psychology of human intelligence* (Vol. 4). Hillsdale, NJ: Lawrence Erlbaum Associates.

(1988b). *The triarchic mind: A new theory of human intelligence*. New York: Viking.

(1990). *Metaphors of mind*. New York: Cambridge University Press.

(1996). Myths, countermyths, and truths about human intelligence. *Educational Researcher*, 25(2), 11–16.

(1997a). Managerial intelligence: Why IQ isn't enough. *Journal of Management*, 23(3), 463–475.

(1997b). *Successful intelligence*. New York: Plume.

(1998) A balance theory of wisdom. *Review of General Psychology*, 2, 347–365.

(2001). Why schools should teach for wisdom: The balance theory of wisdom in educational settings. *Educational Psychologist*, 36(4), 227–245.

(2002). Smart people are not stupid, but they sure can be foolish: The imbalance theory of foolishness. In R. J. Sternberg (Ed.), *Why smart people can be so stupid* (pp. 232–242). New Haven, CT: Yale University Press.

(2003). *Wisdom, intelligence, and creativity synthesized*. New York: Cambridge University Press.

(2004a). Culture and intelligence. *American Psychologist*, 59(5), 325–338.

(2004b). Why smart people can be so foolish. *European Psychologist*, 9(3), 145–150.

(2005). Creativity or creativities? *International Journal of Human Computer Studies*, 63, 370–382.

(2009). The Rainbow and Kaleidoscope Projects: A new psychological approach to undergraduate admissions. *European Psychologist*, 14, 279–287.

(2010). *College admissions for the 21st century*. Cambridge, MA: Harvard University Press.

(2014). The development of adaptive competence. *Developmental Review*, 34, 208–224.

(2016). *What universities can be*. Ithaca, NY: Cornell University Press.

Sternberg, R. J., Bonney, C. R., Gabora, L., Karelitz, T., & Coffin, L. (2010). Broadening the spectrum of undergraduate admissions. *College and University*, 86(1), 2–17.

Sternberg, R. J., Bonney, C. R., Gabora, L, & Merrifield, M. (2012). WICS: A model for college and university admissions. *Educational Psychologist*, 47(1), 30–41.

Sternberg, R. J., Castejón, J. L., Prieto, M. D., Hautamäki, J., & Grigorenko, E. L. (2001). Confirmatory factor analysis of the Sternberg triarchic abilities test in three international samples: An empirical test of the triarchic theory of intelligence. *European Journal of Psychological Assessment*, 17(1) 1–16.

Sternberg, R. J., & Davidson, J. E. (1982, June). The mind of the puzzler. *Psychology Today*, 16, 37–44.

(1983). Insight in the gifted. *Educational Psychologist*, 18, 51–57.

Sternberg, R. J., & Detterman, D. K. (Eds.) (1986). *What is intelligence?* Norwood, NJ: Ablex Publishing Corporation.

Sternberg, R. J., Forsythe, G. B., Hedlund, J., Horvath, J., Snook, S., Williams, W. M., Wagner, R. K., & Grigorenko, E. L. (2000). *Practical intelligence in everyday life*. New York: Cambridge University Press.

Sternberg, R. J., & Gastel, J. (1989a). Coping with novelty in human intelligence: An empirical investigation. *Intelligence*, 13, 187–197.

(1989b). If dancers ate their shoes: Inductive reasoning with factual and counterfactual premises. *Memory and Cognition*, 17, 1–10.

Sternberg, R. J., & Grigorenko, E. L. (2004). Successful intelligence in the classroom. *Theory into Practice*, 43, 274–280.

(2007). *Teaching for successful intelligence* (2nd edn.). Thousand Oaks, CA: Corwin Press.

Sternberg, R. J., Grigorenko, E. L., Ferrari, M., & Clinkenbeard, P. (1999). A triarchic analysis of an aptitude–treatment interaction. *European Journal of Psychological Assessment*, 15(1), 1–11.

Sternberg, R. J., Hedlund, J. (2002). Practical intelligence, *g*, and work psychology. *Human Performance*, 15(1/2), 143–160.

Sternberg, R. J., Jarvin, L., Birney, D., Naples, A., Stemler, S., Newman, T., Otterbach, R., Randi, J., & Grigorenko, E. L. (2014). Testing the theory of successful intelligence in teaching grade 4 language arts, mathematics, and science. *Journal of Educational Psychology*, 106, 881–899.

Sternberg, R. J., Jarvin, L., & Grigorenko, E. L. (2009). *Teaching for wisdom, intelligence, creativity, and success*. Thousand Oaks, CA: Corwin.

Sternberg, R. J., & Lubart, T. I. (1991). An investment theory of creativity and its development. *Human Development*, 34(1), 1–31.

(1995). *Defying the crowd: Cultivating creativity in a culture of conformity.* New York: Free Press.

(1996). Investing in creativity. *American Psychologist*, 51(7), 677–688.

Sternberg, R. J., & Powell, J. S. (1983). Comprehending verbal comprehension. *American Psychologist*, 38, 878–893.

Sternberg, R. J., & The Rainbow Project Collaborators (2006). The Rainbow Project: Enhancing the SAT through assessments of analytical, practical and creative skills. *Intelligence*, 34(4), 321–350.

Sternberg, R. J., Reznitskaya, A., & Jarvin, L. (2007). Teaching for wisdom: What matters is not just what students know, but how they use it. *The London Review of Education*, 5(2), 143–158.

Sternberg, R. J., & Rifkin, B. (1979). The development of analogical reasoning processes. *Journal of Experimental Child Psychology*, 27, 195–232.

Sternberg, R. J., & Smith, C. (1985). Social intelligence and decoding skills in nonverbal communication. *Social Cognition*, 2, 168–192.

Sternberg, R. J., & Sternberg, K. (2017). Measuring scientific reasoning for graduate admissions in psychology and related disciplines. *Journal of Intelligence*, http://www.mdpi.com/2079-3200/5/3/29/pdf.

Sternberg, R. J., Torff, B., & Grigorenko, E. L. (1998). Teaching triarchically improves school achievement. *Journal of Educational Psychology*, 90, 374–384.

Sternberg, R. J., & Weil, E. M. (1980). An aptitude–strategy interaction in linear syllogistic reasoning. *Journal of Educational Psychology*, 72, 226–234.

Tetewsky, S. J., & Sternberg, R. J. (1986). Conceptual and lexical determinants of nonentrenched thinking. *Journal of Memory and Language*, 25, 202–225.

Index

CPSIA information can be obtained
at www.ICGtesting.com
Printed in the USA
LVHW080328280221
680128LV00010B/66